T0319771

Introducing a New Economics

Introducing a New Economics

Pluralist, Sustainable and Progressive

Jack Reardon, Maria Alejandra Madi
and Molly Scott Cato

First published 2018 by Pluto Press
345 Archway Road, London N6 5AA

www.plutobooks.com

British Library Cataloguing in Publication Data
A catalogue record for this book is available from the British Library

ISBN 978 0 7453 3489 9 Hardback
ISBN 978 0 7453 3488 2 Paperback
ISBN 978 1 7837 1217 5 PDF eBook
ISBN 978 1 7837 1219 9 Kindle eBook
ISBN 978 1 7837 1218 2 EPUB eBook

This book is printed on paper suitable for recycling and made from fully managed and sustained forest sources. Logging, pulping and manufacturing processes are expected to conform to the environmental standards of the country of origin.

Typeset by Stanford DTP Services, Northampton, England

Simultaneously printed in the United Kingdom and United States of America

Contents

List of Boxes, Figures and Tables

BOXES

FIGURES

TABLES

Acknowledgements

Jack Reardon:

A warm and fond thanks to my grandfather who taught me about sustainability and the world's environmental problems, long before it was fashionable. I thank Miriam Kennett whose passionate concern for justice has made me a better economist. Thanks to Silja Graupe of Cusanus University, and Prithvi Yadav of NMIMS, for welcoming me at their respective institutions and offering an intellectually thriving home. Thanks to David Shulman at Pluto Press for his vision, and to Alethea Doran for her skill in preparing the manuscript for publication. Special thanks to my wonderful wife Laurie for her enduring and unconditional love and support. And to my delightful children Elizabeth and Patrick for their love and enthusiasm for life; I have learned so much from you. It is for you and your generation that I co-wrote this book: that you may have the wisdom, kindness, and knowledge to solve our growing interconnected problems.

Maria Alejandra Madi:

I am grateful to all of those with whom I have had the pleasure to work during the period while this project has been developed. I would like to offer my special thanks to Prof. Edward Fullbrook and Prof. Grazia Ietto-Gillies from the World Economics Association, and to Dr Miriam Kennet from the Green Economics Institute. I would like to express my gratitude to the many people who provided support, offered comments and assisted in the editing, proofreading and design.

Molly Scott Cato:

I am grateful to all those who have the courage to admit that our economic model is broken and who are working to redesign it rather than papering over the cracks and hoping for the best. I acknowledge in particular the economists of the South who have contributed so much to theorising a solidary economy and to the green economists who have worked to develop a vision of a sustainable economy. Thanks must also go to my family who have supported me so generously and to the Green Party for being my political family.

Preface

A few years ago, one of the authors (Jack) attended a lecture by the novelist and social critic James Howard Kunstler on his 2008 novel *The World Made By Hand*, a chilling dystopian account of life in what used to be the United States. It is a post-oil world, where after a series of disasters, including nuclear war and abrupt climate change, no one knows where the capital city is, or even if one exists. It is a world without cars, planes, electricity and all the accoutrements of what used to be civilisation, with disease rampant and marauders enforcing their own laws. After listening to Mr Kunstler's sobering analysis, a student in the audience asked, 'Why do you assume we won't have the ability, the education and the determination to solve these problems that your generation gave us? We did not create them. We will inherit them. So they will be our problems and we will solve them.'

Jack was impressed by the student's willingness to tackle these problems head-on and assume them as his own. The student was resolved to use his education in order to understand and conceptualise the problems of his generation. He exuded the confidence, certainly not rare, that our problems can be solved not just by relying on markets, technology or some other panacea, but through education, thinking and working together.

As educators it is our job to equip today's students with the knowledge, ability, values and cultural competence to tackle our problems head-on, and to work together to devise solutions. We need big thinkers and educated citizens – not just people trained in narrow competencies or proselytised to think a certain way, but well-educated and well-rounded citizens. We need

> persons of tomorrow [who] embrace the world . . . engag[ing] with their existential reality in a spirit of hope, courage invention and play. Their engagement is conscious, in the moment, not rule-based or rehearsed. They are participants in events, not victims.
>
> O'Hara and Leicester, 2012: 60

Writing this textbook gives us optimism that we can work together to rise and meet the challenges of our generation.

Given that our problems are not delineated by academic discipline, we need educated citizens who can communicate and work with others. The ability and willingness to create and participate in dialogue is central. Amartya Sen (2009: 415), a philosopher and Nobel laureate in economics wrote, 'it is bad enough that the world in which we live has so much deprivation of one kind or another (from being hungry to being tyrannised); it would be even more terrible if we were not able to communicate, respond and altercate.'

Every generation looks at its problems as daunting and uniquely challenging, soliciting its best minds for solutions. Henry George (1879 [1948]: 5–6), for example, wrote more than 150 years ago:

> Discovery upon discovery, and invention after invention, have neither lessened the toil of those who need most respite, nor brought plenty to the poor. . . From all parts of the civilised world come complaints of industrial depression; of labour condemned to involuntary idleness; of capital massed and wasting . . . All the dull, deadening pain, all the keen, maddening anguish, that to great masses of men [sic] are involved in the 'hard times', afflict the world today.

While this is not to deny the significance of any generation's problems, it is clear that our generation is beset with myriad ecological issues, including global warming, rising sea levels, species depletion, etc., that could very well coalesce into an irreversible catastrophe. Such imminence calls for understanding, knowledge, and the ability to conceptualise our problems in a holistic manner, and to communicate and work with others to devise solutions. We believe that economics must play a central role in not only conceptualising the problems of our generation but also in articulating solutions. Knowledge of economics will enable us to take action – but not knowledge of economics as it is currently taught, which ignores the issues of sustainability, pluralism, and justice.

Economics, if it is to be helpful and effective, must be reconceptualised to incorporate the following three issues. First, economics must be consistent with sustainability. As we explain in the text, while many definitions of sustainability exist, a central element uniting them is an ethical concern for the future. Thus, as Klavins et al. write (2010: 267), 'the concept of sustainable development not only looks at short-term processes (to satisfy current needs) but also aims at ensuring equal possibilities for the next generation'.

Second, economics must become pluralist, which, like sustainability, is a multifaceted and complex concept. A simple (and much-used) definition of pluralism is 'respect for different and opposing views'. Pluralism is necessary since there are many ways of conceptualising problems and no one view has a monopoly of understanding. And, pertaining to sustainability, since 'there are different transition routes to sustainable development, and mistakes are possible' (Klavins et al., 2010: 271), pluralism is an essential component of sustainability; that is, the two go hand-in-hand.

Third, economics must concern itself with justice. Economics as currently practised and taught hides the interrelationship of our problems, inures students to human suffering and abnegates thoughtful discussion of the human predicament. John Maynard Keynes (1936 [2010]: 33) explained the ascendancy of modern economics thus: 'that it could explain much social injustice and apparent cruelty in the scheme of progress, and the attempt to change such things as likely on the whole to do more harm than good, commended it to authority'. Economists must step out from the comfortable excuse of positive economics and speak out 'on the side of humanity' (Robinson, 1980: xiii).

Nothing pains us more than to see an eager student wanting to study economics so she can understand her society only to be turned off by overly deductive, axiomatic and ahistorical logic, with textbook authors spinning tales of ideological fancy. Unfortunately this is nothing new, as Henry George (1879 [1948]: 559; emphasis in original) wrote:

> Political Economy has been called the dismal science, and as currently taught, *is* hopeless and despairing. But this . . . is solely because she has been degraded and shackled; her truths dislocated; her harmonies ignored, the word she would utter gagged in her mouth, and her protest against wrong turned into an indorsement [sic] of injustice.

Since the late nineteenth century, economics has turned inward and focused on technique rather than subject, on constructing elaborate deductive models rather than actually studying the economy. This has turned economics into a

> branch of applied mathematics, where the aim is not to explain real processes and outcomes in the economic world . . . [giving the perception of] economics as a technical and rarefied discipline, of questionable relevance and limited practical use.
>
> Hodgson, 1999: 6 & 9

This was done in the name of science, but in doing so economics has renounced its claim of studying the actual economy, and has turned off generations of students looking for wisdom and guidance. Keynes (1936 [2010]: 33) wrote:

> Professional economists . . . were apparently unmoved by the lack of correspondence between the results of their theory and the facts of observation; a discrepancy which the ordinary man [sic] has not failed to observe, with the result of his [sic] growing unwillingness to accord to economists that measure of respect which he gives to other . . . scientists whose theoretical results are confirmed by observation when they are applied to the facts.

Emphasising the dialogue between theory and reality will enhance new perspectives for the discipline of economics.

We need both a new economics and a new economics education. Our future is uncertain, requiring an economics education that is sustainable, pluralist and just. In 2016 the United Kingdom, in a nationwide referendum, voted to leave the European Union (an economic union of 28 nations, which we discuss in Chapter 15) – a phenomenon known as 'Brexit' – throwing the world into economic and political chaos. Brexit requires us to understand the debates and theories which inform political decision-making; and this is why our text is so important.

More foreboding, climate change is accelerating. In 2015, the United Nations issued its 17 Sustainable Development Goals (SDGs), as a hopeful recipe for future living and as a global call to become more sustainable. One objective of this textbook is to increase your understanding of economics in order that you can fully understand the debate about sustainability, so that as citizens you can help successfully implement the UN 17 SDGs within a specific context of pluralism and justice.

We wrote this book anticipating uncertainty and the unknown, looking to the future, yet understanding the past. We sincerely hope that this book will help you conceptualise and solve the problems of this generation, and help you design a more equitable and sustainable economic system that can provision for all. Doing so will hopefully instil a sense of can-do optimism, just like the student quoted at the beginning of this chapter.

And finally, in the spirit of global pluralism, we offer you the perspective of three countries (and three continents) – a much-needed global perspective: Jack (USA), Maria (Brazil) and Molly (UK).

Jack Reardon, Maria Alejandra Caporale Madi and Molly Scott Cato
22 June 2017

1
Introducing Economics with a Judicious Mix of Pluralism, Sustainability and Justice

Alfred Marshall wrote in his best-selling *Principles of Economics* (1890 [1946]: v) that 'economic conditions are constantly changing, and each generation looks at its own problems in its own way'. Our generation is confronted with many problems, including climate change, environmental damage, a global financial crisis, a palpable disparity in income and wealth, escalating debt and a healthcare crisis. These problems are mutually reinforcing and, unless we take radical action, will only worsen. Knowledge and education can help us understand them in order to devise effective solutions.

This chapter will discuss and define economics and its relationship to the other social sciences. We will also discuss how economics is interwoven with sustainability, pluralism and justice – our guiding principles.

1.1 WHAT IS ECONOMICS?

The word 'economics', like so many other English words, derives from the Greek language. It combines 'oikos' (house) and 'nomos' (manager), and literally means 'household management'. Given our text's central focus on sustainability, it is interesting that economics shares a linguistic origin with ecology, which studies the relations of organisms to one another and to their physical surroundings. We are happy to write a textbook that unites the two words by returning them to their common origin.

While managing households is a concern in all societies, the modern discipline of economics is relatively new, dating to Adam Smith and his *The Wealth of Nations* (1776). Originally called political economy, the discipline recognised the interconnection between economics and politics.

While the definition of **economics** has changed over time, we prefer (and will use) the modern definition: Economics is a social science concerned with how societies provision. Or alternatively, 'how societies organise themselves to sustain life and enhance its quality.' (Nelson, 2009: 61)

Three points are obvious from this definition:

(1) Economics is a social science, meaning that it studies human society and its social relationships, as opposed to physics or chemistry, for example, which study the physical world. Nevertheless, the dividing line between human society and the physical sciences (and thus between the social sciences and the natural sciences) is not as clear-cut as first appears. The physical world is changing, affecting human society; conversely, how we act socially and economically changes the physical world. Indeed, this interconnection was noted by The Intergovernmental Panel on Climate Change (IPCC) in their *Fifth Assessment Report* (2014):

> Human influence has been detected in warming of the atmosphere and the ocean, in changes in the global water cycle, in reductions in snow and ice, in global mean sea level rise, and in changes in some climate extremes. This evidence for human influence has grown since 2007. It is *extremely likely* that human influence has been the dominant cause of the observed warming since the mid-20th century.

(2) Economics is concerned with how we provision (from the Latin word *providere*, 'to provide') so that individuals can lead quality lives and reach their full potential.
(3) Economics is also concerned with how *we* organise our societies. Knowledge empowers, enabling us to best construct our societies so that *all* can successfully provision.

So to redress and (perhaps) attenuate climate change, for example, we humans must change our values and behaviour and even our institutions. We believe that economics must and will play a crucial role.

1.2 HOW ECONOMICS RELATES TO THE OTHER SOCIAL SCIENCES

While many of you might have taken, or will be taking, other courses in the social sciences such as sociology, anthropology or psychology, you might wonder how economics fits within the social sciences. Table 1.1 presents a definition of other social science subjects. While each is taught as a separate discipline and is offered as a main degree at most universities, the commonality is striking – every discipline involves the study of human beings. So why do we compartmentalise each discipline? Does that help or hinder understanding the problems of our generation?

One reason for such compartmentalisation within the social sciences is the attempt by economists during the late nineteenth century to emulate contemporary physics by becoming 'scientific'. To do so, 'political' was dropped from 'political

Table 1.1 Definitions of Specific Disciplines Within the Social Sciences

Discipline	*Definition*
Anthropology	The study of peoples and their cultures.
Communications	The study of how individuals and communities devise symbols and languages to communicate with each other.
Economics	The study of how societies provision.
Geography	The study of how human action both affects and is affected by the physical features of the Earth.
Law	The study of custom and rules.
Politics	The study of activities and policies of the government.
Psychology	The study of how the human mind works.
Sociology	The systematic study of society and human action, with a specific focus on groups.

Source: Authors.

economy', to focus almost exclusively on how rational individuals maximise their happiness by allocating scarce resources amongst unlimited wants. Thus, this 'new' economics, or 'neoclassical economics', limited its approach to one narrowly defined as 'scientific', and mostly focused on the question of rational choice rather than the investigation of the economy's ability to provision. Needless to say, not all economists accepted this constricted scope and method, giving rise to the proliferation of many schools of thought within economics, which we will discuss in this chapter.

Other disciplines, particularly sociology and anthropology, formed and developed in order to investigate areas and issues jettisoned by neoclassical economics, such as group behaviour, institutions, property rights, power, culture and the historical evolution of capitalism.

Does such compartmentalisation (within the social sciences) help or hinder? Although we believe in the benefits of specialisation, we also feel that specialisation without cooperation is limiting and self-defeating. Each discipline can and should learn from others. One of the goals of education should be to recognise that in the real world our problems are not demarcated by discrete disciplines. For example, climate change is neither a sociological, environmental nor economic phenomenon. We need the insights of all disciplines to solve our problems, and yet each of the social sciences is a work in progress, since there is a lot we do not yet know. Perhaps one of our goals as social scientists should be to reduce the barriers, blend the disciplines, and/or work across disciplines: that is, to be **interdisciplinary**.

Exclusive reliance on only one discipline gives a misleading and myopic understanding. For example, if we want to study financial bubbles, how can we claim understanding without knowledge of psychology? Or if we want to establish a government that benefits all, how can we do so without knowledge of history, which teaches us what works and what does not, along with sociology, economics, politics and psychology? If we want to effectively address global warming, how can we do so without knowledge of how and why people form and behave in institutions and groups?

To use an analogy of a homeowner, while we respect the property rights of our neighbours, rather than wall off our gardens from each other we prefer an open space to mingle and talk – a commons, if you will – which, among other things, fulfils a basic human need for social contact and interaction. Thus, given a common problem we can come together to develop a solution. It is hard to do so when each garden is walled off, so we don't know our neighbours or any aspect of their lives.

In the social sciences, not only are the 'neighbours' different, they frequently don't speak to each other:

> disciplines and sub-disciplines largely form their own small worlds of methodology, assumptions, language, meaning and identity . . . Disciplines are like tribes, they have a specific culture and specific habits, norms and rules, and they do not easily accept outsiders.
>
> Weehuizen, 2007: 165

1.3 DIFFERENT IDEOLOGIES (OR SCHOOLS OF THOUGHT) WITHIN ECONOMICS

For us, a very emotional and evocative photograph is that of the Earth taken by the Apollo 8 astronauts (titled *Earthrise*) in December 1968. It looks peaceful and somewhat idyllic, and it is hard to imagine that people living so close together against the infinite background of space can be so truculent. To a lesser extent, the same truculence exists within economics. It is a discipline rife with *ideological* disagreement, based on different ideas and visions of how the world works and how it should work. When neoclassical economics was founded, it became **monist** (the opposite of pluralist), espousing only one privileged viewpoint. But, as we explain in the next section, not only is monism inconsistent with democracy but, as we devise effective solutions for our generation's many problems, why constrict our thinking to only one way of seeing the world? Wouldn't we benefit from a healthy discussion involving all viewpoints?

For better or for worse, there are a number of competing ideological positions within the discipline of economics. We believe, however, that disagreement livens economics and enlarges its scope and applicability. Consequently, our approach (consistent with our theme of pluralism) is to make you aware of the existence of the different ideologies and, where appropriate, mention the origin of certain principles and concepts and how they fit in with the overall discipline of economics.

Thus, our goal is to search for commonalities between the different ideologies and across the social sciences. We ask you to be cognisant of the differences and to realise that it is difficult to prove one view superior to others. We offer you a new framework to learn the principles of economics within a pluralist and sustainable context, to help you conceptualise and solve the problems of our generation. It is not expected at this point that you fully understand the major tenets of each view, since most of the concepts will be discussed in later chapters. The major ideologies (or schools of thought) within economics include:[1]

Classical economics: Begins with Adam Smith (1723–90) and includes Jean-Baptiste Say (1767–1832), Thomas Malthus (1766–1834), David Ricardo (1772–1823) and John Stuart Mill (1806–73). The classical economists wrestled with the big-picture questions of their time, especially the advent and development of **capitalism** – a new dynamic system defined as the private (i.e. firms and individuals) ownership of the means of production (i.e. resources used to produce the goods and services that people need) (see Box 1.1). With ownership comes the obligation to decide what to do with the resources and how to use them to produce society's needs. Since it was not immediately obvious how private ownership could ensure that the necessary goods and services would be produced, Classical economists searched for underlying laws of the economy. They also investigated how wealth was produced and distributed between workers, landowners and capitalists. Conflict between different groups and the existence of power was recognised as central and as a legitimate area of study for economics. Classical economists also investigated the source of an item's value, concluding it was labour: the more labour to produce an item, the greater its value. This is known as the **labour theory of value**. According to Adam Smith (1776 [1976], Vol. I, Ch. 5, p.37) and accepted by all classical economists, 'Labour alone . . . never varying in its own value, is alone the ultimate and real standard by which the value of all commodities can at all times and places be estimated and compared. It is their real price; money is their nominal price only.'

Neoclassical economics: Traces its origins to the late nineteenth century. Its principal founders include William Stanley Jevons (1835–82), Leon Walras (1834–1910) and Alfred Marshall (1842–1924). Heavily influenced by eighteenth-century physics, it adopted an ostensibly scientific veneer by divorcing itself from politics and the other social sciences, while limiting its scope to how rational individuals allocate scarce resources amongst unlimited wants. Its three major elements include: (1) individualism – focusing on the behaviour of individual agents (consumers, workers, firms) while trying to understand the economy based on individual behaviour; (2) optimisation – assuming that individual

1. It is impossible here to offer more than a cursory description of each school of thought. For more involved discussion, see Stilwell (2012); Harvey (2015).

Box 1.1 Definitions: Capitalism, Socialism, and Communism

Every nation must ask and answer what type of political and economic system it wants. Pertaining to the later, capitalism is one choice, but not the only choice. **Capitalism**, defined as the private ownership of the means of production (see text above), does not imply that all means of production must be privately owned, only 'most' – although economists disagree what is meant by 'most'. Other central features of capitalism include reliance on the profit motive, competition, and reliance on labour power as a commodity (i.e. labour is bought and sold in the market). With ownership also comes the responsibility of how to use the means of production, unless circumscribed by law. The Netherlands (seventeenth century), England, and the USA (beginning in the nineteenth century) were early examples of capitalist nations.

Socialism is an economic system whereby the means of production are owned by the state. **Communism** is an economic system whereby the means of production are owned by everyone. The former Union of Soviet Socialist Republics (USSR) was the first nation state to adopt socialism; but, based on our definition, a communist system has never existed.

Capitalism usually relies on organised markets to allocate goods and services. A single market is defined, as many dictionaries do, as 'a regular gathering of people for the purchase and sale of provisions, livestock and other commodities'. Whereas single markets bringing together buyer and seller have existed since antiquity, an economic system organised around markets is relatively recent and by no means natural.

History, according to Karl Polanyi (1944) teaches us three important lessons: (1) no economic system is natural; (2) every economic system is constructed by human beings and supported by underlying institutions; and (3) if a system is not just and is not able to adequately provision for all, we can change/modify it.

agents optimise explicit goals such as happiness, income or profits; and that (3) the optimisation of individual agents results in stable equilibrium, in which there is no reason to alter behaviour (Earle et al., 2017: 38).

Neoclassical economics is the only ideology within economics to ignore power, assuming instead that market forces of supply and demand will transform inherent conflict between producers and buyers into a beneficent equilibrium. And it is the only school of thought within economics claiming to be value-free, or non-ideological.[2]

Marxism: Founded by Karl Marx (1818–83) and Friedrich Engels (1820–91). Key publications include the *Communist Manifesto* (1848) and *Capital* (1867).

2. As you will notice throughout this text, ideology has played and continues to play a central role in economics. From the Greek words *idea* (form; pattern) and *logos* (study of), **ideology** is commonly defined as 'the body of ideas reflecting the social needs and aspirations of an individual, group, class or culture. A systematic set of doctrines or beliefs.' Ideology is part and parcel of what makes us human; rather than something odious that must be expunged, it should be welcomed, and understood.

Heavily influenced by classical economics, Marxism utilises the labour theory of value and expands on the inherent class conflict of capitalism to argue that its central conflict is between workers and capitalists. Given that capitalism is defined as private ownership (and hence private decision-making) of the means of production, only a minority of individuals can own these resources, so that those owning nothing but their own ability to labour (the workers) must work for the minority who own resources (the capitalists). The workers are hence dependent on the capitalists, who take advantage of this dependency to exploit workers by extracting **surplus value**, understood as the difference between profits and the wages paid to the workers.

It does not matter if individually such capitalists are benevolent because, as part of the capitalist system, they are driven by its fundamental goal to maximise profit. This profit motive in turn renders capitalism cyclical and unstable. As capitalism expands, labour is replaced by machinery, but since labour is the source of value, the overall profit rate falls, increasing unemployment and decreasing investment. Eventually such conditions will be reversed and temporarily improve (due to falling wages, technical innovations or increased trade), but this will only increase unemployment and eventually lead to a massive crisis in capitalism.

It should be noted that the key concept of 'surplus', significant in understanding how all economic systems function, is central to Marxist economics. The surplus is:

> that part of the total output of an economy that is in excess of what is needed for reproducing and replenishing the [means] of production. There is no reason why a surplus must exist, but it does exist and has existed in all but a few human societies. The surplus product may be used in a variety of ways. It can take the form of cathedrals, palaces, luxury goods, military spending, more or better equipment, higher levels of education, improved health, and many other things.
>
> Bowles et al., 2005: 93, original emphasis deleted

How to use society's surplus to help all provision is a central concern of economics. The recent financial crisis[3] has sparked a renewed interest in Marxist economics.

Institutionalism: Originating in the late nineteenth century in the USA, its principal founders were John Commons (1862–1945) and Thorstein Veblen (1857–1929). It emphasises the important role of **institutions** in any economic system, defined as a rule, custom or pattern of behaviour that simplifies and

---

3. We are referring here (and henceforth in this textbook) to the global financial crisis which began in 2007, with its worst effects in 2008. For many people, however, the effects of the crisis are ongoing, so we would not define it as an event spanning only that time period.

regularises human conduct. Institutions are paramount and should be the focal point of any systematic study of the economy, since 'humans both influence and are influenced by the institutions' (Vatn, 2005: 25). If we want to be able to provision for all, *step one* is to understand and recognise our institutions – institutions that we built and, if necessary, we can change.

The possession of power and its use are central to institutionalists. How power is exercised will influence and determine the evolution of institutions and hence the ability of economic systems to provision. Acemoglu and Robinson (2012), along with many others, argue that institutional factors are critical to sustainable long-term growth. When only a small elite can become rich, countries are unlikely to achieve sustainable growth unless they reform their political, social and economic institutions to make them more inclusive.

Unlike neoclassical economics, which unabashedly trumpets capitalism, and Marxism, which excoriates it, institutionalism expresses no favourite economic system. However, more recently, **'new institutionalism'** has developed, which is, in effect, an extension of neoclassical economics: recognising institutions as being important not in their own right, but rather in terms of influencing and constricting human behaviour.

Feminist economics: Includes studies of gender roles in the economy from a liberatory perspective, and also develops innovative research to address topics such as the economics of households, labour markets, macroeconomics, development, unpaid production in the measurement of gross domestic product (GDP),[4] and the effects of government budgets on gender equity (Nelson, 2008). Tracing its roots to the 1960s, it investigates how unequal distribution and use of power adversely affects women, along with the patriarchal nature of economic relations in capitalism – each ignored by the other ideologies. Thus, feminist economists recognise that subjective biases, social beliefs and structures of power reinforce situations oppressive to women. The International Association for Feminist Economics was formed in 1992 and its journal, *Feminist Economics*, commenced publication a few years later. Considering the dissatisfaction with neoclassical economics, feminist economists propose a re-evaluation of theories and methods in economic courses in order to better reach students with diverse backgrounds and learning styles.

Green economics: Also developed during the 1960s. A holistic vision which advocates careful consideration of the relationship between the economy and the environment. The need to have a stable economic system without constant growth is central, along with sharing resources equitably. Green economists see the economy as essentially enclosed within the environment, which in turn is the source of all wealth, rather than as a source of exploitable resources. The

4. As will be explained in Chapter 12, GDP is defined as the market value of all final goods and services produced within a nation's geographical borders in one year.

recognition of planetary limits challenges the emphasis of economic growth within a conventional conception of economics. This in turn immediately implies the need for greater equality, since if the pie cannot grow overall then the size of each slice becomes much more important. A sustainable approach to economics also requires a more careful stewardship of natural resources and the need to shift from a linear to a circular model of production, so that instead of using energy to extract and transform resources into products that are sold, used and turned into waste, we create a circular model where each product or its components can be reused or recycled (Braungart and McDonough, 2009). Green economists such as Molly Scott Cato (2012a) have written extensively on bioregionalism and economics, exploring elements of current local practices that can prefigure more extensive developments and innovations. Green economics also favours a reflection on the changing nature and rhythm of the transformations of society, knowledge and values (Kennet, 2007). The speed of these changes hastens the search for new connections to offer alternatives based on a more satisfactory understanding of our reality.

The Austrian School: This group is highly critical of the ignorance and omission by neoclassical economics of the role of uncertainty and of the individual entrepreneur. How the individual behaves, particularly in light of uncertainty, determines how an economic system evolves. Austrians stress the highly subjective marginal valuation of assets (i.e. we each value things differently) and, in addition, criticise the overly formal mathematisation of neoclassical economics. Principal founders include Eugen von Böhm-Bawerk (1851–1914), Carl Menger (1840–1921) and Friedrich von Wieser (1851–1926).

Post-Keynesianism: This school of thought developed the ideas of John Maynard Keynes (1883–1946), whose 1936 book *The General Theory of Employment, Interest and Money* revolutionised economics and thinking about the 'proper' role of government. Highly critical of neoclassical economics' belief in the economy's ability to achieve equilibrium at full employment, Keynes argued that the economy was more likely to achieve equilibrium at less than full employment. The Great Depression during the 1930s lent credence to his argument. Keynes also underscored the financial instability of capitalism, particularly the role of credit and the financial sector. Keynes called for government help in stabilising the economy, reducing uncertainty and increasing aggregate demand. Principal Post-Keynesianists include Sidney Weintraub (1914–81), Hyman Minsky (1919–96), Paul Davidson (1930–) and Joan Robinson (1903–83).

As can be seen, the different schools of economic thought tend to emphasise or deny the significance of some concepts and not others, e.g. the entrepreneur, uncertainty, power, patriarchal relations, the environment and the evolution of capitalism itself. It can also be argued that the splintering of economics into different schools was due to neoclassical economics ignoring these concepts. Perhaps the time has come to see if these different ideologies can in some sense

Box 1.2 Adam Smith (1723–90)

Imagine being asked to rank the 100 most influential people who ever lived. How would you proceed? Such an attempt was actually made in an interesting book called *The 100: A Ranking of the Most Influential Persons in History* (Hart, 1992). As the title implies, the author attempted to rank individuals who have most influenced history and the course of human events. Safe to say, if any of these individuals had not lived then human affairs would have been very different. Hart ranked Adam Smith, the founder of economics, #30:

> Adam Smith was not the first person to devote himself to economic theory, and many of his best-known ideas were not original. But he was the first person to present a comprehensive and systematic theory of economics that was sufficiently correct to serve as a foundation for future progress in the field. For this reason, it may fairly be said that *The Wealth of Nations* is the starting point of the modern study of political economy.
>
> Hart, 1992: 148–9

Notice that Hart used the term 'political economy' rather than 'economics'. Indeed, as we have seen, economics originated as the study of both politics and economics, and was known as political economy from the time of Smith to the late nineteenth century, when economists became convinced of the superiority of their scientific credentials and divorced themselves from politics and the other social sciences. One of the motivations for writing this textbook is our shared belief that it is incumbent for economics to return to its political economy roots.

As the title of his book *An Enquiry into the Nature and Causes of the Wealth of Nations* (generally referred to as *The Wealth of Nations*) (1776) implies, Smith wanted to understand what makes a nation wealthy. Heavily influenced by Isaac Newton (1642–1727), who discovered orderly and predictable laws governing the Earth and the heavenly bodies,[1] Smith wanted to do the same for political economy: to discover underlying laws holding economies together. Smith argued that by decentralising control of economic decisions, such as what to produce, how much to produce, etc., a nation could maximise its wealth. But this did not mean that individuals should do whatever they want; on the contrary, as discussed in his earlier book *The Theory of Moral Sentiments* (1759), human beings living together have a moral obligation towards each other as well.

Smith revolutionised the definition of wealth and the role of the individual. Rather than defining wealth as the stock of gold a nation possesses, as was typical then, Smith argued that wealth is a process, so that the amount of wealth is unlimited. Smith argued that the individual matters and is not a mere instrument in producing wealth accruing to the sovereign (or ruler). Since the nation is composed of individuals, the nation is only as wealthy as its citizens.

---

1. Interestingly, Hart ranked Newton #2 in his 'influential persons'.

be integrated or synthesised. It certainly would be a formidable task; one which partly underpins the establishment of *The International Journal of Pluralism and Economics Education* (*IJPEE*), which, in order to find some common ground between the various economic ideologies or schools, applies a methodology based on *pluralism*.

Effective solutions to the problems confronting us today must involve new ways of thinking and cooperation between social scientists, rather than one discipline such as economics insisting on its dominance, and, within economics, only one school of thought. But before economics cooperates with other disciplines, it must learn to recognise and accept diversity within its own ranks; hence the need for pluralism. We believe that enough commonalities exist between the above ideologies to warrant an inclusive and collaborative approach.

1.4 SUSTAINABILITY, PLURALISM, JUSTICE: THE CENTRAL THEMES OF THIS BOOK

As mentioned earlier, the central themes of our book are pluralism, sustainability and justice. Each will now be explained.

(A) Pluralism

In 2001, French economics students petitioned their professors for a more realistic and pluralist teaching of economics:

> Too often the lectures leave no place for reflection. Out of all the approaches to economic questions that exist, generally only one is presented to us. This approach is supposed to explain everything by means of a purely axiomatic process, as if this were THE economic truth. We do not accept this dogmatism. We want a pluralism of approaches, adapted to the complexity of the objects and to the uncertainty surrounding most of the big questions in economics (unemployment, inequalities, the place of financial markets, the advantages and disadvantages of free-trade, globalisation, economic development, etc.
>
> Post-Autistic Economics Network, 2000; emphasis in original

More recently, the student-led organisation Rethinking Economics (2014) argued:

> We need to recognise the plurality within economics. In most courses 'economics' is shorthand for 'neoclassical economics'. There is no recognition of the variety of schools of thought within economics, across history or across the world. Academic integrity requires that alternative economic theories be introduced to students, alongside those currently taught. Economic questions

> cannot necessarily be answered adequately from a single theoretical standpoint, or solely from a mathematical approach.

The call for pluralism has been reiterated in an important new book by recent graduates of the University of Manchester (Earle et al., 2017).

Economics is only one subject among the social sciences; and the social sciences, in turn, is only one area of study among others. To only look at one subject for understanding our economy and then only one viewpoint within that subject short-changes creative thinking and stunts intellectual growth.

Pluralism may be loosely defined as welcoming different and often opposing views; pluralism respects the legitimacy of opposing views. Not to be pluralist is to be monist, which is to recognise only one view as legitimate. To learn in a pluralist manner is to become educated; to learn in a monist manner is to become proselytised. If economics is to help solve our contemporary problems, and we believe it can, then it must become pluralist.

Becoming pluralist does not mean that you must agree with every view; on the contrary, disagreement (and conflict with others) is necessary to forge a fruitful dialogue in which effective policies can be discussed and conceptualised. We feel that

> pluralism instils empathy, dialogue, humility, and understanding. Monism [its opposite], by filtering out different views, prevents one from knowing which view is better in certain situations. Monism is antithetical to pluralism and antithetical to education.
>
> Reardon, 2009: 267

Only pluralism is consistent with democracy and only a democracy in ideas is consistent with the ideals of education.[5] Our world needs educated citizens and economists who understand diversity and are willing to work with others.

It is also important to note that pluralism is primarily a process, a state of mind, a modus operandi. Thus one practises pluralism, one promotes pluralism, one is a pluralist, etc. By focusing on disagreements and the existence of multiple solutions to complex problems, pluralism returns the fun to economics.

Before we proceed, we must make two points about our approach to pluralism. First, there are basically two ways to write an economics text from a pluralist perspective: (1) to discuss every issue and concept from every relevant viewpoint; or (2) to present the text in whole without presenting every ideology's take on every issue. Perhaps an analogy might be going to a restaurant and ordering a meal. The first approach involves the chef explaining how every step of the recipe (and ingredient) differs from the approaches of other chefs, whereas the second

5. For a multifaceted discussion of pluralism, see Heise (2017) and Reardon (2017).

approach involves the chef presenting the meal with a general overview of her philosophy. Our approach is the latter: we offer you a textbook that is pluralist, emphasising the themes of sustainability and justice. We use the necessary ingredients to offer you a satisfying and useful product without cluttering the text.

Having said that, our second point about our approach to pluralism is that, throughout the text, the reader might feel we are overly critical toward neoclassical economics. To an extent this is correct: neoclassical economics is silent on sustainability and justice, and has been consistently anti-pluralist.[6] Yet, at the same time, we emphasise what is useful in that school of thought.

(B) Sustainability

Imagine checking into a hotel room and finding the room littered with trash, the bed unmade and the toilets clogged. How would you react? Would you calmly dismiss this as the right of previous owners to enjoy themselves, or would you be angry that no one had the decency to care about you? Most of us would be angry at the previous tenants and at the management for allowing this to happen.

In a way this captures the essence of sustainability: the hotel room is analogous to our Earth. We check in when we are born and (hopefully) enjoy our stay and then leave. In what condition should we leave it? Why should I care for someone who comes after me? Isn't such an individual capable of cleaning up on their own?

We believe that we should care for others both now and in the future, for three reasons. First, caring for both humans and non-humans is what makes us human; it allows us to consider ourselves as sentient and self-conscious beings. Imagine a society in which no one cared for anyone. How inviting would this be? Second, we need to respect those who come after us; to ensure that the planet is liveable, and perhaps in a better condition than we received it. And third,

6. So the reader doesn't think we have an axe to grind, consider the titles of the following texts, all of which are highly critical of both neoclassical economics and its pedagogy: *A Guide to What's Wrong with Economics* (2004); *The Economics Anti-Textbook: A Critical Thinker's Guide to Microeconomics* (2010); *Debunking Economics* (2011); *What Every Economics Student Needs to Know and Doesn't Get in the Usual Principles Text* (2014); *The Econocracy: The Perils of Leaving Economics to the Experts* (2017). Steve Keen begins his widely read *Debunking Economics* with, 'Economics may make our recessions deeper, longer and more intractable, when the public is entitled to expect economics to have precisely the opposite effect' (Keen, 2011: 1). And the authors of the influential *The Econocracy* write, 'Having graduated now we are all keenly aware that our economics education has not equipped us with the knowledge or skills to justify any authority we [have been] given. In fact we were so frustrated with how little our education was helping us understand the world that midway through our second year at university we began a campaign to reform economics education' (Earle et al., 2017: 2).

research indicates that one reason why societies have failed in the past is because human demands on Earth's natural resources outstrip the planet's capability of supplying them or replenishing those that can be renewed or regrown (Diamond, 2005). Through history, inattention to sustainability has affected large empires, from the Roman Empire to the present-day United States. Consider, for example, the fall of the Roman Empire:

> Roman society prominently exhibited status and prestige-driven patterns of conspicuous consumption. But with [its] over-expansion, problems with regard to the quantity and reliability of food supplies arose. Rome was largely a grain-based empire, sustained largely by slave labour. Subject to diverse social-military, ecological and climatic stresses . . . Growing food imports caused economic crises and contributed to the strains which led to the eventual decline of the Roman Empire. Roman emperors could no longer finance the customary free distribution of food. Unable to pay its soldiers, Rome was no longer capable of stopping the barbarian incursions in the north. Ultimately the overextended and financially strapped empire collapsed.
>
> Broswimmer, 2002: 44–5

In the past, one nation's failures were more or less self-contained, but today, globalisation means that national economies are interconnected; and unsustainability, along with climate change, is no respecter of national boundaries.

While many definitions of sustainability exist (e.g. one Earth; to give something to the next user in no worse condition than it was given to you), we prefer the definition offered by the Brundtland Commission. In 1987 the Brundtland Commission (chaired by Norwegian Prime Minister Gro Harlem Brundtland) explored, among other things, how to achieve a workable balance between economic development and the sustainable use of natural resources. Its report, *Our Common Future* (WCED, 1987: 16) defined the term **sustainable development**, which has since become extremely popular: 'development that meets the needs of the present without compromising the ability of future generations to meet their own needs'. Importantly, a key element of sustainable development is ethical concern for others, especially non-humans, those of future generations and the poor:

> Meeting essential needs requires not only a new era of economic growth for nations in which the majority are poor, but an assurance that those poor get their fair share of the resources required to sustain that growth. Such equity would be aided by political systems that secure effective citizen participation in decision-making and by greater democracy in international decision-making.
>
> WCED, 1987: 16

Sustainable development is frequently envisaged as consisting of three intersecting circles, which denote the economic, the social and the environmental (Figure 1.1). Given this, sustainability is sometimes referred to as a goal or an 'end in view', whereas sustainable development is the processes whereby we seek to achieve this goal. Both concepts are multifaceted, but 'sustainable development' is an especially contested concept, often meaning different things to different people. For example, economic growth may be viewed as perhaps more important than, or maybe incompatible with, living within the ecological limitations of our planet.

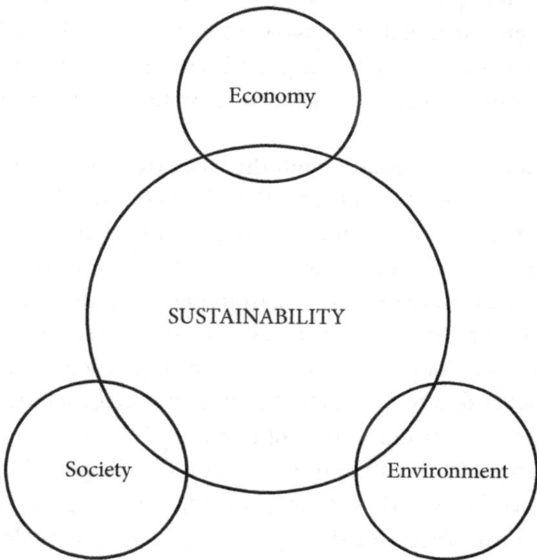

Figure 1.1 Venn Diagram of Sustainable Development
Source: Elaborated by the authors.

So how does one develop a modus vivendi for sustainable development and sustainability? How does one incorporate sustainability into one's life and the organisation of our interconnected national economies? One key means is to recognise that sustainability and development are not mutually contradictory but mutually dependent: healthy economic development cannot exist without a healthy supporting environment. Economic development, in this context, means being more concerned with economic well-being than simply producing more stuff, using more of the world's natural resources, creating more and more waste, etc.

A person's commitment to sustainability – how she acts and implements its values – can range from reluctant acceptance to a radical change in one's lifestyle. Peter Söderbaum (2008: 14–15) identifies three such levels of commitment:

- **Business-as-usual:** Supporters might adopt the language of sustainability but without changing any underlying values and ideology. Reports about ecological and social problems are considered to be exaggerated, and any future problems can be handled within the traditional paradigm of economic growth and reliance on technology.
- **Social and Ecological Moderation:** Environmental and social problems are acknowledged but they can be solved within the current economic system. All we need is specific policies to attenuate the most unethical behaviour and nudge consumers, firms and workers in the 'correct' direction.
- **Radical Change:** Our way of life is on a collision course with the environment, such that business-as-usual policies will result in ecological disaster. We need a major change and rethinking of our values. We must rethink the heretofore acceptance of continued economic growth.

This book is concerned primarily with the latter two levels. We argue that our current economy is unsustainable and that if we continue business-as-usual, a collision course with the environment is inevitable. This situation is partly due to our values: we are conditioned to want more while assuming the environment to be infinitely resilient, always recovering from the demands we place upon it and always providing the necessary resources to meet our ever-growing wants and needs. Given an insuperable problem, we assume technology will be our saviour. Partly, this belief is due to the current dominance of neoclassical economics, which was conceived in the nineteenth century 'when economists thought, wrote, and prescribed as if nature did not [exist]. . . The growth fetish, while on balance quite useful in a world with empty land, shoals of undisturbed fish, vast forests and a robust ozone shield, helped create a more crowded and stressed one' (McNeil, 2000: 335, 336).

Just when you thought you understood the important concept of sustainability, we need to add an additional layer of complexity: that between weak and strong sustainability.

- **Weak sustainability** assumes that if we deplete our resources such as air, water, fisheries, ecological systems, etc., we can replace them with human-made capital, i.e. machinery, factories, tools, computers, etc. made by people; thus, human-made capital is substitutable for natural capital.
- **Strong sustainability** assumes that different types of capital are not substitutable. Natural capital must be preserved and passed on to future generations.

Weak sustainability comports with the 'business-as-usual' approach and to some extent Söderbaum's 'social and ecological moderation', whereas strong sustainability is consistent with the radical interpretation.

Probably one of our most pressing problems is climate change. How (and if) we respond depends on whether we can become sustainable and adopt sustainable values. We need the urgent cooperation of all the sciences and social sciences in order to devise effective and sustainable solutions to prevent the worst effects from happening. Hopefully this book will give you the necessary background in economics in order to understand and to help develop effective solutions.

Box 1.3 What Does 'Parts Per Million' Mean?

Scientists claim that if we are to avoid cataclysmic and irreversible damage to our climate, we must prevent the Earth's mean temperature from rising more than 2 degrees Celsius (3.6°F) by 2100, from its 1800 level (at the dawn of the Industrial Revolution). According to the National Aeronautics and Space Administration (NASA), since 1800 the Earth's temperature has risen by 0.16°C (0.29°F). And, according to the UN Intergovernmental Panel on Climate Change the Earth's temperature increase by the end of the twenty-first century is *likely* to exceed 2.0°C (3.6°F). Currently, according to NASA, the Earth's temperature is the warmest in 800,000 years.

While global warming has many interrelated causes, a primary causal factor is the concentration of gases (such as carbon dioxide, methane and water vapour) in the atmosphere, which acts as a greenhouse effect, trapping warmth. A preponderant global warming gas is carbon dioxide (CO_2), which is a natural and constituent component of the atmosphere. Burning carbon-based fuels such as oil, coal and natural gas releases CO_2 into the Earth's atmosphere.

The atmospheric presence of CO_2 is measured in parts per million (ppm). According to the *Business Dictionary*, parts per million means concentration (by volume) of one part of an entity (gas) per million parts of another entity. One part per million is roughly equivalent to 5 litres of material in an Olympic-size swimming pool.

Based on data from NASA, current CO_2 ppm stands at 406, meaning that if we were to divide the atmosphere into a million parts, 406 parts would be carbon. We passed the 400 ppm threshold in 2015. According to NASA, we don't know the critical CO_2 ppm threshold that would trigger catastrophic damage – but we do know that as the ppm increases, so does global temperature.

Sources:
Business Dictionary: www.businessdictionary.com/definition/parts-/
NASA: http://climate.nasa.gov
IPCC: *Climate Change 2014: Synthesis Report*. Summary for Policymakers. http://ipcc.ch/report/ar5/syr/

In 2015, the UN promulgated (after countless hours of debate and talking with various individuals around the world) 17 sustainable development goals (SDGs), which is a central theme of this textbook. These goals are built on the Millennium Development Goals (MDGs) adopted in 2000, aimed at an array of issues that included slashing poverty, hunger, disease and gender inequality, and improving access to water and sanitation. The UN 17 SDGs go much further, and are connected to the United Nations Development Programme (UNDP) Strategic Plan focus areas: sustainable development, democratic governance and peace building, and climate and disaster resilience. The UN 17 SDGs, taken together, reinforce and exemplify the three main themes of our textbook: pluralism, justice and sustainability. They are:

1. End poverty in all its forms everywhere.
2. End hunger, achieve food security and improved nutrition, and promote sustainable agriculture.
3. Ensure healthy lives and promote well-being for all at all ages.
4. Ensure inclusive and quality education for all and promote lifelong learning.
5. Achieve gender equality and empower all women and girls.
6. Ensure access to water and sanitation for all.
7. Ensure access to affordable, reliable, sustainable and modern energy for all.
8. Promote inclusive and sustainable economic growth, employment and decent work for all.
9. Build resilient infrastructure, promote sustainable industrialisation and foster innovation.
10. Reduce inequality within and among countries.
11. Make cities inclusive, safe, resilient and sustainable.
12. Ensure sustainable consumption and production patterns.
13. Take urgent action to combat climate change and its impacts.
14. Conserve and sustainably use the ocean, seas and marine resources.
15. Sustainably manage forests, combat desertification, halt and reverse land degradation, halt biodiversity loss.
16. Promote just, peaceful and inclusive societies.
17. Revitalise the global partnership for sustainable development.

Think of these 17 goals as a recipe for future living, although with a sense of urgency. They underscore the point that sustainability involves a lot more than concern with the environment. Notice the wording: 'all', inclusive', and 'urgent'; and the active verbs: end, ensure, achieve, promote, reduce, conserve, revitalise. This is the language of the SDGs, this is the language of urgency, and this is the language of your textbook.

The SDGs are interrelated; so by tackling one, we tackle others. One example: consider the use of charcoal for fuel. It is cheaper and easier to use than firewood, natural gas and coal, and charcoal collecting and selling is now one of the biggest economic drivers of Africa, helping many people earn money in order to survive. But since charcoal comes from wood and wood comes from trees, as more charcoal is used, more trees are cut down, the greater the forest loss, and the greater the loss of biodiversity. Given that women in developing countries are the principal gatherers of firewood, spending an additional 2 to 20 hours per week (UN, 2015d); as more trees are felled, women spend more time looking for wood – time which could be devoted to other issues. But if Africa invests in clean, renewable energy (Goal #7) then we don't have to deforest; which in turn will increase biodiversity (meeting Goal #15) and help to increase quality education (Goal #4), since women and girls do not have to spend more time gathering firewood; which will help achieve gender equality and empower all women and girls (Goal #5); which would help make cities more inclusive (Goal #11) and reduce climate change (Goal #13); which will promote just, peaceful and inclusive societies (Goal #16). Of course, whether these goals are achieved is a function of Goal #17: Revitalize the global partnership for sustainable development.

We hope that your textbook will provide a necessary foundation of knowledge to reach these goals, so you can contextualise our problems and engage in dialogue with others towards a solution. We also feel that this is a wonderful opportunity – a once-in-a-lifetime opportunity for all of us to collectively embrace our future.

Sustainability is intricately related to justice, the third theme of this book.

(C) Justice

In the nineteenth century, a scientist was assumed to be a neutral observer, standing aloof from his or her experiments without influencing them with his or her values. In the early twentieth century, this notion of value neutrality was jettisoned by physics and the other sciences – except for neoclassical economics, which has inexplicably retained this quaint assumption. All scientists have ideas and values which shape the research field they enter, along with the basic questions asked, which determine which stones are turned and which are not. There is nothing wrong with admitting that our values influence our interests; it is common sense. But it is wrong and ethically unacceptable to insist on value neutrality – something that is not humanly possible. In fact, insisting on value neutrality is itself articulating a value judgment. In her book *What are the Questions?*, Joan Robinson (1980: xiii), urged her fellow economists 'to speak up on the side of humanity'. We intend to do so in this book.

All authors have values, and in our case we are very much concerned with justice. But what is it? The word 'justice' is derived from the Latin *jūstitia*, and, like sustainability, is multifaceted and contestable. Essentially, it means fair, equitable, due treatment according to custom and the law. More specifically, we feel that a just society ensures that basic human needs are met, investing in the social well-being of all of its members, especially those unable to provide for themselves. We share Adam Smith's value judgement that

> Servants, labourers and workmen of different kinds, make up the far greater part of every great political society. But what improves the circumstances of

> the greater part can never be regarded as an inconveniency to the whole. No society can surely be flourishing and happy, of which the far greater part of the members are poor and miserable.
>
> (Smith 1976 [1776], Vol. I, Bk. I, Ch. 8, p.88)

Jean-Jacques Rousseau, an eighteenth-century Swiss philosopher, wrote, 'if we look at human society with a calm and disinterested eye, it seems, at first, to show us only the violence of the powerful and the oppression of the weak. The mind is shocked at the cruelty of the one, or is induced to the blindness of the other' (Rousseau, 1755 [1973]: 48). He famously suggested that humans are born free but live everywhere in chains.

The philosopher Stanley Benn (1967b: 298) noted that 'although justice is sometimes used as a synonym for law or lawfulness, it has a broader sense closer to fairness'. John Rawls (1971), for example, used an interesting thought experiment: He asked, what type of society would you like to live in and what place would you like to have in it? Now plan out that society – its social structure, economic arrangements, political institutions, legal codes, power relationships and social dynamics relating to wealth and inequality, without knowing your position in that society, without knowing your status, power or wealth. To attempt such a thought experiment, suggests Rawls, is for most people a practical demonstration of the desirability of living in a fair and just society.

Justice, like democracy, equality and freedom, is a complex and multifaceted concept. Consider the commonly defined definition of justice:

> The quality of being just; fairness. The principle of moral righteousness, equity; the upholding of what is just, especially fair treatment and due rewards in accordance with honour, standards or law; the administration and procedure of law; conformity to fact or sound reason.

Even if we could agree on which facet of justice deserves emphasis, can we agree on exactly what is meant by 'fairness', 'facts' or 'sound reason'? These terms are subjective, and without an objective measuring stick we must rely on democratic discussion and dialogue to arrive at agreement. Amartya Sen (2009: vii), a Nobel laureate in economics, admitted that agreeing on what is just is difficult; but at the same time it is easier to recognise and understand injustice:

> What moves us, reasonably enough, is not the realisation that the world falls short of being completely just – which few of us expect – but that there are clearly remediable injustices around us which we want to eliminate.

Injustice is an individual not able to provision for herself; or a nation unable to provide decent livelihoods for its citizens or, in the course of producing goods and services, destroying the environment. Injustice is individuals without access to food, shelter or education. And so on.

Although our textbook discusses the traditional concepts of economics, such as savings, investment, consumption, money, trade, etc., it also focuses on poverty, inequality, debt, dispossession and sustainability within a pluralist theoretical framework. Contemporary global challenges force us to seek justice and articulate the concerns of the Global South, along with the interests of future generations. As a result, the book is largely written from a global perspective, and considers how actions today will impact the lives of others in different parts of the world. We hope this book will be read and utilised by all those concerned with justice and with redressing situations of injustice.

CONCLUSION

Knowledge of economics can elucidate the central problems of our time as well as provide solutions. This can happen only if economics is fundamentally reconstituted and reconceptualised along the three elements of pluralism, sustainability and justice. This is what we offer in this book. It does not mean that you will be equipped to solve all the world's problems immediately after reading it. After all, we offer only an introduction to economics, which in itself is only an introduction to the social sciences. Successfully dealing with the serious problems affecting us all will require hard work, cooperation and a lot of intellectual investment. We hope this book is the first of many fruitful steps to help you think like an educated citizen of the twenty-first century.

THINKING QUESTIONS

How might you handle disagreements between different points of view or economic perspectives?

Think of your typical day. Which actions do you consider sustainable and which do you consider unsustainable?

What has economics in common with justice?

CLASS ACTIVITY

Is there a common denominator between the various economic ideologies?

AREAS FOR RESEARCH

How might you define and conceptualise a just healthcare system? Or a just distribution of income?

UN SDG FOCUS

Please read carefully the 17 UN SDGs. What is your initial reaction? Do they fit well together? Do some of the goals contradict each other? What are the concrete action words? Which words are ambiguous? What should be the initial steps in implementing these goals?

FURTHER READING

Blewitt, J. (2014) *Understanding Sustainable Development*. London: Earthscan.

Diamond, J. (2005) *Collapse*. New York: Penguin.

Lovelock, J. (1979 [2000]) *Gaia: A New Look at Life on Earth*. Oxford, UK: Oxford University Press.

Söderbaum, P. (2008) *Understanding Sustainability Economics: Towards Pluralism in Economics*. London: Earthscan.

United Nations (2015) 'UN Sustainable Development Goals'. https://sustainabledevelopment.un.org/?menu=1300

2
Knowledge and the Construction of Economic Models

Just like the confident student we encountered in the Preface, we believe that knowledge enables and empowers. This chapter addresses how knowledge is obtained and how it is used to construct economic models – a necessary first step in understanding our economy. Just like using a 2-D GPS to find your bearings, a model is a necessary first step in understanding our economy.

2.1 WHAT IS KNOWLEDGE AND HOW IT IS OBTAINED?

In a provocative yet disturbing book, *The Climate Change Challenge and the Failure of Democracy* (Shearman and Smith, 2007), the authors argue that our most important problem, bar none, is climate change. However, to avoid cataclysmic climate change, or perhaps at least to attenuate it somewhat, they suggest dismantling our current higher education system and replacing it with colleges and universities that will produce 'philosopher-warriors' who can understand our ecological predicament and thus enact targeted solutions:

> The conventional university trains narrow, politically correct thinkers who ultimately become the economic warriors of the system. Our proposal is to counter this by an alternative framework for the training and complete education of a new type of person, who will be wise and fit to serve and to rule. Unlike the narrowly focused economic rationalist universities of today, the real university (special institutions in which the opportunity is provided for the much-needed ecowarriors to develop and be nurtured) will train holistic thinkers in all of the arts and sciences necessary for tough decision-making that the environmental crisis is confronting us with. These thinkers will be the true public intellectuals, with knowledge well-grounded in ecology. . . We must accomplish this education with the dedication that Sparta used to train its warriors. As in Sparta, these natural elites will be especially trained from childhood to meet the challenging problems of our times.
>
> Shearman and Smith, 2007: 134–5

Aside from the perhaps undemocratic nature of such training, a fundamental objection is 'who is going to educate the educators?' Needless to say, we strongly disagree with this elitist, anti-democratic proposal: education must be broad-based and democratic. Solutions can and must germinate from an educated, rather than a narrowly trained, elite.

Education needs to be conducted within a community of learners. As college students and professors, we are active members of this community. So the first item of business is to welcome each other and to look forward to learning together co-operatively and collaboratively. No one has all the answers. In addition, our active community of economics learners must extend across time, so that we can access the wisdom of those who preceded us, and hopefully we can offer new knowledge to future generations.

This nexus between the past, present, and future is a fundamental tenet in education, and a key ingredient in progressing knowledge forward. Having access to contributions from the past means we do not have to learn everything from scratch: we can share and communicate, and hopefully learn from others.

Is there a specific requirement for membership in a learning community? Only one: the willingness to join and become an active member – it is impossible to coerce someone to do either. By 'active' we mean interacting with others, not working in isolation, and eager to learn. But active also requires one to be proactive: we don't learn as passive recipients of knowledge; we are not empty vessels waiting to be filled with wisdom. Becoming educated requires a good deal of effort, but at the same time being a member of a learning community is enabling, which makes it fun.

The Brazilian Paulo Freire (1921–97) has influenced us, along with other educators and community developers. While Freire's original work was on adult literacy, his approach to education identifies issues of positive action for change and development. For Freire, the educational process is not neutral, and people need to link knowledge to action so that they actively work to change their societies. As a result, people can engage in a 'problem-posing' approach in which they become active participants. Indeed, in his book *Pedagogy of Freedom: Ethics, Democracy, and Civic Courage* (1998), Freire argued that *engaged* learning and teaching is central to the creation of the individual, culture and history.

Are there strict boundaries to individual communities of learning, and if so, how are they determined? There is widespread disagreement on this issue. Our view is that society needs the specialised knowledge of economics in order to solve our generation's problems. Yet, at the same time, these boundaries should not be hermetically sealed, barring contact with other learning communities. Each community (think of the individual social sciences discussed in the last chapter), with fluid borders and a welcoming attitude, is the perfect antidote for the self-destructive assumption that only one discipline has all the answers.

A related issue is whether we should become specialists in one particular field, like economics, or even a sub-discipline like labour economics, or become more of a generalist, a 'jack-of-all-trades'. This gets to the crux of the pedagogy of economics: is the goal to think like an economist or like a citizen of the world? Once again, there is no right or wrong answer. Given the explosion of knowledge, being a generalist risks being superficial, although sustainability educators argue that it is important to embrace a holistic view of the world and its interactions. For these educators, breadth is as important if not more so than depth or super-specialisation. Of course, a disciplinary specialist, such as an economist or sociologist, can provide a solid basis for understanding reality, although a super-specialist with little knowledge of other disciplines might be too optimistic or adamant about the efficacy in his or her field, and consequently not able to work well with others. Indeed, the more specialised we become, the less knowledgeable we are of other intellectual disciplines. Alfred Marshall (1842–1924), a leading economist of the nineteenth century whose influence is still widely felt today, addressed his fellow economists:[1]

> It is the duty of those who are giving their chief work to a limited field, to keep up close and constant correspondence with those who are engaged in neighbouring fields. Specialists who never look beyond their own domain are apt to see things out of true proportion; much of the knowledge they get together is of comparatively little use; they work away at the details of old problems which have lost most of their significance and have been supplanted by new questions rising out of new points of view; and they fail to gain that large illumination which the progress of every science throws by comparison and analogy on those around it.
>
> Marshall, 1890 [1946]: 770–71

Our position is an attempted compromise. We feel that a traditional discipline, e.g. economics or sociology, is a legitimate starting point for a learning community; thus, study of an individual discipline can and should provide a solid intellectual basis. However, it is important for the educator to encourage humility about any individual discipline's efficacy, and to provide a systematic means to communicate across intellectual boundaries. This is why we advocate pluralism. The borders between individual disciplines, and of intellectual learning communities, must remain open and fluid, with practitioners willing and able to listen to others. Openness and the willingness to listen and learn from others – the essence of pluralism – leads to new and fruitful insights.[2] Pluralism requires an open-mind-

1. This is not just an indictment of the economics profession, although we agree that it rings very true today, but, as Thomas Kuhn argued in his important book *The Structure of Scientific Revolutions* (2012 [1962]), the narrowness that Marshall condemned typifies normal science.

2. A great example is Arturo Hermann's *The Systemic Nature of the Economic Crisis: The Perspective of Heterodox Economics and Psychoanalysis* (2015). His interdisciplinary title is self-explanatory. He writes, 'an interdisciplinary perspective does not imply that each

edness, often noticeably absent in traditional economic pedagogy. Pluralism is often misidentified as requiring knowledge of every subject, but on the contrary, its essence is the ability to listen and to engage in dialogue, especially with those you disagree with.

2.2 WHAT ARE THE PROPER TOOLS TO ACQUIRE KNOWLEDGE?

If you want to build a house, you need tools; likewise, to become an active member of a learning community it is necessary to develop and acquire a set of tools – concepts, theories, methods, philosophies, processes, etc.– i.e. an intellectual toolbox. Such a toolbox is not fixed in size or shape, but evolves as our knowledge and understanding evolve. The acquisition and development of tools makes us human and allows knowledge to progress; and, of course, we should always be willing to use improved and/or additional intellectual tools.

To become a good and critical learner one must acquire facility with the following three tools: the ability to doubt and to ask good questions; the willingness to imagine; and the ability to listen and engage in constructive dialogue. It is asking questions via a pluralist dialogue that enables us to conceptualise effective answers.[3] Thus, the goal of education is to encourage thinking – not so much *what* to think (for this is proselytisation) but, specifically, *how* to think.

While some of us might admire people with unflinching faith, for our purposes the ability to doubt well-established beliefs and concepts is the essence of learning and knowledge development. Are existing institutions as good as they could be? Is an existing theory problematic and unable to explain reality? If, for example, our economic system is unable to provision for all, can we make it better? Or do we automatically assume that the existing economic system is as good as it gets? We do not advocate disagreeing with everything for the sake of disagreement; rather, our objective is to promote a healthy scepticism, and not to doubt everything or allow our learning journey to degenerate into a ceaseless and irreverent questioning.

This leads us to the second tool for acquiring knowledge: the willingness to imagine. To imagine is to venture beyond the constricting confines of accepted values and accepted lines of thought. To imagine is to ask what is, what if, and why not? To give one memorable example: for centuries, scientists studied mass and energy as if they were separate entities; admittedly there was no compelling

---

discipline would lose its distinctive features. Quite the contrary, a more comprehensive approach such as this, by broadening the horizon of the observer, can also contribute to a better appraisal of the specific characteristics of his/her main fields of specialization' (Hermann, 2015: xvii).

3. For a good example, see Robinson (1980).

reason to think otherwise. Albert Einstein (1879–1955) postulated that, rather than being separate, energy and mass were intricately related, devising the simply elegant yet powerfully relevant formula $E = MC^2$.

Interestingly, as a youngster, Einstein often imagined what it would be like to sit on a beam of light and travel the universe astride it. This wondering led to the development of the special theory of relativity (1905) and the general theory of relativity (1915), both of which have profoundly affected our understanding of the universe.[4] On the other hand, and at the risk of oversimplification, thinking like an adult is constricted by peer pressure, prior conceptions or biases and, for some, a timidity to question.

Our third tool is the willingness to discuss, listen and enter into constructive dialogue, which in turn is the modus operandi of pluralism. Dialogue can occur with fellow students, family and friends, and hopefully with people from other disciplines. This can be as simple as sharing with a colleague a draft of your paper; or, if at a dead end, looking to jumpstart your thinking. Sometimes we are reluctant to discuss our work with outsiders, and sometimes as outsiders we are reluctant to comment on other's work. But the interchange between different learning communities can be profoundly fertile. As one example, after developing his special theory of relativity, Albert Einstein was convinced that the concepts of space/time and mass/energy were directly related, but could not link them. After years of thinking, he turned to his good friend the mathematician Marcel Grossman, who suggested using non-Euclidean geometry. This enabled Einstein very quickly to conceptualise the framework for the general theory.

Thus, our overall goal in developing our tools is not to reach a final state of knowledge in which everything is known, but to consistently refine and modify our tools in order to advance our understanding of the world.

2.3 HOW DOES ONE ACQUIRE KNOWLEDGE?

One of the more fascinating debates in philosophy is 'How do we acquire knowledge?' At birth is the human mind a blank slate, or do we have certain

4. For a fascinating historical development of the 'world's most famous equation', $E = MC^2$, see Bodanis (2000). Incidentally, it was Einstein's special theory of relativity which destroyed the once-vaulted position of value neutrality. This occurred (almost) simultaneously with the invention of Cubism in art by Pablo Picasso and Georges Braque, which impugned the notion of a single, aloof, neutral, privileged perspective. For a fascinating (and essential) account of the intersection of art and physics, and its implications for our current values, see Shlain (1990). For an extended discussion of art and physics and its interrelationship with modern economics, see Boyd and Reardon (forthcoming).

preconceived notions? Is knowledge acquired through our senses? How do we know what is out there and how can our minds make sense of it?[5]

We acquire knowledge through experience, through reading, observing what we consider to be reality, making sense of it with concepts and theories, and discussing and developing our understanding with others. Our minds equip us with the ability to synthesise, abstract and simplify – a necessary tool to help us build models to understand our economy. Dialogue helps us to compare and contrast; to develop. Dialogue or engagement may be with a past writer or a current one, your teacher, a documentary film, a lab experiment, your personal experience, etc. You may wish to reflect on what you have learnt and to see what else you need to learn; to know and to understand. It is not always easy. Sometimes complex issues take time to understand, and sometimes it is important to have more than one head involved.

There is no shortcut to obtaining knowledge and understanding; it is a difficult and, at times, an arduous task, as Marx himself wrote in the preface to the French edition of *Capital* (1867 [1967]: 21): 'There is no royal road to science, and only those who do not dread the fatiguing climb of its steep paths have a chance of gaining its luminous summits'. Fortunately, as members of learning communities, we don't have to climb alone.

2.4 HOW CAN WE ENSURE THAT KNOWLEDGE IS NOT USED FOR SOCIALLY DESTRUCTIVE ENDS?

A fundamental question that all human societies ask is: are there things we should not know, either because such knowledge comes perilously close to the quintessence of life, and/or because human beings cannot be trusted with such knowledge if obtained? There is no better example than Einstein's famous $E = MC^2$, which led quickly to the development of the atom bomb. Would it have been better if such knowledge had never been discovered? But then who determines what knowledge is, and what knowledge is forbidden? What are the criteria? And if such dangerous knowledge *is* obtained, how can we ensure that it will not destroy human beings?[6]

Perhaps a more fundamental question is: can we ensure that knowledge produced now will not result in its use for destructive ends in the future? An illustrative example is the invention of Freon (the first of the chlorofluorocarbons

5. Fully discussing these questions is beyond the confines of this book. For a brief but helpful introduction, see Shlain (1990: 84–96).

6. Two fascinating and must-read novels which directly address this important issue are *Faust* (1999) by Johann von Goethe and *Frankenstein* by Mary Shelley (1816 [1992]). *Faust* was published in several parts during 1790–1832; the reference cited here contains the complete *Faust*.

– CFCs – which we now know damage the Earth's ozone layer).[7] But back in 1930, when Freon was invented, it was hailed as a wonder chemical, since it was highly stable and inert, and did not react with anything. In fact these two properties proved 'useful in refrigerants, solvents, and spray propellants . . . Freon replaced dangerously flammable and toxic gases previously used in refrigeration, and made air conditioning practical' (McNeil, 2000: 111). Although Freon solved an immediate practical problem, enabling many to enjoy the benefits of refrigeration and air conditioning, it wasn't until much later (during the 1970s) that we realised that its desirable properties of stability and inertness also abetted its drifting upward into the stratosphere, where sunlight broke the chemical apart, releasing agents that ruptured ozone molecules (Ibid.).

The inventor of Freon, Thomas Midgley, a chemist working for General Motors, also invented lead gas during the 1920s, which reduced engine knocking and made high-compression auto and aircraft engines possible. Because of these two inventions, McNeal writes that 'Midgley had more impact on the atmosphere than any other single organism in earth history' (Ibid.). Certainly this was not Midgley's intention. From the vantage of hindsight, how could we have foreseen Freon's deleterious consequences? And, perhaps more importantly, how can we prevent future Freons?

The alternative – to stifle and prevent new knowledge – is certainly not palatable, desirable, nor practical; and who would monitor this process? And what about the opposite problem: the inability to solve a future problem, given current suppression of knowledge? We believe that knowledge can't (and should not) be suppressed, but that we should engage in dialogue with each other carefully to monitor its usage and effects (particularly regarding sustainability). This can only happen with educated citizens.

There are two motivations for acquiring knowledge. (1) The acquisition of pure knowledge, which by definition does not have any immediate applications; after all, human beings have a natural curiosity: we want to explore and investigate what lies above, below or within us; we are seekers, discovers, explorers.[8] (2) We want to improve existing ways of doing things. Historically, attempts have been made to distinguish between these motivations as pure and applied research respectively, but in practice the dividing line is blurred.

Turning to economics, economists spend much of their time developing theories (from the Greek *theorein*, 'to look at'), which attempt to explain how economic systems function. Theories, based on underlying knowledge, are

---

7. This discussion of Freon and its harmful effects is based on McNeil (2000: 111–15).
8. For examples of the myriad seekers and discovers in history, see Boorstin (1983); Boorstin (1998). Boortsin writes, 'We are all seekers. We all want to know why. Man [sic] is the asking animal . . . it is the seeking that continues to bring us together, that makes and keeps us human' (1998: xiii).

important in an economist's intellectual toolbox. But many economists are not simply content to explain the world in various ways; they wish to engage practically, to change how the economy operates, to prevent certain things from happening, or to find solutions to existing problems. In this way, economists work with policymakers to fashion practical ways to intervene in the economy via financial or environmental regulation; the development and application of economic instruments or macroeconomic techniques that may alter the monetary supply; levels of private and public investment, etc.

Box 2.1 Doesn't Everyone Have the Same Values?

Thomas More gives the amusing example in his novel *Utopia* of first-time visitors to the island on which the novel is set, who are unaware of local customs and assume that gold would be highly esteemed as in their home country, and why not? Doesn't everyone value gold? More (1516 [1965]: 87–8) wrote that the visitors, 'who were great men [sic] in their own country [naively adorned themselves] with cloth of gold, with great chains round their necks, gold earrings dangling from their ears, and gold rings on their fingers. Their very hats were festooned with glittering ropes of pearls and other jewels'. But they quickly learned, much to their chagrin, that in this island, gold adornments were not admired but despised.

Several lessons emerge from this: (1) the folly of assuming that one's own values are uniformly applicable; (2) the importance of understanding local culture; and (3) the folly of gold and money. The word 'utopia' comes from the Greek *ou* (not) and *topos* (place), meaning 'no place', currently suggesting an ideal perfect place; or sometimes, pejoratively, an impractical ideal scheme.

2.5 MODELS AND THEIR USEFULNESS IN ECONOMICS

A **model** is a simplification of reality, as well as an abstraction; it omits a lot in order to distil its essence. In many ways a model is like a map, which gives a two-dimensional picture of a three-dimensional world – if reasonably accurate, it will help navigation. Nonetheless, we expect the map to present the essence of reality in a somewhat recognisable form, which in turn makes it useful. Both a map and a guidebook capture the concentrated essence of a society, but, as anyone who has used a guidebook realises, no two guidebooks are alike: each is written by authors with different visions and perspectives. An economic model functions in similar ways.

Is a model necessary for understanding the economy, or can we study the economy without one? Surprisingly, this is one of the few issues that all schools of thought within economics agree. Given the complexity of the economy, a model is a necessary aid to understanding. While economics students are most anxious to get their hands dirty and jump right into studying the economy, it's important to keep in mind that an economy is itself a social construct that we have devised in order to achieve our objective of provisioning for all. In other words, 'economic systems are not natural systems. An economy is a social organisation created either through legislation or by an evolutionary process of invention and innovation' (Hyman Minsky, 2008: 7).

As we learn more about models, keep in mind the following three caveats. First, because models are simplifications of reality, we trade off realism for manageability. We need to keep some things simple. Consequently, to criticise a model for its simplification is mistaken. We can't expect a model to cover all aspects of reality, but nevertheless we expect it to capture its essence. Second, models are developed by individuals, or teams of individuals, working together, meaning that a model reflects their underlying assumptions and ideologies; thus, to criticise a model because it is ideological is also mistaken. Third, since the economy changes over time, we expect our models to change as well. What could be worse than using a nineteenth-century map to navigate around twenty-first-century London? To blindly assume that one model can explain all situations in all time periods is not only lazy but also intellectually dishonest, and potentially dangerous, especially if it is intended to influence public policy.

Models also encompass particular types of reasoning. In her book *Foundations for New Economic Thinking*, Sheila Dow (2012) writes of the use and abuse of mathematics in economics; that is, the insistence that economic theory must be expressed in the language of formal mathematics. In this regard, it is important to note that the use of maths involves adopting a particular type of reasoning, which in neoclassical economics takes the form of *deductive reasoning*. In other words, economic relations are derived deductively from a common set of assumptions about rational, optimising individuals. As rational behaviour is based on information that is known with certainty, predictions are made using deductive mathematics. Unfortunately, as we shall see, in the real world information is not always certain or complete, and neither do people always act rationally.

2.6 ELEMENTS OF A MODEL

Let's assume that you want to construct a model of the economy, say of the United States. Admittedly this is a daunting task, with 320 million citizens, millions of businesses and a complex and active government. So, where do you begin? The first element in constructing a model is to begin with your assumptions and ideology. What motivates you to study the economy in the first place? Why the US? Do you have any preconceived notions about the US – perhaps as a paragon of efficiency, or of unsustainability? Amartya Sen (1999: 262) wrote:

> The use of formal economic models to understand the operation of market mechanisms, as is the standard practice in economic theory, is to some extent a double-edged sword. The models can give insight into the way the real world

Box 2.2 The First Model In Economics: the Physiocrats and Their 'Economic Table'

From the Greek words *phýsis* (nature) and *kràtos* (power), 'physiocrat' literally means 'power of nature'. The physiocrats emerged during the mid-eighteenth century in pre-revolutionary France. This was a time of economic, political and social disorder, culminating in the French Revolution in 1789. The intellectual leader of the physiocrats, François Quesnay (1694–1774) is credited with constructing the first economic model with his *Tableau Économique* (1758). This model, based on his own knowledge as a surgeon, fused metaphors of body and motion with that of (economic) value, reflected the economic and political system of pre-industrial France. The model helped the physiocrats search for deeper and more orderly meaning, especially the interconnectedness of the various sectors of the economy. Not surprisingly, given the importance of land and agriculture in eighteenth-century France, land was assumed to be the ultimate source of value and the only productive sector. Manufacturing was seen as sterile and therefore not producing any value, and landlords as idle, consuming the value produced by agricultural workers.

The physiocrats have an important place in the history of economic thought for several reasons. First, for developing an economic model as an abstract and simplified depiction of reality. Second, because of the importance they attached to land as the only source of value, which reflected contemporary economic conditions. Third, they directly influenced Adam Smith, who while travelling in France consulted Quesnay for medical treatment and was impressed, and undoubtedly influenced by his ideas. Fourth, the physiocrats' insight into the role of money in the economy was revolutionary. They argued that, just like blood circulating through the body, money was the conduit through which value flowed between the productive and unproductive sectors. The physiocrats argued that if at any particular stage money was hoarded, then the functioning of the whole system was disrupted – an idea later incorporated by Keynes and Minsky to explain why capitalism is unstable (Hunt and Lautsenheiser, 2011; Reynolds, 2000).

> operates. On the other hand, the structure of the model conceals some implicit assumptions . . .

It is very important in the construction of an economic model that any assumptions be carefully (and honestly) articulated. Consider, for example, three different individuals: one who believes in the harmonising forces of the economy, so that even though firms and employees have different interests they can work together to achieve a beneficent outcome; another believing that all economic decisions should be made by the entrepreneur or the firm; and a third assuming every business wants to exploit workers and pocket the surplus in order to enrich themselves. Each individual would construct a very different model, but isn't it intellectually dishonest claiming each as value-free? Practising pluralism enables each of these three individuals to engage in dialogue with the other two, enabling understanding of each model's strengths and weaknesses.

The second element in building a model is to describe in words what you want to model, i.e. what you want to describe. Then, later, proceed from words to more abstract thinking.

Third, we need to decide if the model should be static – a snapshot at a moment in time – or dynamic and evolving over time. Each type is useful, but each gives a different perspective of reality. Each has its strengths and weaknesses, with neither intrinsically superior. In building a model, it might be helpful to begin with a static picture. But keep in mind that to do so we must hold all things constant, particularly the influence of outside factors. A problem arises if we want to depict a relatively dynamic economy, like that of the United States, with a model that is basically static: it will be misleading to the extent that it withholds information. We will return to this discussion at the end of this chapter.

The fourth element is to list the variables of interest and how they relate to one another. Just like in a recipe, it isn't enough to list the ingredients in any haphazard order; it is also important to suggest how they fit together. This should first be attempted in words, and then, if need be, mathematical language should be substituted, especially if the words have some ambiguity. What variables are **endogenous** (to be explained by the model) and which variables are **exogenous** (outside of the model's explanation)? Which variables are to be included and which variables excluded? Undoubtedly, careful model construction is extremely important. It requires diligent study and empirical understanding of how the economy works.

The fifth element is to consult with others – from other schools of thought within economics and also (ideally) from other social sciences.[9] Does the model make sense? Is something missing?

If your original objective was to construct an explanatory picture, your task is complete. However, if you wanted to explain the relationship between different variables – say, for example, why income inequality has increased in the USA, or the casual factors of unemployment, then more careful modelling is necessary. If, the model is to be empirically tested, then data must be gathered.

Fortunately, as members of a learning community we do not have to construct models from scratch (although some of us do); instead, we learn from past contributions. Typically, our task is confined to using existing models with minor variations. We must also be mindful that our model is unlikely to be completely realistic and thus unlikely to be the final word on how the economy works. So we should continuously and rigorously revise and test it against the data we have

9. Earle et al. rightly criticise (neoclassical) economics for becoming 'so detached and obscure [that] citizens often cannot even assess whether or not elites are serving them well' (2017: 151). They suggest (quite persuasively) that we should actively engage the public in a two-way dialogue to produce a new generation of citizen economists (2017: 151–8).

gathered from our observations and other studies.[10] It is therefore important for a congruence to exist between the economy and the model; otherwise a model lacks explanatory power.

A particular embarrassing moment for neoclassical economists occurred when Queen Elizabeth visited the London School of Economics, one of the UK's most prestigious higher education institutions, in late 2008. Quite reasonably, she asked why economists had not anticipated the financial crisis, and why they were asleep on watch during the most serious economic crisis in a century. After the Queen raised this question there was a flurry of letter-writing to various national newspapers, with neoclassical economists concluding they had the right response: market failure means that we need more markets! But more revealing is that neoclassical economics could not predict the crisis, since its very existence was deemed not possible and thus not worthy of inclusion in their models. As Minsky (2008: 323) warned:

> for an economic theory to be relevant what happens in the world must be a possible event in the theory. On that score alone, standard economic theory [neoclassical economics] is a failure; the instability so evident in our system cannot happen if the core of standard theory is to be believed.

2.7 NEOCLASSICAL ECONOMICS AND THE CONCEPT OF EQUILIBRIUM

The word 'equilibrium' was first used in the early seventeenth century to suggest a 'well-balanced state of mind'. As we noted in Chapter 1, the existence of equilibrium and the tendency of market systems towards equilibrium is a central element of neoclassical economics. All other schools within economics have rejected equilibrium as a foundational concept, as have the other social sciences.

But why has neoclassical economics tenaciously clasped this metaphor and made it the crux of its ideology? Two reasons. First, the nineteenth-century founders of neoclassical economics were heavily influenced by Isaac Newton's three laws of motion, which, taken together, assume a body is at rest (i.e. equilibrium) until acted upon by a force; which in turn generates an equal but opposing force; with motion continuing until the force ceases, resulting in a new equilibrium (Newton, 1687 [1995]: 2–3).

The neoclassical founders enthusiastically adapted Newtonian physics in order to understand their world and to clarify how economic systems work; for them, and the general public, it was intellectually stimulating. This emulation, however,

10. This is the essence of one of the guiding principles of institutional economics: 'that direction is forward which provides for the continuity of human life and the noninvidious re-creation of community through the instrumental use of knowledge' (Tool, 2001: 293; original emphasis deleted).

soon became locked in and ossified (Hodgson, 1999: 70), with future generations of neoclassical economists parrying and then ignoring developments in physics such as quantum mechanics, which impugned the notion of equilibrium and posited that our very investigation of matter can influence its behaviour.

Box 2.3 Alfred Marshall (1842–1924)

Among Keynes' preponderant 'intellectual influences' was Alfred Marshall, his teacher and mentor at Cambridge University. Originally educated as a mathematician, Marshall studied physics and philosophy, giving him a more holistic and more compassionate understanding of political economy. His *Principles of Economics* (1890) became the standard text for the next 50 years. Generations of economics students can thank Marshall for developing the concepts of demand and supply, elasticity, consumer surplus, the theory of the firm, partial equilibrium analysis, and much more.

Marshall was also chiefly responsible for the *neoclassical synthesis* by retaining some of the more 'acceptable' elements of classical economics, such as price theory, abstract/deductive reasoning, applicability of universal laws and distribution, while jettisoning the more controversial items, such as the labour theory of value, the wage fund and inherent class conflict.

This **neoclassical synthesis** constricted the accepted domain of economics and served to legitimise capitalism as the only acceptable economic system and the only system consistent with markets. The neoclassical synthesis was also responsible for spawning other schools within economics, especially institutionalism, due to the deliberate omission of the interesting topics from classical economics. With the neoclassical synthesis, economics became divorced from classical economics and turned inward, focusing more on its own deductive methodology. Nonetheless, there was subtlety in Marshall's thought; an awareness of the limitations of mathematics, the importance of time and the limitations of partial equilibrium analysis. Marshall, and the other founding fathers[1] of neoclassical economics,

> were pioneers in a new way of thinking, and yet, in contrast to their modern disciples, they were often aware of possible limitations of the theory they were trying to construct. They expected their heirs to extend the boundaries of economic analysis, and they expected economics to develop from the precocious but hobbled child to which they gave birth into a vibrant and flexible adult (Keen, 2012: 34).

Although a staunch believer in capitalism, Marshall believed that government could temper the worst abuses of capitalism, very much in evidence during the late nineteenth century. But this temperance and amelioration could happen only very slowly, in an evolutionary rather than revolutionary process. For Marshall, successful change requires the learning and apprehension of new values, which in turn requires time.

1. Yes, fathers: they were all male.

A second reason why neoclassical economics insists on the equilibrium metaphor is the ideological belief that only capitalism, and only a laissez-faire variation of capitalism, is capable of achieving equilibrium on its own, thus rendering government intervention unnecessary. In this sense, neoclassical economics and capitalism have 'rarely been at "scientific" arm's length; they have always been incestuous to some degree, and most shamelessly as we approach the present' (Dowd, 2004: xiii). Not only do neoclassical economists assume, rather than empirically investigate, that free-market capitalism naturally gravitates toward equilibrium, but they also assume that this equilibrium is as good as it gets. The danger is that the model is confused with reality and, more importantly, that the ideology prevents understanding of how our world really works.

Let's illustrate this confusion with the idea of the **minimum wage**, defined as a legal wage established (by the government) above the market wage. Whether we should implement a minimum wage, and who will be affected (both positively and negatively) is an important yet contentious question, given that the discipline of economics is concerned with provisioning. Such a question necessitates an empirical investigation. Neoclassical economists, however, begin by assuming the economy is in equilibrium, so that any interference will distort the beneficent outcomes of the market. They define equilibrium as that price (or wage, as the price of labour) in which the quantity demanded of labour equals the quantity supplied; in other words, at equilibrium there is no surplus labour.

Given a minimum wage which by force of law is greater than the existing wage, it is then deductively assumed that the amount of labour demanded by firms decreases, while the amount of labour supplied by workers increases, cumulatively causing **unemployment**, i.e. a surplus of labour. Just as Newton assumed that an object reacts automatically to an imposed force, neoclassical economists assume that workers and firms will react automatically (without thinking) to a wage change.

Thus, by assuming an initial equilibrium, the model ignores the possibility that the existing labour market might not be in equilibrium and thus that government intervention could bring the economy closer to equilibrium (if we want to use that term).

We are wary of using the term 'equilibrium' except in specifically defined circumstances, since our dynamic world is constantly changing, and it is the process of change that is most interesting. In ecology, for example,

> there is no equilibrium tendency that is automatically manifested in natural systems. Indeed their normal movement is simply the product of one isolated disturbance outcome followed by another isolated disturbance outcome in a somewhat unpredictable and even random fashion.
>
> Nelson, 2010: 175–6

From a sustainability perspective, much more relevant and practical than the concept of equilibrium is the carrying capacity of our planet and of ensuring that our level of economic activity is compatible with the available natural resources and our ecosystems. More on this in the next chapter.

2.8 THE IMPORTANCE OF TIME IN ECONOMICS

We conclude this chapter with a discussion of the importance of time, which to you might seem obvious, but time has been neglected in much of neoclasical economics. As Keynes (1936 [2010]: 46) wrote in his *General Theory*, 'Time usually elapses, however – and sometimes much time – between the incurring of costs by the producer (with the consumer in view) and the purchase of the output by the ultimate consumer.'

To understand how we move from the 'incurring of costs by the producer to the purchase of the output by the consumer', it is necessary to include the passage of time: only then can we understand the process of change, including what and who has caused it. Constructing sophisticated models, such as system dynamics, can certainly incorporate time, but time can also be included in simple static models often used at the principles level, so that 'each functional relationship in a theory – each link in a model – is really a hypothesis that can and should be tested in many different ways' (Wheat, 2009: 73).

Let us assume, for example, that price increases for a particular good. The *No Time* model assumes that the quantity demanded decreases simultaneously with an increase in the quantity supplied, resulting in an increase in price, and a new equilibrium. What is ignored is the process of attaining the new equilibrium, that is, how we get from one static picture (A) to another (B). To use the **feedback method** (i.e. understanding how endogenous behaviour derives from the initial structure of the model), it is useful to deconstruct the process into steps and ask at each step what happens. Put yourself in the position of either the producer or consumer facing uncertainty and risk, each of which involves the passage of time and the pervasive uncertainty as to whether to make the adjustments:

> Adjusting prices involves serious and uncertain risks because of the immediate impact on sales and revenue and the longer-term effects on customer loyalty and market share. Such decisions take time [. . .] after a pricing decision is made. . . implementing that decision requires an additional flurry of activity that could take days or run into weeks . . . [While] some consumers would react immediately to a price change, [o]thers would take longer to observe and respond . . . and change their spending habits . . . Gearing up production in response to higher prices or cutting back production when prices are falling could take several months, depending on labour market conditions, institutional arrangements, and norms surrounding overtime and temporary layoffs or the hiring and firing of workers.
>
> Wheat, 2009: 78

Specifically, what happens as the price changes? The quantity demanded by the consumer decreases; the supply/demand ratio decreases; price increases; changes must occur to ensure the supply/demand ratio goal is met; the quantity supplied increases. We cannot be sure *a priori* that a new equilibrium will be met, given the uncertain reactions of producer and consumers along any step. Thus, in such a dynamic context captured by the feedback method, 'price, supply, and demand are *mutually dependent over time*, and that a distinction between so-called independent and dependent variables is meaningless' (Ibid.: 79; emphasis in original).

The feedback method also incorporates *unintended* as well as intended consequences of actions. It is quite possible to model unintended consequences, although this is not necessarily easy, since the consequences of some actions may not be apparent immediately and indeed may take time to work their effects. Climate modellers understand this quite well. Software programmes of varying degrees of complexity and sophistication are now routinely used to identify and map a range of dependent, lagged and other types of variables that manifest themselves over time. Needless to say, current 'institutional arrangements, and the case for particular institutional arrangements can be better evaluated by noting the likelihood of various unintended consequences' (Sen, 1999: 257). Indeed, economists, like meteorologists, often 'run' their models in computer simulations to see what might happen if certain variables interact and certain feedbacks consequently result. As Wheat (2009: 87) notes, such simulation can help us to 'encourage investigation of how markets change over time [while focusing] on processes that influence dynamics rather than presuming end results'.

2.9 ECONOMICS AND COMPLEXITY THEORY

In addition to supply and demand, consumer surplus, elasticity and other topics that have become ossified in neoclassical thought, Alfred Marshall popularised the technique of **partial equilibrium**, i.e. illustrating a single part of a complex system while holding everything else constant. Its attraction is partly due to simplification, and partly to our ignorance of the operation of the whole system. Proponents of partial equilibrium argue that students are more receptive to simplification. We disagree. Our present-day economic system is inherently complex, and its complexity in all dimensions must be understood. Pursuing a partial and simplified analysis will often mislead, especially when couched in equilibrium terms.

Complexity theory has developed as an alternative, and we believe it is a much more fruitful method of understanding complex systems. It is distinguished by the following elements: (1) rejection of the assumption of order in favour of chaos, i.e. disorder; (2) equilibrium is specious, misleading and 'quaint' (Keen, 2012:

454); (3) the progression of the complex system depends on initial conditions; variations thereof can influence its direction; (4) mutual interaction and interdependence between the system and its environment is of crucial importance. While the construction of complexity theory requires sophisticated mathematics that takes us beyond the confines of this book, it is useful and informative and 'among the glamour areas' (Ibid.) of contemporary science, including issues of environmental sustainability, and should form the basic foundation of future courses in economics.

THINKING QUESTIONS

What is meant by 'community'? How would you define a community of learners?

Can all economists be considered members of a specific community?

CLASS ACTIVITY

Devise an economic model to explain how your community of learners operates.

AREAS FOR RESEARCH

How influential was J. M. Keynes in the past? How influential is he now? How do you account for the difference?

Is equilibrium a useful concept in economics?

Explore further the idea of complexity theory in economics.

UN SDG FOCUS

In order to implement any of the UN 17 SDGs, is a model necessary? What are the necessary ingredients for such a model? Should the model be static or dynamic? Which variables would be exogenous in your model, and which would be endogenous?

FURTHER READING

Boorstin, D. (1993) *The Discovers*. New York: Random House.

Boorstin, D. (1998) *The Seekers: The Story of Man's Continuing Quest to Understand his World*. New York: Vintage Books.

Dowd, D. (2004) *Capitalism and its Economics*, 2nd ed. London: Pluto Press.

Keen, S. (2012) *Debunking Economics*. London: Zed Books.

Sen, A. (1999) *Development as Freedom*. New York: Anchor Books.

3
Sustainability, Resources and the Environment

If the purpose of economics is to help people provision, what resources are available to help us achieve this important objective? This chapter begins with a classification of resources: what are they and how should they be used? We then introduce two individuals central to our themes of sustainability and justice: Thomas Malthus, whose population thesis predicted that global population will increase far more than the supporting resources, causing calamity; and Karl Polyani, who argued quite persuasively that an economy is artificially constructed and needs to be embedded within the broader society. This chapter also introduces the important concepts of the laws of demand and supply and of elasticity. Each is a helpful working tool, essential in constructing economic models.

3.1 LIVING WITHIN OUR MEANS

Politicians, experts and many others use the phrase 'living within our means'. What does this meant? On one level, we have been enjoying a better standard of living than our resources and our work efficiency have warranted, especially in the developed world. The affluent lifestyle of many Western countries has been funded by a boom in cheap energy and the creation of easy credit; and, because of how this credit was created, many of the world's richest societies have accumulated significant amounts of public and private debt. But we are also living beyond our means on a deeper, more fundamental level, since our accustomed lifestyle is exhausting the Earth's resources and poisoning the natural systems we rely on.

The common English definition of a **resource** is 'a source of support or help'. The word is derived from the Latin *resurgere*, meaning to 'rise again', suggesting that resources are not dropped down from heaven but become resources as our knowledge, technology and culture progresses. A **natural resource** is something found in nature – trees, coal, wind, etc. Our present economic arrangements mean that we are using more materials, creating more waste and pollution, and using more (fossil fuel) energy than we can actually sustain. The global population, especially in the affluent countries, is using finite resources as if there was a never-ending supply – or, putting it another way, using resources as if we had three or more Earths to plunder rather than just the one. We feel that our global society needs to respect the limits of what the planet can provide – and there is a plethora of evidence that we humans have overstepped our bounds. We also believe that a central task of the economics profession is to become aware of these limits and to conceptualise policies that work within them rather than ignore them. And, in the interest of sustainability, we believe that we owe discussion and consideration of these issues to future generations.

As Table 3.1 shows, we can divide nature's resources into four kinds: renewable, non-renewable, replenishable and recyclable. From an economic point of view, the important question is how we harvest and steward these resources. Renewable resources should not be used more rapidly than they can regenerate, so we should not use, for example, more timber than we can plant trees to replace it; replenishable resources should not be used at a faster rate than they can be replenished. There is a subtle difference between replenishable and renewable resources, relating to the speed of use compared with the speed of replacement. This means that replenishable resources must be stewarded with more care than renewable resources because it takes much longer for their supply to be replenished. To illustrate: consider the difference between the time needed to form an underground aquifer and for a tree to grow.

Table 3.1 Defining Resources

Type of resource	*Definition*	*Examples*
Renewable	Resources that can grow and therefore regenerate themselves.	Timber, food crops, fisheries.
Non-renewable	Resources that are finite within the planetary system and cannot be restored once used.	Petroleum, gas, coal, uranium.
Replenishable	Resources that can be renewed over a long time.	Groundwater, soil.
Recyclable	Resources that are limited within the planetary system but can be reused.	Copper, gold, iron ore.

Source: Authors.

Recyclable resources are limited, but once used they can be retrieved and used again. However, we should note that retrieving and recycling materials still requires energy inputs, so we should use them only when necessary and with care. Finally, we have non-renewable resources, primarily fossil fuels. Since their supply is limited and cannot be replaced, we should carefully steward their remaining reserves.

That resources are limited may seem self-evident, but neoclassical economists assume that no resource is so essential that a substitute will not be found as it nears depletion. They rely on market forces to allocate scarce resources, while ignoring the importance of power and sustainability. Specifically: as a good becomes scarcer its price will increase, inducing users to demand less, existing producers to find more (or produce more, or make available more), and potential producers to offer substitutes.

Evidence of impending resource shortages was offered by *The Limits to Growth* (Meadows et al., 1972), published by The Club of Rome, an organisation comprised of businesspeople, scientists and politicians. The most arresting aspect of the study was its computer model that simulated our future based on a number of assumptions about population, resource endowments and usage. Its conclusion was stark: sustained increases in consumption and economic growth would lead to an 'overshoot' of the Earth's 'carrying capacity'. As it turns out, many of the predictions were unduly pessimistic, as resources have lasted longer than predicted in many cases, although predictions for continuing and accelerating increased resource use and pollution have been reasonably accurate. The reason for the increased supply of once 'scarce' resources is that technological developments enable additional extraction, while reducing the quantity demanded of the resource. However, in 2005 the original authors reviewed their earlier findings and made a number of amendments in the face of criticisms and new evidence, and reaffirmed their vital message about necessary ecological limits to economic growth. Continuing research from the Stockholm Resilience Centre on planetary boundaries seems to confirm the validity of the Club of Rome's position, although the Centre's emphasis is a little different – not limits to growth but growth within limits (Rockström and Klum, 2015).

The Limits to Growth was peremptorily dismissed by neoclassical economists for ignoring market forces. They replaced its circumspection with exuberance while ignoring ecological limits; however, their disregard is no longer shared by many, including global management consultants. A report from the global consultancy McKinsey (Dobbs et al., 2011), *Resource Revolution*, for example, argued that the twenty-first century will see increased resource depletion and a rising price for most resources.

Of course, if we accept this argument that resources are becoming scarce, it raises important questions about how remaining supplies will be shared between today's citizens and those of tomorrow. The McKinsey report takes the pro-market position that market systems and market forces are the most effective methods for allocating resources, while green economists argue that resources should be treated as the common property of local communities (Cato, 2012a). In contrast, institutionalists argue that we need to study the institutions that have developed around the allocation of resources in order to determine who benefits and who loses.

Cheap energy has enabled us to live beyond our means, while resulting in spectacular growth in population and GDP. But an increasing number of economists realise that economic growth is a threatening problem and that we need to restructure our economy away from constant growth. Not only has the effect of pollution on our planetary systems become apparent but it is also increasingly clear that easily available energy sources, particularly oil, are being exhausted. In addition, we need to drastically reduce our consumption of fossil fuels, especially oil and coal, if we are to avoid causing increased concentrations of carbon dioxide and other greenhouse gases in the atmosphere. Climate change is the best evidence yet of how our economy as presently structured fails to keep within natural limits. As Sir Nicholas Stern stated in his famous report for the UK Treasury, *The Economics of Climate Change* (2007), it is a clear and potentially very expensive example of market failure.

Another important book, *Prosperity Without Growth* (2009), argued that not only must growth end, but no basis exists for optimistically assuming improvements in technical efficiency as a panacea. The book's author, Tim Jackson (2009: 188) wrote, 'This delusional strategy has reached its limits. Simplistic assumptions that capitalism's propensity for efficiency will stabilise the climate and solve the problem of resource scarcity are almost literally bankrupt.'

3.2 THOMAS MALTHUS' *ESSAY ON POPULATION* AND THE GREAT LAND GRAB

Economics is not teleological, meaning that economics has not systemically evolved since Adam Smith such that today's ideas and concepts are superior to yesterday's. In fact, we believe the opposite: there is a lot of wisdom in the past, and that we can learn much from history. At the same time, however, economic laws and principles are seldom constructed in a vacuum; on the contrary, they are specific in terms of time and place in their objectives, and thus, not surprisingly, are highly ideological. There is nothing wrong with being either ideological or passionate about reform; this makes us human. However, if we use a concept, principle or theory today, we must not automatically apply it without first understanding its historical origins, initial objectives and underlying ideology. There is no better example than Malthus's *Principle of Population*:

> Malthus lived in tumultuous times of intense class conflicts, and his writings reflect his positions on these conflicts. . . [He] was an outspoken champion of the wealthy, and his theory of population provided the framework within which he defended them.
>
> Hunt and Lautzenheiser, 2011: 65, 71

When the Reverend Thomas Malthus (1766–1834), a professor of political economy, wrote his famous *Essay on Population* (1798), England was in the beginning stages of the Industrial Revolution. Not surprisingly, the dominant agricultural interests at the time were not keen to cede their power and control of the British Parliament to the burgeoning capitalists. In his *Essay*, Malthus was replying to the earlier arguments of William Godwin and Marquis de Condorcet, both bothered by the inequities and undue sufferings of many people during the Industrial Revolution. Each advocated reforms, including a primitive social security, limiting credit and even abolishing private property. Malthus, defending the interests of the wealthy, would have none of that. Not only is the separation of people into capitalists and workers classes natural, he argued, but such separation is also necessary for social progress and development. And furthermore, since only capitalists are socially virtuous, any attempts to improve the lot of workers will only make the situation worse by increasing their propensity to breed.

Stated succinctly, **Malthus' Law of Population** is: Population, if unchecked, will increase faster than the means of subsistence. In other words, population has a greater rate of change than the means of subsistence. Ironically, the use of coal by England during the Industrial Revolution, and oil later in the century, allowed us to increase our means of subsistence geometrically, thanks to cheap energy.

Malthus' ideas remain influential today, with some neo-Malthusians arguing that we should carefully check population growth. However, if the environmentally focused economists are right, then as the population increases and resources become scarce we will see more competition for remaining resources. Some economists see this already happening in the growing attempt by global corporations and national governments to acquire land in other countries to feed their populations. The problem is most severe in Africa, where some countries are seeing vast areas of their agricultural land fall into the hands of foreign owners. Arguments can be made that such land purchases represent investments in poor countries, perhaps creating jobs. But in many cases the land is used to grow biofuels, which then exhaust the soil, while people using the land to support themselves through subsistence agriculture are displaced and forced into poverty. As de Schutter (2011) has argued, targeted countries become increasingly vulnerable to price shocks, and the development of the market for land rights has destructive effects on livelihoods dependent on 'the commons', such as grazing land and fishing areas.

This raises fundamental questions about who owns the land and whether, if land is a gift from nature, it should be allocated differently from products bought and sold on the market. In 1879 the US economist Henry George (1839–97) published his best-selling *Progress and Poverty*, in which he asked many challenging questions including why anyone should be excluded from the land. He argued that since land is scarce and provided free by nature, individuals fortunate enough to own land and receive rents, in exchange for allowing others to use it should pay the community as a whole in return for this privilege. His idea of a land value tax was taken up in Australia and Canada, and is currently under discussion in other countries among many green groups as an ethical means to gain revenue for national investment.

3.3 KARL POLANYI AND *THE GREAT TRANSFORMATION*

Karl Polanyi (1886–1994) was a Hungarian economist who spent much of his life in London. His most famous book is *The Great Transformation* (1944). What makes Polanyi's economic theories unusual and particularly interesting is that he actively conducted research, undertaking anthropological studies of how people in different human communities engaged in the most fundamental economic task of provisioning. He learned that the market system, which many of his contemporaries assumed to be the basic form of economic organisation, was in fact extremely unusual and only an historically recent development. He called it a 'utopian myth' that a society relies entirely on the market for meeting needs. Indeed, Polanyi (1944: 48) was convinced that in most human communities the social life was more important than economic structures:

> The outstanding discovery of recent historical and anthropological research is that man's [sic] economy, as a rule, is submerged in his social relationships. He does not act so as to safeguard his individual interest in the possession of material goods; he acts so as to safeguard his social standing, his social claims, his social assets. He values material goods only in so far as they serve this end.

Polanyi thought that economics should be 'embedded' within social relationships. Later economists with a concern for the environment have suggested that this idea of 'embedding' can be extended, arguing that economies are also embedded within their natural environments. Polanyi believed that traditional economies are closely embedded within their local land – 'an element of nature inextricably interwoven with man's [sic] institutions' (Ibid.: 187). He believed that this connection was only lost when the market economy developed and parts of the natural world were turned into commodities (what he termed 'fictitious commodities') in order to be sold in the market. Polyani was convinced (Ibid.) that the market had utterly distorted the relationship between human communities and the land:

> Traditionally, land and labour are not separated; labour forms part of life; land remains part of nature, life and nature form an articulate whole. Land is thus tied up with the organisations of kinship, neighbourhood, craft and creed – with tribe and temple, village, guild and church. One Big Market, on the other hand, is an arrangement of economic life which includes markets for the

> factors of production. Since these factors happen to be indistinguishable from the elements of human institutions, man and nature, it can be readily seen that market economy involves a society the institutions of which are subordinated to the requirements of the market mechanism.

Polanyi argued that land and labour have an intrinsic value that can never be lost, and that the denigration and degradation of nature and people by their transformation into 'fictitious commodities' is harmful, both socially and ecologically. Real commodities are 'objects produced for sale on the market' (Ibid.: 75). Land, by contrast, 'is only another name for nature, which is not produced by humans [while] labour is only another name for a human activity'. (Ibid.: 75). To refer to these basic economic elements as equivalent to goods that were produced specifically to be sold he considered a fiction.

3.4 RESOURCES, OR FACTORS OF PRODUCTION

In this section we focus on how various resources become available for human use. This question concerned the early classical economists, like Adam Smith (1723–90) and David Ricardo (1772–1823). They defined resources in terms of 'factors of production', and more specifically as land, labour and capital. These are fundamental productive resources necessary to make anything that can later be sold in a market. According to the classical economists, the most fundamental economic resource was **land** (see our discussion of the physiocrats from the previous chapter): this comprised obviously the soil itself but also everything it contained, such as minerals, petroleum, diamonds, etc., along with the seas and inland water.

It is important to notice that their definition is rather limited, and instrumental, since it considers land in terms of what it can do for us. Thus 'the economic notion of resources is strictly *anthropocentric*. That is, the economic value of any resource is defined by human needs and nothing else' (Hussen, 2000: 4). This strongly contrasts with the view of land for much of human history, and still held by many indigenous people today, that land is our 'mother'. Today we are accustomed to thinking that the land belongs to us, whereas many Native American people, for example, feel that they belong to the land.

While lumping people with different beliefs, skills, loves and ambitions into the simple factor of **labour** is problematic, the third conventional factor of production, **capital**, poses even greater definitional problems. For Hussen (Ibid.), capital refers to 'a class of resources that is produced for the purpose of creating a more efficient production process. In other words, it is the stock of produced items available not for direct consumption but for further production purposes'. Examples include machines, buildings, computers and education (acquired skill).

Classical economists paid much more attention to land and labour, the more concrete sources of value, than to the rather more abstract and confusing 'capital'.

The UK-based sustainability consultancy and think tank Forum for the Future has further developed the notion of capital to encompass a range of other factors. Forum's **Five Capitals Framework** is fully explained by Parkin (2010), with the five 'capitals' explained in Table 3.2. 'Natural capital' is primary, embracing all other capitals. The environment, an extended version of 'land', appears as natural capital, and money appears as 'financial capital', which has been separated from 'manufactured capital' – the equipment and machinery needed to produce goods. People feature in this model in two ways: first, their skills and expertise as individuals reflected in 'human capital'; second, as 'social capital' or their shared institutions and culture – so important in making economic activity successful and efficient.

Table 3.2 The Five Capitals

Type of capital	*Definition*
Financial	Includes shares, bonds or banknotes; it is useful to facilitate exchange of the other capitals. Has no intrinsic value.
Manufactured	Machines and equipment.
Social	Civil society organisations and the relationships of trust they create.
Human	Health, knowledge, skills, motivation and spiritual ease of individuals.
Natural	The environment, including its available resources, and the natural systems supporting life.

Source: Adapted from Parkin (2010).

This model arises from a 'strong definition' of sustainability, such that any one capital cannot be substituted for another. But what is meant by 'substitution'? A good illustration is the idea of carbon offsetting. If you take a flight, you know it is producing carbon emissions (or do you?) and, if you have a conscience, you might feel guilty. A carbon offsetting company allows you to pay money to balance out the damage resulting from the pollution, thus substituting financial for natural capital. These examples, however, raise the important questions of how we value such damage, and can such damage even be measured?

3.5 DEMAND, SCARCITY, SUFFICIENCY AND ABUNDANCE

Allocating resources to members of a society is a crucial concern of all economic systems. Every society establishes rules of the game to determine how goods are allocated and who gets what. Much of the world is now organised according to some form of market economy, meaning that we purchase goods and services in

Box 3.1 The Jevons Paradox and Rebound Effects

Although many economists today are technological optimists (not concerned about resources becoming depleted), traditionally this was a central concern of economics. In 1865, for example, William Stanley Jevons[1] (1835–82) wrote *The Coal Question: An Inquiry Concerning the Progress of the Nation, and the Probable Exhaustion of Our Coal-Mines*. The British Empire depended on coal to fuel industry and exports (as well as domestic heating and transportation), so this was a fundamental concern for the country's policy-makers.

Jevons' conclusions were unduly pessimistic, since later in the same year new sources of coal were found in South Wales, but he is remembered for sophisticated thinking about the complexity of resource use. Specifically, Jevons noticed that if we develop ways to use energy more efficiently, then its price decreases, and, all else equal, we are likely to use more. His ideas have contemporary relevance in terms of policies to reduce fossil-fuel usage and hence CO_2 emissions. An example of such a policy might be to better insulate our homes to reduce the need for burning fossil fuels to heat them. This will lead to decreased fuel bills, but would we respond by setting the thermostat higher, rather than keeping our house the same temperature? Another example is how improved design of trains and aircraft has reduced energy use per mile, but has also improved the speed and comfort of travel and reduced costs. The outcome has been more travel and far more transport-related emissions than before. These behavioural responses to technological improvements are known as **rebound effects** and indicate the importance of including human behaviour and social and cultural understanding when theorising about economics or designing economic policies (Cato, 2011).

1. Yes, this is the same William Stanley Jevons whom we noted in Chapter 1 as a co-founder of neoclassical economics.

exchange for money. Such markets are based on the interaction of the amount of a good available (the **supply**) and the people who want to buy it (the **demand**).[1] How this process works is the focus of a central debate in economics: what determines the price of an object? Remember that classical economists argued that the main determinant of price was the amount of labour needed to produce it: the more labour needed, the greater its price, and vice versa. Neoclassical economists, however, argue that its main determinant is how much people value the good: If more people value a good, its price will increase, all else being equal, and vice versa. Whether it does and by how much will, first of all, depend on the amount of the good: if it is unlimited, then an increase in demand does not matter. There is enough to satisfy everyone. But a limited amount means that not everyone who wants the good will be able to obtain it.

Under capitalism, a distinction is made between those who want an item and those who can actually demand it. This distinction is made by money, enabling

1. Supply and demand, as well as the concept of elasticity, is based on Newton's three laws of motion (see Chapter 2).

those who want the good to actualise their demand; conversely, those without money are excluded from participating in the market. (Is possession of money the most just way to distinguish between want and demand?) Consider a person living on the street in Calcutta (Kolkata), India's seventh-largest city. She sees new high-rise luxury towers being built, but without any money she is excluded from this market and cannot articulate a demand. How to provision for such people and how to re-include them are crucial questions that every economic system must answer. This doesn't mean that every person should be able to demand any good. Certainly we can distinguish luxury goods from necessities.

We will have much to say on this in later chapters, but for now, let us return to our basic issue. In a market economy, if an individual wants a good (or service) and possesses money, then she will translate her desire into a demand for that good. Its price will increase depending on a number of factors: the available supply; the power of those controlling the good; the power of those demanding it; the relevant institutions affecting demand and supply; and the culture and values of the economic system, i.e. do we help those in need, or is everyone on their own?

The interaction of supply and demand is key to illustrate how a market functions. Neoclassical economic theory suggests that as the price of a good increases, an individual will demand less of that good, all else equal, and vice versa. One reason is that an individual's budget is limited, so for a given price increase, she will have less money to spend on something else, all else equal. If, for example, the price of petrol doubles and my income is not unlimited, and if I continue to purchase the same amount of petrol, I must devote less of my income to other goods and services. This understanding of how people react to the limited nature of their spending power is based on the concept of **opportunity cost**: the cost of obtaining an item is equivalent to the next-best offer. If I am reading this textbook than I am not socialising, so the opportunity cost of reading is the missed socialising. In attending university, in addition to the direct costs, the opportunity cost is what I give up – perhaps the income I might have obtained from paid employment.[2]

The other side of the theory focuses on the price and the quantity supplied, specifically how much of the product to make available for sale, as a function of price. If we experience particularly cold weather, for example, more people will want to buy gloves, meaning that the price of gloves may rise. This will

2. Interestingly, the concept of opportunity cost is heavily influenced by the nineteenth-century Newtonian value of binary opposites. For example, an electron can be either a wave or a particle but not both; an object can be either mass or energy but not both. Black versus white; male versus female; and, in the above example, I'm either studying or socialising, but not both. But quantum physics teaches us that polar opposites are often more complementary rather than antithetical.

encourage clothes manufacturers to shift to glove production because they can achieve higher sales and higher profits.

Price changes illustrate how demand and supply interact. In Europe, for example, when the price of oil and therefore petrol increases, quantity demanded tends to fall, with people buying more fuel-efficient cars. In the USA, when the price of oil increases, efforts have been made to increase its supply by unconventional means such as using additional energy to crack rock deposits to release oil and gas, commonly known as 'fracking'. 'Fracking' is short for **hydraulic fracturing**, and involves cracking rocks (deep in the Earth's crust) which contain oil and natural gas deposits; injecting a mixture of sand, chemicals and water, causing the rocks to break and allowing the oil and gas to flow to the surface. While fracking obviously increases the supply of fossil fuels (and, all else equal, reduces their price), it comes at a significant cost of adding to global warming gases (via mining, transportation and consumption), contamination and depletion of local water resources, and the relatively unknown effects of fissured underground rock on the local environment.

In the United States, although fracking has provided additional jobs and income and reduced dependence on foreign oil, it is not sustainable and postpones efforts to develop renewable energy (remember Jevons' Paradox). In spite of the central message of the Paris Climate Talks in December 2015 that human societies across the world are transiting to phase out fossil fuels by the middle of this century, we should not underestimate the huge social and economic changes this will entail:

> If the world agrees to limit the burning of . . . fossil resources, then that would wipe out the wealth of fossil fuel businesses, governments reliant on fossil fuel incomes and individuals whose pensions and savings are invested in those fossil fuel companies. . . it would mean wiping out US$20 trillion of wealth.
>
> Birch et al., 2017: 145

This doesn't mean that we should not transition; just that doing so has significant obstacles in terms of costs.

In neoclassical economics, the interaction of the desire to consume and the desire to profit is often portrayed via the **Laws of Demand** and **Supply**. The interaction of these two laws is referred to as **market forces**. Really the 'laws' are just generalisations of human behaviour and a simple way of understanding people's market behaviour. The **Law of Demand** assumes that given a price increase, the quantity demanded will decrease all else equal; conversely, a price decrease will enable consumers to increase the quantity demanded. The **Law of Supply** assumes that given a price increase the quantity supplied will increase, all else equal; conversely, a price decrease will result in a decrease in quantity supplied, all else equal.

In reality, however, people respond to price changes in a number of different ways. If, for health reasons, politicians encourage people to smoke less, then an increase in the price of cigarettes might achieve this. But some people might be unwilling and unable to respond to price signals, which also depends on the nature of the commodity. Like the price of water, for example: however high, people still need it. Perhaps some goods are so basic to human survival that they should be beyond the confines of any pricing system? We can also question whether market forces are the most ethical way to allocate scarce resources, especially as this involves placing a price tag on nature.

3.6 *TECHNIQUE 1*: UNDERSTANDING BASIC MARKET FORCES

Notwithstanding the reservations outlined above, we can introduce five generic templates to understand market forces:

- With demand constant, and all else equal, if the supply of a good increases, its price will decrease. *Example:* after the recent financial crisis, additional unconventional oil supplies decreased the price of oil. Keep in mind that this is only a first approximation. And, as Jevons' Paradox predicts, reduced prices, all else equal, will then increase the quantity demanded.
- With demand constant and all else equal, if the supply of a good decreases, its price will increase. *Example:* it is predicted that a decreasing supply of conventional oil within the next five years will increase its price.
- With supply constant, and all else equal, if the demand for a good decreases, its price will decrease. *Example:* decreased demand for coal, due to heightened awareness of global warming has decreased its price.
- With supply constant, and all else equal, if the demand for a good increases, its price will increase. *Example:* vigorous economic growth will increase the demand for oil, increasing its price.
- If both demand and supply change in the same direction (e.g. demand and supply increase), then the effect on price depends on which effect is greater: if demand increases more than supply, then, all else equal, the price will rise, and vice versa. But if demand and supply change in opposite directions (e.g. demand decreases, causing the price to fall, while supply increases, also causing the price to fall), the two effects reinforce each other.

How much (and if) a quantity changes due to a 'stimulus change' can be predicted by *elasticity*, which we explain in the next section.

3.7 *TECHNIQUE 2*: CALCULATING ELASTICITY

A basic tenet of neoclassical economics is that consumers respond to incentives, especially changing prices, so that a price increase causes consumers to buy less of a commodity, and vice versa. How much the reaction (in this case quantity demanded) changes due to a change in the stimulus (i.e. price) is measured by **elasticity**, defined as a response to a given stimulus. Such information guides firms as to how much to charge for their goods, when to increase or decrease prices, or how the demand for the good is expected to change as incomes change.

Elasticity of a good (or service) is determined by a number of factors:

- the need for the good
- the number of substitutes
- the good's importance in one's budget
- the length of time under consideration.

Each will now be explained.

If you usually drink orange juice every morning for breakfast, but a freak snowstorm in Florida reduces the supply, causing the price to double, you might switch to apple juice or another substitute. So goods with close substitutes will likely have a greater elasticity of demand. But if you are addicted to something, like tobacco or coffee, by definition the number of workable substitutes is limited, causing the demand to be inelastic. This is one reason why firms devote large sums of money to advertising and marketing: to convince you that you need the product.

As a general rule, the more important the good in one's budget, the more aware the consumer is of the item and the greater is the elasticity of demand: thus, demand for big-ticket items like housing and cars tends to be more elastic.

When it comes to the time period under consideration, the elasticity is likely to be greater in the longer term than in the short term, since one is more able to change one's preferences, and suppliers have more time to develop additional supplies or provide substitute products.

The general formula for any elasticity is:

% change in response ÷ % change in stimulus

So the **Price Elasticity of Demand** (PED), for example, can be defined mathematically as:

$$\frac{\text{\% change in demand for good X}}{\text{\% change in price of good X}}$$

To calculate this elasticity (or any elasticity), we need two data points: (1) the initial price and quantity demanded; and (2) the final price and quantity demanded. Now, two questions arise: (1) If we have all four pieces of data, why do we need the formula? Can't we see how the data moves? While this is true, the formula gives a precise number, easily amenable to interpretation. (2) How difficult is it to estimate the final quantity, since this occurs after the initial decision is made? For example, if Delta Air Lines increases its fare from Minneapolis to London, the initial price and final price are obvious and easy to obtain, as is the initial quantity, but what about the final quantity? Several methods are available, including past similar price changes, small sample survey, or statistical estimation.

In the above formula, if the absolute value of the PED is greater than 1, the demand is responsive to changes in price, and the good is **price elastic**. Conversely, if the absolute value of the PED is less than 1, then demand for the good is relatively unresponsive to changes in price and the good is **price inelastic**.

While elasticity is a somewhat useful idea, it is a limited way of considering how consumers really make decisions about their purchases. Elasticity assumes that people are rational and automatically react to incentives, while holding all else equal. Thus, elasticity eschews any complex or holistic analysis of human behaviour. For example, you may have established habits about purchasing that you are unwilling to change, or you may choose certain branded products and pay more for them although you are aware that they are of equivalent or even lower quality than similar substitutes. The discussion of elasticity also hides the power relationships between buyer and seller, and how desperate a person might be to obtain the good.

John Steinbeck's epic Depression novel *The Grapes of Wrath* tells the story of the Joad family: they become dispossessed from their land in Oklahoma and travel to California looking for work. With very limited resources and a low budget, the family has a continuous angst, easily read on their faces. Consider this scene where the family desperately needs an automobile tire – a desperation easily read by the tire seller: 'We got to get a tire, but Jesus, they want a lot for a ol' tire. They look a fella over. They know he got to go on. They know he can't wait. And the price goes up' (Steinbeck, 1939 [1996]: 120). Alas, very typically in market reactions there is a psychological element in pricing, based on the relational power between buyer and seller.

The above example discussed one specific elasticity: elasticity of demand. Other elasticities include elasticity of supply, elasticity of income and cross elasticity. For each, the general formula is the same:

% change in response ÷ % change in stimulus

But the specific response and stimulus is different. For elasticity of supply, the stimulus is a change in price and the response is the amount supplied; for elasticity of income, the stimulus is a change in income and the response is quantity demanded; for cross elasticity, the stimulus is a change in the price of one good, and the response is the quantity demanded of either a complement or a substitute.

In addition, the interpretation is different for each elasticity. For income elasticity, an answer greater than 1 means this is **luxury good**; an answer less than 1 but greater than 0 means the good is a **necessity**. A negative answer means the good is an **inferior good**: as income increases we demand less, and vice versa, as with the demand for lottery tickets, hamburger meat or potatoes. For cross elasticity, a positive answer means that the two goods are **substitutes** (think of Delta Air Lines increasing prices, with a resultant increase in demand for American Airlines); and a negative answer means that the two goods are **complementary**, that is, they go together.

3.8 MEETING OUR NEEDS

We began this chapter by noting that our planet's resources are limited, suggesting the need to steward them carefully and to ensure that they are shared fairly. However, neoclassical economists believe that rather than thinking about limits we should think of resources in terms of scarcity. The difference between these two concepts is critical to how we respect and preserve the planet we share.

This distinction is important because whether you focus on scarcity or limits depends on whether or not you try to limit your desires. If your desires are infinite then scarcity is ubiquitous, whereas if your desires are small you will find the world abundant. It is for this reason that the anthropologist Marshall Sahlins (1972) referred to the hunter-gatherer communities he studied as 'the original affluent society'. They defined their needs very frugally, and so met them easily with a few daily hours gathering food and the occasional hunting expedition. By contrast, he found a great deal of scarcity in his own society (the USA in the 1970s), where people defined their needs excessively and devoted lots of time trying to satisfy them, usually without success.

It is important to recognise that expectations about the scarcity or abundance of resources significantly affect economic behaviour. For example, if you are expecting something to run out, or expecting not enough to meet your needs, you might choose to buy more and hoard it. You might deprive somebody of access to the resource whose need is actually greater than yours because of your perception of scarcity, which might not even be well-founded. In the worst case, the panic-buying and hoarding behaviour of a large number of people can actually create a shortage which did not previously exist. Such an example occurred in the UK in 2012 when the government took a critical position towards the lorry-drivers' (truckers') union for threatening a strike over pay rates. The government stated that the union members were creating a shortage, which caused people to buy extra supplies of fuel.

Capitalism is a system of allocating scarce resources, goods and services, via the fundamental laws of supply and demand, within a context of private ownership. However high the level of demand, it is assumed that there will always be enough supply because price would effectively ration the supply to those who could afford it. The assumption is that the good is scarce: if it were freely available, it would have no price.

Hence capitalism cannot function without scarcity. This has led commentators such as Panayotakis (2012; 2011) to suggest that scarcity is artificially created, and that we are encouraged to think of ourselves as having unmet needs. In particular, he is concerned with how the advertising industry constantly creates demand for new products, such as the mobile phone or tablet computer. He concludes that this creation of scarcity undermines attempts to achieve a sustainable economy and so must be ended.

The other side of the coin is the question 'Where do our economic desires (our needs) come from?' Although it may feel as if we are incomplete without our mobile phones and tablet computers, we were not born with a desire for these high-tech products. In modern societies our patterns of consumption form an important part of our identity. So does the advertising industry's artificial creation of our perceived need for the good, suggesting that it will bring us happiness, friendship or human warmth, even though such things can never be gained through the purchase of a material item.

Instead of infinite desires and limited products leading to a situation of scarcity, many economists advocating sustainability propose the idea of a 'sufficiency economy', based on the understanding that nature offers abundance but not an infinite supply of resources. Its motto might be Mohandas Gandhi's adage that 'Earth has enough to satisfy the needs of all but not the greed of some'. This insight has been developed by Molly Scott Cato (2011) as well as the ecofeminist economist Mary Mellor (2012), who describes a sufficiency economy thus:

> Arguments for de-growth raise questions about what level of consumption is sustainable. One principle offered is 'sufficiency' or 'enough', where the economic system would remove incentives for over-production and over-consumption above the level necessary for a needs-based economy. A sufficiency green economy would aim to provide enough goods and services to enable each person to flourish without destructive growth. As sufficiency for one must mean sufficiency for all, it would be necessary to meet human needs on an egalitarian basis. Sufficiency economics would remove the impetus for environmentally damaging growth and create the potential for socially just de-growth.

A framework for considering satisfaction within such an economy is provided by Manfred Max-Neef in his theory of 'human-scale development'. He argues that

Box 3.2 Climate Finance: Highlights

According to the World Bank, **climate finance** refers to financial resources invested in climate mitigation and adaptation measures via loans, grants and guarantees. The amount of such resources has steadily increased, now standing at US$741 billion[1] (UNFCC, 2016). **Climate mitigation** is any action taken to eliminate or reduce the long-term risks of climate change; **climate adaptation** enhances the economy society's ability to adjust to climate-change outcomes. In other words, climate mitigation tackles the causes, while climate adaptation tackles the effects. Table 3.3 shows some examples.

Table 3.3 Uses of Climate Financing: Mitigation and Adaptation Strategies

Mitigation	*Adaptation*
Renewable energy generation	Water-supply management
Energy-efficiency in industry and buildings	Climate-resilient infrastructure
Sustainable transport	Costal protection
AFOLU (Agriculture, forestry and other land use) and livestock management (how farms and ranches operate)	Disaster risk reduction

Source: Cordova (2015).

East Asia and the Pacific, mainly China, is the largest recipient of climate finance, with Western Europe the second. According to Buchner et al. (2014), the private sector provides approximately 61 per cent of total climate finance resources. The main private actors are:

- project developers: national/regional utilities / independent power producers
- corporate actors: manufacturers, corporate end-users
- private households: high net-worth individuals
- commercial financial institutions

Although the public sector provides only 39 per cent of climate resources, its role as a key driver in covering risks and bridging viability gaps is important. The main public actors are:

- governments and bilateral aid agencies, export credit agencies and UN institutions
- development finance institutions: multilateral development banks, national development banks and bilateral financial institutions
- climate funds: global environment policies, adaptation funds, climate investment.

According to the UNFCC (2016), mitigation-focused finance represented more than 70 per cent of public-sector climate finance in developing countries in 2014.

1. A billion is 1,000,000,000 (one thousand million).

when we buy material products to find satisfaction, we are actually seeking to meet a deeper emotional need. If we could clearly delineate our basic 'subsistence' needs, we might be able to meet them with considerable less use of materials and energy, but in a capitalist economy it is the process of making and selling actual products that generates profits. As an example, we might be seeking identity, which could be met by buying certain branded goods. Max-Neef (1991) suggests we could instead develop the sense of belonging and self-esteem that brings us the identity we crave by enjoying deeper relationships with other people and within our local place. As Max-Neef (quoted in Cato, 2012a: 140) explains:

> in conventional economics we have two links: wants and goods. In Human Scale Development Theory we have three links: needs, satisfiers and goods. For instance, there is the need for Understanding, whose satisfier is literature and whose good is a book.

It is interesting to note that the idea of 'human-scale development' arose from an economist based in the Global South, whereas it is the countries of the over-developed Global North whose consumption patterns threaten the future of life on Earth. We make clear that the principle of reducing consumption is aimed at countries that already have the basic health and social security systems in place, as well as a high level of material security.

THINKING QUESTIONS

What is a resource? How would you define it? When does an item become a resource?

What other needs and satisfiers could be added to Max-Neef's formulation?

CLASS ACTIVITY

Discuss how the concept of 'capital' can be rethought so that it helps create a more sustainable world. How does the Five Capitals Framework do this?

AREAS FOR RESEARCH

Are the terms 'economic growth' and 'sustainable development' mutually contradictory? Might your geographical location, say Global South or Global North, influence how you tackle that question?

UN SDG FOCUS

Goals #6, #7 and #13 call for:

6. Ensure access to water and sanitation for all.
7. Ensure access to affordable, reliable, sustainable and modern energy for all.
13. Take urgent action to combat climate change and its impacts.

How would you conceptualise, define and measure 'modern, affordable and reliable'? What is meant by 'urgent action'? Research the UN's findings on Goals #6, #7 and #13. How would you recommend implementation?

FURTHER READING

Jackson, T. (2009) *Prosperity Without Growth: Economics for a Finite Planet*. London: Earthscan.

Mellor, M. (2006) 'Ecofeminist political economy', *International Journal of Green Economics*, Vol. 1, Nos. 1–2, pp.139–50.

Panayotakis, C. (2011) *Remaking Scarcity: From Capitalist Inefficiency to Economic Democracy*. London: Pluto.

Panayotakis, C. (2012) 'Scarcity, capitalism and the promise of economic democracy', *International Journal of Pluralism and Economics Education*, Vol. 3, No. 1, pp.104–11.

4
Power and the Distribution of Resources

In *The Wealth of Nations*, Adam Smith (1976 [1776]: Vol. I, Bk. I, Ch. 8, pp.74–5) noted that in the determination of wages, masters (i.e. business owners) have a clear advantage over workmen:

> The masters, being fewer in number, can combine much more easily; and the law, besides, authorises, or at least does not prohibit their combinations, while it prohibits those of the workmen . . . In all such disputes the masters can hold out much longer. A landlord, a farmer, a master manufacturer, or merchant, though they did not employ a single workman, could generally live a year or two upon the stocks which they have already acquired. Many workmen could not subsist a week, few could subsist a month, and scarce any a year without employment.

Given these cumulative advantages, at least for Smith, it was not 'difficult to foresee which of the two parties must, upon all ordinary occasions, have the advantage in the dispute, and force the other into a compliance with their terms' (Ibid.: 74).

If neither masters nor workmen possessed any inherent advantage over the other, then the outcome of any contest would be random, decided by other factors; perhaps not even decided by a contest but by mutual agreement, that is, a cooperative endeavour recognising and incorporating the interests of both parties.

The ability of one party to force another into compliance with its terms is unfortunately more typical than atypical in any economic system. This ability to exercise one's will over others is **power**. This chapter examines how power is defined and exercised in the economy. It concludes with a brief look at impending water shortages, which not only underscores the interrelatedness of climate change, population growth, carbon emissions and unsustainable agriculture but also highlights the importance and ubiquity of power in determining solutions. Who owns access to the resources? What is the power configuration? How is this supported by the underlying institutions? What is an equitable price? What are the most effective institutions to ensure adequate access for all?

4.1 UNDERSTANDING POWER IN AN ECONOMIC CONTEXT

Power is an important concept and is a central aspect of just about everything that happens in our economy. Ascertaining the sources of power, how power is obtained, how it is used and its effects are important objectives of a thorough study of economics. Power is a multifaceted word, much like democracy, sustainability and pluralism – rich in meaning, yet hard to define. Nevertheless, a good working definition that we like and will use in this text is offered by Benn (1967a: 426):

> Power is the generalised potentiality for getting one's own way or for bringing about changes (at least some of which are intended) in other people's actions or conditions.

Given the importance of power in economics, and its ubiquity in economic systems, let's take a few moments to dissect this definition into its constituent components:

- **Power is contextual:** it involves a specific time, place and actors. Change the time and place, and most likely the initial configuration of power no longer exists.
- **Power is relational:** that is, power occurs between two or more parties.

In a relational context of power, the two (or more) parties are unequal: the stimulator possesses advantages which are contextual vis-à-vis the reactor, i.e. 'power generally implies a difference of standing between the two parties: the one stimulates and the other reacts' (Ibid.: 424). Given unequal advantage, a conflict of interest exists between the stimulator and the reactor, so that the latter acquiesces to the wishes of the former even if against the reactor's wishes. In fact, one person forcing another to act contrary to the other's wishes in order to enforce one's will is the essence of power.

Power is supported by underlying rules, values and institutions which, if changed, could tilt the balance of power in another direction. Recognising the foundation of power is an important purview of economics. If we can ascertain the foundation of power, we can see who benefits and who does not from existing institutions, and perhaps we can change the way the world works to improve the situation for all.

But what if force is not involved? In political science a distinction is usually made between power and authority, where power can ultimately rely on force but invariably includes authority, which refers to a certain dependency on having the right to govern and consent in being governed.

In the employment relationship in capitalism, as Adam Smith recognised, the employer has far greater power over the employee than the employee has over the employer. The employer has the power and the authority to recruit, select, reward, promote, demote and fire the employee. Admittedly there are employment laws and regulations, professional associations and trade unions that mediate the exercise of this power relationship, but it is exceptionally rare for the employee to sack the employer.

According to neoclassical economics, the market is an unbiased judge of an individual's wage or a firm's worth, so that if a worker earns a low wage, it is considered just, since she is therefore making a rather low contribution. And if a firm goes out of business, it is not the market's fault but the firm's for not adequately meeting demand. But markets do not exist in the abstract: they are composed of real people making everyday decisions. Markets operate because people – employers, investors, regulators – make decisions and act on them in certain ways. How power is used in economic relationships is an important conceptual element of economics and a central theme of our textbook.

4.2 POWER AND INSTITUTIONS

Power can be manifested in many areas of life: the workplace, the family, the social setting, and the political arena, with perhaps the latter receiving copious attention in both West and East.

Perhaps the best-known piece of writing on the exercise of power, at least in the West, is Niccolò Machiavelli's *The Prince*, first published in 1532. Written during a long period of internecine struggle between warring states in what is now Italy, Machiavelli offered clear guidance for a prince to retain and strengthen his power: 'men [sic] should either be caressed or crushed; because they can avenge slight injuries, but not those that are very severe. Hence any injury done to a man must be such that there is no need to fear his revenge' (Machiavelli, 1513 [1988]: 9).

From Machiavelli we obtain the word *machiavellian*, defined in *The American Heritage Dictionary* as that 'which holds that craft and deceit are justified in pursuing and maintaining political power'. Thus, to call someone 'machiavellian' is both complimentary, since the person is adept at obtaining and/or holding on to power, but also pejorative, in the sense that the person is bereft of morals.

Ascertaining the existence of power, how it is supported by underlying institutions, and who benefits from it should be the focal point of economics and the main task of economists. In particular, given a configuration of power, what are the supporting (and enabling) institutions? What alternative institutions can we can implement to either diffuse the existence of power or ameliorate its negative effects? Who benefits (and who loses) from an existing configuration of power? How does the relative power of states and individuals affect our ability to provision fairly for all?

Configurations of power are determined and upheld by existing rules and values, i.e. institutions, that many of us take for granted. Institutional economics developed during the late nineteenth century largely due to the neglect of neoclassical economics in studying power. For the American economist John Commons (1862–1945), the economy consisted of a web of institutional relationships and interests, with business corporations, organised labour and government as major players. Fluctuating business cycles would often lead to labour conflict, and large corporations would seek monopoly control in order to secure and guarantee their future profitability, even at the expense of the wider society. Commons argued that government had to mediate disputes between business and labour, and between big and small businesses who were liable to be victims of such actions.

The locus of power in any economic system is a function of the underlying institutions that enable and legitimise unequal relations between buyer and seller. Capitalism is an economic system which relies on many institutions such as markets, money, and private property enforced by the legal system, each giving rise to unequal configurations of power.

4.3 KARL MARX ON POWER

Another classical economist who viewed power as central to understanding the economy was Karl Marx (1818–83). Although Marx was very critical of capitalism, he also praised it on two accounts. First, its productive capacity, which far surpassed that of any other economic system, 'creat[ing] more massive and more colossal productive forces than have all preceding generations together' (Marx and Engels, 1848 [1992]: 7–8). And second, capitalism freed the worker from the bondage of feudalism, which had inextricably bound the serf to the lord. Capitalism thus created ostensibly free and independent workers who could go anywhere to sell their labour-power in order to earn their living. This 'freedom' caused considerable social disruption, depriving not only individuals but also households and communities of their previous source of livelihood rooted in the land. They sought employment in the new factories and workshops in the growing towns and cities. Known as the 'enclosure movement', this ripping of peasants from the land:

> viewed by many historians as 'the revolution of the rich against the poor', was carried out in England between the sixteenth and early nineteenth centuries, fundamentally altering the economic and political landscape. Millions of peasants were uprooted from their ancestral lands and forced to act as

> free agents whose labor power would henceforth be available for hire in the budding medieval marketplace.
>
> Rifkin, 2014: 31

Although incipient capitalists benefited from cheap and willing labour, the enclosure movement was precipitated and structured by landlords in the countryside, responding to higher prices for both wool and fuel, rather than by capitalists themselves. Consequently, with industrialisation came urbanisation, and as a result of being 'free' these workers were at the mercy of the market and the power of the capitalist.

According to Marx, this led to a society divided into antagonistic classes, the *bourgeoisie* and the *proletariat*, based on their relationship to the ownership of the means of production. This unequal power relationship meant that the workers (the proletariat) depended on the bourgeoisie, who in turn extracted the *surplus value* produced by workers in the form of profit. Simply put: the worker receives far less value in wages than he or she actually creates through his or her labour.

For Marx, an economic system built on dependency and exploitation could not be stable. The profit motive as the modus operandi would lead to an aggregation of capital and replacement of labour with machinery. Profit rates would fall, increasing unemployment and the immiseration of the working class. Workers would have no choice but to overthrow the chains of the bourgeoisie oppressor. Indeed, Marx and Engels end their famous *Communist Manifesto* (1848 [1992]:

Box 4.1 Extracting Surplus Value

Here, we let Marx speak directly from *Capital*:

> Suppose that a capitalist pays for a day's labour-power at its value; then the right to use that power for a day belongs to him, just as much as the right to use any other commodity, such as a horse that he has hired for the day. To the purchaser of a commodity belongs its use, and the seller of labour-power, by giving his labour, does no more, in reality, than part with the use-value that he has sold. From the instant he steps into the workshop, the use-value of his labour-power, and therefore also its use, which is labour, belongs to the capitalist. By the purchase of labour-power, the capitalist incorporates labour, as a living ferment, with the lifeless constituents of the product. From his point of view, the labour process is nothing more than the consumption of the commodity purchased, i.e. of labour-power; but this consumption cannot be effected except by supplying the labour-power with the means of production. The labour process is a process between things that the capitalist has purchased, things that have become his property. The product of the process belongs, therefore, to him, just as much as does the wine which is the product of a process of fermentation process completed in his cellar.
>
> Marx, 1867 [1967]: 185)

39, emphasis in original) with a call to revolution: 'Let the ruling classes tremble at a Communistic revolution. The proletarians have nothing to lose but their chains. They have a world to win. WORKING MEN OF ALL COUNTRIES, UNITE!'

Contemporary Marxists such as David Harvey (2010) have interpreted the erosion of welfare and labour rights, the growth in social and economic inequality, and the dominance of global corporations both before and after the recent financial crisis as a reassertion of class power and class domination. The economic exploitation of many workers in the developing world is for critics like Harvey a continuation of the unequal power relations that Marx wrote about.

4.4 THE COMMODIFICATION OF NATURAL RESOURCES

The word **commodity** is derived from the Latin *commodus*, meaning convenient. A commodity is defined as something useful that can be turned to commercial advantage. In the business world we are familiar with exchanges, such as the Chicago Board of Trade and the London Metal Exchange, which buy and sell commodities like cotton, wheat, cocoa, coffee, etc. For Marx, commodification was very important and meant transformation of something into a good that could be bought and sold in the market. (The opening chapter of *Capital* is on commodities.) During the enclosure movements and the Industrial Revolution in England, labour was transformed into a commodity, something we take for granted today. As we saw in Chapter 3, with the discussion on land grabbing in the developing world, land once held and used in common is still being commodified. Businesses routinely commodify nature in agriculture, mining and other industrial sectors, and even, through the activities of scientists working in the field of genetic modification, commodify life itself.

The commodification of natural resources is readily apparent looking at events in Brazil. Between 2002 and 2008, mining, energy and food were identified as strategic sectors in Brazil, largely due to the surge in demand from China and other developing countries. This augmented demand for commodities strengthened some Brazilian corporations. For example, in 2004 the private minerals corporation Vale and the public petroleum corporation Petrobras were among the 50 most important transnational corporations in the newly emerging economies of the world. This increase in corporate power and wealth has been accompanied by growing levels of social and economic inequality in Brazil, along with conflicts involving indigenous communities and peasants whose land rights have been ignored or dismissed. The commodification of natural resources and the ensuing power relationships are crucial elements in determining how, or whether, we can actually become environmentally and socially sustainable.

4.5 DEFINING PROPERTY RIGHTS AND PRIVATE PROPERTY

In Ivan Turgenev's mid-nineteenth-century short story 'The Loner', the main character, a peasant overseer of a forest owned by an absentee landlord, ruthlessly guarded his master's forest. In fact, as Turgenev tells the tale (1835 [1990]: 175):

> [T]here wasn't a better master of his job in the world: He won't let you take so much as a bit o' brushwood! It doesn't matter when it is, even at dead o' night, he'll be down on you like a ton o' snow, an' you'd best not think of puttin' up a fight. . . An' you can't bribe him, not with drink, not with money, not with any trickery.

In the story, the overseer hears an axe felling a tree and immediately confronts the would-be thief: a pitiful and destitute peasant. The peasant pleads for mercy. He is hungry and his horse is his only possession, to which the overseer coarsely replies, 'I know your sort . . . You're all the same where you come from, a bunch of thieves . . . I'm telling you I can't. I'm also the one who takes orders and I'll have to answer for it. And I've got no reason to be kind to the likes of you' (Ibid.: 179).

Although fiction, this short story faithfully recreated the conditions of the mid-nineteenth-century Russian countryside and adroitly captured the power, exploitation and vulnerability inherent in the class relationships. Indeed, Turgenev was exiled during the 1850s due to his realistic portrayal of Russia's powerful landowning class. This cogent short story underscores the power of fiction. Although more than 150 years old it still resonates, makes us think, and raises a number of questions for debate:

- Why is an exclusive right to own nature assumed, when nature was given as a gift to all?
- Why should only a few expropriate and profit from nature while excluding the majority?
- Can we reconcile the bounty of nature with the poverty of individuals?
- What is the role of property rights in causing and extending poverty?
- How might property rights be aligned with the rights of people in order to ensure a decent living for all?
- Are there resources common to all that should not be privatised?

As an economic system, capitalism relies on the private ownership of the means of production to provide incentives in order to produce goods and services that people need (or think they need). Its modus operandi is profit maximisation, assuming that a private owner can manage resources better than the community, the local government body or the national state. However, capitalism has also begotten serious environmental consequences which have disproportionately affected the poor.

A **property right** 'is a relationship between the *rights holder* and the rights *regarders* under a *specific authority structure* like the state granting legitimacy and security to a specific resource or benefit stream' (Vatn, 2005: 254; emphasis in original). In other words, a right to own property is a social relation conceptualised, defined and protected by the state. Three important points are clear from this definition: first, the state has a clear role in defining and enforcing a property right; second, the converse of the right to own is the right to exclude; and third, since the right is a social relation and social relations change, so do property rights.

Vatn suggests four possible property regimes (Ibid.: 255–60), each understood as 'the structure of rights and duties characterising the relationships between individuals with respect to a specific good or benefit stream' (Ibid.: 255):

- **Private property:** An individual owns the asset and is able to exclude others from ownership.
- **Common property:** A set of individuals own the asset, which is 'private property for a group of co-owners' (Ibid.: 256). The co-owners collectively establish rules of access/exclusion.
- **State owned:** The asset is owned by the state.
- **Open access:** There is no ownership and thus no property relationship between owner and rights regarder; it is 'what was there in the beginning' (Ibid: 256.).

There has been considerable debate about whether capitalism is actually compatible with creating a sustainable world. Capitalism needs growth in order to survive, but economic growth is closely associated with an increase in the use of material resources, which has enabled us to live beyond our ecological means. However, many businesses and a number of sustainability advocates suggest that scientific and technological innovation, new modes of doing business and different ways of running the economy can lead to a virtuous circle of increased productivity, increased resource efficiency and green growth (Rifkin, 2014). Socialism, according to sustainability advocates highlighting the abysmal environmental record of the USSR and Eastern Europe, may have created an industrial system but it also created a considerable amount of environmental degradation.

Some argue that in order to create a more sustainable world we must abandon the ideology of continuing economic growth – whether in capitalism or socialism. And we must severely curtail the operation of the profit motive and the private accumulation of wealth, while seeking forms of economic ownership and control that respect ecological limits; valuing the significance of the commons while retaining the benefits of individual and collective enterprise and innovation.

In an important article 'The Tragedy of the Commons', Garrett Hardin (1968) admitted that perhaps discussion of the commons (owned by all) was not necessary in an earlier age, when population was not a problem. However, given today's global population of 7.2 billion, with 2 billion more expected by 2050, and the correspondingly increased demands on water, food and energy, it is important to discuss how we understand and regulate the commons and open-access resources. Will our resources benefit all humanity or only a select few lucky enough to own them?

Hardin (1968) criticised Adam Smith's concept of the **invisible hand**: that the pursuit of individual self-interest would promote the public good and economic well-being. And certainly, the notion of the invisible hand has been plundered by neoclassical economics in order to praise the workings of the market system. In Turgenev's short story, described earlier, each character pursued his self-interest, but there was no coalescing of the public or common interest. Although implicitly assumed by neoclassical economists, there is actually no connection – empirical, ethical or otherwise – between private ownership, blind pursuit of self-interest and the overall benefit of society. To assume otherwise is not only blithely disingenuous but ignores the existing contours of power, along with issues of justice and sustainability.

Before we discuss Hardin's article, it is highly beneficial to examine Smith's concept of the invisible hand. The concept is important, even though it is mentioned only once in *The Wealth of Nations* and once in *The Theory of Moral Sentiments*.[1] Here is the passage from *The Wealth of Nations* (1776 [1976], Vol. I, Bk. IV, Ch. 2, p.477):

> As every individual, therefore, endeavours as much as he [sic] can both to employ his own capital in the support of domestic industry, and so to direct that industry that its produce may be of the greatest value; every individual necessarily labours to render the annual revenue of the society as great as he

1. Here is the quote from *The Theory of Moral Sentiments*: 'The rich only select from the heap what is most precious and agreeable. They consume little more than the poor; and in spite of their natural selfishness and rapacity, though they mean only their own conveniency, though the sole end which they propose from the labours of all the thousands whom they employ be the gratification of their own vain and insatiable desires, they divide with the poor the produce of all their improvements. They are led by an invisible hand to make nearly the same distribution of the necessaries of life which would have been made had the earth been divided into equal portions among all its inhabitants; and thus, without intending it, without knowing it, advance the interest of the society, and afford means to the multiplication of the species' (Smith, 1759 [2000], Pt. IV, Ch. 1, pp.264–5).

> can. He generally, indeed, neither intends to promote the public interest, nor knows how much he is promoting it. By preferring the support of domestic to that of foreign industry, he intends only his own security; and by directing that industry in such a manner that as its produce may be of the greatest value, he intends only his own gain, and he is in this, as in many other cases, led by an invisible hand to promote an end which was no part of his intention. Nor is it always the worse for the society that it was no part of it. By pursuing his own interest he frequently promotes that of the society more effectually than when he really intends to promote it. I have never known much good done by those who affected to trade for the public good. It is an affectation, indeed, not very common among merchants, and very few words need be employed in dissuading them from it.

This illustrates why it is necessary to critically examine the foundational rationale for a given concept and/or theory in economics. Smith ignored (or probably had no idea about, like most of his contemporaries) the connection between individual economic activity and the global environment.

Indeed, concerning the commons, self-interest is the crux of the problem. Each user is assumed to take from the commons an amount that will maximise her utility, with little regard for the institutional survival of the system. Unfortunately, the more users, the greater the demand on the system and the less its ability to survive. Hardin calls for some type of enforced behaviour to regulate the usage of the commons. Perhaps one could also gather from Hardin that we should privatise common resources, which in effect means establishing property rights and allowing each owner the opportunity to use a resource and thereby exclude others. Aside from the ethical consideration of owning and excluding others from something that should be enjoyed by all, private ownership does not necessarily mean that resources will be used sustainably, or to the benefit of all. While Hardin has been criticised quite extensively (not the least for confusing 'open-access' and 'commons'), discussion over managing the commons has come a long way in the last 50 years. How to manage the commons sustainably is an important topic in economics, which we will return to in later chapters.

4.6 CLIMATE CHANGE, POPULATION GROWTH, ENERGY USE AND WATER

Most of the projected increase in human population is expected to occur in developing nations. As nations develop economically, they hope to both provision for their citizens and increase their ability to do so (with the Western nations offering alluring and perhaps unattainable living standards). Given that fossil fuels comprise 80 per cent of global energy use, increased provisioning for the extra 2 billion people expected by 2050 will require more energy, which in turn will increase the emission of greenhouse gases. Energy use is predicted to increase by approximately 30 per cent within the next 20 years, with a corresponding increase in greenhouse gases (United States Energy Information Administration, 2016: 7).

Looking ahead to 2035, fossil fuels are projected to account for 77 per cent of global energy consumption, with the remainder comprised of nuclear (5 per cent), hydro (7 per cent) and renewables (10 per cent) (British Petroleum, 2017: 96). How to reduce reliance on fossil fuels and emissions of greenhouse gases while not jeopardising the ability of developing countries to provision is a central question; some might argue that it is our most important question.

Given climate change, both the availability and the usage of water will also be affected, since

> climate change is to a large extent water change. [It] affects all aspects of the water cycle and water is the main way through which the impacts of climate change will be felt. Its impact includes shifting precipitation patterns, rising water temperatures, deteriorating water quality, increase in evaporation, and increases in frequency and intensity of extreme events.
>
> OECD, 2013: 25

The ability to provision, economic development, energy use, the ability to feed the global population, climate change and water usage are all interrelated. It is difficult if not impossible to discuss any one of these factors in isolation. Agriculture, for example, accounts for 70 per cent of fresh water use, and as population increases, more people must be fed, increasing the demand for energy and water, and thus increasing the emission of greenhouse gases.

Water is ubiquitous on Earth, which itself is composed of 97 per cent water, although only 3 per cent is freshwater, and only 1 per cent is readily available for consumption, with the rest locked up in glaciers. It should not be surprising that future water scarcities are predicted, given increased population and increased demand for food and therefore agriculture. According to the World Bank (2016d), the world will face a 40 per cent shortfall between forecast demand and available supply of water by 2030, and by 2025, about 1.8 billion people will be living in regions or countries with absolute water scarcity. Table 4.1 below surveys the world's current and expected water problems.

As Table 4.1 makes clear, climate change and attendant water changes will affect the world differently. Although exact prediction is elusive, it is a safe prediction at this point that dry areas will become drier and wet areas will become wetter.[2]

2. According to Jean-Louis Chaussade, Chief Executive of the French utility Suez, whose company recently purchased General Electric's water unit, water will become a more valuable commodity than oil (Ward, 2017).

Table 4.1 Water Scarcity and Policy Setting, by Global Region, 2016

Region	*Main issues to be addressed*
Sub-Saharan Africa	• Severe water scarcity: people in rural and peri-urban areas lack adequate access to water for agriculture and even for drinking and household needs. • Weak institutional, financial and human capacities for managing water. • Lack of coordination among public entities. • Lack of harmonisation of regulations and policies on water management. • Rising surface temperatures.
North Africa	• Increasing physical water scarcity. • Weak water governance. • Lack of technical and human resource capacity. • Rising surface temperatures.
Latin America and the Caribbean	• Lack of capacity for addressing declines in water quality. • Increased competition for water. • Low water-use efficiency in agriculture. • Rising surface temperatures.
Central Asia	• Political disagreements to manage water scarcity. • Lack of capacity to manage water resources effectively. • Rising surface temperatures.
Asia and Pacific	• Suboptimal water distribution, salinisation and other forms of land degradation. • Issues related to equity, resilience, governance, demand management and water allocation. • Lack of water infrastructure for irrigation in rural areas. • Rising surface temperatures.

Sources: Food and Agricultural Organization of the United Nations (FAO, 2016); World Bank (2016d).

Potential trouble spots for water scarcity include sub-Sahara Africa, the Middle East, much of China and India, and the southwestern US. As Vahid et al. (2009: xix) noted, another safe prediction is that developing countries will suffer disproportionately, given their

> weak institutions and limited institutional capacity, high levels of poverty, insufficient stock of water management and services infrastructure, lack of access to technology and capital to invest in risk reduction, and dependence on climate-sensitive sectors such as agriculture, forestry and fisheries.

This presents us with a host of complex and interconnected problems. Our traditional habit of looking at these issues as compartmentalised, based on ignorance of climate change, is no longer tenable; likewise, doing nothing is no longer an option. We must develop new ways of thinking that recognise the importance of complexity and the value of taking a holistic view. The Food and

Agriculture Organization of the United Nations (FAO, 2009: 9), for example, argued:

> Land water institutions have not kept pace with the growing intensity of river basin development and the increasing degree of inter-dependence and competition over land and water resources. Much more adaptable and collaborative institutions are needed to respond effectively to natural resource scarcity and market opportunities.

This statement is reinforced by the International Water Management Institute (IWMI, 2009: 1):

> What is clear is that today's water management challenges – and tomorrow's – differ greatly from those of 50 years ago, or even 25, and thus require new approaches. Those approaches will be broader [. . .] They will be more participatory and involve informed multi-stakeholder dialogues to deal with the many trade-offs. And they will embrace diverse interests and institutions to increase the equity of water's use.

And finally, and most importantly, as the World Bank (2016d: vi & vii) notes:

> Water is the common currency which links nearly every SDG, and it will be a critical determinant of success. Abundant water supplies are vital for the production of food and will be essential to attaining SDG 2 on food security; clean and safe drinking water and sanitation systems are necessary for health, as called for in SDGs 3 and 6; and water is needed for powering industries and creating the new jobs identified in SDGs 7 and 8. None of this is achievable without adequate and safe water to nourish the planet's life-sustaining ecosystem services identified in SDGs 13, 14 and 15.

4.7 CONCLUSION

Traditional solutions to resource problems such as markets, property rights and open access might have been viable during the twentieth century, but are not necessarily so now. Predicted impending shortages underscores the interrelatedness of climate change, population growth, CO_2 emissions and unsustainable agriculture, but also highlights the importance and ubiquity of power in determining equitable solutions: Who owns access to resources? What is the power configuration? How is this supported by the underlying institutions? What are the most effective institutions to ensure adequate access for all?

Developing new solutions across intellectual fields is a central objective of the three authors of this textbook. At this point we wish we could offer you a panoply of tailor-made solutions. Instead, we invite you to put your thinking caps on and work with us.

THINKING QUESTIONS

What is power? Who has it, and who doesn't? In what ways do social classes have, and exercise, power?

Is capitalism a solution to our myriad problems, or is it part of the problem?

Should all resources be considered 'means to production', or should some resources be held by all for the common good of humanity?

How should we manage resources? Who benefits from their use and who decides whether these resources should be privatised or owned in common by all?

What does 'commonly owned' mean?

CLASS ACTIVITIES

What are the economic implications of Hardin's 'tragedy of the commons'?

To what extent is Hardin arguing for private property?

AREAS FOR RESEARCH

What alternative forms of ownership exist? How do they function?

UN SDG FOCUS

How does the existence of power affect the ability to achieve the 17 SDGs? Are there specific SDG goals that are more susceptible to the exercise of power than others? Select an individual goal. What are the existing configurations of power? Who owns the resources? Are the relationships of equal power? Are the existing configurations a help or a hindrance in attaining the goal?

FURTHER READING

Harvey, D. (2010) *The Enigma of Capital and the Crises of Capitalism*. London: Profile Books.

Vahid, A, Qaddumi, H. M., Dickson, E., Diez, S. M., Danilenko, A. V., Hirji, R. F., Puz, G., Pizarro, C., Jacobsen, M. and Blankespoor, B. (2009) *Water and Climate Change: Understanding the Risks and Making Climate-Smart Investment Decisions*. Washington: World Bank.

Vatn, A. (2005) *Institutions and the Environment*. Cheltenham, UK: Edward Elgar.

5
Inequality, Poverty and Disempowerment

In 1962, Michael Harrington's book *The Other America* shocked the USA out of its complacency. The book's title underscored Harrington's thesis that beneath the veneer of opulence, another America existed, mired in hopeless poverty, invisible to policymakers and with little hope for the future. After reading Harrington's book, the reader is not sure which America is the 'other' America – rich or poor. It is also clear that if pervasive and intransigent poverty can exist in America, it can exist anywhere.

Sir Thomas More's 1516 novel *Utopia* envisioned a blissful society without poverty: a mythical society without money, unemployment or private property, in which

> [E]verything's under public ownership, no one has any fear of going short, as long as the public storehouses are full. Everyone gets a fair share, so there are never any poor men [sic] or beggars. Nobody owns anything, but everyone is rich – for what greater wealth can there be than cheerfulness, peace of mind, and freedom from anxiety?
>
> More, 1516 [1965]: 128

In imagining a world without poverty, More's book suggests how ubiquitous and intransigent poverty is. It has existed in all societies. So why have we failed to understand its nature and devise effective solutions? Why does poverty still exist and why do we tolerate it? Since economics is defined as the study of how we provision, the continuation of poverty suggests the failure of economic theory as well as economic practice.

In this chapter we first discuss how poverty is defined, conceptualised and measured; then we discuss why poverty exists, and its extent in the world today. We also suggest some changes to economic systems that might allow us to tackle the massive global inequality that poverty represents. A central theme of this chapter and this book is that poverty, power, inequality, justice and climate change are interconnected.

5.1 POVERTY: DEFINITIONS AND CONCEPTS

Poverty is another multi-dimensional concept, much like pluralism and justice. We know poverty when we see or experience it: a visit to a poor community in Latin America, Africa or Asia, or inner cities in the USA, reveals a poignant picture of social vulnerability. But what is poverty? How do we define it? In this section we discuss three different conceptualisations of **poverty**. First, poverty as deprivation of income. Here we need to distinguish income from wealth. Income is a flow (measured over time) and wealth is a stock. More specifically, **income** is earned from work, dividends, interest, and any rents or royalties on properties (Domhoff, 2012). **Wealth**, however, includes the value of everything owned (**assets**), minus what is owed (**liabilities**). Assets include real estate owned by the household, cash and demand deposits, financial assets (savings deposits, certificates of deposit, money market accounts, government bonds, corporate bonds, foreign bonds, and other financial securities), pension plans, corporate stock, mutual funds and equity in trust funds. Liabilities include mortgage debt, consumer debt, loans and other debt.

In this conceptualisation, poverty is a threshold line demarcating a minimum level of income needed in order for a person to survive, so that a person with less than this level is officially designated 'poor', and a person earning more is not. This is usually referred to as *absolute poverty*. A person who is poor in this sense does not have sufficient resources to remain alive and well; her very survival is threatened.

A second conceptualisation of poverty is relative to a societal norm, such as the median level of income (i.e. the income most commonly earned by people in that society). So a person is poor not because her absolute level of income is low per se, but because she earns less than the norm. From this perspective, those in poverty fall below a certain 'poverty line', perhaps represented by 40 per cent of the median income. This leads us to *relative poverty* rather than absolute poverty.

A third conceptualisation (and very different from the first two) of poverty is to focus on the lack of freedoms to attain one's potential, i.e. 'deprivation of basic capabilities rather than merely as lowness of incomes' (Sen, 1999: 87). This conceptualisation, known as 'the capability approach', shifts the focus away from means (income and wealth) toward ends (reaching one's potential) and the freedom to satisfy those ends.

The first two conceptualisations are ostensibly simple, yet present difficulties when practical measurement is attempted. An obvious problem is deciding what measure to be used to assess what is, and who is in, poverty. Furthermore, as Sen discusses, given two individuals with identical incomes, each might spend their income differently depending on age, gender, illness, physical and environmental conditions, existing public healthcare, education, social values, etc. (Sen,

2009: 88–9). Depending on their skills and social networks, different people can maintain a decent existence on very different monetary incomes.

The first two conceptualisations are contextual, since they depend on the existence of a monetary economy, where the income earned determines the extent of participation in the economy; and without an income one is excluded from participation. The capability approach gets right to the heart of the matter by ascertaining an individual's capability to live a full and meaningful life. Although the capability approach focuses on ends rather than means, it is much more difficult to measure; hence the preference by economists to use either of the first two approaches, 'the standard criterion of identification of poverty' (Sen, 2009: 87).

Having addressed the conceptualisation of poverty, let us move on to its measurement. The World Bank (2016b) first introduced a global poverty line in 1990. Extreme poverty was initially defined as at or below $US1.25 a day; in 2015 the World Bank increased it to US$1.90 a day. The recent change accounts for the latest estimates of how prices of goods and services vary across countries, based on 2011 US dollars. According to the most recent estimates from the World Bank,[1] in 2013, 761 million people (10.7 per cent of the world's population) lived on US$1.90 or below a day, down from 1.85 billion (35 per cent of global population) in 1990. As the World Bank notes, regional progress has been uneven, with China, Indonesia and India the main drivers for poverty reduction. Yet in sub-Saharan Africa the number of extreme poor fell by only 4 million, with 389 million people living in extreme poverty – more than all other regions combined.

5.2 POVERTY AND THE DEVELOPING WORLD

Climate change, increasing water scarcity, poor sanitation services, population growth, demographic changes and urbanisation are expected to affect the evolution of poverty in developing countries (WHO, 2013). Table 5.1 indicates the incidence of poverty as a percentage of total population in developing countries in selected regions between 1981 and 2013. The most striking feature is the East Asia and Pacific region, where the incidence of poverty decreased from 92.4 per cent to 3.4 per cent of the population (which, although not evident here, includes China's precipitous decrease from 97.8 per cent to 29.4 per cent.)

The highest levels of incidence of poverty are in South Asia and sub-Saharan Africa.

Despite the overall decrease in extreme poverty, the challenge, as The World Bank writes:

1. Data on extreme poverty in this section is obtained from World Bank (2016c).

> is far from over . . . it is becoming even more difficult to reach those remaining in extreme poverty, who often live in fragile contexts and remote areas. Access to good schools, healthcare, electricity, safe water and other critical services remains elusive for many people, often determined by socioeconomic status, gender, ethnicity and geography. Moreover, for those who have been able to move out of poverty, progress is often temporary: economic shocks, food insecurity and climate change threaten to rob them of their hard-won gains and force them back into poverty. It will be critical to find ways to tackle these issues as we make progress toward 2030.
>
> World Bank, 2016c

In other regions, despite the decreasing incidence of poverty, social exclusion has occurred with increasing marginalisation and deprivation in urban areas. Social exclusion is a challenge to urban sustainable development, since coverage of basic needs still remains far from universal, especially when people do not own basic assets like a home or land.

Table 5.1 Percentage of the Global Population Under the Official Poverty Line

Region	*1981*	*1996*	*2008*	*2013*
East Asia and Pacific	92.4	64.0	33.2	3.4
Europe and Central Asia	8.3	11.2	2.2	2.1
Latin American and the Caribbean	23.8	21.0	12.4	5.4
South Asia	87.2	80.7	70.9	15.1
Sub-Saharan Africa	72.2	77.5	69.2	41.0

Note: Five countries – Bangladesh, Cabo Verde, Cambodia, Jordan and Lao PDR – use 2005 data and the corresponding US$1.25-a-day and US$2-a-day poverty lines.

Source: World Bank (2016e).

Indeed, the urbanisation of poverty is significant in developing countries. One important explanation is that people in rural areas still have access to land and can grow food for their own needs, whereas people in cities often fail to find employment or are only able to find intermittent or informal employment. According to the United Nations (UN, 2014), the global rural population is now close to 3.4 billion and is expected to decline to 3.2 billion by 2050. Africa and Asia are home to nearly 90 per cent of the world's rural population; India has the largest rural population (857 million), followed by China (635 million). Considering migration trends, just three countries – India, China and Nigeria – together are expected to account for 37 per cent of the projected growth of the world's urban population between 2014 and 2050. India is projected to add 404 million urban dwellers, China 292 million and Nigeria 212 million. One of the outcomes is that slums[2] are a reality globally, as we can see in Table 5.2.

Table 5.2 Percentage of Urban Population Living In Slums in 2014

Region	*Percentage living in slums*
Arab World	33
East Asia and Pacific (developing only)	26
Latin America and Caribbean (developing only)	21
Least developed countries (UN classification)	63
South Asia	31
Sub-Saharan Africa (developing only)	55

Source: World Bank (2016a).

Another related urban problem for the poor is access to water. By 2025, half of the world's population will be living in water stressed areas. In developing countries, where at least 20 million hectares are irrigated using wastewater, this practice enhances health risks from exposure to untreated and partially treated waste. Indeed, increasing reliance on groundwater and alternative water sources, such as wastewater could expose people, (mainly poor) to dangerous levels of biological contaminants and chemical pollutants in their drinking water due to inadequate management of urban infrastructure.

The concern with this scenario is particularly relevant since, because of the recent financial crisis, the pace of poverty reduction has slowed.

5.3 MEASURING POVERTY

Data on poverty has taken on greater significance since 2000, when the United Nations, the World Bank and the Inter-American Development Bank (IDB) joined national governments to develop the Millennium Development Goals (since replaced by the Sustainable Development Goals, or SDGs), a key objective of which was to reduce the 1990 poverty rate by half before 2015. Traditional measures of poverty used by economists use household income or expenditure, indirectly reflecting access to goods and services that affect well-being. The World Bank's data are perhaps the most widely cited for international comparisons.

2. While many definitions exist for a **slum**, a most illuminating one is from Wikipedia: 'A slum is a heavily populated urban informal settlement characterised by substandard housing and squalor. While slums differ in size and other characteristics, most lack reliable sanitation services, supply of clean water, reliable electricity, law enforcement and other basic services. (https://en.wikipedia.org/wiki/Slum.) For a viscerally humane description of daily life in an Indian slum, see Roberts (2003).

Box 5.1 UN Sustainable Development Goal No.1: End Poverty in All its Forms Everywhere

By 2030, eradicate extreme poverty for all people everywhere, currently measured as people living on less than $1.90 a day; reduce at least by half the proportion of men, women and children of all ages living in poverty in all its dimensions according to national definitions; implement nationally appropriate social protection systems and measures for all, and by 2030 achieve substantial coverage of the poor and the vulnerable.

In addition, by 2030, ensure that all men and women, in particular the poor and the vulnerable, have equal rights to economic resources, as well as access to basic services, ownership and control over land and other forms of property, inheritance, natural resources, appropriate new technology and financial services, including microfinance. And, by 2030, build the resilience of the poor and those in vulnerable situations, and reduce their exposure and vulnerability to climate-related extreme events and other economic, social and environmental shocks and disasters.

Source: Adapted from United Nations (UN, 2015a).

In Latin America and the Caribbean, the UN Economic Commission for Latin America and the Caribbean (ECLAC) has developed country-specific poverty lines based on the estimated costs of a basic food basket, intended to capture the widely varying costs of living among the poor. ECLAC's poverty rates are generally higher than the World Bank's but also tend to show greater improvement.

Its 'extreme poverty' line reflects the income necessary to buy a minimally nutritious basket of food, as defined by the World Health Organization's standards and local dietary customs. The ECLAC's 'moderate poverty' line is set at twice this level for urban areas and 1.75 times this level in rural areas.

Recently, poverty in Latin America has continued its downward trend, but at a decreasing rate. As of 2014, poverty affected 28 per cent of Latin America's population, revealing the overall context of economic deceleration (ELAC, 2015). Given the current demographic growth rate, the number of poor people increased in absolute figures to 167 million people. In 2014, of the 167 million officially poor people, 71 million suffered extreme poverty or indigence.

5.4 POVERTY ALLEVIATION

It is sometimes said that income poverty has been significantly reduced by government programmes that make **transfer payments** – a form of income for those in need, which includes unemployment compensation, Social Security, Temporary Assistance to Needy Families (welfare), food stamps and Medicaid. In Latin America, there is great variation from one country to the next, and regional trends are dominated by the two largest countries, Mexico and Brazil. Brazil's cash transfer programme Bolsa Família (described in the next chapter) has been considered a success. Cash transfer as a social policy can be understood broadly as government intervention policies directly related to social protection, redistribution and production of material life. According to the World Bank, the state has to provide a safety net for the very poor, redressing its social policies in the form of pensions, aid, educational and public investments from the richest to the very needy. Economic growth is assumed to reduce absolute poverty and, even in a context of low growth, different qualitative and institutional aspects of markets could affect distributive policies.

Investment in education is the most efficient and adequate structural policy action to achieve more equitable income distribution and reduced poverty levels. Indeed, philosopher and economist Amartya Sen (1999, *passim*) stressed the importance of education and investment in a sound social infrastructure to attain and sustain growth. He argued that no nation has achieved prosperity without ensuring the basic needs of its people, especially basic education. There are several reasons why:

- General expansion of education allows participation in a global economy.
- Literate people can invoke their legal rights and participate in the political arena in order to express their demands effectively.
- Basic education (due to increased knowledge and information) can improve health and fertility rates.
- Women's empowerment is strongly influenced by literacy since it enhances their participation in decisions within and outside the family.

Governments are not the only bodies that can address poverty. Recently, international development organisations have supported microfinance to reduce poverty by enlarging access to financial services (banking accounts, saving, credit, insurance) to poor people lacking access to regular banking services. Microcredit policies aim to extend credit access to self-employed and household-based entrepreneurs. The thinking is that aid creates dependency, whereas small loans might facilitate independence.

Microcredit borrowers receive loans to invest in a diverse range of small enterprises, including small retail shops and street stalls. By enhancing the ability to expand these businesses, microcredit loans could initiate a series of 'virtuous spirals' of economic empowerment and increased well-being for households. Access to microfinance services has increased over the past two decades (Maes and Reed, 2012). As of December 2013, 3,098 microfinance institutions reported reaching 211,119,547 clients (Microcredit Summit Campaign, 2016).

Table 5.3 Enrolment Ratio, Secondary and Primary school, Both Sexes (in Percentage), 2011–2014

Region	*Gross Enrolment Ratio, Secondary School*		*Adjusted Net Enrolment Ratio, Primary School*	
	2011	*2013*	*2012*	*2014*
Arab World	72	71	86.1	85.3
East Asia and Pacific (developing only)	81	85	96.2	96.0
Europe and Central Asia (developing only)	94	99	95.1	94.6
Latin America and Caribbean (developing only)	89	93	98.7	98.5
Middle East and North Africa (developing only)	77	76	94.9	94.0
South Asia	62	66	95.9	94.3
Sub-Saharan Africa (developing only)	42	43	93.0	93.5
World	73	75	77.5	78.8

Note: 'Gross primary or secondary school enrolment ratio' refers to the number of children enrolled in a level (primary or secondary), regardless of age, divided by the population of the age group that officially corresponds to the same level. 'Adjusted net enrolment ratio' refers to the total number of students of the official primary-school age group who are enrolled at primary or secondary education, expressed as a percentage of the corresponding population.

Source: World Bank (2016a).

5.5 INCOME INEQUALITY

Income inequality is often measured by the Gini Coefficient,[3] which measures the extent to which the distribution of income among households within an economy deviates from a perfectly equal distribution. The Gini Coefficient ranges between 0 and 100. In a country with a totally equal income distribution – every person receives the same income – the Gini Coefficient equals 0; in a country with a completely unequal distribution, with one person receiving the entire income, the Gini Coefficient equals 100.

Income inequality has increased in Eastern Europe due to socioeconomic changes following the collapse of socialism. Former socialist nations favoured less inequality, advocating egalitarian values and policies. The end of socialism led to a variety of structural changes in the labour market. Most notable was the decline of employment in government-owned businesses and the emergence of private entrepreneurs. In Poland, by late 1994, people in high-status occupations earned around 3.5 times as much as ordinary workers, increasing to 3.7 times

3. The Gini Coefficient was developed by the Italian sociologist Corrado Gini in 1912. (See Chapter 12 for further discussion.)

by 1997 and as much as 7 times by 1999. Most dramatically, by 1999 the 'owner/manager of a large factory' earned 14 times as much as an ordinary worker. The same patterns appeared in Hungary. By 1992, Hungarians already thought factory owners ought to earn 7 times as much as ordinary workers; by 1999, this perception had increased to no less than 10 times (Kelley and Zagorski, 2003).

Table 5.4 Gini Coefficient: Selected Countries In Latin America and Eastern Europe, 2007 and 2014

Country	*2007*	*2014*
Latin America		
Argentina	47.4	42.7
Brazil	55.9	51.5
Costa Rica	49.2	48.5
El Salvador	46.9	41.8
Honduras	56.2	50.6
Paraguay	53.3	51.7
Peru	51.6	44.1
Uruguay	47.6	41.6
Eastern Europe		
Poland	34.0	32.1
Ukraine	29.6	24.1

Source: World Bank (2016a).

In examining Table 5.4, it is clear that globalisation has led to an increase in economic and social inequalities globally, despite a decreasing trend in extreme poverty.

5.6 RECENT GLOBAL TRENDS IN POVERTY AND INEQUALITY

Within many countries, income inequality, according to Thomas Piketty (2014), has significantly increased since the early 1990s. Piketty's 15-year empirical study, conducted in conjunction with other scholars, analysed the evolution of income and wealth (which he calls 'capital') over the past three centuries in several high-income countries. Among the lessons learned are the following:

- There is no general tendency towards greater economic equality.
- The relatively high degree of equality after the Second World War was partly a result of deliberate policy, especially progressive taxation, but even more a result of the attenuation of inherited wealth, particularly within Europe, between 1914 and 1945.
- In Europe, a 'patrimonial capitalism' – the world dominated by inherited wealth – of the late nineteenth century is being slowly recreated.

- Inequality within generations remains vastly greater than between them.
- Perhaps the most extraordinary statistic is that 'the richest 1 per cent appropriated 60 percent of the increase in American national income between 1977 and 2007'.

Despite high employment in the United States before the recent crisis, productivity increases have not been matched by increases in real wages, increasing profits but not wages. In the USA, the most striking numbers on income inequality pertain to the dramatic change in the ratio of the pay of the average chief executive officer (CEO) to that of the average factory worker over the past 40 years (Domhoff, 2012), which today is 200 times higher, with some CEOs earning as much as 1000 times more than the average worker.

In Europe, increased poverty has been associated with more precarious work employment opportunities, including shorter hours and **zero-hour contracts** (i.e. the employer is neither obliged to accept any hours offered nor required to offer any), as well as the difficulties of single-parent family arrangements and an ageing population. In the Global North, the management of fiscal budgets and the crisis in welfare systems have also contributed to growing inequality. To give just one example, the politicisation of medicine could stimulate unequal access to medical assistance and threaten social cohesion (Fremstad, 2013).

In the Global South, the effects of the **Washington Consensus**, emphasising open markets and unrestricted movement of financial and physical capital,[4] along with aligning domestic policies to the **structural adjustment programmes** (SAPs) mandated by the IMF and World Bank (see Chapter 12), including liberalisation, privatisation of state infrastructure and services, fiscal austerity and the search for competitiveness, with macroeconomic stabilisation and fiscal austerity as preponderant objectives, has increased inequality. The expectation is that more jobs and higher rates of economic growth would be generated. This has not occurred, although the incidence of social vulnerability, particularly in developing nations during the 1980s and 1990s, is clearly evident. This has led to the growth of the **informal economy** (see Chapter 7), the expansion of low-wage service industries and the increase in jobs without any legal protection. In India, large sections of the labour force have working conditions that are not legally protected. In Latin America, informality increased due to the impact of the new international division of labour, while industrial production and formal employment declined as firms struggled to face foreign competitors. Changes in

4. 'Washington Consensus' was coined by the economist John Williamson in 1993 to refer to 'accepted agreement that unfettered free markets work best to promote economic growth; a wisdom accepted by all US policy makers and global financial institutions such as the IMF, World Bank and the WTO (Birch et al., 2017: 124).

working conditions and pensions, and increasing labour market informalisation, among other factors, have fostered poverty and inequality.

Despite significant and unprecedented economic growth, income inequality increased in China. Data from Peking University found that in 2012, households in the top 5 per cent income bracket earned 23 per cent of China's total household income, whereas households in the lowest 5 per cent accounted for just 0.1 per cent of total income. In urban areas, the average annual income for a family in 2012 was about US$2,600, while in rural areas it was $US1,600. Indeed, China's recent growth policies, which lifted millions from poverty, have also resulted in an uneven distribution of wealth (Wong, 2013).

In the aftermath of the global financial crisis, the recession has also affected wealth distribution, which is more unequal than before the crisis. In the United States, median household net worth decreased by $12,993, or 16 per cent, between 2000 and 2011 (US Census Bureau, various years; nominal data). At the same time, median household debt has increased over the past decade: from $50,971 in 2000 to $70,000 in 2011 (Ibid.). In the US, there is significant difference in wealth deterioration between blacks and whites, with the former suffering disproportionately more, since their wealth is almost exclusively comprised of housing. Many homes have declined in value or have been repossessed by banks. Indeed, the gap between the rich and the rest of the American population increased even more.

Since the 1970s, the strategies of financial managers have been important in understanding the general trend towards greater inequality. **Financialisation** (i.e. the increased importance of finance, credit, money and those who regulate and lend it) has increased incomes derived from share dividends and investments. In this context, labour markets have become a key variable in macroeconomic and business adjustments. Given the increased power of capitalists versus workers in recent decades, it is not surprising that both the process and outcomes have favoured capitalists. The percentage of labour income in GDP has generally trended downward, whereas capitalist income has trended upwards. Economic growth has been accompanied by worsening working conditions and deep economic insecurity, with employment conditioned to private investment decisions searching for increasing profits. In contemporary capitalism, the international institutional architecture has favoured capital mobility and short-term investment decisions – increasingly subordinated to rules of portfolio risk management, favouring those with capital. While recent changes in productive organisation have been based on competitiveness and the salience of the profit motive, job instability and fragile social protection have forced the reorganisation of survival strategies. Thus, workers must redefine their skills or become informal entrepreneurs (Madi and Gonçalves, 2013: 239).

5.7 WOMEN AND POVERTY

Today there are 66 million more men than women on the planet. The surplus is concentrated in the youngest age groups and diminishes until the age of 50. China and India are the world's most populous countries, and hence the large surplus can be found within these countries. Although women live longer than men, social, cultural and economic factors favour disempowerment. Two-thirds of the 775 million adult illiterates worldwide are women, a proportion which has not significantly changed since 1990 (UN, 2017).

Table 5.5 Adult Literacy Rate, 2010 (Percentage of People Aged 15 and Above)

Region	*Total*	*Male*	*Female*
Arab World	77.4	84.7	69.2
East Asia and Pacific	95.1	97.1	93.1
Europe and Central Asia	99.0	99.4	98.6
Latin America and Caribbean	92.6	93.1	92.2
South Asia	66.7	76.0	57.0
Sub-Saharan Africa	60.9	69.2	53.0

Source: World Bank (2016a).

The lack of gender balance is a worldwide reality not only in the number of adult illiterate women but also in decision-making positions in government, science and the top levels of many big businesses. According to the UN (2017), only 22.8 per cent of all national parliamentarians were women as of June 2016, a 'slow increase' from 11.3 per cent in 1995, with ten women serving as Head of State and nine serving as Head of Government.

However, as we write this book, an increasing number of nations are witnessing women either running for national office (Hillary Clinton, USA) or elected (Theresa May, Great Britain; Nicola Sturgeon, Scotland; Angela Merkel, Germany; Beata Szydło, Poland; Erna Solberg, Norway); or achieving a good position to challenge and win elections: Ursula Leyden, Germany; Marine Le Pen, France; Ayelet Shaked, Israel) (Johnson 2016). Perhaps the tide may be changing. According to Johnson, what unites 'the younger generation of women rising to power across Europe, Asia and America is a determination to make the world a better place' (Johnson, 2016: 29).

Interestingly, the UN (2017) notes that women's representation in local government can make a difference, but that 'the global proportion of women elected to local government is currently unknown, constituting a major knowledge gap'. Nevertheless, the UN is currently constructing a database on women elected to local government under the auspices of UN SDG #5: 'Achieve gender equality and empower all women and girls.' Sadly, only 28 of the CEOs of the Fortune 500 companies, or a dismal 5.6 per cent, are women.

In less developed countries, poor infrastructure and housing conditions affect women disproportionately. In sub-Saharan Africa, more than 50 per cent of rural households and almost 25 per cent of urban households do not have easy access to drinking water. In general, the burden of water collection rests on women; as a result, the amount of time spent on income earning or educational or leisure activities is significantly reduced. In fact, the provision of public childcare is a key factor in whether mothers start or return to work outside the home. In sub-Saharan Africa and parts of Southern and Southeast Asia, women are exposed to smoke from burning solid fuels while cooking and care for children indoors, increasing health problems and exacerbating disempowerment. In sub-Saharan Africa, North Africa and the Middle East, women constitute the majority of HIV-positive adults. Table 5.6 highlights some important political and economic differences between men and women.

Table 5.6 *Women at Work*, 2016: Global Highlights

Selected features	*Status of women at work*
Unemployment	Women are more likely to be unemployed than men, with global unemployment rates of 5.5% for men and 6.2% for women.
Informal work	In 2015, a total of 586 million women were own-account (i.e., self-employed) or contributing family workers. Many working women remain in occupations that are more likely to consist of informal work arrangements.
Wage and salaried jobs	52.1% of women and 51.2% of men in the labour market are wage and salaried workers.
Jobs and occupations by economic sectors	Globally, the services sector has overtaken agriculture in employing the highest number of women and men. Since 1995, women's employment in services has increased from 41.1% to 61.5% in 2015.
High-skilled occupations	High-skilled occupations expanded faster for women than for men in emerging economies, where there is a gender gap in high-skilled employment in women's favour.
Part-time jobs	Globally, women represent less than 40% of total employment, but make up 57% of those working on a part-time basis.
Hours of work	Across the globe, one quarter of women in employment (25.7%) work more than 48 hours a week, mainly in East, West and Central Asia, where almost half of women employed work more than 48 hours a week.
Gender wage gap	Globally, women earn 77% of what men earn.

Source: International Labour Organization (ILO, 2016).

5.8 POVERTY AND CLIMATE CHANGE

Vulnerable groups in all parts of the world will suffer adversely from the anticipated extreme weather patterns brought by climate change. If global temperatures rise as much as 4°C since 1800, as is possible, no amount of mitigation will be of use to the world's poor and vulnerable. A report from the World Bank, *Shock Waves: Managing the Impacts of Climate Change* (Hallegatte et al., 2016), states that rising temperatures could mean 100 million or more people falling into 'extreme poverty'. Recent natural disasters including floods, typhoons and tsunamis have already affected the poor disproportionately. Poor countries in warmer and drier regions will experience decline in crop yields, leading to malnutrition; in addition, higher food prices and increase in waterborne diseases and destitution are likely to be far more common than at present. The Report states that policies and actions to stabilise climate should also incorporate policies to eradicate poverty, like social safety nets and the provision of universal healthcare. To do this, the world must invest US$1 trillion (£645 billion) more every year to develop key infrastructure projects.

In 2009, the Global Humanitarian Forum published its *Human Impact Report*. It stated clearly that climate change is already acting as a multiplier of human impacts and risk. It indicates that every year climate change leaves over 300,000 people dead, 325 million people seriously affected, and economic losses of US$125 billion (2009: 3). Indeed, four billion people were vulnerable, and 500 million people were at extreme risk (Ibid). According to the *Report* (Global Humanitarian Forum, 2009: 3):

> The populations most gravely and immediately at risk live in some of the poorest areas that are also highly prone to climate change – in particular, the semi-arid dry land belt countries from the Sahara to the Middle East and Central Asia, as well as sub-Saharan Africa, South Asian waterways and Small Island Developing States.

5.9 WOMEN AND CLIMATE CHANGE

According to the United Nations (UN, 2015b), in developing countries, women and girls constitute 50 per cent of people in poor households, compared with 53 per cent in developed nations. However, such aggregated statistics, as the UN notes, fail to adequately document the increased **feminisation of poverty**, defined as the current higher share of women among the poor, and/or the increase in the proportion of women among the poor over time,[5] which can

5. We highly recommend the United Nations' *The World's Women 2015: Trends and Statistics*, an interesting book which discusses the complex and multidimensional dimensions of the world's women and poverty.

vary significantly by region and household characteristics (Ibid.: 190). For example, according to the UN, 'three-quarters of one-parent families are lone mothers with children and . . . in most countries with data available, families of lone mothers with children are more likely to be poor than families of lone fathers with children' (ibid.: 183). As for the reasons: women continue to remain dependent on their spouses; women are institutionally disadvantaged, which restricts female ownership of land, other resources, and inheritance rights; and an overall lack of female empowerment (Ibid.).

Added to this, two-thirds of the female labour force in developing countries is engaged in agriculture, which is most susceptible to climate change, suggesting that women will bear a disproportionate burden. Climate change will increase the unpredictability of water sources, hence the unpredictability of food sources. As agriculture prices increase due to scarcity, women and girls are more susceptible, both due to the higher prices and to being excluded (United Nations, 2015d: 1).

The UN also recommends that 'in order to preserve biodiversity, indigenous communities and indigenous women should be greater included' (Ibid.: 2–3). We agree and also recommend a greater inclusion of women in economic and political decision-making in order to meet the UN SDGs.

5.10 GLOBAL MIGRATION AND REMITTANCES

One of the more difficult and emotional decisions an individual can make is whether to leave one's native country. Perhaps because it is so difficult, we should not be surprised that the number is so low. According to the UN, in 2013, 232 million people, or 3.2 per cent of the world's population, were international migrants, compared with 154 million people in 1990, or 2.8 per cent of the global population. Migration[6] has become a highly contentious political issue in many countries. In 2013 the United Nations Under-Secretary-General for Economic and Social Affairs, Wu Hongbo, stated, 'Migration, *when governed fairly*, can make a very important contribution to social and economic development, both in the countries of origin and in the countries of destination' (UN Information Service 2013, emphasis added). This generic statement is hard to disagree with, but the key phrase is 'governed fairly'. What does 'fair' mean, and who does the governing?

Following the International Labour Organization's Fair Migration Agenda, we highlight the following topics as intrinsic to 'governed fairly':

6. 'Migrate' comes from the Latin word *migrare* (to wander; to move). Unless stated otherwise, **migration** can refer to either internal movement from one region of a country to another, or to movement from one nation to another. **Emigration** refers to leaving one's country, while **immigration** refers to entering a country.

- Respecting the human rights, including labour rights, of all migrants.
- Ensuring fair recruitment and equal treatment of migrant workers to prevent exploitation and level the playing field with nationals.
- Countering unacceptable situations through the promotion of the universal exercise of fundamental principles and rights at work.
- Promoting social dialogue by involving ministries of labour, trade unions and employers' organisations in policy-making on migration.

Indeed, inhumane living and working conditions and physical (and sexual) abuse that many migrant workers must endure should be addressed by the reaffirmation of basic freedoms and prohibition against degrading treatment. Migrant workers should be treated as equal to domestic workers regarding remuneration and conditions of work – such as overtime, hours of work, weekly rest, holidays with pay, safety, health, termination of work contract, minimum wage. In addition, migrant workers should benefit from social security benefits and emergency medical care, and should be allowed to globally transfer their earnings and savings.

Some of the more significant events increasing the likelihood of emigration include war, revolution, persecution, political upheaval, poverty, lack of economic opportunity and, increasingly, environmental factors brought on by climate change, including persistent drought, desertification in some areas or flooding, and other forms of habitat destruction. It is quite possible that many migrants in the near future will be environmental refugees.

On the other hand, factors making a country a destination for immigration include relatively favourable economic, political and social conditions, the absence of war and instability, and a more equitable climate. The key word is 'relative'. This suggests that unless conditions are the same across all countries, or there are strict prohibitions against migration, the will to migrate will always exist.

Global migration of healthcare workers has intensified, partly caused by an increase demand for healthcare services in richer developed countries (most of which are experiencing an ageing population). This has increased the emigration of healthcare workers from developing nations, especially in Africa, where, given the prevalence of AIDS, hunger and malnutrition, the need is most acute. This results in a 'brain drain', underscoring, as Connell (2010: 203) notes, that the costs of global mobility are unevenly borne by the poorer source countries, with the primary benefits elsewhere. Migration emerges from inequality, and contributes to it (especially as skilled migrants ply their skills elsewhere), stimulating an institutionalisation of social and economic inequality that may ultimately entrench social problems.

In many instances, migrants send a considerable part of their earnings back to their families. This private income transfer is known as a ***remittance***, and financial costs involved in sending money across national borders is defined as the ***remittance cost***. Unsurprisingly, given the laws of supply and demand, increased remittance transfer fees decrease overall remittances.

The World Bank's Migration and Development Unit Report (World Bank, 2017b) noted that officially recorded remittances to developing countries reached US$601 billion in 2015, over three times the amount provided by official aid. As remittance flows include unrecorded flows through formal and informal channels, the actual amount of money transferred cross-border to family members might be significantly higher.

In 2014, diaspora members living in the United States sent more remittances than diaspora members based in any other country, with an estimated US$56 billion in outward flows. The United States was followed by Saudi Arabia (US$37 billion) and Russia (US$33 billion). In 2015, India was the largest remittance-receiving country. According to the World Bank (2017), diaspora members sent almost US$72 billion in remittances to India and US$64 billion to China in 2015. The Philippines and Mexico received almost US$50 billion in officially recorded remittances.

However, remittance flows to developing countries registered a decline of 1 per cent in 2015, followed by 2.4 per cent in 2016. Factors responsible, according to the World Bank, include weak economic growth, increasing regulatory burdens on money transfer operations and the discouragement of hiring foreign workers (World Bank, 2017b).

High unemployment rates in Europe have impacted outward remittance flows. An analysis of labour markets indicates that migrant unemployment rates are higher than those of native-born workers in France, Greece, Italy, Spain and the UK. This trend has dampened the level of remittance outflows from major remittance senders in Europe, such as the UK, Spain, and Italy; as a result, Eastern Europe and Central Asian countries have received weak remittance inflows.

A striking contrast to weak remittance outflows from Western Europe has been the outflows from Russia, a country that benefited from elevated oil prices until the last few years. In 2012, the main beneficiaries of growing remittance outflows from Russia have been migrants from Armenia, Georgia, the Kyrgyz Republic, Moldova and Tajikistan.

Compared with private capital flows, remittances have shown remarkable resilience since the global financial crisis, indicating the importance of migrants giving money to their families. Remittances increase disposable income and are generally spent on consumption, especially food, clothing, medicine, shelter and durable goods. As a result, remittances help lift people out of extreme and moderate poverty by enabling them to maintain a higher level of consumption, especially during economic adversity.

However, what might be good for an individual household is not necessarily good for the overall economy (Chami and Fullenkamp, 2013). In some developing countries, policy-makers have considered remittances as a source of funding for economic development. In the Caribbean, for example, local governments have increased imports, financed by official remittances, instead of domestic production. Consequently, the increase in remittances has reduced the opportunities of employment and increased migration to other countries in the Caribbean region.

Perhaps remittances assuage any guilt on the part of the individual, for in one sense 'remittances have partly replaced the morality of return' (Connell, 2010: 208). But does this raise an obligation by the home country to improve economic and social conditions in order to prevent the need to emigrate? Obviously there is a problem of affordability here, and of course one country can do very little to arrest or even mitigate the impact of climate change, though some countries and regions, such as the USA, China and India, have a greater impact than others, suggesting multi-regional and global cooperation.

THINKING QUESTIONS

To what extent has increased inequality resulted from current economic and financial policies?

How could social and financial policies alleviate poverty and empower women?

To what extent can microcredit schemes ensure income creation?

CLASS ACTIVITY

Conduct research on a specific nation's recent (i.e. in the last five years) poverty and inequality indicators, considering the World Bank website; then construct a critical analysis of the causes and consequences of its poverty.

AREAS FOR RESEARCH

Using material published online from the United Nations International Children's Emergency Fund (UNICEF), United Nations Development Programme (UNDP), United Nations Research Institute for Social Development (UNRISD), International Monetary (IMF) and the World Bank, explore the current extent and nature of childhood poverty in the developing world.

Select a country. Why are its people poor? Are there unique factors in its history? What is the government doing to solve the poverty?

UN SDG FOCUS

Goals #1 and #2 call for:

1. End poverty in all its forms everywhere.

2. End hunger, achieve food security and improved nutrition, and promote sustainable agriculture.

How would you define and measure poverty, hunger and sustainable agriculture? How would you 'end' poverty and hunger?

Research the UN's findings on Goals #1 and #2. How would you recommend implementation? Is there any particular school of thought that you find most helpful?

FURTHER READING

Chami, R. and Fullenkamp, C. (2013) 'Beyond the Household'. *Finance & Development*, Vol. 50, No. 3, pp.1–25.

Hallegatte, S., Bangalore, M., Bonzanigo, L., Fay, M.; Kane; T., Narloch, U., Rozenberg, J., Treguer, D. and Vogt-Schilb, A. (eds). (2015) *Shock Waves: Managing the Impacts of Climate Change on Poverty.* Climate Change and Development Series. Washington DC: World Bank.

Tudge, C. (2007) *Feeding People is Easy*. Grosseto, Italy: Pari Publishing.

United Nations (2015) *The World's Women 2015: Trends and Statistics*. New York: United Nations, Department of Economic and Social Affairs, Statistics Division.

6
Livelihoods and Work

Our objective in this chapter is to introduce a conceptualisation of work. How is work used to affect the basic economic goal of provisioning? How does work provide meaning and self-worth in an individual's life? Since the nature of work is changing globally, it is crucial to understand the contemporary dynamics of capitalism. Indeed, current working conditions are increasing insecurity and unease. In this context, we will ask: Is work a means to an end rather than an end in itself? What about work in the informal sector? What is unpaid work? Is caring in the family fulfilling? How can work become both fulfilling and sustainable? Could a basic income be an effective and sustainable solution?

6.1 WHAT IS WORK?

It is not our general purpose to criticise one particular school within economics, for in the spirit of pluralism we feel that each school has something to offer. However, pertaining to work and its many attendant issues, we feel an initial criticism of neoclassical economics is justified. As discussed in Chapter 1, neoclassical economics is deductive (based on axiomatic assumptions) rather than empirically based. In other words, rather than investigating how the economy operates, and the labour market in particular, neoclassical economics gratuitously (and rather dogmatically, we might add) assumes that it operates in a particular way. Specifically, individual workers are assumed to trade off between work and leisure: leisure is a positive good to be enjoyed, something that everyone wants more of; whereas work is not desirable in itself, but only instrumental – we work to earn money in order to buy goods and services. Thus, workers are mere cogs, and

> 'labour' or work [is] little more than a necessary evil. From the point of view of the employer, it is . . . simply an item of cost, to be reduced to a minimum if it cannot be eliminated altogether, say, by automation. From the point of view of the workman [sic], it is a 'disutility'; to work is to make a sacrifice of one's leisure and comfort, and wages are a kind of compensation for the sacrifice.
>
> Schumacher 1973 [1989]: 57

We find this gratuitous assumption of a labour–leisure tradeoff highly insulting. We view labour and leisure as complementary and intricately related: one is fulfilling only if the other is. Schumacher (Ibid.: 58) again:

> to strive for leisure as an alternative to work would be a complete misunderstanding of one of the basic truths of human existence, namely that work and leisure are complementary parts of the same living process and cannot be separated without destroying the joy of work and the bliss of leisure.

Not only does such a trade-off give the wrong message about what work entails, but it ignores the rich tradition of Eastern thought, particularly Buddhism, on the satisfying potential of work:

> The Buddhist point of view takes the function of work to be at least threefold: to give a man [sic] a chance to utilise and develop his faculties; to enable him to overcome his ego-centredness by joining with other people in a common task; and to bring forth the goods and services needed for a becoming existence.
>
> Ibid.

This richer and more holistic view of work calls for the design of jobs that are fulfilling for the individual, enabling her to meaningfully connect to the larger society. Not to do so is to

> organise work in such a manner that it becomes meaningless, boring, stultifying or nerve-wracking for the worker [and] would be little short of criminal; it would indicate a greater concern with goods than with people, an evil lack of compassion and a soul-destroying degree of attachment to the most primitive side of this worldly existence.
>
> Ibid.

Heavy stuff. But, nevertheless, for many people work *is* nothing more than labour: it is meaningless, boring – just a means of earning a pay cheque. Why? What went wrong?

Capitalism's modus operandi is to maximise profits, to accumulate more capital, to expand, to grow. Not only is this unsustainable but it also stultifies human creativity and destroys the 'joy of work and the bliss of leisure'.

In *The Great Transformation*, Karl Polanyi (1944) argued that land, labour and money are 'fictitious commodities' because they were never intended to be 'produced' and sold in a market. Now, selling our labour for a wage in order to buy goods and services is second nature for many of us, and we may think it normal and even natural. But this did not happen until the Industrial Revolution, which at the time surprised and angered many people. One's labour cannot be reduced simply to a commodity, since it is a human activity. Life is not sustained by market forces but by a process of transferring aspects of society from generation to generation: in households, in communities, in society. Land is not simply a commodity, because it is part of nature.

Polanyi argued that the dehumanisation of capitalism is a result of the particular institutional construct of a market society, which of course is not natural. This is important since it suggests that we can develop new institutions to push the economy in a more human and sustainable direction.

Beginning with the classical economists, we get two different views of labour: (1) labour is the most important factor of production; (2) labour is instrumental to capitalism as the source of both profits and exploitation. Each will now be explained.

(1) Labour is the most important factor of production

The importance of labour underlies the **labour theory of value**, as explained in Chapter 1. The labour theory of value was subsequently challenged by neoclassical economists later in the nineteenth century, who argued that the source of value of an item is the **utility** or satisfaction obtained from it. Utility theory is an important concept in neoclassical economics and deserves a brief explanation. Deeply rooted in intellectual thought, it stems from the assumption of human beings as combative, alone, isolated, disconnected with others, forced to specialise in order to survive, yet at the same time dependent on a well-functioning economy (Hunt and Lautzenheiser, 2011: 125–9). Taken together, these factors laid the foundation for neoclassical economics 'as a theory of social harmony' rather than a system that pitted different class interests against each other (Ibid.: 127).

Jeremy Bentham (1748–1832), in his *Introduction to the Principles of Morals and Legislation* (1780), developed the rationale for utility theory.[1] According to Bentham, every individual is subject to both pleasure and pain (i.e. negative pleasure); thus, in order to maximise her happiness, she should avoid pain and increase pleasure.

Bentham assumed this guiding principle explained all human motivation in all times and in all places! (Hunt and Lautzenheiser, 2011: 130). Using this principle as a foundation, he thought governments should implement policies to maximise

1. William Jevons, one of the founders of neoclassical economics, wrote in the introduction to his influential *The Theory of Political Economy*, 'The theory which follows is entirely based on a calculus of pleasure and pain; and the object of Economics is to maximise happiness by purchasing pleasure, as it were, at the lowest cost of pain' (Jevons, 1871 [1931]: 23).

total utility, and should discriminate between different policies according to which increased total utility more.

But utility is subjective, existing in the minds of individuals.[2] So how can a society base economic policy on something so intrinsically subjective?

(2) Labour is the source of both profits and exploitation

The second view of labour is more pejorative: labour is instrumental to capitalism, the source of profits and of exploitation. Thus, labour is no different from any other factor of production: something to be minimised – forgetting, of course, that labour is unique since it is possessed (at least initially) by the individual. But capitalism strips the work from the worker and makes labour a commodity, and in doing so alienates one's labour from oneself. This notion of alienation is important to understand contemporary capitalism:

> it is a problem arising from how our particular economic system is organised, with workers divorced from control over their own labour process and from the products of their work... Numerous studies of working conditions over the last century have shown the ongoing links between alienation in the workplace and an array of industrial and health disorders . . . It now takes more diverse forms, as social, environmental, and political alienation. As market criteria increasingly dominate our lives, their clash with a holistic view of ourselves in relation to nature, society and polity becomes an ever-more profound source of discontent.
>
> Stilwell, 2012: 397

The focus on labour as instrumental to producing goods and services led logically to the **division of labour**: subdividing labour into minute tasks, each performed by a different worker, which theoretically leads to increased accumulation of profits; which, in turn, at least as this argument goes, increases the wealth of the nation. While Adam Smith was not the first to advocate a division of labour, his account in *The Wealth of Nations* (which is the book's opening passage) is most eloquent and deserves reading:

> The greatest improvement in the productive powers of labour, and the greater part of the skill, dexterity, and judgment with which it is any where directed, or applied, seem to have been the effects of the division of labour [...] To take an example, therefore, from a very trifling manufacture; but one in which

2. This did not stop many people, including Bentham himself, from (unsuccessfully) trying to invent devices to actually measure utility, much like a thermometer measures temperature.

> the division of labour has been very often taken notice of, the trade of the pin-maker; a workman not educated to this business (which the division of labour has rendered a distinct trade), nor acquainted with the use of the machinery employed in it (to the invention of which the same division of labour has probably given occasion), could scarce, perhaps, with his utmost industry, make one pin in a day, and certainly could not make twenty. But in the way in which this business is now carried on, not only the whole work is a peculiar trade, but it is divided into a number of branches, of which the greater part are likewise peculiar trades. One man draws out the wire, another straights it, a third cuts it, a fourth points it, a fifth grinds it at the top for receiving the head; to make the head requires two or three distinct operations; to put it on, is a peculiar business, to whiten the pins is another; it is even a trade by itself to put them into the paper; and the important business of making a pin is, in this manner, divided into about eighteen distinct operations, which, in some manufactories, are all performed by distinct hands, though in others the same man will sometimes perform two or three of them... But if they had all wrought separately and independently, and without any of them having been educated to this peculiar business, they certainly could not each of them have made twenty, perhaps not one pin in a day; that is, certainly not the two hundred and fortieth, perhaps not the four thousand eight hundredth part of what they are at present capable of performing, in consequence of a proper division and combination of their different operations.
>
> Smith, 1776 [1976]: Vol. 1, Bk. I, Ch. 1. pp.7–9

So here we have it from the beginning of capitalism: that labour to be meaningful must be squeezed, trimmed, divided and specialised. It makes one wonder if capitalism is consistent with meaningful work. How can work be conceptualised as sustainable if it is merely instrumental to maximising profits?

6.2 THE CHANGING NATURE OF WORK

Work is contextual: that is, the nature of work is a function of specific economic conditions. As technology changes, so does work. The best we can do here is to give a brief overview of the changing conditions of work and their most important drivers – to do otherwise would require several volumes on the subject.[3]

The Industrial Revolution, which began in England in the late eighteenth century, saw the rise of the **factory** (from the Latin *factotum*: 'to do everything'),

3. For a good thoughtful exposition, see Rifkin (1995: xviii). He writes: 'For the whole of the modern era, people's worth has been measured by the market value of their labour. Now that the commodity value of human labour is becoming increasingly tangential and irrelevant in an ever more automated world, new ways of defining human worth and social relationships will need to be explored' We will expand on this in future chapters.

Box 6.1 A Sampling of Historic Contributions on Work and Leisure

Early contributions in political economy to the ideas of work and leisure were developed in the context of moral philosophy. The concept of happiness was highlighted by **David Hume** (1955: 21):

> Human happiness, according to the most received notions, seems to consist in three ingredients; action, pleasure and indolence. And though these ingredients ought to be mixed in different proportions, according to the particular disposition of the person; yet no one ingredient can be entirely wanting, without destroying, in some measure, the relish of the whole composition.

According to **Jeremy Bentham**, as described earlier, individuals choose actions that generate the highest level of pleasure and the lowest level of pain. Also known as utilitarianism, this concept is fundamental in classical and neoclassical economics. Accordingly, work is a means to obtain goods in the market, while leisure offers intrinsic utility. This is the genesis of the neoclassical assumption of a trade-off between work and leisure.

Joan Robinson (1903–83) criticised this rational-choice methodology for not understanding the actual behaviour of workers. In her *Essays in the Theory of Employment* (1937 [1947]), she noted that the choice between earnings and leisure does not depend entirely, or even mainly, on the preferences of the individuals. Instead, she argued that features of working conditions such as the length of the working day, educational requirements and nominal wages are the result of collective (rather than individual) decisions.

where power, technology, machines and specialised occupations were brought together under one roof. Factory-based work was characterised by division of labour, with manual work separated into its fragmented constituent tasks. In this setting, work specialisation stimulated the invention of new machinery. Factory owners not only exercised control over the pace and quality of work but also shaped workers' attitudes towards discipline, commitment and punctuality, dictated by the pace of the machines. Consequently, workers gradually realised the power of the workplace, developing a class consciousness. In addition, a feature of the factory system was the employment of women and children.

After the mid nineteenth century, work became more intensive and controlled by 'scientific management' principles, known as **Taylorism**, an extension of the division of labour. Work and workers were moved to increasingly large and centralised factories owned by corporations. Steam-powered factories, railroads, steamships and telegraphs were introduced in order to speed up work, cut time and increase productivity (Greenbaum, 2004). Bringing work under one roof led to mass production as well as assembly-line production, also known as **Fordism**. Taylorism and Fordism (elaborated in Box 6.2 below) were made possible by the development of the telegraph, which not only enabled global markets but also facilitated the railroad and the large corporation, controlled from a central office (Standage, 1998: 210).

Box 6.2 Business Management History

Taylorism and Fordism are considered 'classical' work organisations, representing the earliest contributions to modern business management (Bratton et al., 2010).

Taylorism was pioneered by Frederick Taylor (1856–1915), an American mechanical engineer who devised methods to improve industrial efficiency. Based on his analysis, management 'scientifically' analysed all tasks to be undertaken within a job, then dissected and designed each to be efficient as possible. Not surprisingly, workers' autonomy shrank.

Fordism was pioneered by Henry Ford (1863–1947), who applied Taylor's principles in his car factories. Ford borrowed the idea of an assembly line, first used in the bicycle and meatpacking industry.[1] The assembly line is the ultimate control over work: no need to go to the workbench for a tool; no need to bend over, since the task is presented to you; and no discretion for speed – the assembly line can be sped up at will. Little wonder that wherever the assembly line was introduced, it precipitated the formation of trade unions.

Both Taylorism and Fordism have been criticised for fostering an oversimplification of work, increasing workers' dissatisfaction, absenteeism and turnover. Alternative approaches include the *human relations school of industrial relations*, which developed during the 1920s, and shifted attention towards the psychological and social needs of workers. In the 1970s and 1980s, the *quality of working life* movement criticised specialisation and aimed to provide a variety of tasks for workers in order to improve satisfaction. In addition, *team working* developed during the 1980s, based on a multi-skilled and multi-tasking workforce.

Post-Fordism emerged as a response to the crisis of Fordism. Post-Fordism is defined as a production process based on flexible machines or systems and an appropriately flexible workforce. Its crucial hardware is micro-electronics-based information and communications technologies.

Redefining the role of the individual in a near workerless society is likely to be the single most pressing issue in the decades to come. New approaches to providing income and purchasing power will have to be implemented. Greater reliance will need to be placed on the emerging 'third sector' to restore communities and build a sustainable culture.

Source: Bratton et al. (2010), Jessop (1992).

1. For a lucid and realistic depiction of the assembly line in the meatpacking industry, see Upton Sinclair's *The Jungle* (1985 [1906]). Incidentally, Sinclair's lurid description of the horrible conditions in the US meatpacking industry led directly to the passage of the US Federal Meat Inspection Act of 1907.

Since the mid-1970s, work organisation has shifted away from Fordism to post-Fordism, with more emphasis on smaller production units and consumer-demanded production. The main features of each work organisation and employment relationships are delineated in Table 6.1. More recently, the Internet has enabled transformation of traditional work, under Fordism, to knowledge work, characteristic of post-Fordism. Table 6.2 shows a comparison between traditional and knowledge work.

Table 6.1 Historical Evolution of Work Organisation and Employment Relationships

	Craft/artisan	*Taylorism/Fordism*	*Post-Fordism (since the mid-1970s)*
Work organisation	Specialist work. High-skill.	Repetitive work. Low-skill.	Knowledge work. High-skill. Fragmentation of tasks.
Employment relations	Workers on their own.	Wage contracts. Formality. Control of workers.	Wage contracts. Increasing informality. Outsourcing. Crowdsourcing. More control of workers.
Major economic trends	Agriculture as main economic activity.	Industrial Capitalism. Closed economies. Managerial 'scientific principles'.	Financial-led capitalism. Expansion of global competitive markets. Expansion of the global labour market, including China. Availability of digital technologies. Demographic and educational changes. Managerial 'scientific principles'.

Source: Elaborated by the authors from Bratton et al. (2010) and Bauer (2004).

In knowledge work, multi-tasking workers are integrated into flat hierarchical structures, compared to the centralised large corporation, e.g. General Motors. As a result, communication channels have been redefined, with greater involvement of lower-level employees in decision-making (Bauer, 2004). Knowledge work features flexitime, teleworking, alternative payment schemes, employee empowerment and autonomy, task rotation and multi-skilling, teamwork and team autonomy. Potential consequences include fragmentation of work, crowdsourcing and virtualisation of work.

Jeremy Rifkin (1995; 2014) has analysed the technological impact on the future of work; accordingly, we are facing a new phase of history characterised by the steady and inevitable decline of jobs in the production and marketing of goods and services. As a result of the high-technology revolution, the number of people underemployed or without work will continuously increase. In an increasingly automated world likely to be dominated by the Internet, and production at near-zero **marginal cost** (the extra cost of producing an additional unit of a good or service), the labour market is polarising into two forces: (1) an elite that controls and manages the high-tech global economy; and (2) increasingly displaced workers with few prospects for meaningful employment.

Table 6.2 Traditional Work and Knowledge Work: Main Differences

	Traditional work	*Knowledge work*
Skill/knowledge scope	Narrow-skilling.	Multi-skilling.
Work dynamics	Around individuals.	Teamwork around projects; teleworking; task rotation.
Skills	Gradual obsolescence.	Rapid obsolescence.
Performance evaluation	Task deliverables.	Targets.
Development of human resources	Internal to organisation.	External to organisation.

Source: Elaborated by the authors from Bratton et al. (2010) and Bauer (2004).

Among today's notable changes in the labour market is **crowdsourcing**: the outsourcing of tasks to a large, undefined group of people in an open call (Howe, 2006). This 'cloud-based' work environment is characterised by five essential characteristics: on-demand service, broad access, resource pooling, rapid elasticity and measured service (Ipeirotis, 2012). Low wages, lack of rights, unprotected jobs and increasing informality are the flipside of cloud labour. Paul Markillie noted in *The Economist* (2012) that crowdsourcing platforms operate under no regulation and tend to drive down wages.

Crowdsourcing is fundamentally associated with the virtualisation of work. Technologies such as instant messaging, teleconferencing and video calls make it less necessary for co-workers to gather together physically, which in turn allows the creation of virtual teams, along with teleworking, co-working and the use of social media. However the effects of teleworking on livelihoods are controversial. While for some workers teleworking fosters a better work–life balance, it might not be suited to other workers, especially those who prefer interacting with colleagues at a physical workplace. And many teleworkers complain about their inability to set a clear dividing line between work and private life. Adverse effects on health resulting from technological changes and management strategies in the virtual universe require new forms of care in order to prevent workers' health problems.

Management strategies are also transforming working conditions. Thanks to globalisation, the quick and instant flow of investment funds has reconceptualised many jobs and work practices to comport with management prerogatives. This has already occurred in healthcare, engineering and computer science with highly paid and skilled professionals. For example, trained nurses are allowed to assume the routine tasks of doctors. This fragmentation process extends the Taylorist principles of scientific management in order to increase efficiency by the reassignment of repetitive tasks.

More flexible strategies also include outsourcing of jobs. **Outsourcing** is essentially subcontracting workers outside a company instead of hiring workers in-house; when done across international borders, it is **offshoring**. Both large and small companies outsource work in order to restrain payroll and overhead costs. For example, in the USA, companies of all sizes hire lower-paid workers in emerging markets. The advantage: the company can become more competitive in the global marketplace by reducing costs. The disadvantage: it can cause immediate unemployment in the home country.

Needless to say, these trends taken together produce precarious work, reduce full-time jobs and attenuate workers' rights and protection. Not surprisingly, horror stories exist about working conditions in such companies. Here we can mention two examples: Foxconn in China, and the Bangladesh garment industry.

Foxconn, the manufacturer responsible for assembling tech products for Apple and Samsung, among other corporations, is one of China's major employers. It has been accused of violating labour rights for many years: Overcrowded dormitories run by military-like security forces, excessive hours and excessive management control over workers' lives. After a rash of suicides between 2009 and 2011, Foxconn reduced employee overtime. In the garment industry of Bangladesh (Dhaka), which supplies garments to North America, Europe and Australia, the catastrophic collapse of the Rana Plaza factory killed more than 1,100 workers. In spite of this (or maybe because so), workers currently complain of physical assault, verbal abuse, forced overtime, unsanitary conditions, denial of paid maternity leave, and failure to pay wages and bonuses on time or in full (Human Rights Watch, 2015).

6.3 THE INTERNET OF THINGS: THE THIRD INDUSTRIAL REVOLUTION

Today, we have another industrial revolution, brought about by digital technology, which is leading to many changes in both the nature and extent of work. These changes are already affecting previously secure professional groups. According to Susskind (2015), systems and machines can do much of the traditional professional tasks without human experts. In 2014, almost 48 million Americans used online tax preparation software; while legalzoom.com, an online legal advice and document-drafting service, has become the best-known legal brand in the USA. And Associated Press and Forbes both use algorithms to write sports commentary.

In *The Future of the Professions*, Richard and Daniel Susskind (2016) identify two different futures for technology-based professions. The first is a version of the traditional professions, with the adoption of new systems that improve the efficiency of traditional work. For example, accountants using such new systems to perform difficult computations, and engineers to design more complex buildings. The second future is related to the introduction of a range of systems that will replace the work of traditional professionals. For example, new systems and machines can be used to diagnose illnesses, offer legal advice and teach children.[4] Although both futures develop in parallel, the second type of future will dominate and will lead to the gradual dismantling of the traditional professions in the long run.[5]

These changes call for reflection on and redefinition of the connections between the changing characteristics of employment and the nature of work. In his book *Farewell to the Working Class*, André Gorz (1982) states that the changing work and labour process at the end of the twentieth century (including the growth of capitalist power over working conditions, working relations, and the duration and intensity of work) has weakened workers' power in society. While capital succeeded in reducing workers' power, their role in reducing oppression and inequalities has been taken up by social movements such as the women's movement and the green movement.

According to Rifkin (2014), the Third Industrial Revolution (TIR) is a convergence of the Internet and renewable energy in order to build a new infrastructure that will change the distribution of economic power in the twenty-first century. The Revolution will fundamentally reorder our relationships, from hierarchical to lateral, significantly affecting how we conduct economic and social activities.[6]

---

4. We expand on this in the next two chapters.

5. Neoclassical economics makes a sharp distinction between the short run and the long run, assuming that an individual can conceptually separate the two, while operating in either one or the other. Partly this is due to assuming that individuals are rational, deciding what to do free from crippling uncertainty. But, as Keynes wrote, 'the state of expectation is liable to constant change, a new expectation being superimposed long before the previous change has fully worked itself out; so that the economic machine is occupied at any given time with a number of overlapping activities, the existence of which is due to various past states of expectation' (1936 [2010]: 50).

6. According to Klaus Schwab (2015), the founder and Executive Chairman of the World Economic Forum, the Internet of Things is part of a *fourth* Industrial Revolution, characterised by a fusion of technologies between the physical, digital and biological spheres. Velocity, scope and systems impact are three reasons why today's transformations cannot be considered as a mere prolongation of the Third Industrial Revolution – the so-called digital revolution. Indeed, the breadth and depth of these changes foster the

The intelligent TIR infrastructure – the 'Internet of Things'[7] – will connect virtually every aspect of economic and social life via sensors and software to the TIR platform. The connections will feed 'Big Data' to every node – businesses, homes, vehicles, etc. – in real time.[8] In turn, the data will be analysed with advanced analytics, transformed into predictive algorithms, and programmed into automated systems. This will improve efficiencies, increase productivity, and reduce the marginal cost of producing and delivering a full range of goods and services to near-zero across the entire economy (Srnicek, 2017; Rifkin, 2014).

Among the initiatives, according to Rifkin (2014: 14) are:

> General Electric's 'Industrial Internet', Cisco's 'Internet of Everything', IBM's 'Smarter Planet', and Siemens' 'Sustainable Cities', [which] bring online an intelligent Third Industrial Revolution infrastructure that can connect neighborhoods, cities, regions, and continents in what industry observers call a global neural network. The network is designed to be open, distributed and collaborative, allowing anyone, anywhere, and at any time, the opportunity to access it and use Big Data to create new applications for managing their daily lives at near zero marginal cost.

Here we need to mention an interesting development that we believe will intensify quickly in the near future: platform capitalism. A **platform** is a 'digital infrastructure that enables two or more groups to interact. It is an intermediary bringing together different users: customers, advertisers, service providers, producers, suppliers and even physical objects' (Srnicek, 2017: 42). Companies that either use or build platforms, such as Airbnb, Uber, Zipcar, Google, Facebook, GE, Siemens, John Deere, AWS, Salesforce, Rolls Royce, Spotify, Monsanto, TaskRabbit and others, are restructuring markets, and also capitalism. These companies 'thrive on the most efficient way to monopolise, extract, analyse, and use increasingly large amounts of data' (Ibid.). Driven by the profit motive and **network effects**

---

transformation of entire systems of production, management and governance. While we don't dispute Schwab's analysis, and, if anything, we feel these events will intensify in the near future, for now we refer to our current revolution as the Third Industrial Revolution.

7. This phrase originated in 1999, by Keven Aston from Proctor and Gamble.

8. Here's an interesting statistic: In 1995, there were 16 million Internet users across the globe (0.4 per cent of the global population); today there are 4.7 billion (49 per cent of the global population). With the development of free Wi-Fi, this number will be much higher, as Rifkin writes: 'In the near future, everyone will be able to share Earth's abundant free air waves, communicating with each other for nearly free, just as we will share the abundant free energy of the sun, wind, and geothermal heat. . . It's just too beneficial for the human race to turn down, regardless of the push back by conventional wired carriers. The notion of communicating over proprietary, centralized, wired communications networks is going to be little more than a historical curiosity to young people living in the mid-twenty-first century' (2014: 149).

(the more customers and users, the better to reduce costs), platform capitalism creates a 'powerful new type of firm' (Ibid.), with troubling implications for privacy, surveillance, bigness, monopolisation, power and control, and exclusion.

6.4 DEVELOPING COUNTRIES AND THE INFORMAL ECONOMY

In developing countries, informality has been a central and important feature of capitalist development. The definition of **informal employment** includes not only unregulated enterprises but also employment not legally regulated or protected. For a long time, particularly in developed countries, there was a widespread misconception about the informal economy as somehow illegal or tantamount to the underground, or even criminal (Chen, 2007). But informal unemployment includes self-employment in small unregistered enterprises, unpaid workers, own-account operators and also unpaid work in family businesses. Considering wage employment in unprotected jobs (workers without benefits or social protection), informal workers include: employees of informal enterprises, casual or day workers, domestic workers, some temporary or part-time workers, industrial outworkers and homeworkers.

Based on estimates in 2000, the average size of the informal economy as a percentage of Gross National income (GNI) ranged from 18 per cent in OECD (Organisation for Economic Co-operation and Development) and European countries to more than 40 per cent in Latin America and Africa. As of 2000, in the Economies in Transition (economies formerly part of the Soviet Union), the average informal economy was 38 per cent (Schneider, 2002).

In developing countries, the informal economy involves a significant percentage of the economically active population. By 2010, the informal economy accounted for 33–40 per cent of urban employment in Asia, 60–75 per cent in Central America and 60 per cent in Africa (Sundquist, 2011). According to more recent data from the International Labour Organization (ILO, 2012), while ignoring China, for which there is no data for the whole country, six countries (India, Brazil, Mexico, Vietnam, Pakistan and the Philippines) have three-quarters of total global informal employment. The lowest percentages of informal employment are in Central and Eastern Europe.

In terms of gender, the share of women in informal employment in the manufacturing sector is generally much higher than that of men. In India, for example, the percentage of women with an informal job in manufacturing is 93 per cent. In Brazil, 49 per cent of women have an informal job in the manufacturing sector, compared with 32 per cent of men. This is partly due to the lower wages paid to women.

Extreme poverty is a preponderant structural feature of the informal economy in developing nations. Typically, workers in the informal economy generally lack birth certificates, legal documents, and even addresses or market stalls. In this context, self-provisioning is crucial, and monetary incomes, when considered, often determine one's poverty status. Table 6.3 lists a sampling of informal employment in selected nations.

While central to developing countries, the informal economy is increasing in developed countries. Indeed, economic relations of production, distribution and employment belong to a continuum between pure *formal* relations (i.e. regulated and protected) and pure *informal* relations (i.e. unregulated and unprotected) (Chen 2007: 236).

Table 6.3 Informal Employment in Agriculture and Non-Agriculture in Selected Countries, 2013–2015, as Percentage of Total Workers

Country	*Year*	*Agriculture*	*Non-agriculture*
Bangladesh	2013	44.2	49.2
Colombia	2013	87.1	63.7
Colombia	2014	90.2	–
Colombia	2015	84.5	55.5
Greece	2015	5.8	3.3
Russian Federation	2015	54.4	16.9
South Africa	2013	76.0	39.3
South Africa	2014	69.9	38.6
South Africa	2015	77.7	39.7
Thailand	2013	94.1	42.8
Thailand	2014	36.5	8.9
Turkey	2013	87.6	17.2
Turkey	2014	88.9	18.3
Turkey	2015	81.2	21.2
Ukraine	2014	68.5	17.6
Ukraine	2015	38.6	61.4
Uruguay	2015	28.8	24.3

Note: Workers in the informal economy comprise all workers of the informal sector and informal workers outside the informal sector. Statistics refer, to the extent possible, to the main job of employed persons.

Source: International Labour Organization (ILO, 2015b).

The growth of the informal sector is a combination of historical conditions and macroeconomic policies. In Latin America, for example, data from the Caribbean countries indicate that the relationship between the formal sector of tourism (hotels, restaurants and other service providers) and the local economy (agriculture, manufacture, fishing and construction) is limited, defining the expansion of 'tourist enclaves' (such as cruises and all-inclusive hotels) in which the restricted access of tourists to local markets decreases the possibility of economic growth (World Trade Organization, 2002). In rural areas, tourism seldom benefits the local population, given the tenuous link between the formal and informal economy. The relationship between the formal sector of tourism and the informal economy also relies on poor access conditions to education and health. And new social risks have emerged, given the absence of adequate conditions of employment and social protection (Ocampo and Martin, 2003). Schneider and Enste (2000) document the deepening nature of this phenomenon in Latin America.

In the 1990s, neoliberal economic reforms (i.e. tariff liberalisation and labour market flexibilisation) fostered the informal economy in developing countries. The structural adjustment programmes (SAPs) imposed by the International Monetary Fund (IMF), the World Bank and the World Tourism Organization (WTO)[9] led to massive layoffs in the formal employment sector. In addition, urbanisation has expanded informal jobs and increased rural-to-urban migration, which in most countries is significant. In many developing countries, rural migration is a result of globalisation, since agriculture competes directly with heavily subsidised agricultural exports from developed nations. In rural areas of developed countries, the adoption of capital-intensive agriculture has in turn reduced the number of agricultural jobs.

Difficulties in becoming an entrepreneur in developing countries also expands the informal economy. Small and micro-entrepreneurs are usually subject to complex regulatory barriers, along with restricted access to credit. As a result, such enterprises fare poorly in competitive environments, and have a lower capacity for innovation and a weak international orientation.

Table 6.4 The Cost of Regulation to Start Up a Legal Business, June 2015

Economic region	*Number of procedures to register a firm*	*Duration (days) to register a firm*	*Cost as percentage of income capita*
East Asia and Pacific	7.0	25.9	23.0
Europe and Central Asia	4.7	10.0	4.8
Latin America and the Caribbean	8.3	29.4	31.0
Middle East and North Africa	8.2	18.8	25.8
OECD high-income	4.7	8.3	3.2
South Asia	7.9	15.7	14.0
Sub-Saharan Africa	8.0	26.8	53.4

Notes: (1) The total number of procedures required to register a firm: A **procedure** is defined as any interaction of the company founders with external parties (for example, government agencies, lawyers, auditors or notaries). (2) The total number of days required to register a firm captures the median duration that incorporation lawyers indicate is necessary to complete a procedure with minimum follow-up with government agencies and no extra payments. (3) Cost is recorded as a percentage of the economy's income per capita; it includes all official fees and fees for legal or professional services, as required by law. Each business assumes between 10 and 50 people one month after the commencement of operations.

Source: World Bank (2017).

9. These global institutions are discussed in Chapter 16.

Among other obstacles to survival and expansion in the formal economy, the costs of starting up a formal enterprise are very significant in developing countries. Table 6.4 indicates some of the costs confronting entrepreneurs in different world regions. As indicated, Africa and Latin America countries face the highest costs.

6.5 UNPAID WORK AND FAMILY CARE

Unpaid work is essential for family survival, and hence a family's ability to provision. It includes the inter-personal world of caring for other household members, and, in countries that lack sufficient infrastructure, collecting water and fuel for household needs. Though males contribute somewhat, a socially constructed division of labour assigns the major responsibility for this work to females (Elson, 2007). Gender-differentiated work is affected by many factors, including age and gender of household composition; seasonal considerations; regional and geographic factors, including ease of access to water and fuel; availability of infrastructure; and distance to key economic and social services such as schools, health centres, financial institutions and markets. Social, demographic and cultural norms also define and sustain rigidity in gendered division of labour, especially with basic provisioning.

While income is the most commonly used indicator of poverty, broader indexes including non-monetary aspects of deprivation have been proposed and measured, incorporating unpaid work. While the usual poverty threshold is calculated as the amount of income to buy the minimum required goods and services, incorporation of unpaid work allows for a better understanding of its connections with the economic system. Vickery (1977) argued that 'time poverty' and 'income poverty' are interrelated, with negative reinforcing consequences for the individual and for household well-being. Specifically, the sheer drudgery of labour-intensive activities reduces the availability of time for household members to engage in more productive economic activities, reducing the expansion of capabilities through education and skills development. In strictly neoclassical terms: time spent gathering fuel/food has a high opportunity cost, reducing the effective time that females (especially) could be investing in human capital.

The social and economic impacts of unpaid family care must be considered in our understanding of the synergies and tradeoffs between market-oriented and household-oriented activities. Many researchers believe that the examination of time-use data (see below) gives policymakers a more complete and comprehensive picture of employment and labour effort. Examples of unpaid activities, that is to say, of the production of goods and services by family members, and not sold on the market, include routine housework (cooking, gardening, cleaning, laundry), care for household members, care for non-household members, volunteering, fixing the car, etc. Indeed, non-market labour is of particular importance from a gender standpoint, since, among family members, women typically have extra household burdens.

A time-use survey is a statistical survey which empirically estimates how, on average, people spend their time. Neoclassical economics assumes that an individual's (and his or her household's) choice of work time and non-market activities depends on market wages and input prices used to produce non-market activities. In particular, non-market time and consumer goods used in the production of non-market activities is chosen so as to maximise utility (i.e. an individual's satisfaction) subject to constraints imposed by income and the price of consumption goods. Time allocation is influenced by gender, public infrastructure (transportation, efficient energy sources, water and sanitation facilities), geographic location, income status and education level.

It is challenging to collect, analyse and utilise time-use data and statistics for measuring unpaid work (which remains unaccounted for in existing labour-force surveys.) Until now, time-use statistics have not been sufficiently integrated into the formulation of public investment policies and alternative growth strategies. Such an effort, however, is important given that climate change is most likely to disproportionately affect women in developing countries, as we discussed in the last chapter.

6.6 WORK AND SOCIAL SECURITY

From the end of the Second World War until the early 1970s, many capitalist governments, particularly in the developed world, actively reduced the economic and social risk of individuals. This was in stark contrast to the periods before and after, and thus an aberration in the evolution of capitalism. During this period, governments actively mitigated risk for the aged by providing social security, for the unemployed with unemployment compensation, and for the sick with universal healthcare coverage. Not only was this assumed to benefit the individual from a humanitarian perspective, but the economic system would also benefit, since it was assumed (correctly from our perspective) that reduced risk would increase confidence and hence investment.

This period of economic growth ended with the energy and the dollar crisis of the early 1970s. The reconfiguration of the world economy involved increased globalisation and financialisation (for a discussion on financialisation, see Chapter 7), and changes in work technology, causing national governments (along with corporations) to reduce their safety nets (see Chapter 14). Indeed, the opposite values are now entrenched: increased individual risk increases insecurity, which in turn increases effort, with the beneficial by-product of making individuals more subservient to the interests of capital. As the historian Eric Hobsbawm (2007) noted, this current scenario differs significantly from the 'Golden Years' where economic growth could support social inclusion (Gonçalves and Madi, 2009).

Insecurity breeds fear of job loss and uncertainty about accessing income, along with social vulnerability, especially among young people. As a reaction, some governments, in many developing countries such as Brazil, have implemented a citizens' basic income programme (see below). The governments of India and South Africa, for example, have integrated employment schemes into economic growth and development strategies, e.g. the National Rural Employment Guarantee Scheme in India (NREGA) and the Expanded Public Works programme in South Africa (now called the Community Works Programme). In some countries, the labour force is growing rapidly, pressuring governments to provide more jobs, while others have an ageing population that restrains labour-force growth, with direct implications for social protection systems. These changes have reduced the ratio between the absolute population and the labour force since 2000.

6.7 BASIC INCOME

Basic income is offered as solution to automation, alienation, loss of decent jobs, reduced employment, under-employment and unsustainable consumption. It has also been praised as being just, equitable and sustainable; its criticism being its opportunity cost and where to obtain the requisite funds. This section will briefly discuss this important topic.[10]

Guy Standing (2017: 3) defines basic income as:

> a modest amount of money paid unconditionally to individuals on a regular basis. . . It is often called a universal basic income because it is intended to be paid for all.

From this definition, four essential elements deserve mention (Ibid.: 3–7):

- While many of us disagree over how basic a basic income should be, it does not mean 'total security or affluence. . . [it] surely constitutes what any "good society" should provide equally, and as certainly as it can' (Ibid.: 3–4).
- Basic income is a right, meaning it cannot be withdrawn at will.
- It is universal, paid to every resident of the nation.
- It is unconditional: There are no conditions, quid pro quo, or strings attached.

10. We rely on Standing's (2017) comprehensive and easily accessible discussion of basic income. The book also provides suggestions to incorporate a basic income pilot and initiative, along with extensive references.

- The payment of basic income is regular: 'Predictability is a crucial component of basic security. Unlike most other forms of state benefit, basic income would be both guaranteed and known in advance [In other words], it is "an economic right to basic income security"' (Ibid.: 7).

By freeing up individuals from having to labour in the market, basic income allows for active work in the commons and social sectors, which today are hardly considered, or even measured, as worthwhile economic objectives. By shifting attention away from paid labour, which today is largely underwritten by cheap availability of fossil fuels, and deductions, subsidies and give-aways in the tax code,[11] a basic income can attenuate climate change while also redirecting us away from ever-increasing and unsustainable consumption. Standing writes: 'by making income less dependent on employment, basic income would encourage people to question the drive for jobs at any cost and encourage a rethink on the relationship between jobs, production and consumption' (Ibid.: 180–81).

Standing (Ibid.: 60–61; and *passim*) discusses in detail the following benefits of a basic income in terms of strengthening basic freedoms:

- To refuse a job that is onerous and boring, low-paying or just nasty.
- To accept a job that is none of the above, but which could not be accepted if financial necessity dictated.
- To stay in a job that pays less than previously or that has become more financially insecure.
- To start a small-scale business venture, which is risky but potentially rewarding.
- To do care work for a relative or friend, or voluntary work in the community, that might not be feasible if financial necessity required long hours of paid labour.
- To do creative work and activities of all kinds.
- To risk learning new skills or competencies.
- Freedom from bureaucratic interference, prying and coercion.
- To form relationships and perhaps set up 'home' with someone, often precluded today by financial insecurity.
- To leave a relationship that has turned sour or abusive.
- To have a child.
- To be lazy once in a while – a vital freedom.

11. Either individually or combined, these are substantial. In the USA, Standing notes, there are over 200 selective tax reliefs: the ten biggest cost federal coffers more than $900 trillion in 2013, approximately 6 per cent of GDP (2017: 134).

Mention the concept of basic income today, and many people have preconceived notions: it can't work; we can't afford it; it reduces work incentives, etc. But Standing makes a convincing case that it can work (and that it already has in many areas);[12] and that given poverty, growing inequality, automation, sluggish demand and climate change, it is our only effective choice.

Will it work? Yes, we believe so. The bottom line of affordability 'comes down to the priority society gives to social justice, republican freedom and economic security. In those terms, not only is a basic income affordable; we cannot afford *not* to afford it' (Ibid.: 44; emphasis in original).

In Brazil, the basic income (cash transfer) programme Bolsa Família aims to alleviate income deprivation of poor and extremely poor households. The enforcement of health and education conditions is part of the success of the programme in breaking down intergenerational inequalities (Soares et al., 2007). After the global financial crisis, the coverage of the Bolsa Família was expanded and the number of families involved increased by almost 2 million, covering 12.4 million households in 2009 (Sicsú, 2011). In addition to women's challenges in the labour market, the increasing burden of unpaid work is more likely when women become unemployed and return to their homes and take more responsibility for housework, or because loss of family income makes it impossible to support the remuneration of domestic workers (OBIG, 2011). In this setting, the expansion of the Bolsa Família was instrumental in reducing women's vulnerability, with the number of women benefiting from the programme reaching almost 27 million in 2010 (DIEESE, 2011).

As of 2016, the monthly benefit received by Brazil's poor and extremely poor families was based on a set amount (US$22) and a variable amount that depends on the number of children and teenagers living in the household between 0 and 16 years. Guy Standing (2017: 169–70) sums up the beneficial aspect of Brazil's Bolsa Família, and its potential positive contributions to justice for women in other developing nations:

> In Brazil, the *bolsa familia* cash transfer scheme has boosted women's economic activity outside the home by helping to pay for childcare and fares for public transport. In many developing countries, a basic income would also increase women's ability to claim equal priority for healthcare, counteracting the tendency to give priority to 'the breadwinner'. Better healthcare would enable women to do more work and, if they chose, more paid labour, simply because they would have less ill-health. This is another instance of a basic income not 'obviously' diminishing the incentive to work.

12. For specific references, including pilot projects, see Standing, 2017: 249–78.

6.8 SUSTAINABLE WORK

As of 2014, 54 per cent of the world's population lived in urban areas, a proportion that is expected to increase to 66 per cent by 2050. Projections show another 2.5 billion people will be added to urban populations by 2050, with almost 90 per cent of this increase concentrated in Asia and Africa (UN, 2015a). (See Table 6.7.) Between 2000 and 2025, the urban population in developing countries is expected to nearly double from almost 2 billion to more than 3.5 billion, surpassing the rural population by 2020. After 2025, about 90% of global population growth is expected to occur in the urban areas of developing countries.[13]

Chaotic and unplanned urban growth, infrastructure deficits (due to the absence of strategic urban plans) and growing slums are manifestations of the global urban transformations. The intense urbanisation has increased real estate prices in city centres, forcing low-income population into urban peripheries with lack of infrastructure (water, sewers, light, public transport). Urbanisation aggravates environmental problems due to unsustainable patterns of production and consumption, worsened by the lack of urban planning. This requires new solutions for helping people living and working in urban areas.

Peasants and others working in rural areas are among the most marginalised groups. Indeed, 80 per cent of the world's hungry live in rural areas – with half subsisting on plots of land in marginal farming areas, unable to achieve self-sufficiency because they are denied access to sufficient land, water and seeds. The majority of people in Africa live in rural areas and subsist from agriculture, with many suffering from hunger and malnutrition. Food security is a challenge, since soils are getting poorer, while the legislation on land occupation and tenure is weak. As a result, more people have no access to land.

Rural workers including small-scale farmers, fishers and pastoralists face other challenges including volatile food markets, climate change, environmental degradation, loss of biodiversity, and increasing competition for resources from much larger businesses. Such workers have restricted access to information and are usually excluded from freedom of expression, assembly and association; and from basic social services, including health, education and social security. Indeed, the persistent lack of rights negatively affects the sustainability of these communities, along with the development potential of individuals.

Several years ago the international movement La Via Campesina focused attention on the challenges to peasant communities. International cooperation is essential to promote and protect the human rights of peasants and other workers in rural areas (see UN SDG #17). Excess CO_2 emissions, also caused by soil

13. For a well-thought discourse on the problems of urban area and urban economics from a pluralist and sustainable perspective, see Obeng-Odoom (2016), especially pp.201–27.

Table 6.5 Percentage (and Projected Percentages) of Population Living in Urban Areas in Major World Regions, 2010–2050

Major area, region or country	*2010*	*2020*	*2030*	*2040*	*2050*
World	51.6	56.2	60.0	63.2	66.4
More developed regions	77.1	79.3	81.5	83.5	85.4
Less developed regions	46.1	51.6	56.2	59.8	63.4
Sub-Saharan Africa	35.4	40.4	45.4	50.1	54.8
Africa	38.3	42.6	47.1	51.5	55.9
Eastern Africa	23.5	27.9	32.8	38.1	43.6
Middle Africa	41.5	46.5	51.5	56.2	60.8
Northern Africa	50.5	52.9	55.9	59.5	63,3
Southern Africa	59.1	64.0	68.1	71.4	74.3
Western Africa	41.6	48.3	54.1	58.5	62.7
Asia	44.8	51.2	56.3	60.3	64.2
Eastern Asia	54.3	64.8	71.5	75.1	77.9
South-Central Asia	33.0	37.2	42.0	47.2	52.5
Central Asia	40.4	41.1	44.1	48.9	53.9
Southern Asia	32.7	37.1	42.0	47.2	52.5
South-Eastern Asia	44.5	50.6	55.8	60.2	64.5
Western Asia	68.1	71.4	74.1	76.7	79.2
Europe	72.7	74.7	77.0	79.5	82.0
Eastern Europe	68.9	70,1	72.2	75.0	77.8
Northern Europe	80.1	82.3	84.2	85.9	87.5
Southern Europe	68.9	71.3	74.0	76.8	79.5
Western Europe	77.7	80.0	82.1	84.1	85.9
Latin America and the Caribbean	78.4	81.0	83.0	84.7	86.2
Caribbean	67.5	72.7	76.1	78.5	80.7
Central America	72.2	75.2	77.7	79.8	81.8
South America	82.1	84.3	86.0	87.4	88.7
Northern America	80.8	82.5	84.2	85.9	87.4
Oceana	70.7	70.9	71.3	72.2	73.5

Source: United Nations (UN, 2014a).

destruction, for example, could be addressed by more sustainable agricultural practices common to peasant farming communities, such as diversified cropping systems, the integration of crops and animal production, and a shift to local markets. These practices are more labour-intensive and rely less on fossil fuels.

In 1948, the general assembly of the United Nations proclaimed the Universal Declaration of Human Rights as a common standard for all people. The UN supports a working group to reflect and guide the international community to promote the rights of people working in rural areas. This is not only to discuss a wide range of existing civil, cultural, economic, political and social rights but also to recommend 'new' rights such as the right to land, the freedom to determine price and the markets for agricultural products, the right to protect agricultural values and the right to biological diversity. A sustainable livelihood in rural areas depends on a comprehensive, human-rights-centred development paradigm.

Box 6.3 Cultural Values and the Ideology of Work

Cultural values influence the dynamic evolution of economies. In particular, the role of religion and its impact on economic growth and entrepreneurship has been influential. Max Weber (1864–1920) proffered an interesting and provocative thesis in his book *The Protestant Ethic and the Spirit of Capitalism* (1930): the reason the Industrial Revolution began in northern Europe, and England in particular, was the influence of the Protestant religion, especially Calvinism. It fostered a work ethic favouring the accumulation of capital and money, along with literacy, which increased education. While not everyone accepts Weber's thesis, it suggests that values are important in shaping a culture and an economic system.

Religion and the evolution of capitalism are intertwined. Evidence suggests that in capitalist countries, a disenchanted society, its devastating consumption of natural resources, and the insecurity of urban life fosters the support of spiritual experiences (Meyer and Moors, 2006). In the USA, the number of Protestants is currently approximately 51 per cent of the total population. Protestant churches are characterised by internal diversity: evangelical Protestant churches (26.3 per cent of the adult population); mainstream Protestant churches (18.1 per cent) and historically black Protestant churches (6.9 per cent). Pertaining to American Catholicism, emigrating Latinos may account for a larger share of US Catholics in the future. Due to immigration, Islam and Hinduism are rapidly increasing, although each still accounts for less than 1 per cent of the adult population.

How religion affects economic systems and how economic systems affect religion is an interesting topic, which we feel will assume increased importance. As we move towards sustainability, how will religion affect society's underlying economic institutions? And, conversely, how will changing economic systems affect religion? Can religion help or hinder the transition to sustainability? How will changing patterns of religion affect society? The underlying common denominator is values, which in turn are a function of culture and society. And what about the growth of religious fundamentalism, which is part and parcel of every religion? How does fundamentalism affect the ability to reach out and understand others?

6.9 SUSTAINABLE WORK AND CORPORATE SOCIAL RESPONSIBILITY

Promoting sustainable growth is our most important current global issue. With the gap between capitalist power and working conditions wider than ever, pressure for more sustainable organisations and work styles has increased. Capital mobility, price stability and risk management have fostered individual performance and corporate profitability rather than workers' rights.

While the need to promote economic changes is well recognised, the emergence and dissemination of solutions has been slow. New approaches are needed to create jobs, and to enhance employees' well-being and employability. Docherty et al. (2002) pose a critical question to begin discussion: How might corporations create a work system – the system of roles, responsibilities and relationships – that could achieve a life/work balance?

Corporate social responsibility is a key feature in the context of **neoliberalism**, an important and widely used term, which means a

> political-economic system based on the idea that (free) market interactions – i.e. those with no or limited state or social intervention – are the most efficient way to organize the economy *and* to coordinate all social institutions . . . The state's role is to create new markets, maintain the rule of law (especially when it comes to competition) and ensure social stability through penal policies. As such, neoliberalism does not simply imply 'de-regulation' of the economy, but rather its 're-regulation' as new rules are instituted.
>
> Birch et al., 2017: 111; emphasis in original

Guy Standing expands:

> At the heart of neoliberalism is a contradiction. While its proponents profess a belief in free unregulated markets, they favour regulations to prevent collective bodies from operating in favour of social solidarity. That is why they want control over unions, collective bargaining, professional associations and occupational guilds.
>
> Standing, 2016: 12

Some corporations assume that long-term economic performance demands a solid commitment to sharing trustworthy information with shareholders and maintaining high-quality products and services, which in turn will increase economic growth, maintaining, at the same time, a balanced relation between profitability, the protection of human beings and nature. However, we feel that these objectives could be achieved through projects developed in partnerships with institutions and nongovernmental organisations (NGOs), while involving governments and suppliers.

In 2000, the United Nations Global Compact was launched to facilitate within business the practice and associated mentality of inclusive economic development and a living code of ethics. In order to express social responsibility, banks, for example, would support social, environmental and educational projects; and corporations would examine sources of greenhouse-gas emissions in order to define sustainable working conditions. However, such practices have not surmounted tensions inherent in capitalism. One problem is that some corporations might be tempted just to present a veneer of social responsibility while practising business as usual. While speculative and short-term-profit decisions predominate in business strategies, we believe practices of social responsibility actually support the profit motive, searching for growing efficiency instead of defeating inequalities.

In 2007, the United Nations launched the Principles for Responsible Management Education (PRME). This initiative is the first organised relationship between the United Nations and business schools whose mission is to transform management education, research and leadership globally. As a result, the PRME initiative serves as a framework for gradual, systemic change in business schools and management-related institutions. The principles of PRME foster academic commitment to advance social responsibility through incorporating universal values into curricula and research. The objective is to develop a new generation of business leaders capable of managing today's complex challenges. In spite of the relevance of the subject, this initiative has not yet reached the economics curriculum.

THINKING QUESTIONS

How does technological change influence the nature of work?

How should policy-makers manage social and other impacts of technological change?

What is sustainable work?

Why is work so important for an individual and the community?

What are the arguments in favour of a basic income? And what are the arguments against?

CLASS ACTIVITIES

If you could design an ideal workplace, what would it be?

In your town or city, how would you implement a basic income?

AREAS FOR RESEARCH

What areas of work are outsourced? And why? And where to?

UN SDG FOCUS

UN SDG #8 is: 'Promote inclusive and sustainable economic growth, employment and decent work for all.' What do 'inclusive' and 'decent' mean? How does one promote this goal? Is achieving this 'for all' realistic?

Is a basic income consistent with the 17 UN SDGs?

FURTHER READING

Ocampo, J. and Martin, J. (Eds) (2003) *Globalization and Development: a Latin American and Caribbean Perspective*. Stanford: Stanford University Press.

Rifkin, J. (1995) *The End of Work: The Decline of the Global Labor Force and the Dawn of the Post-Market Era*. New York: Putnam.

Schumacher, E. F. (1973 [1989]) *Small is Beautiful: Economics as if People Mattered*. New York: Harper Perennial.

Schneider, F. (2002) *Innovative Policies for the Urban Informal Economy*. UN-Habitat, Nairobi, Kenya: United Nations Human Settlements Programme.

Standing, G. (2017) *Basic Income: And How We Can Make it Happen*. London: Penguin.

7
Unemployment and Employment

This chapter will discuss the roots, evolution and shifting conceptualisation of unemployment in the context of a pluralist approach. Is the current conceptualisation of unemployment sufficient to understand the trends in global capitalism? In addition, we will discuss recent employment trends in labour markets and how involuntary unemployment is an increasing challenge. We then discuss the need for developing a sustainable perspective on work and employment. Considering economic policy we also introduce the concepts of the minimum wage, the living wage, and decent work.

7.1 THE SHIFTING DEFINITION OF UNEMPLOYMENT

Whereas under Fordism, the typical employment relationship was viewed as permanent (or as permanent as one could get at the time), today's typical employment relationship is transient and amorphous. The typical worker today does not work for a large corporation, but contracts with several firms and individuals under a number of different working arrangements including flexitime, teleworking, employee empowerment and autonomy, task rotation and multi-skilling, teamwork and team autonomy, and platforms. Given the changing employment relationship, the meaning of unemployment is also different. It is no longer tied to the industrial sector; rather, today's typical worker shifts between different jobs and different working arrangements. Unfortunately, when conceptualising, defining and measuring unemployment, the old definitions are still used. If unemployment is considered to be a problem, but it is misconceptualised and incorrectly defined, we will fail to understand the root causes of the problem and hence offer ineffective solutions.

The word 'unemployment' first appeared in the 1870s, and, while it was known to be a problem, particularly in urban areas, it could not be adequately measured at the time without a definition. It wasn't until the massive unemployment during the Great Depression of the 1930s that a concerted effort was made to define unemployment. The prototypical employed worker at the time was assumed to be male and employed at a large factory in an industrial setting, working fixed hours with an indefinite contract (Baxandall, 2004: 233). From this it followed that a person unemployed would either be let go temporarily or be searching full-time for work in the industrial labour market. While many able-bodied workers were available, it was decided to distinguish between being *able* to work and being *willing* to work. Hence the current prerequisite of **unemployment** to be actively searching for work rather than just available.

With the shift to post-Fordism, the prototypical worker no longer works for a large industrial firm but within a more decentralised and amorphous setting. If the key element of post-Fordism is flexibility and working for several firms and individuals, then what does it mean for a person to be laid off? If a person works in teams, then how can unemployment be more meaningfully specified? Baxandall expands (Ibid.: 234–5):

> subcontracting, consultancies, multiple job-holding, youth internships, and working out of the home, as well as more multiple wage-earning families and early retirees . . . [Such] workers do not easily fit into the traditional categories] of the unemployed, employed, or those out of the labour force . . . [Their] income is ever more decoupled from traditional employment relationships.

And given cloud sharing and job sharing, with no sharp distinction between work and leisure, then what does **employment** mean specifically? Baxandall again (Ibid.: 3):

> The concept of unemployment is in flux. We knew when the post-war steelworker was unemployed, and that this was politically destabilising; but it is not at all clear how we should apply these categories to today's Internet consultant, temp-worker, or independent sub-contractor. The future political economy of unemployment will depend very much on the changing world of work and how it is regulated.

New definitions of employment and unemployment are currently being researched, but many people, institutions and governments are stuck in the old way of thinking and, thus any transition to a new conceptualisation will not be easy. An important lesson, however, is that in order to solve a problem we first must conceptualise and define it. This must be contextual, that is, we must define the problem not in an absolute sense but in the context of current economic conditions. Indeed, Baxandall (Ibid.: 4) writes:

> Unemployment is a socially-constructed benchmark used for evaluating the competency of economic rule. In different places and in different times the category of 'unemployment' has included different kinds of joblessness and excluded others. It has implied different kinds of commitments or accountability by the state.

Not to change or revise our ideas is to risk misdiagnosis of the problem. As economic systems evolve, so must our thinking. But for now we must work with the current definitions, while understanding their shortcomings and helping to devise new conceptualisations.

In addition to the current disconnect between the prototypical worker and the definition of unemployment, several other problems exist. The first problem relates to the idea of actively searching for work, discarding the earlier notion of simply being able to work. So, if a person gives up searching for work, despite being able and even willing to work, he or she is no longer in the labour force and hence no longer unemployed.

In the United States, the labour force participation rate (LFPR)[1] has steadily declined after peaking in the late 1990s at 67.1 per cent. It is currently (in mid-2017) at 63.0 per cent. At the start of the recession in December 2007, the US LFPR was 66.0 per cent; after reaching a low of 62.4 per cent in September 2015, it has since rebounded to 63.0 per cent. What is worrying is that, contrary to previous recessions, in which the LFPR initially declined, then increased after the official end of the recession surpassing its pre-recession level, the LFPR has steadily declined.

We are not exactly sure of the reason(s) for a steadily decreasing US LFPR, other than a lack of new jobs being created, underscoring the fact that the current economy is created and run for corporate profit rather than human need. Accordingly, Larry Summers (2015) argued that the scale and significance of the 'persistent jobless growth' problem mainly results from the transformations and job displacements associated with technology and automation, with robotics and 3D printing revolutions accelerating this trend. However, following the OECD's (1996) broader analysis, technology is only part of a general restructuring process in the world economy, which also includes changes in the world division of labour between countries and regions; greater degree of international integration of production, trade and finance; the increased role of multinational companies; the rise of the service sector to become the major source of employment and employment growth; and the intensification of competition, which has led to the rationalisation of production and cost-cutting.

A second problem with the current definition of unemployment is that it doesn't account for **underemployment**, which in our view is a growing global phenomenon. Underemployment has

> two distinct, but not mutually exclusive, categories. . . someone is underemployed if he or she is employed but working less than a desired number of hours, and someone is also considered underemployed if he or she is overqualified for the job he or she is working.
>
> Reardon, 2014: 494

1. The data was obtained from the US Bureau of Labor Statistics, www.bls.gov

A significant problem is that 'there is no official government measure of underemployment; [thus] there is also no official manner in which the underemployment rate is to be calculated' (Ibid.: 495).

Box 7.1 Key Concepts: Labour Market Indicators

The unemployment rate is the most visible and perhaps best-known barometer of the labour market. It generally increases during recessions and decreases during expansions; thus, typically, the longer the expansion, the lower the unemployment rate. The current global conceptual framework for measuring the labour force was officially adopted by the 13th International Conference of Labour Statisticians in 1982. Whether a person is categorised as unemployed is determined by a survey questionnaire asking about his or her activities during a specific reference point, e.g. a specific week during the previous month. The following are some commonly used definitions:

- **Working-age population, or economically active population:** the total number of people aged 16 years and over.
- **Labour force:** the number of people employed, plus the number unemployed from the working-age population, over the age of 16.
- **Labour force participation rate:** the percentage of the working-age population who are members of the labour force; to obtain the rate, the latter is divided by the former.
- **Unemployed population:** all persons who, during a specified week, had no job and were available for work and had made efforts to find employment.
- **Unemployment rate:** the percentage of people in the labour force who are unemployed. It is calculated by dividing the number of unemployed by the number of people in the labour force, then multiplying by 100. *Question:* If workers give up their search for work, what happens to the unemployment rate?
- **Vulnerable employment:** According to the International Labour Organization (ILO), such workers are less likely to have formal work arrangements, and are therefore more likely to lack decent working conditions, adequate social security and 'voice' through effective representation by trade unions and similar organisations. Vulnerable employment is often characterised by inadequate earnings, low productivity and difficult conditions of work that undermine workers' fundamental rights.

Source: Reardon (2014).

7.2 *TECHNIQUE 3*: CALCULATING THE UNEMPLOYMENT RATE, THE EMPLOYMENT RATE AND THE LABOUR FORCE PARTICIPATION RATE

Consider the following data obtained from the United States Bureau of Labor Statistics for the month of May, 2017:

Employed:	152,923,000
Unemployed:	6,861,000
In the labour force:	159,784,000
Civilian noninstitutional population [working-age population]:	254,767,000

To calculate the rate of unemployment:
(1) Divide the unemployed by the labour force
(2) Multiply by 100

(6,861,000 ÷ 159,784,000) x 100 = 0.0429 x 100 = 4.3%

To calculate the employment rate:
(1) Divide the employed by the working-age population
(2) Multiply by 100

(152,923,000 ÷ 254,767,000) x 100 = 0.6002 x 100 = 60%

To calculate the labour force participation rate:
(1) Divide the labour force by the working-age population
(2) Multiply by 100

(159,784,000 ÷ 254,767,000) x 100 = 0.6272 x 100 = 62.7%

7.3 EMPLOYMENT TRENDS IN LABOUR MARKETS

As previously discussed, due to globalisation, changing work technology and the increased focus on profitability, work has become more flexible. But what does **flexibility** mean? The term has three dimensions: wage, employment and job (Standing, 2011). **Wage flexibility** generally means downward adjustments in offered wages. **Employment flexibility** means a reduction in employment security and protection; involving variability in working time, such as changes in holidays, in the length of the working week, and in working patterns and overtime. Alternatively, it involves increased part-time work, temporary employment contracts, outsourcing, home-working and consultancies. **Job flexibility**, by contrast, involves multi-tasking, reduction in job demarcation, employee participation, and the subcontracting of production for external actors.

Flexibility in any dimension flattens organisational hierarchies while reducing bureaucratic overhead, requiring new skills and competences for workers while increasing anxiety and stress among workers. These issues have been long debated within the disciplines of sociology, industrial relations, organisational behaviour and management, but are largely absent in neoclassical economics. This is because of the central belief (based on ideology; certainly not on evidence) that involuntary unemployment cannot occur, so any unemployment is due to workers demanding a higher wage than the market equilibrium. Indeed, at the beginning of the Great Depression, neoclassical economists advocated reducing wages to reduce unemployment! This is a classic example of analysing a problem with the wrong lens and a concomitant misperception of how the actual economy works.

Even during the economic expansion previous to the recent global crisis (late 2001 to 2007), most economies did not create enough decent and productive jobs, due to downsizing and labour-saving techniques. The structural changes in labour relations have increased the precariousness of employment and the informalisation of labour. The current global labour market is characterised by persistent inequality and precarious work and employment, and **precarity** (defined as a precarious existence, lacking in predictability, job security, and material or psychological welfare); the latter being the current characteristic mode of exploitation (Standing, 2011).

As globalisation and the flexibilisation of the labour market proceeds, the number of people in insecure forms of labour has multiplied. The earlier labels 'working class' or 'proletariat' suggest a society consisting mostly of workers in long-term, stable, fixed-hour jobs with established careers in traditional professions, subject to unionisation and collective agreements. But perhaps becoming more common is the term 'precariat', first used to describe temporary or seasonal workers by French sociologists in the 1980s. According to Guy Standing (2011: 10) the **precariat** worker lacks:

- **Labour market security:** Adequate income-earning opportunities.
- **Employment security:** Protection against arbitrary dismissal; regulations on hiring and firing.
- **Job security:** Opportunities for upward mobility in terms of status and income.
- **Work security:** Protection against accidents and illness at work.
- **Skill reproduction security:** Opportunity to gain skills by training and to make use of competencies.
- **Income security:** Assurance of an adequate stable income, protected via income policies (minimum wage, wage indexation) and social security.
- **Representation security:** Participation in independent trade unions, with a right to strike.

Standing (2016: 27–8) writes of the emergence of a new global class structure due to globalisation, neoliberalism and automation, comprised of elites at the top (a tiny plutocracy; a 'salariat' in relatively secure salaried jobs and freelance professionals); a shrinking middle, comprised of traditional workers (relying mainly on labour), and a growing bottom, comprised of precariats and the 'lumpen-precariat', an underclass of social victims relying on charity, often homeless and destitute, suffering from social illness including drug addiction and depression.

The impact of the 2008 financial crisis was quickly felt in labour markets globally, and the current precariousness of employment and working conditions is a political challenge. The number of unemployed worldwide increased by 38 million in 2009, and the global unemployment rate surpassed 7 per cent. The crisis has already affected exporting industries dependent on American and European markets. As a result, in developing countries that rely heavily on exports, significant job losses have occurred. As the global financial crisis began, employment fell by over 3 per cent in export-oriented sectors in India.

Table 7.1 Sectoral Distribution of Employed Persons in the World (Percentage of Total Employed), 2015 and 2021 (Estimates and Projections)

Year		*Agriculture*	*Industry*	*Services*
2015	Total	29.5	21.5	48.9
	Male	28.5	26.6	45.0
	Female	31.2	13.7	55.1
2021	Total	27.4	21.5	51.2
	Male	26.2	26.7	47.1
	Female	29.2	13.4	57.4

Note: **Agriculture** covers farming, animal husbandry, hunting, forestry and fishing. **Industry** comprises mining and quarrying; manufacturing; electricity, gas, steam and air-conditioning supply; water supply, sewerage and waste management and remediation activities; and construction. **Services** covers wholesale and retail trade; repair of motor vehicles; transportation and storage; accommodation and food-service activities; professional, scientific and technical activities; administrative and support-service activities; public administration and defence; compulsory social security; education; human health and social-work activities; arts, entertainment and recreation; and other service categories.

Source: International Labour Organization (ILO, 2015).

According to the ILO, vulnerable employment will increase, particularly in South Asia and sub-Saharan Africa. Indeed, quality of employment remains a big challenge in the developing world, with approximately 56 per cent of workers in vulnerable employment. Many people, especially in the Global South, must engage in the informal sector through small-scale employment and insecure 'survival' activities. This trend is starkly visible in Latin America, where according to the ILO (2012), between 40 per cent and 75 per cent of workers are in the informal sector. Furthermore, the growth of the service sector has also contributed to more precariousness in employment and working conditions, which in turn has greatly weakened workers' capacity to negotiate better conditions.

The gap between employed men and women remains a challenge globally. Female labour-force participation has increased in the last decades mainly in industry and services. In spite of increasing women's education, much of women's employment remains characterised by lower pay and more precariousness compared with men's employment.

The global labour market is characterised by differentiated employment and social outcomes from a gender perspective. In developing countries, the high participation of women in export-oriented activities deepened the precariousness of women's employment in industry sectors like clothing, footwear and processed foods, as well as micro-circuits and electronic products. Women's vulnerability is linked to casual and temporary employment and to their preponderant role as family care providers, in addition to their earning lower wages than their male counterparts.

Indeed, gender remains an important factor in determining employment and earnings. Although women have increased their participation rate in the labour market in the last decade, they have entered into more precarious occupations, such as domestic work, along with occupations in the service and trade sectors, where working hours are longer and wages lower.

In addition to the wage gap, women face an increased job turnover. More recently, the expansion of female formal jobs in trade and services is characterised by precarious jobs, mainly based on short-term contracts with low earnings. In metropolitan areas, female workers lost proportionately more jobs than male workers. Indeed, policies have not been able to prevent women from suffering the greater proportion of company workforce adjustments in industrial manufacturing. When a woman belongs to an ethnic minority, she suffers from double discrimination. For instance, in urban Brazil, non-white women on average earn the lowest income, followed by white women, and non-white men (Otobe, 2014).

Research on financial crises reveals that the group most vulnerable to job loss, in addition to women and migrant workers, are young people. Between 1997 and 2007, the share of employed people in the world's working-age population (aged 16 years and older) declined, with the decrease largest among young people (aged 16 to 24 years). Despite the recent economic recovery, the youth unemployment

Table 7.2 Global Indicators: Youth Unemployment Rates, as Percentage (and Projected Percentage) of Working-Age Population, 2007–2019

Economic Region	*2007*	*2010*	*2013*	*2019p*
World	11.7	13	13	13.2
Developed Economies and European Union	12.5	18.1	17.7	15.1
Latin America and the Caribbean	14.1	15.0	13.4	13.8
North Africa	25.2	24.2	30.2	30.7
Sub-Saharan Africa	12.3	12.2	11.6	11.6
East Asia	8.2	9.3	10.4	11.9
South Asia	8.9	9.7	9.9	10.1

Notes: (1) p = projection. (2) Youth unemployment rate refers to the age group 16–24. The calculation of youth employment is the same as for adults: the number of unemployed divided by the total number of people in the labour market.

Source: International Labour Organization (ILO, 2015).

Box 7.2 Historical Insights on Wealth, Capital, Labour and Markets

Labour specialisation paves the way for increased production and, therefore, the expansion of the market, but often at the expense of workers' well-being. Here are just a few samples from economic thought:

Adam Smith (1723–90) defended free markets as a driver of economic growth thanks to labour specialisation. But at the same time he advocated free public education, since the specialisation of labour would severely stunt the intellectual development of workers:

> In the progress of the division of labour, the employment of the far greater part of those who live by labour, that is, of the great body of the people, comes to be confined to a few very simple operations... But the understandings of the greater part of men [sic] are necessarily formed by their ordinary employments. The man whose whole life is spent in performing a few simple operations... has no occasion to exert his understanding, or to exercise his invention... and generally becomes as stupid and ignorant as it is possible for a human creature to become. The torpor of his mind renders him, not only incapable of relishing or bearing a part in any rational conversation... [or] forming any just judgement concerning many even of the ordinary duties of private life . . . this is the state into which the labouring poor, that is, the great body of the people, must necessarily fall, unless government takes some pains to prevent it.
>
> Smith, 1776 [1976], Vol. II, Bk. V, Ch. 1, pp.302–3

David Ricardo (1772–1823), in his *The Principles of Political Economy and Taxation* (1817), discussed factors affecting the price of grain and the connections between land, rent and profits. Ricardo developed a theory of international trade based on comparative advantage, advocating specialisation in goods produced at lower costs in a context of free markets. However, Ricardo was ideologically motivated to do so, primarily to prevent developing nations like Portugal from overtaking Great Britain. Ricardo believed that total production generates income to be divided into wages, profits and land rent. He supported the theoretical discussion initiated by Adam Smith on the relative value of goods, the labour theory of value and the distribution of income.

Karl Marx's (1818–83) *Capital* analysed capitalism as a social organisation based on an exchange system and the division of labour. For Marx, capital is a social relation. The only value-adding factor in the process of capital accumulation, however, is labour. Thus social wealth creation is dependent on labour employed or, more properly, on labour power exploited to appropriate surplus value. This is the source of profit. Marx, never known for mincing words, wrote:

> all methods for raising the social productiveness of labour are brought about at the cost of the individual labourer... they mutilate the labourer into a fragment of a man [sic], degrade him to the level of an appendage of a machine... they estrange him from the intellectual potentialities of the labour-process . . . subject him during the labour-process to a despotism the more hateful for its meanness...
>
> Marx, 1867 [1967]: 645

rate stabilised at 13 per cent and remains well above its pre-crisis level of 11.7 per cent, according to the ILO (ILO, 2015). The number of unemployed youth dropped to 73.3 million in 2014, 3.3 million less than the number of unemployed youth at the peak of the global financial crisis in 2009. In 2014, the youth unemployment rate has increased in East Asia, Southeast Asia and the Pacific, the Middle East and North Africa. Globally, youth unemployment is higher than adult unemployment. This raises a crucial question: is the state obligated to provide jobs for young people? If not, then who is?

7.4 THE CAUSES OF INVOLUNTARY UNEMPLOYMENT

Before the 1930s Great Depression, neoclassical economists assumed that a perfectly flexible labour market, free from rigidities and/or restrictions imposed by employers, trade unions and government regulations for job protection, unions, labour market segmentation or discrimination, could achieve full employment.[2] Neoclassical economists assumed thus that unemployment could only be 'frictional'. Arthur Pigou in *The Theory of Unemployment* (1933 [1968]) for example, studied 'frictional unemployment' as unemployment arising from normal labour turnover from the ongoing creation and destruction of jobs and from people entering and leaving the labour force.

During the Great Depression, John Maynard Keynes (1883–1946) argued that the capitalist system cannot obtain full levels of spending, income and employment; and that at any one point in time it is highly unlikely that the economy will operate at full capacity. He distinguished 'frictional unemployment' from 'involuntary unemployment'; the latter ignored and assumed not to exist according to neoclassical economists, but which according to Keynes presented a fundamental social and economic problem. Simply defined, involuntary unemployment occurs when a worker wants a job but is unable to attain one, since not enough are offered. This is usual during recessions.

At this juncture it is important we understand and define the different types of unemployment.

Frictional unemployment occurs when workers switch jobs or change occupations. According to Keynes, this includes 'various inexactnesses of adjustment . . . so that there will always exist in a non-static society a proportion of resources employed in 'between jobs' (Keynes, 1936 [2010]: 6). If a worker switches her job, she can either switch jobs immediately from the old to the new, or quit and search for a new one. Only the latter counts as unemployment.

Voluntary unemployment occurs when workers quit their present job to look for something different, and presumably better, than their present job. A

---

2. This conclusion is based on faulty deductive reasoning. Correction of the logical errors leads (perhaps surprisingly) to the opposite conclusion (Reardon, 2006).

paradox here is that as the job market improves, voluntary unemployment can increase, which, all else being equal, will increase the overall unemployment rate. Why quit your job to search for a better one unless you believe something better exists? Another type of voluntary unemployment, at least according to neoclassical economists, occurs when a worker insists on a wage higher than the 'market-clearing equilibrium wage' (i.e. where the quantity supplied equals the quantity demanded) – which is due, as Keynes explained, to the

> refusal or inability of a unit of labour, as a result of legislation or social practices or of combination for collective bargaining or of slow response to change or of mere human obstinacy, to accept a reward corresponding to the value of the product attributable to its marginal productivity [i.e. the worker's worth as determined by the efficacy of the market as judge].
>
> Ibid

It also presumes, of course, the existence of an 'equilibrium wage', known to both workers and firms.

Involuntary unemployment results when a worker wants a job but not enough jobs are available. According to Keynes:

> Men [sic] are involuntarily unemployed if, in the event of a small rise in the price of wage-goods relative to the money-wage, both the aggregate supply of labour willing to work for the current money wage and the aggregate demand for it at that wage would be greater than the existing volume of employment.
>
> Ibid.: 15, emphasis in original deleted

Structural unemployment results from technical change and increased productivity, or from changes in the composition of domestic output. Thus, as capitalism evolves, some goods and services are replaced by others, with labour demand increasing in expanding industries and decreasing in declining industries.

Cyclical unemployment refers to loss of jobs due to decreased demand during decreased economic activity, i.e. recessions.

To explain involuntary unemployment, Keynes argued that employers make decisions about the amount of labour hired based on expected returns, which is clouded in uncertainty. Due to future uncertainty, firms might postpone spending decisions and search for alternative investments for their cash. Thus, a tension exists between increasing individual wealth and expanding employment in the capitalist system. Due to uncertainty, instability and unemployment are inherent in capitalism; thus capitalism has no tendency for self-regulation to achieve full employment.

For Keynes, it logically followed that the government should decrease involuntary unemployment by effectively managing aggregate demand, i.e. the sum total of demand made by consumers, firms, foreigners and the government (see below). The government could restore (and increase) effective demand via public expenditures, subsidies and the minimum wage, and by encouraging the existence of trade unions. In addition, the government could dampen both consumer and firm uncertainty, with positive effects on employment.

Given the severity of the Great Depression, with US unemployment peaking at 25 per cent of the labour force in 1933, all these policies were tried and implemented.

7.5 KEYNES ON EFFECTIVE DEMAND

The roots of neoclassical orthodoxy can be found in Jean-Baptiste Say (1767–1832), who argued that there could be no general glut in a free-market economy, since supply creates its own demand. This 'Law of Markets' became part of the neoclassical core theory: the rational (and accepted) explanation for unemployment became the inflexibility of wages; conversely, wage flexibility would ensure labour market equilibrium.

Keynes flipped Say's Law on its head by focusing on the inadequacy and instability of aggregate demand. Keynes argued in *The General Theory of Employment, Interest and Money* (1936) that the primary driver of economic expansion is demand; deriving the Principle of Effective Demand (PED) to explain the causes of unemployment.

To understand PED we must understand the interrelationship between time, uncertainty and money regarding production. Each of these elements, believe it or not, was ignored by neoclassical economics! First of all, time and uncertainty are intricately related: the past is irrevocable and the future is unknown, beset with uncertainty; so every action is predicated on uncertainty. Money affects the economy both as a medium of exchange and a store of value (see Chapter 8). Thus, given an uncertain future, it is entirely rational to hold wealth as money, but to do so reduces aggregate demand. And since the future is unknown and uncertainty is rife, the demand for money is unstable (Davidson, 1978).

In discussing demand we need to understand the following important concepts:

- **Aggregate demand:** The sum of demand of household consumption, business investment spending, government spending and net exports. (See Chapter 12.)
- **Aggregate supply:** The total value of production of final goods and services offered for sale in a given period, produced by firms and entrepreneurs.
- **Liquidity preference:** The demand for money resulting from speculative decisions in a context of uncertainty. Its amount depends on expectations about the returns of financial and non-financial assets.

- **Interest rate:** A price paid for the use of borrowed money. The interest rate is also the reward for the renunciation of liquidity for a certain period of time.

Investment, a key component of aggregate demand, is simply defined as deferred consumption. Investment links the above concepts of time, uncertainty and money. Specifically, investment has a dual nature: (1) it increases aggregate demand in a particular period of time; and (2) it expands the productive capacity of the economy. Firms have two types of expectations about the future: short-term and long-term. The former relates to the existing productive capacity and to the demand for labour, which in turn is based on future sales (aggregate demand). More specifically, the demand for labour depends on expected profit (revenue minus cost). If expectations per future sales were confirmed (i.e. no uncertainty), aggregate demand would equal aggregate supply. If future sales were lower than expected, firms would accumulate stocks of unsold products; then, in the next production period, they would decrease the level of utilisation, decreasing the demand for labour. This process of adjustment results in short-term fluctuations in the levels of production and employment, along with fluctuation in the demand for money.

Firms also have long-term expectations about the future. It is conceivable that the purchase of capital goods could be postponed given changing expectations, and that firms, as a result, might prefer to maintain their wealth in liquid assets, especially money (i.e. a liquidity preference). Thus, aggregate demand might become insufficient to ensure the level of investment required to achieve full employment. After all, a firm's goal is to maximise profit by matching investment plans as close as possible to future expectations, rather than to maximise overall employment. Thus, a mismatch exists between firms following their self-interest and the overall well-being of the economy.

This raises an obvious contradiction between the modus operandi of capitalism and UN SDG #8: Promote inclusive and sustainable economic growth, employment and decent work for all.

Reduced or unfavourable long-term expectations are endogenous (i.e. to be explained by the model, rather than assumed as given). A high liquidity preference could decrease expected returns on capital goods. When the speculative demand for money increases, or the demand for other financial assets increases (due to increased uncertainty about future returns on investment), firms could reduce their demand for capital goods, and hence investment.

In a specific historical setting, the average assessment of firms about the future is based on a precarious set of expectations about aggregate demand. Keynes argued that expanding productive capacity depends on the degree of confidence, which affects the expected return on investment – the **marginal efficiency of capital** (MEC). The MEC is of fundamental importance, since it affects future expectations, which in turn influence current investment decisions. Today, for example, investment decisions are influenced by Internet technology and renewable energies, and the 'Internet of Things' that will virtually connect every aspect of economic and social life via sensors and software (see Chapter 6). As this investment trend will increase productivity and reduce the marginal cost of producing goods and services across the entire economy, the expected return on investment will be affected.

Capital goods are considered within other financial and non-financial assets in the context of a firm's investment decisions; hence the importance of time and uncertainty. The firm purchases capital goods, for example, if the expected rate of return is at least equal to the interest rate, which represents either the cost of borrowing capital or its opportunity cost. The interest rate is the reward for the renunciation of liquidity for a certain period of time. As a result, the level of employment is conditioned by the expected profits in the market of goods and the expected returns on financial assets, which in turn affect aggregate demand.

7.6 POLICY ANALYSIS: CONCEPTUALISATION OF UNEMPLOYMENT

In solving a problem it is imperative to conceptualise it, discuss the reasons for its existence, engage in dialogue with others to get different points of view, and then develop an effective solution. And, once this is implemented, to regularly monitor the problem: 'Are we making progress or should we go back to the drawing board?' In a dynamic economy some unemployment is normal: future expectations are not perfect and there will always be a disconnect between available jobs, information and the supply of workers. And, ironically, the more dynamic an economy, the higher the unemployment, due to structural, frictional and voluntary reasons. Would we want to live in a society with perfect certainty?

Table 7.3 lists the reasons and solutions for each type of unemployment. Some unemployment is normal although economists disagree on what normal

Table 7.3 Conceptualisation of Unemployment (Based on Conventional Definitions)

Type	*Reason*	*Solutions*
Involuntary	Lack of aggregate demand.	Increase aggregate demand.
Frictional	Inevitable mismatches.	Better information.
Voluntary	Misaligned expectations; Imperfect information.	Better information.
Frictional	Changing economy.	Worker education/training.
Cyclical	Recessions.	Reduce severity of by government policy.

Source: Authors.

is. The least serious and least bothersome type of unemployment from a policy perspective is voluntary, since this is mostly due to the volition of the worker. On the other hand, the most serious type is involuntary, signaling that the economy is unable to adequately provision for all of its members, and requires the most concerted public policy effort.

Box 7.3 Unemployment in Neoclassical Models

As neoclassical economics developed, it emulated the physics of Isaac Newton and, interestingly, parried the new physics of the twentieth century. If neoclassical economics had followed the path of the new physics – particle physics, the principle of uncertainty, etc. – economics would be very different today, eschewing equilibrium and becoming much more humble and pluralistic. Alas!

A key belief of neoclassical economics is that the economy tends towards equilibrium, and that if this is unattained, it is due to systematic interference with the laws of supply and demand, such as a trade union increasing the wage above the market-determined wage, or the imposition of the minimum wage. This belief is based on deductive reasoning –albeit, as it turns out, quite faulty: see Reardon (2006) – rather than empirical evidence. It is assumed as a matter of faith that price adjustments will guarantee full employment, and that worker and firm reactions are based on an automatic and unthinking reaction to market forces.

But the problem here is assuming that the market is initially at equilibrium, so that any adjustments can only interfere (and distort) a naturally obtained market result. This is an ideological assumption guaranteed to give a predetermined outcome: neoclassical economists don't necessarily like trade unions, so they devise a model that disparages or obviates them. (Note: the same analysis for a trade union is equally applicable to the minimum wage, as discussed in Chapter 2.)

Unfortunately, this is not the world we live in. In *The General Theory*, Keynes consistently scolds neoclassical economists for their inattention to how the economy actually works, 'whether logical or illogical, experience shows that this is how labour in fact behaves . . . These facts from experience are a prima facie ground for questioning the adequacy of the [neo]classical analysis' (1936 [2010]: 9; original emphasis deleted). Perhaps a more intellectually honest method is to investigate the actual economy (and labour market) in order to ascertain why trade unions exist and why unemployment occurs.

7.7 FINANCIALISATION OF CAPITAL AND UNEMPLOYMENT

As Keynes warned, capitalism is particularly influenced by finance. The linkages between finance and unemployment have reinforced unemployment and inequality (for a discussion on inequality, see Chapter 5). This 'social precarity' underscores the fact that the 'labour market has not only lost its capacity to promote integration and social mobility but has also become one of the main sources of vulnerability and social exclusion for large, growing sectors of the population' (Bayón, 2006: 126).

We can define **financialisation**[3] as 'A process whereby financial services, broadly construed, take over the dominant economic, cultural, and political role in a national economy' (Phillips, 2006: 268).

Let's explore why this term is used and its significance. New rules on corporate finance fostered the growth of institutional investors, such as pension funds or private equity firms, as relevant shareholders. These investors influenced the corporate governance of firms and, consequently, their strategies retreated from reinvestment towards maximising short-term value for shareholders. Many shareholders began investing as a form of speculation, hoping to gain a quick and substantial profit. The drive to increase shareholders' value and the incorporation of management share options shifted (and reduced) long-term investment in favour of short-term mergers and acquisitions, fostering financial speculation.

As a result, there has been a noticeable slowdown in real production (Stockhammer, 2008). Furthermore, domestic monetary policies increasing real interest rates made financial accumulation more attractive, expanding it, and thus restoring and increasing the wealth (and power) of the owners of capital whose assets are embodied in securities, bonds, shares, etc. And finally, due to liberalisation, mergers and acquisitions have increased the size and power of financial capital. The concentration and centralisation of capital favour the reordering of finance whereby financiers aim to maximise their short-term returns rather than building long-term sustainable businesses.

Investors search for capital accumulation. Their goal is to make profits quickly from investments in other firms, which can be achieved more easily by

> intercorporate sell-offs; spin-offs, where the divested part of the company is floated and shares distributed to shareholders of the parent; purchases by internal management (MBOs) or external management (MBI); and leveraged buyouts (LBOs), which are a particular form of buyout heavily financed by debt . . . Even without transfer of corporate assets, restructuring can take place in the form of 'rightsizing' via closures, outsourcing, management incentive schemes based around share options, and financial engineering through share buy-backs and substitution of debt for equity.
>
> Froud et al., 2006: 771

3. Phillips argues, quite persuasively, that 'historically, top world economic powers have found 'financialisation' a sign of late-stage debilitation, marked by excessive debt, great disparity between rich and poor, and unfolding economic decline' (2006: 268). For a fascinating discussion of the intricate relationship between financialisation and the historical decline of global superpowers, see (Phillips, 2002: 171–200).

Financialisation not only makes the above practices easier but also provides a rationale. It has pressured firms to downsize, restructure, reduce costs, and focus on short-term gains. In practice, this means a whole-scale attack on employment and labour conditions, while increasing outsourcing and plant closures, and intensifying pressure on supply-chain producers in global markets. The level of employment is also strongly related to the development of 'on-demand' or 'just-in-time' work patterns. The main motivation of employers for contingent workers is to control costs by reducing the time that paid workers are idle or working below capacity (Polivka and Nardone, 1989: 12). Another motivation is to reduce 'worker compensation and administrative costs' as well as training costs. As recognised by Froud et al. (2006: 771) 'labour is usually the first casualty of restructuring at company level'. The costs fall disproportionately on labour because the new priorities of shareholder value limit the social responsibility of firms. Thus, financialisation disproportionately reduces worker wages and weakens worker rights. This explains why growing numbers of economists advocate a *minimum wage* and a *living wage.*

7.8 THE MINIMUM WAGE AND THE LIVING WAGE

The minimum wage, defined as a legally imposed wage above the market wage, was first enacted in 1894 in Victoria, Australia. It was not a universal minimum wage; instead, it was only adopted by six industries. New Zealand enacted compulsory national minimum wage laws later in the same year. In the United States, early minimum wage laws were enacted at the state level during the first two decades of the twentieth century, applicable only to women and children, given that men had access to trade unions. In 1938 the US Congress passed the Fair Labor Standards Act. The Act's title underscores the disconnect between neoclassical economics and the reality of the labour market, in which power in the labour market was used disproportionately to favour capitalists at the expense of workers. During this time the United States also passed the Social Security Act (1935), which implemented a social security system (essentially a compact between young and old, with the former providing funds to decrease the risks of the latter), and the Wagner Act (1935), which made it easier for trade unions to organise. This mirrored the trend in other developed nations. Noticeably absent in the United States was passage of a universal healthcare law; and to this date the United States is the only developed country without one. The reasons are complex but are basically due to: (1) undue attachment to individualism while ignoring the greater good for society; and (2) the extensive lobbying power of the AMA (American Medical Association) and the AHA (American Hospital Association).

In most countries, recent policies to reduce unemployment have emphasised nominal wage flexibility. (**Nominal** means measured in current prices; **real** holds prices constant; so for example, real income measures how much goods and services your nominal income can actually buy. So, if you earn five dollars an hour, that is your nominal wage; and how much you can buy with that wage is the real wage.) According to this thinking, labour markets should be made flexible in order to eliminate rigidities and imperfections that could prevent the market from achieving full employment. Under this approach, it is believed that flexibility redistributes income from wages to profits, providing the foundation for capital formation according to Say's Law. More specifically, reducing nominal wages increases profits, which favours capital accumulation and economic growth. Conversely, if wages are increased, profits are reduced, thereby reducing investment, and vice versa. Thus, the level of nominal wages constitutes a limit to capital formation, since Say's law is based on the 'preservation of purchasing power' created by production (supply).

Keynes, however, warned that the reduction of nominal wages would not necessarily generate more profits and jobs. A nominal wage reduction could very well do the opposite: reduce consumer demand. Thus, the main question to be asked is: What are the consequences of declining nominal wage levels, declining real wages and proportionately declining price levels?

Post-Keynesian economists defend minimum wages not only in order to increase workers' standard of living, and to reduce inequality, but also to increase business expansion. According to Keynes (1936 [2010]), the increase in minimum (nominal and real) wages could foster positive expectations about future aggregate demand, thereby increasing expected return on investment. And raising nominal minimum wages (together with declining or constant prices) could affect the levels of consumption because real wages and, thus, workers' real income would be increased.

Keynes argued that the minimum wage can significantly foster economic growth by increasing expected aggregate demand and thus future investment; and, conversely, that falling nominal and real wages would certainly reduce effective demand, increasing inventories and reducing investment, resulting in a vicious cycle of unemployment. **Inventories** are stocks of goods (finished or not) held by firms to meet temporary or unexpected fluctuations in production or sale (World Bank, 2016).

At the beginning of the twenty-first century, the importance of the real wage and real income is evidenced by the concept of a **living wage**, i.e. a wage that enables an individual to live a decent life; or in other words, a wage that allows one to adequately provision. A living wage (despite its ambiguities and generalities) attempts to connect the means (income) with the ends (capability). Of course, what is considered an acceptable quality of life is time- and place-specific.

The right to earn a living wage is a human right, included in the ILO Declaration on Fundamental Principles and Rights at Work (1998). According to the ILO, the income to ensure a living wage is estimated by: (1) the cost of basic necessities such as a nutritious diet, basic housing and adequate clothing/footwear; (2) the cost of other needs, such as transportation, children's education, healthcare, childcare, household furnishings and equipment, recreation and cultural activities, communications, and personal care and services; and (3) a margin for unforeseen events, such as illnesses and accidents (Anker, 2011). Although the living wage is considered a human right, in most countries the legal minimum wage is far below the amount required to meet a worker's basic living needs, i.e. the living wage.

7.9 MEASURING DECENT WORK

We need now to understand what constitutes **decent work** and how it can be measured. Given recent trends in global flexibilisation, decent work is conceptually relevant for both developing and developed countries. The word 'decent' is subjective, meaning different things to different people. Can we design and measure decent work? Currently, the ILO's Decent Work Agenda asks governments and policy makers for a set of policies and actions to promote employment, rights at work, security and income support, equality in opportunity and access in a gender-sensitive approach. The ILO's understanding is that labour-market regulation affects the kind of society we live in and is important in building institutions to achieve the balance between capital accumulation and social needs. An important question becomes: Who should construct and determine decent jobs?

Statistical indicators on work and working conditions, such as employment and wage conditions, are insufficient to monitor progress towards decent work. The multidimensional nature of decent work creates measurement challenges, since the Decent Work Agenda is not only concerned with paid productive work and the workplace but also with the living conditions of workers and their families. That is why research needs to go beyond statistics on work and the workplace. Data from unpaid care work, access to healthcare and rights at work should be also considered.

Table 7.4 displays some indicators, main implementation issues and shortcomings related to the Decent Work Agenda. As definitions are not universally applicable, this sample presents a lean set of indicators of decent work; it is not exhaustive, rather, it aims to stimulate research on decent work data. Decent work is an important area of research in Europe, but not so much in the United States. This suggests the need for concerted research across developed and developing countries, and perhaps attainment of a universal definition and a global database.

Table 7.4 Selected Substantive Elements of the Decent Work Agenda

Substantive elements of the Decent Work Agenda and their indicators	*Main implementation issues*	*Shortcomings*
Employment opportunities/ Employment indicators:		
Labour force participation rate. Employment/population ratio. Unemployment rate. Youth unemployment rate. Share of wage employment in non-agricultural employment.	Improve comparability.	Ongoing efforts to improve international comparability should be incorporated into the indicators as improvements become available.
Work that should be abolished/ Unacceptable work indicators:		
Children not in school by employment status (percentage by age). Children in wage employment or self-employment (percentage by age).	Need to establish when factors other than work cause non-attendance, such as absence or poor quality of local school.	Neglected aspects for future development: forced labour, hazardous and other worst forms of child labour. Total work time, including non-economic household work, may be relevant. Regular attendance and progress in school.
Adequate Earnings and Productive Work/Earnings and training indicators:		
Inadequate pay rate (percentage of employed below half of median hourly earnings or absolute minimum, whichever is greater, by status in employment). Average earnings in selected occupations. Employees with recent job training (percentage with job training during last 12 months provided or paid for by employer or state).	Improve comparability of earnings data, mainly earnings distribution. Appropriate selection of occupations. Improve comparability and include country coverage.	Earnings often poorly measured for self-employed workers, therefore useful to report indicator by status in employment. Key neglected aspect: irregularity of employment/ earnings. Superficial portrayal of training.

Source: Adapted by the authors from Anker et al. (2002).

THINKING QUESTIONS

Have you, or one of your immediate relatives, ever experienced unemployment? If so, how did it feel?

To what extent is unemployment an individual, social and economic problem?

What *can* governments do to address unemployment? What *should* they do? What can businesses do? What should they do?

CLASS ACTIVITY

To what extent can labour flexibilisation ensure full employment? What are the downsides of flexibilisation?

AREAS FOR RESEARCH

To what extent is technological innovation a cause of involuntary unemployment?

UN SDG FOCUS

Goals #5 and #8 call for:

5. Achieve gender equality and empower all women and girls.
8. Promote inclusive and sustainable economic growth, employment and decent work for all.

What is meant by 'equality'? How would you define 'decent' work? What is meant by 'gender'? How does one 'achieve', 'promote' and 'empower'?

FURTHER READING

Akyüz, Y. (2006) *From Liberalization to Investment and Jobs: Lost in Translation.* UNCTAD Working Papers. Available online at IDEAs: www.networkideas.org/featart/feb2006/fa28_Lost_in_Translation.htm

Folkman, P., Froud, J., Johal, S. and Williams, K. (2007) 'Working for themselves: capital market intermediaries and present day capitalism'. *Business History*, Vol. 49, No. 4, pp.552–72 (also available as CRESC Working Paper, No 25).

Ghosh, J. (2003) 'Exporting Jobs or Watching Them Disappear? Relocation, Employment and Accumulation in the World Economy'. In Ghosh, J. and Chandrasekhar, C. P. (Eds.) *Work and Well-Being in The Age of Finance*. New Delhi: Muttukadu Press. pp.99–119.

Rama, M. (2003) 'On Globalization and the Labor Market'. *World Bank Research Observer,* Vol. 18, No. 2, pp.159–86.

8
Money

Money is the 'oil' of a capitalist economy: without money, a modern economy cannot function; at the same time, too little money and too much money are both problematic. But what is money? How is it defined? Who controls it? Traditional neoclassical textbooks tend to provide a functional definition of money, i.e. defining money in terms of what it does. While this is important, it is not a sufficient explanation. We also need to consider who has the power to create money and the resulting consequences. Following convention, we will begin with what money does before moving on to these other equally important questions.

8.1 WHAT IS MONEY?

It would be very difficult to operate in a complex society without money, because money enables us to exchange goods with each other. Rather than swapping goods directly, we price them in terms of money, enabling more rapid and complex exchanges to take place. This function of money is called the **medium of exchange**. It is clear that capitalism could not function without the ability to exchange in this way, and so money has developed hand-in-hand with capitalism. Although other non-capitalist societies had forms of money, they were not as flexible as the money that is central to a capitalist economy.

Imagine that I am a farmer and I grow carrots. You want to buy carrots and offer me a woollen jumper, but I am allergic to wool and want to buy a new chair. We can imagine infinitely complex series of needs and offerings which would be very complicated to resolve without money. The medium-of-exchange function of money enables exchanges, but it is important to note that this also introduces the idea of a money price, over which some producers might have more influence (i.e. power) than others.

So we have learned that when we want to exchange, we can use money, but how do we know the appropriate price for something? Money also functions as a **unit of account**, that is to say, we can measure an item's value in terms of money. However, money is not a particularly good measure, since, unlike a measure of length, say a metre rule, money does not have a fixed value. For example, in a high-inflation economy the price of a loaf of bread might double within a week, but this does not mean that the value of bread has increased, only its price. To continue our analogy of the carrots, we could imagine measuring the length of a table in terms of carrots, but since carrots are of different sizes, this would not help us to compare different tables. Money is intended as a fixed measure of value, but again we should exercise caution here, since money can change in value relative both to other goods and to other currencies.

Lastly, economists suggest that money can operate as a **store of value**, which is the most problematic of all its functions. Clearly, paper currency is not a very good way to store value, as anybody who has left a £10 note in their trousers before putting them in the washing machine can tell you. But if you consider the use to me as a carrot farmer in storing carrots in a sack under the bed, you can see that the paper money is more useful to store value. With luck and a good root cellar, the carrots might last until the spring, but I could not hold the value of my surplus for long in carrots (unless they were gold carats of course!). But even money held in a bank can lose its value in times of financial instability or inflation. Indeed, the whole currency itself can collapse, such that savers find that the apparent value they had stored in a currency in the bank disappears, as with the Argentinian peso in 2001 and the Icelandic krónur in 2008.

But there is a deeper problem with money as a store of value. In a simple peasant economy, very few people will have access to the sorts of commodities that can store large amounts of value, e.g. precious metals. But once a market economy develops an accessible currency that can be deposited and held in a bank, many people begin to accumulate wealth. They can use this wealth to accumulate further wealth through the payment of **interest** (the price paid for the use of borrowed money), and can even bequest it to their children or friends after death. The money enables them to exercise an unequal share of power within their society and, conversely, disempowers other people. This is only possible because money, and the banking system, facilitate the storing of value.

In concluding this section we should note that there are two problems with a functional definition of money: first, it does not explain how money originated; and second, the three functions identified may not be compatible with each other. Let's look at the second problem and think about how money moves in our economy. Recently, we have seen how money has found its way into speculative finance, sometimes referred to as the 'casino economy'. Those who control money have been keen to gain the maximum return, which is achieved not by investing in manufacturing plants or health services, but by trading in foreign exchange or buying cocoa futures, for example. From a social and ecological perspective this might be called a 'misallocation of resources', since money is not achieving the greatest benefit for the greatest number of people; rather, a very small number of people benefit while the resulting inequality results in social distress.

While a functional definition of money can be helpful, unfortunately it excludes the social aspect of money, so that money is defined as such only because people have confidence in its acceptance. Although a political authority is likely to back up this confidence, it is people's mutual agreement to accept money that gives it

Box 8.1 A Short History of Money

There are two conflicting stories of how our modern money system developed. One relates money back to gold and how this was handled by medieval merchants ('fractional reserve'). The other is a story of money as a social phenomenon.

The story of fractional reserve banking dates to the Middle Ages, when wealthy merchants deposited their savings with goldsmiths with secure vaults where they could keep it safe. The goldsmiths began to operate as money lenders, lending the money deposited with them to others who might need it for investment. For the sake of convenience the goldsmiths did not lend the gold itself, but what became known as 'promissory notes', effectively IOUs which the goldsmiths promised to redeem for gold if requested. Over time, the goldsmiths realised that they could lend more money than they had deposited in their vaults, since it was unlikely that all customers would return for their gold at the same time. This is how the modern banking system was born, as a system relying on long-term deposits to support shorter-term borrowing. If all depositors seek their money at the same time, the bank will have insufficient funds; and if depositors know this is happening they will likely swamp the bank, fearing that their deposits will be lost. This is known as a 'run on the bank' and was common in the nineteenth century, when banks were poorly regulated and there were large numbers of small, private banks. The failures often arose from speculative lending, so the banks could not guarantee the value of their depositors' money. In times of uncertainty such failures are likely, since depositors will suffer insecurity and may seek to withdraw their deposits.

So how did banks know how much money they could lend relative to their deposits? Enter the idea of 'fractional reserve'. Banks estimated how much of their deposits, or what fraction, they needed in reserve to meet the demand of their depositors. It is important to understand that the money system today, with private banks creating money through issuing debt, effectively functions without a fractional reserve. There are some international restrictions on the amount of money that banks are allowed to issue relative to their reserves, known as the Basel Accords, after the Swiss town where they were agreed (see Chapter 14). However, these are lax, and national regulatory authorities allowed their banks to create as much money as they thought 'prudent'.

Critics of the story of money-as-gold use the irrefutable argument that money existed before gold coins were ever created. The first forms of money were accounting devices, such as the clay tablets used by Babylonian accountants to record transactions and money or tax owed between parties. The early medieval economy in Britain grew rich without the use of any gold money. Instead, several kings, beginning with Henry I, produced 'tally sticks', with notches to indicate how much was owed between two parties. The stick was then split in two so that both sides had a record: one was called the 'stub' and the other the 'counterfoil', as in contemporary chequebooks. Because the king was prepared to accept only these tally sticks for payment of taxes, they were able to circulate as money, indicating again the importance of trust within a community supporting any form of money, and the consequent unimportance of the value of what the money is made from.

its power. Hence, we can define **money** as the circulating medium of exchange, either in paper or digital format within a community of economic agents in a defined geographical area and time period.

8.2 WHO CONTROLS MONEY?

We have discussed what money does and how important it is in a complex society, but where does money come from? Why do we believe that pieces of paper or digits on a computer screen can be accepted in exchange for real goods and services? What makes money acceptable is that we have confidence in it – and, incidentally, it is no coincidence that the word 'credit' comes from the Latin word *credere*, which means 'to believe'.

To function effectively, money must have authority, and through history this authority has had various different origins. Most money in existence today is defined by economists as **'fiat' money**, from the Latin word *fiat* meaning 'let it be'. This is because such money has been brought into existence by a political authority rather than having any intrinsic value.

The original authorities whose money was trusted were usually sovereigns. You may know the expression 'As rich as Croesus'. Croesus was a King of ancient Lydia (located in today's Turkey) who became rich by controlling the money used for trade in nearby kingdoms. It is important to understand that this wealth did not rely on the availability of gold within his kingdom, but rather on his canny decision to issue a form of money that had credibility. Sovereigns from ancient times to the early modern period issued money usually in the form of coin, both to facilitate trade and exchange and so that they could collect taxes. As we have already seen, taxes in the form of carrots or other perishable commodities are not very useful. If a sovereign can issue and guarantee the value of a currency, then he can receive taxes in that currency and spend it as he chooses, either on weapons or luxurious living.

However, in most cases modern states do not have that power, because they have privatised the function of money creation and allowed it to be exercised by private banks. While banks have long had the power to create private money, in the late nineteenth and the twentieth centuries states increasingly reduced the amount of money they created directly and allowed debt-based bank money to dominate as the medium of exchange.[1] This is partly the result of the expansion of electronic money, since the **seigniorage** (i.e. the difference between the currency's exchangeable value and the cost of making it) of circulating money, whether paper or coin, always remained with the state; but it was also due to a political decision. However, at some point the private and state forms of money became confused, so that both were considered 'legal tender', meaning that the

1. We will discuss the important topic of how banks create money in Chapter 14.

ultimate guarantee of both rested with the state. The consequences of this became clear during the recent financial crisis, when central banks felt obliged to support their banks financially to prevent the whole financial system from collapsing. Following this, an increasing number of people are questioning whether states should reclaim control over such an important tool as money. A consequence of this is that some local communities are now taking control and producing their own money.

So although many people think that money is a public resource and that the government is somehow responsible for it, in reality the decision to create money occurs when banks make loans. This has two very serious consequences: first, the money is always accompanied by a corresponding debt, so that we cannot have money without debt, and as the amount of money in circulation expands, so does the volume of debt. Second, the privatisation of the credit-creation function has important implications for where the money goes, or how it is allocated. Banks are private businesses owned by their shareholders; when they create money, they do so by lending it to clients whom they think will repay. So money tends to flow to the wealthier sections of society, exacerbating existing inequality. If governments created money themselves, they could choose to spend it in areas of greatest social need, perhaps paying it to citizens as a form of basic income, or using it to pay for home-insulation programmes or to improve health or transport services.

8.3 MONEY, DEBT AND EXPONENTIAL GROWTH

Money provides an excellent means of understanding the mathematical phenomenon of exponential growth. This is an unexpected way in which your student loan will support your education: by enabling you to study the process by which the money you owe will rapidly increase year after year through the process of **compound interest**. When you borrow money, there is an understanding that you will pay a charge for that service, and that this charge will relate to the amount you have borrowed: it will be quoted in percentage terms, so that the more you borrow, the more you will pay. Let us imagine that you borrow £100 and are quoted an interest rate of 10 per cent. At the end of the first year, ignoring other charges, you will owe £10 as a fee for borrowing the £100. But the nature of compound interest means that at the end of the second year, if you have not paid anything back, you will owe not just twice £10, but also the interest on the charge you have not paid in the first year, so £20 plus 10 per cent of £10. Each year you will accrue interest on the unpaid interest as well as on the original loan, which accountants call the 'principal'. This is what is known as 'compound interest', and it explains why debts can expand rapidly and cause people to fall into arrears i.e. payments owing that have not been paid on time.

8.4 *TECHNIQUE 4*: COMPOUNDING INTEREST

The following is a worked example of the process of compounding.

If we borrow £100 at a rate of interest of 10 per cent per annum, then 10 per cent of the value of the principal we have borrowed will be added to it each year. But each year the interest due will be calculated on the basis of the new sum owing: the principal plus the interest accrued in the previous year(s). As the following calculations show, this means that the amount owing will increase very rapidly.

After 1 year the amount owing will have grown to £100 x 1.1 = £110.
After 2 years the amount owing will have grown to £100 x 1.1 x 2. = £121.
After t years the amount owing will have grown to £100 x 1.1 x t.

We create a formula that expresses how the amount owed increases over time:

The amount owed (D) resulting after t years of accruing interest is:

$D_t = S_0(1+r)^t$

Where r is expressed as a decimal, S_0 is the initial loan and t is the number of time periods.

Based on the formula, you can work out the increase in the cost of a student loan, borrowed over 25 years, at an average rate of interest of 4 per cent. Then substitute different numbers (higher and lower) for the interest rate, principal, and number of time periods.

8.5 MONEY AND CAPITAL

Ostensibly an oxymoron – why would anyone pay interest to keep money in a bank? – negative interest rates have recently (at least since the recent global crisis) become less uncommon. Sweden first imposed a negative interest rate in 2009, followed by Japan, Denmark, Switzerland and Finland. Remember we had earlier defined an interest rate as 'the price paid for the use of borrowed money'. This is a concept we all familiar with: If you deposit 1000 euros at your local bank, with a (positive) interest rate of 2 per cent, at the year's end you will collect an additional 20 euros. A **negative interest rate** is defined as the price paid for depositing money, i.e. the depositor pays the bank for the privilege of depositing her money. But with a negative interest rate of 2 per cent, at the year's end you must give the bank 20 euros. This raises the obvious question: Why? The negative interest rate is charged either by the central bank to member banks, and/or by a bank to member customers. The objective is twofold: to decrease the cost of a bank making a loan, and to increase the incentive for a consumer to purchase goods

Box 8.2 Silvio Gesell and the Amazing Circulatory Money System

Silvio Gesell (1862–1930) was a German businessman and money theorist. He wanted to create a form of money called **free money**, the supply of which was determined socially and which exactly matched the local economy's economic activity. This was to counteract how existing money systems enabled the extraction of value through speculation (investing in risky schemes) and the earning of interest, creating economic instability, with an inherent tendency to depress economic demand. Gesell set three objectives for his new currency: to secure the exchange of goods so that there were no boom-and-bust cycles; to accelerate the rate of economic exchange; and to close the value gap between producer and consumer, thus avoiding profiteering by middlemen.

Gesell directly observed the problems of boom and bust while running his family business in Germany and Argentina. His theory was that money was not circulating rapidly enough because of the mistaken belief that money increases its value if left alone. To ensure rapid circulation of money, Gesell suggested that, rather than people being rewarded for holding money, through interest, they should be charged for holding it, a process he called **demurrage**. His concept of demurrage is like negative interest (see text), so that money slowly loses its value over time. This is achieved by effecting a staged reduction in the face value of the money over time: it has initial validity of a fixed period, after which its value can only be extended by purchasing a stamp, costing some percentage of its value. Since it earns no interest, there is no incentive to hoard or invest, meaning that the currency will instead be spent, increasing economic activity. Money generated from the extension and exchange charges can be used to fund local social projects. Gesell's theories strongly supported the design of Germany's *Regiogeld* or 'regional money' systems, which we discuss later in this chapter.

rather than keep her money idle. But, as Robert Skidelsky (Keynes' biographer, and a member of the British House of Lords) wrote:

> negative interest rates are simply the latest fruitless effort since the 2008 global financial crisis to revive economies by monetary measures . . . the real case against negative interest rates is the folly of relying on monetary policy alone to rescue economies from depressed conditions. The truth, however, is that the only way to ensure that 'new money' is put into circulation is to have the government spend it. The government would borrow the money directly from the central bank and use it to build houses, renew transport systems, invest in energy-saving technologies, and so forth.
>
> Skidelsky, 2016

We agree, as long as the government spends on either renewable energy infrastructure or necessary investment to obtain the 17 UN SDGs.

The economic system that dominates most of the world today is capitalism, which indicates how important money is. But economists mean something different from money when they use the word 'capital'. **Capital** has the power to bring resources together so that they can be combined to make products to be sold. So one part of capital might be the investment capital that enables entrepreneurs to buy machinery and land, and to employ workers; but the land and machinery is also considered to be 'capital' because it too can support the production of goods and services. Some economists go even further and create concepts such as 'social capital' or 'human capital' to draw attention to how people's skills and their working relationships are important to the success of productive enterprise (see Chapter 3).

We usually think of money in its retail function, that is, how we use it as citizens to receive our wages and pay our bills. However, in a capitalist economy, how money is controlled and can be created at will is crucial to the ability of the economy to innovate and expand. Before the system of creating money came into existence, economic development had to wait until there was sufficient capital for funding. In the case of a person wishing to start a business or buy a house, she would have to save enough money from earnings to invest in the business or house. Imagine how economic activity could be accelerated by creating the money first, as an expectation of future returns, and then paying it back once the business had been a success. This method of making money on the basis of future expectations rather than past achievements was critical to the development of capitalism and to the boom in activity and rapid innovation known as the Industrial Revolution. It is also vital for the development of international trade and globalisation.

It is helpful to think of money and banking in terms of two different kinds of activities: **personal retail banking**, to support citizens in paying their bills and receiving their salaries; and **commercial banking**, representing the investment of money at risk and in expectation of a healthy return if the business is successful. It is clear that the second type of banking is far more risky, and the rewards are correspondingly higher. Traditionally, governments have underwritten retail banking, since the social consequences to all citizens and to the national economy are potentially disastrous if the retail money system collapses: people lose their savings and sometimes their homes as well.

However, commercial banking is related to business investment: those with spare money undertake a risk to increase returns on their investment, also known as '**venture capital**', precisely because the risks (and potential rewards) are so great. What became clear during the 2008 crisis is that these two types of money and banking had become confused. Governments were underwriting massively risky financial schemes which, when they collapsed, threatened the whole system of money, including the savings and bank accounts of ordinary people. This is why one of the most persistent demands following the crisis is for the clear separation of retail and commercial banking to ensure monetary stability.

However, we can also argue that radical changes to the banking system are necessary to ensure sustainability as well as stability. We saw earlier how the ability of money to store value enables people to accumulate wealth in one time period, and use it as a call on goods and services in the future. So money that is created as debt by being borrowed from banks makes a claim on goods and services. This means that money created as it is in the current system automatically creates a pressure for the economy to grow, both because of the need to repay interest and because the money is created in advance of being supported by products of real economic value. But such products need to repay the debts created when that money is made.

So creating money through the parallel issue of debt creates pressure for economic growth. During the initial stages of capitalism, this provided an extraordinary boost, and turbo-charged innovation and industrial expansion, but today this rapid growth is now causing an ecological crisis. So our current money system must be changed if we are to achieve sustainability.

Consequently, we think it helpful to realise that capitalism has always used money as a fuel: the speculative power of money, enabling innovation and productive expansion, has been the dynamic force behind economic growth. But it has also led to inequality and instability, with no connection between the real and financial economies, and to an allocation of money not responsive to social or ecological priorities. In a sustainable and just economy we will need money that acts rather like the oil in the engine, lubricating economic activities and exchanges but with limits, and according to priorities determined democratically and in the interest of all.

8.6 BOOMS AND BUSTS; BUBBLES AND BULBS

We have seen the close connection in a capitalist economy between economic development and the creation of money. This is sometimes referred to as **speculation**: investing money in risky schemes to grow rich faster than by working and earning a salary or wage. The history of capitalism is littered with the corpses of such investment schemes, and the pattern of them is always the same. First, an entrepreneur discovers or creates an 'investment vehicle', which must be convincing enough to carry the hopes of investors. Then he or she creates excitement around this 'investment opportunity' to attract investors. As their money floods in, the value of the scheme rapidly increases, making it attractive to other investors in a self-fulfilling process.

A **bubble** is defined as unwarranted or unjustified inflation of an asset's real value. All bubbles have been financed (or perhaps 'fueled' is the better word) by an injection of credit. As the investment expands, it outstrips whatever was of true value that created the excitement in the first place. It has now become a bubble, and by this stage people are trading on their expectations in a pyramid-selling scheme, since they can continue to profit so long as more investors are attracted; here the buying becomes a mania or a frenzy. This is the riskiest stage of the scheme, since at some point expectations will change, investors will take flight, and the bubble will burst. This is what Warren Buffet meant when he famously said that 'only when the tide goes out do you discover who's been swimming naked' (quoted in *The Economist* online, 2007). During an economic boom such schemes prosper, but in a crisis people seek assets of real value, for example land or productive enterprises, and those holding only paper assets in over-inflated speculative schemes are likely to lose their shirts.

The worthy and sturdy Bank of England (established in 1694) was created by a Scottish entrepreneur who was responsible for such a speculative scheme: the Darien project. In 1693, William Paterson established the Company of Scotland Trading to Africa and the Indies, which sold shares of a proposed colony on Darien in Panama. The Scots were keen to see their own advantage from expanding international trade, and so there was no shortage of investors: about half a million pounds, half Scotland's national capital, was invested. Darien was in fact the original Mosquito Coast, and most of the settlers died within the year. Thanks to Paterson, the Scottish economy was nearly bankrupted, preventing Scottish entrepreneurs from competing with the British Empire.

Paterson's plan for the Bank of England was based on the creation of the national debt, which provided the capital for the bank, backed by the English citizenry. In 1719 the South Sea Company offered to assume the government debt (then at £31 million) in return for trading concessions, offering an official £3 million lump sum as a sweetener, as well as substantial unofficial bribes. It outbid the Bank of England and acquired the debt in 1720. These costs were met by share issues, and although the company had virtually no value, a policy of talking up its prospects, and the speculative fever this caused, increased the share's value from the initial £120 to £950 in July of the same year. Directors of the Company increased share values by purchasing their own shares. Once word leaked that the directors had sold all their stock, there was panic selling by investors, most of whom (including the scientist Sir Isaac Newton and the writer Jonathan Swift) lost sizeable fortunes.

The most improbable debt was backed by the bulbs of a beautiful but financially worthless flower: the tulip frenzy of the Netherlands, which peaked in 1637. The Dutch were mad for these beautiful flowers, which rapidly became status symbols: the more unusual the colour or pattern, the more valuable the bulb. By the height of the mania, a single tulip bulb was worth the equivalent of £35,000 today. Tulips were exchanged on the stock exchange, and again ordinary people were sucked into the speculative madness. In February 1637 the bubble burst, when confidence was destroyed by some investors drawing the obvious conclusion that these values could not be sustained.

Problematic, at least at the early stages of an incipient bubble, is that in a dynamic economy we would expect demand to increase (at least initially for new innovative products), causing the product's price to increase. But how to differentiate between ordinary price increases and those of an incipient bubble? To do so requires diligent empirical observation, as well as knowledge of underlying trends. Contemporary examples are typically associated with new technology companies, where the assets are intangible forms of 'intellectual property' that are also technically complex, as in the dot-com bubble; or with companies engaged in such arcane and technically sophisticated financial engineering that investors can be misled about the real value of the company.

8.7 LOCAL CURRENCIES: A FAD OR THE WAVE OF THE FUTURE?

In recent years, and increasingly since the credit crisis in 2007–08, communities have taken the power to create credit into their own hands by issuing their own local currencies. Such currencies have a long history and are **counter-cyclical**, meaning that they flourish at times when the capitalist economy is in crisis and/or when liquidity is consequently scarce. The first boom in such currencies in modern times occurred during the Depression of the 1930s. In the USA, where the economic crisis caused mass unemployment and widespread hardship, communities across the country issued their own money. Many forms of local money were created by individual states in the USA, and came to be known as 'scrip'. This was issued by local authorities to finance their own expenditures, and then accepted back in tax. These currencies were designed in different ways, some funded from a local purchase tax, which required users to buy stamps each time they used the money; others funded from anticipated tax revenues. It has been estimated that as much as one billion dollars' worth of local currencies may have been created during the Depression years and that at its most widespread, in 1933, the movement involved up to a million people.

The recent wave of community currencies began with the **LETS schemes** (Local Exchange and Trading Schemes), which took off in the UK in the 1990s. As their name suggests, these are clubs of people who agree to exchange services, rather like an extended baby-sitting circle. Rather than using a physical currency, they often just exchange time, which is recorded in a computer system. Many of these LETS schemes were highly successful in enabling people without access to jobs, or with a shortage of pounds sterling, to be part of a flourishing local exchange system. Time banks are similar systems, where the money is derived directly from people's time.

In an economy in recession, the money system fails to connect people with spare time with people who need help and support. Both sides can lose out: elderly people might be deprived of care and parents might not be able to pay for people to look after their children; meanwhile the unemployed become socially isolated and lose self-esteem. A time bank allows them to exchange time without becoming involved in the formal money system.

Local currencies in Japan have exploded in the last two decades, where the stagnation of the economy in the 1990s and 2000s led to a proliferation of currencies with a wide variety of designs and purposes. Japanese local currencies tend to be designed as coupons which are received in return for voluntary work and can then be spent in local shops. The first Japanese currencies were organised as 'voluntary labour banks' similar to time banks. These currencies exemplify how different types of money can be very important to an economy in a recession. In a country with such a strong work ethic, recession has led to considerable social problems, including mental illness. Local currencies have enabled people to work and make a contribution to their community even when conventional jobs paid in the national currency are not available. In this way many social needs have been met that would otherwise have been left unresolved.

More recently, community currency schemes have developed in Europe. They have been particularly successful in Germany and Austria, with 73 local money systems known as *Regiogeld* or 'regional money'. In total these regional currencies have injected some €750,000 equivalent into circulation, providing an important stimulus to their local economies. The most successful is the Chiemgauer in Bavaria (Germany), which uses Silvio Gesell's concept of demurrage to increase its velocity of circulation (see Box 8.2). This is achieved by effecting a staged reduction in the currency's face value over time. It has initial validity of three months, after which its value can only be extended by purchasing a stamp costing 2 per cent of its value. Since it earns no interest there is no incentive to hoard or invest, meaning that the currency will instead be spent, increasing economic activity. Money generated from the extension and exchange charges is used to fund local social projects. The Chiemgauer is currently widely used. It has 600 shops participating in the scheme, 1,800 consumer members and 200 charitable associations who receive donations every time the local currency is purchased. Around 430,000 Chiemgauers are in circulation, generating a transaction volume value of more than €4m.

So what should we conclude about local currencies? Are they just a whimsical fad or could they help to support a transition to more sustainable and stronger local economies? First, evidence indicates that such currencies generally find it hard to compete with strong national currencies. They succeed best when those currencies are under pressure, as in the case of the local Greek currency – the TEM – which is a response to the crisis in the Eurozone. However, the Chiemgauer shows what is possible in a highly successful capitalist economy when a local community supports its local currency. Given what we know about the importance of national currency, we should perhaps think of the local currencies as complementary to national currency; and, however successful they may be, they do not undermine the importance of asking questions about how the national currency is issued and controlled. Nevertheless, central to well-functioning local currencies is the strong underlying bonds of trust and commitment, effectively producing the much-needed social capital for a fully functioning commons. As Rifkin writes, 'the currency a society uses to enable its members to trade goods and services with one another is a good marker of the underlying values held by the community' (2014: 259). While traditional debt-based currencies are the 'oil' of today's capitalism, local currencies might very well become the 'oil' of tomorrow's commons-based economy.

Bank transactions by internet and mobile banking have sharply increased since the 2008 global financial crisis. The current wave of financial innovations is increasingly oriented to more friendly digital channels through apps in the context of mobile banking strategies privileging the development of open bank softwares and the interaction with social media. Concomitant with this increased digitalization of financial transactions is the growth of fintechs – startup companies organized as digital platforms emphasising costumer relationships in the areas of payment systems, insurance, financial consultancy and management. An advantage of their business models are low operating expenses, greater operational agility and the ability to generate data for the design of customized financial products and services – such as the digital currency BITCOIN.

THINKING QUESTIONS

Are you satisfied that the existing currency serves your interests, or would you desire a new currency? If you want a new currency, what would be its objectives? How would you decide the following: Who issues the currency? Who makes decisions about its operation?

Would you allow everybody to use the currency, or exclude some groups? Would it be backed by another currency or something of value? If so, which or what? Would you include demurrage in the design? Would you allow everybody to swap it for the backing currency? Would you charge a redemption fee?

CLASS ACTIVITY

Explore the possibility of creating local money to fulfil a number of objectives, given different interest groups such as a local unemployed support organisation, an environmental campaign group, a local supermarket, the chamber of trade, etc.

AREAS FOR RESEARCH

What have been the effects of introducing local currencies in some communities? Explore some real-world examples and construct a case study which would enable other communities to successfully introduce their own local currency.

UN SDG FOCUS

UN SDG #16 states: 'Promote just, peaceful and inclusive societies.' Which money system discussed in this chapter could best promote/achieve this goal? How could a money system be made 'inclusive'?

FURTHER READING

Cato, M. S. (2012) *Local Liquidity*. Weymouth: Green House.

Graeber, D. (2012) *Debt: The First 5,000 Years*. New York: Melville House.

Mellor, M. (2010) *The Future of Money*. London: Pluto Press.

North, P. (2010) *Local Money: How to Make it Happen in your Community.* Cambridge: Green Books.

Ryan-Collins, J. and Greenham, T. (2012) *Where Does Money Come From?* London: New Economics Foundation.

9
Economic Value

The questions we raise in this chapter are still subject to ongoing discussion and debate amongst economists, which is to be expected since the issue of what is valuable and how to measure it is at the heart of the subject of economics. We explore how previous societies and theorists assessed the essential sources of value, and then bring the discussion up to date with the practice of pricing nature.

9.1 CONTROVERSIES ON THE SOURCES OF ECONOMIC VALUE

Whether or not money has intrinsic value or only acts like a token to enable the exchange of goods with value is a key source of disagreement within economics. The Scottish philosopher David Hume (1955: 33) argued that money did not have intrinsic value but was useful as a tool to facilitate exchange:

> Money is not, properly speaking, one of the subjects of commerce; but only the instrument which men [sic] have agreed upon to facilitate the exchange of one commodity for another. It is none of the wheels of trade: It is the oil which renders the motion of the wheels more smooth and easy.

Adam Smith argued that traditional societies exchanged goods directly through a barter system, but, as Graeber (2012) has shown, there is no anthropological evidence of early societies relying on barter as a formal system of exchange. But as economies became more complex, money became the dominant commodity. As we saw in Chapter 8, money functions as a unit of account, meaning money can add up the value of the production of an economy, with the value of different goods/services represented by the market price. But if the value of money changes through time, how can we use it to measure anything? Indeed, summing the value of the production of an economy is clearly not as objective as using a tape measure to measure the length of a piece of cloth. Yet many economic theories assume that economic production can be measured by summing prices and quantities in this way.

The physiocrats were the first group of economists to propose a theory of value. As discussed in Chapter 2, they wrote about the economy in which they lived, which was mostly agrarian. Since people's livelihoods were derived from the land directly, or from craftwork based on products derived from the land, they assumed that value only comes from land, which is a gift from nature. The physiocrats had ongoing disputes with rival schools of economics, including the mercantilists, who sought national advantage through trade and the accumulation of money rather than through natural resources.

The mercantilists favoured policies to support industry, including the granting of exclusive rights to certain companies; they favoured trade and the accumulation of surplus through selling industrial products. They also favoured the availability and even the subsidy of basic food to maximise the production of saleable goods. The mercantilists' preponderant goal was to run a trade surplus (exporting more than they imported), which would attract gold and silver into the country.

In traditional societies, a direct relationship existed between people and their land in the production of food and other commodities. However, with the advent of industrialisation, this relationship broke down and a large number of people were forced to sell their labour to ensure their survival. This economic change had a major impact on economic theory, with economists seeing people's work as the main productive force in the economy. Indeed, this changing social and economic background led to the development of a labour theory of value (as discussed in Chapter 1), especially amongst those who sought to improve the conditions of the industrial working class. The classical economists found value not in land but in labour: in the work and skill of ordinary people. The labour theory of value was expounded and developed by all the classical economists, but found its denouement in Marx.

Marx wrote about the industrial economy in which he lived. He distinguished economic actors on the basis of their 'relationship to the means of production'. The bourgeoisie control capital and therefore own the means of production; proletarians are not owners, and so must sell their labour to survive. In the Marxist tradition, the standard to explain the relative value of a commodity is the amount of labour socially required to produce it. Implicit in the classical labour theory of value is the inherent conflict between classes over how the product is produced and its distribution. For classical economists, including Marx, class conflict was assumed intrinsic to capitalism and central to its methodological analysis.

The neoclassical revolution of the late nineteenth century rejected the labour theory of value, and by doing so swept the labour/capital conflict under the carpet in favour of the much more benign assertion that the interaction of market forces obviates class conflict by producing an outcome beneficent to all (Dowd, 2004). The nineteenth-century founders of neoclassical economics assumed that an item's price had nothing to do with intrinsic properties, only with the amount of satisfaction (or 'utility') that an individual derived from its use. And, more specifically, it is the utility at the margin, that is, the **marginal utility** – or the additional utility obtained from the purchase of an additional commodity – that gives an item its value. Hence, a good's value is its price, reflected by marginal utility.

The neoclassical revolution also transformed value and pricing from something objective –the labour theory of value – to something subjective, like utility, existing only in the mind of individuals. Neoclassical economists conflated value and price, assuming the two to be equal: a mistake that has continued to this day.

9.2 JOAN ROBINSON: THE PRODUCTION FUNCTION AND THE CAMBRIDGE CAPITAL CONTROVERSY

Joan Robinson (1903–83) is a rare example of a female economist who achieved great esteem during her lifetime (we had to wait until 2009 for a woman (Elinor Ostrom) to win the Bank of Sweden Prize in Economic Sciences, although she was a political scientist by training, and she had to split the prize with Oliver Williamson). Robinson worked in Cambridge with a group of economists deeply influenced by John Maynard Keynes. We like her book, actually a compilation of essays, *What are the Questions and Other Essays*, which is thought-provoking and just as relevant today as it was in 1980, but is sadly largely unheeded.

In 1954 Robinson published an article, 'The production function and the theory of capital', in which she attacked the view propagated by neoclassical theorists that capital can easily be measured and then summed to produce an aggregate or total capital. She was joined by other economists working in Cambridge, UK, most notably Piero Sraffa, and was opposed by the economists Robert Solow and Paul Samuelson, based in Cambridge, Massachusetts. Hence the disagreement became known as the Cambridge Capital Controversy.

About this controversy, Robinson (quoted in Cohen and Harcourt, 2003: 1) wrote:

> the production function has been a powerful instrument of miseducation. The student of economic theory is taught to write Q = f (L, K), where L is a quantity of labour, K a quantity of capital and Q a rate of output of commodities. He [sic] is instructed to assume all workers alike, and to measure L in man-hours of labour; he is told something about the index-number problem in choosing a unit of output; and then he is hurried on to the next question, in the hope that he will forget to ask in what units K is measured. Before he ever does ask, he has become a professor, and so sloppy habits of thought are handed on from one generation to the next.

Indeed, Robinson criticised the simplistic and unrealistic nature of the neoclassical growth model and in particular its production function, which was based on one produced good, Q, that can either be consumed or accumulated as capital, K. The economists in Cambridge UK effectively undermined neoclassicism thus:

- They stressed that capital and labour were complementary but could not be considered to be perfect substitutes, as neoclassical theory required. In other words, no matter how efficient machines might be, it is impossible to imagine an economy where production involved no workers at all.
- They also challenged the idea that the total amount of capital can be quantitatively determined and monetarily valued in a stable and consistent way.

And their critique was also based on three additional points:

- The 'fallacy of composition', which assumes that it makes sense to talk about production in terms of one homogeneous good, as if all goods produced in the economy were identical.
- The assumption that since goods produced in an economy are exchanged for money, we can consider them homogeneous and that their total amount, or even their total value, can be definitively established.
- That a model which claims to be focused on material production actually relies on a pricing system that cannot have any meaning without a system of money, which is absent from the theory.

9.3 INFLATION AND DEFLATION

Inflation and deflation are key concepts in economics and frequently are topics for discussion among politicians, policy-makers and businesspeople. **Inflation** is defined as an increase in the average level of prices. Notice two elements of this definition: (1) prices have to be increasing for inflation to occur – it is not enough to have only high prices; and (2) to measure inflation we consider an average level of prices. Thus, it is quite possible and quite typical that during periods of inflation some prices increase while others decrease. If we can think of inflation as too much money chasing too few goods, then inflation is caused either by too few goods in relation to the supply of money; or too much money chasing the existing goods. The solution depends on the cause. Inflation is a problem since higher prices reduce the standard of living, especially if the inflation is unanticipated.

Inflation is not new; it has existed in all cultures. In the sixteenth century, for example, when Spanish explorers remitted gold and silver to Spain following their conquests of the Americas, Spaniards noticed that prices were increasing. Although this was certainly not the first instance of inflation and not the last, it affected many people, and the causal link between increased gold and higher prices was quite palpable.

Hyperinflation occurs with severe inflation, usually as a result of excessive monetary creation. Although 'severe' is, of course, subjective, one accepted lower limit is a monthly inflation rate in excess of 50 per cent (Carlin and Soskice, 2015: 517).

Box 9.1 Values and Prices

Oscar Wilde famously defined a cynic as a person who 'knows the price of everything and the value of nothing'. This epigram is witty because it exploits the double meaning of the English word 'value' – and it offers a salutary lesson in the context of this chapter because, as just explained, neoclassical economists have confused these two meanings. In neoclassical economics, as we will shortly discuss in the context of cost–benefit analysis, only items with a price are included. A similar understanding lies behind the willingness of environmentalists to accept the practice of 'costing' nature through the valuation of ecosystem services, because of their belief that money talks, and therefore if something has a price it will acquire enhanced importance.

This is strangely ironic, since for most of us our ethical system of values suggests that the most valuable aspects of life – whether the natural world or the people we love – are priceless. Green economists seek to protect these ultimate sources of value and set them above the melee of the market. Environmental economists define these ultimate values as having 'intrinsic value' but, unlike green economists,[1] they do not find it spiritually problematic to attempt to put a price tag on them. Groucho Marx (1890–1977; no relation to Karl!) quipped about values in this joke: 'These are my principles; if you don't like them, I have others.' Like values, principles are the subject of deep commitment. If they are not, then they serve no purpose. In this sense, the values that we are committed to, the ultimate values by which we lead our lives, are beyond price because no amount of money would persuade us to abandon them.

1. While green and environmental economists might seem to be quite similar, they are not. To give one example: the former rejects neoclassical economics, while the latter is based on it.

Since inflation generally harms people on fixed budgets, you might assume that deflation is much preferred. **Deflation** is defined as a decrease in the average level of prices. The same two elements described above in the inflation definition apply. Actually, however, deflation is worse than inflation, since not only prices decline but also firm profits, asset values, wealth and wages. Deflation usually occurs during depressions (e.g. in the USA during the 1880s and 1930s; in Japan during the 1990s), and its solution requires a dramatic break with existing institutions.

Inflation is caused by too much money chasing too few goods; thus it is solved by either producing more goods and making them available, or by decreasing the amount of money. Since it is easier to do the latter, this is usually the choice. Deflation is caused by not enough money, and, like running an engine without enough oil, there is no quick and painless solution; it often requires an abrupt change from the existing economic regime.

It is interesting that in the USA, periods of deflation were associated with labour strife and social tensions. This should not be surprising, given the definition of deflation. During the 1870s many trade unions of all types formed – capitalist, socialist and anarchist. In addition, the American Federation of Labor (AFL) was born (1886) as a federation of pro-capitalist trade unions. Likewise, during the 1930s deflation, aggressive unionisation of the nation's mass production industries (such as automobiles, steel, rubber, etc.) occurred, culminating in the formation of the Congress of Industrial Organizations (CIO) in 1937. In 1955 the AFL and the CIO merged to form the AFL-CIO, the most important voice of today's American labour movement.

Of course, no discussion of American deflation is complete without reference to the *Wizard of Oz*. The movie was produced in 1939, based on the book by Lyman Frank Baum (1900). Baum was an avid supporter of women's suffrage (as was his mother-in-law), and *The Wonderful Wizard of Oz* was published in a series of Oz books intended for children, yet the references to the economic and political issues of the day were numerous and quite obvious. Baum published his book in the middle of heated debate on the fairness of the US gold standard.

A gold standard directly links the amount of paper money circulating in the economy to the amount of gold. Thus, the amount of paper money available for everyday transactions can only increase with the amount of gold. Since gold was (and is) scarce, this benefited creditors and bankers but disadvantaged debtors (since the nominal value of the debt remained the same, but the real value of the assets used to repay the debt declined – in other words, the borrower was squeezed). Many people wanted to replace the gold standard with silver, given that it was obviously in greater supply.

The gold standard versus silver was a major theme in the 1896 and 1900 US elections. Here are just a few symbols from the *Wizard of Oz* book/movie. The Tin Man: the industrial worker of the Midwest, whose joints were enervated from disuse. The Scarecrow: the Midwest farmer saddled with debt. Dorothy: representing traditional values (it is interesting that Baum was an ardent suffragist, and, at least in our view, Dorothy is infused with progressive values). The yellow brick road: the gold standard. Oz: abbreviation for ounce – gold is measured in ounces. The Cowardly Lion: William Jennings Bryan, presidential candidate. The Wicked Witch of the East/West: financial interests of the east and west. In the book, Dorothy wears empowering silver shoes, which were replaced by ruby slippers in the movie, for cinematic effect.

From time to time, a gold standard is suggested as a means to instil monetary discipline, but if we are to progress toward sustainability, why lock one's currency – which should be local and energetic – with a scarce, artificially created commodity?

9.4 *TECHNIQUE 5*: COMPARING COSTS AND BENEFITS

Because economics as a discipline prides itself on its ability to measure, and on its willingness to deal in costs and prices, economists (especially neoclassical ones) are often asked to calculate the costs and benefits of new projects. Their preferred technique is cost–benefit analysis (CBA), and in this section we explain how it works, along with its limitations. Like the concept of 'utility' that we discussed earlier, CBA is derived from the philosophical approach known as 'utilitarianism' (see Chapter 6). This philosophy suggests that our likes and dislikes in life can be counted, costed and aggregated. Policy-makers can then simply compare costs and benefits, assessing which is greater. If the benefits outweigh the costs, then the project should be undertaken. Although the first CBA study was conducted in France in 1747, on whether to build a bridge, a rigorous methodology did not develop until the 1960s. The steps in CBA include the following:

- **Define the project.** Define the problem, its scope and objectives. What is the event that will occur? What is the null situation (i.e. what exists without the event)? How can we compare them? For example, if we are considering constructing a tunnel under the River Thames, the null situation is not building a tunnel. At this stage it is crucial to ask if there are other alternatives to constructing the project.
- **Determine the relevant time period.** Since by definition the project occurs at a moment in time, the costs and benefits will also occur over time. Thus it is crucial to identify the time period.
- **Identify all stakeholders.** Living, non-living, past, present and future. What about the destruction of habitats which all projects involve? Who represents their interests? And what about stakeholders from the future?
- **Identify and predict the impacts,** both positive and negative. Neoclassical economics assumes that defining and measuring impacts is value-free and, since no ideology is involved, estimates can be made scientifically by the experts.
- **Monetarise all impacts.** All calculations are in monetary values, which means that a monetary cost must be calculated for any positive or negative impact of the proposed action. But why is money used? Although it represents a common metric, it is certainly not without problems. For example, money assumes that all values are *commensurable* – they can be readily transformed into one measurement scale, e.g. dollars; and that all values are *compensable* – a loss in one attribute can be compensated by a gain in another.
- **Compute 'net present value' (NPV) for each alternative.** NPV will depend on the chosen discount rate (see the next section). To calculate NPV we first calculate present value (PV) of all future costs and benefits, then subtract the initial outlay costs. (To calculate PV, see Technique 6 below.)
- **Conduct a sensitivity analysis.** Ask if slight changes in the beginning assumptions result in significant changes in the end results.

- **Choose the project with the lowest costs and the highest benefits.**
- **Revisit the project from time to time** to assess its progress or lack thereof.

While apparently straightforward and easy to use, the CBA approach has significant problems, calling into question its usefulness:

- The CBA assumes not only that we can monetarise costs but also that they can be measured with certainty. But many aspects of the natural world and human community that people value most highly are, literally, 'priceless'. What is the value of clean water? What is the value of functioning wetlands, forests and the ozone layer?
- The CBA is based on an elitist and outdated conception of scientific progress: an expert conceptualises the project and can, without bias, measure its costs and benefits. Since the 'scientist' is an expert, little input is needed from the subjects. It is also assumed that the expert is rational and non-emotional, and is calmly able to compare costs and benefits.[1] The CBA is antithetical to a democracy, in which decisions are made by the people.
- The CBA gives the appearance of being objective and transparent, and it often yields simple numbers that policy-makers can use to justify their actions. But is this really the way people make (or want to make) decisions affecting their livelihoods?
- Research shows that people find it extremely difficult to cost nature or put a price on the loss of a view, for example, because ordinarily they do not make decisions this way. Only the 'rational economic man' makes such decisions, as opposed to real flesh-and-blood people who have to live with the consequences of such decisions.
- Finally, a *discount rate* is used, since costs and benefits may not have equal real value at different periods in time.

The concept of a discount rate is important in economics and will now be explained.

9.5 *TECHNIQUE 6*: DISCOUNTING

The consequences of environmental losses and impacts are likely to be felt many years into the future. In the case of climate change, we may be talking about a generation from now, although, quite clearly, the effects have already started. This represents a significant problem for economists whose techniques are based on markets and prices, since they need to be able to predict prices many years

1. See Earle et al., 2017: 9–11 for an interesting critique of CBA from a student perspective.

ahead. To ostensibly achieve this they use a technique known as **discounting**. This translates the environmental impact from the future into the present. A discount formula is as follows.

If measuring a benefit:

$$PV(B) = B_T/(1+r)^T$$

where r is the discount rate, and B is the benefit accruing in T years' time.

If measuring a cost:

$$PV(C) = C_T/(1+r)^T$$

where r is the discount rate, and C is the cost accruing in T years' time.

This formula diminishes the impact of environmental destruction caused today by making our current actions appear less costly to future generations. One justifying reason is that today's economic growth will provide the necessary pecuniary resources for future generations to devise effective solutions.

When determining the costs and benefits of any economic policy or production process over time, the bottom line (and the most crucial question) depends entirely on the chosen discount rate. The higher the discount rate, the lower the future costs of current actions. But what discount rate should be chosen? Economists differ in their choices: some favour a descriptive approach, which assumes that the discount rate should equal the prevailing interest rate. If interest rates are relatively high, say 5–10 per cent, then the future environmental costs of current actions will weigh very little, since the discount rate significantly diminishes the present value of the distant future.

Here is one example. In November 2011, the UK's Department for Environment, Food & Rural Affairs (DEFRA) conducted a CBA of building a new tunnel under London's River Thames. Its estimated benefits were taken from an earlier study and then revised in line with general growth in GDP and adjusted using a standard discount factor, assuming that the tunnel will last for 100 years.

Relying on estimates from previous studies is known as **benefit transfer**, and is widely used, given that 'conducting a CBA can be both time-consuming and expensive. Often federal and state agencies require quantification of environmental costs and benefits but lack the resources to fund original analyses' (Harris and Roach, 2018: 163). But just because such practice is common, is it intellectually acceptable?

> Of course primary studies are preferable . . . if the resources are available. But benefit transfer does provide an estimate when information would not be available otherwise. Benefit transfer may be more suitable for some situations,

> such as preliminary screening or policy options, and less suitable for other applications, such as determining damages in a legal case.
>
> Ibid.: 162

The economists in the Thames project also increased the estimate of benefits on the assumption that incomes will increase, and because (theoretically) rich people value environmental benefits more. Immediately we can see two of the major criticisms of CBA: it is not a transparent process, instead relying on a number of accounting adjustments (and assumptions) that are difficult for laypeople to understand; and, even worse, it gives the impression of scientific detachment, when it is obviously not (Earle et al., 2017).

Environmental and ecological costs are seldom considered in such projects. There is an obvious cost of greenhouse-gas emissions in the construction of the tunnel. No costs were included for the impact on wildlife or ecosystems, although it is hard to imagine how such a large infrastructure project could fail to impact on local habitats. The 'whole life costs' of the tunnel was estimated at £4.1 billion, while the benefits were estimated between £3 billion and £5.1 billion. In spite of the high uncertainty, it was concluded that the benefits would outweigh the costs. The report accepted that a large number of potential benefits and costs could not be priced and so were not included in the calculations. This was a judgement, based on unproven assumptions about unproven benefits, but one can easily see how these numbers will be used without the limitations cited in the report and in this critique, and then used to rationalise the construction of the Thames tunnel.

A more effective technique, we believe, for assessing the viability of a project from a pluralist and sustainable perspective, is the **deliberative evaluation process** (DEP) coupled with positional analysis.[2] Rather than experts making a decision, a facilitator guides the discussion, giving equal consideration to all stakeholders and all competing ideologies – no one ideology receives preferential treatment. Monetary and non-monetary impacts are separated. The methodology involves system analysis and system dynamics rather than partial equilibrium. Emphasis is on path dependency, irreversibility and the uncertainty principle. The facilitator can guard against the proceedings being usurped by a dominant interest or a powerful speaker. Compared to the elitist CBA, the DEP coupled with positional analysis is pluralist and democratic, although certainly not perfect.

9.6 *TECHNIQUE 7*: DISCOUNTING AND THE CONCEPT OF PRESENT VALUE

If you received $100 today, how much would it be worth in the future? It depends on two factors: the length of time the money is invested and the rate of interest.

2. For an extended analysis from a pluralist perspective, see Söderbaum, 2008: 99–119.

Obviously, the longer the length of time the money is invested, the more the money will be worth; likewise, the higher the rate of interest, the greater the future worth. The following simple formula enables us to calculate the future value (FV) of a present sum of money (PV):

$$(1)\ FV = PV(1 + i)^n$$

Where i equals the rate of interest and n equals the number of time periods.

As can be seen from the above equation, **Present value** – the value today of an amount of money received in the future – works backwards: it begins from a certain amount of money received in the future and determines its worth now. The rate of interest relates the present and future values. Notice from the formula that if the money is not invested (where $i = 0$), then the future and present sums are equal. If we divide both sides of equation 1 by $(1 + i)^n$ then we obtain a formula for calculating the PV:

$$(2)\ PV = FV/(1 + i)^n$$

Three things to notice in equation 2:

- Since the term $(1 + i)^n$ is in the denominator, the process works in reverse from the calculation of the future value; that is, the greater the interest rate, the less is PV now –since today's money can be invested for use in the future.
- The longer the time period (n), the less the PV, given that there is more time to invest.
- This underscores the role of uncertainty – pervasive in everyday life, but assumed away by neoclassical economists: How can anyone know the future with precision? And how can anyone know future interest rates? What does this suggest about inter-temporal pricing?

Let us work out a simple example:

Let's assume we are to receive $100 at the end of two years. We would like to calculate its present value, assuming that 8 per cent is the appropriate interest rate. Using the present value formula, our answer is **$85.73**. This amount tells us that receiving $100 in two years is the same as receiving $85.73 today. Question: What happens to our PV if we increase/decrease the interest rate? Or increase/decrease the number of time periods?

9.7 VALUING NATURE AND THE IDEA OF 'ECOSYSTEM SERVICES'

We have already made clear that our perspective in this textbook is that nature is the ultimate source of value, economic and otherwise; and that our current ecological crisis suggests we are not effectively protecting our vital inheritance. Over the past two decades environmentalists have grown increasingly concerned about this failure to protect the environment, and some have argued that their case would be strengthened if policy-makers understood the value of nature in economic terms. This is how the idea of 'ecosystem services' arose: as a way of communicating the value of nature to people who speak the language of money.

A useful example is pollination and the threat to the world's bees. In all agricultural communities many plants are pollinated by bees, but bees are suffering a collapse in numbers as a result of habitat loss and pollution. Without bees, farmers would have to pollinate by hand. Economists have attempted to value the cost of this labour as an ecosystem service.

Several attempts have been made to calculate the global value of ecosystem services. One of the better known was by Costanza et al. (1997). After acknowledging the difficulty of valuing ecosystems, they estimated the total value of ecosystem services at US$33 trillion[3] within a range of US$17–49 trillion, more than triple the value of conventionally measured global GDP at the time.[4]

There are two problems with valuing ecosystem services:

- First, it assumes that the world and its creatures exist only to serve the human race – what critics call 'anthropocentrism'. Human beings are assumed to be at the centre of the world; everything else, non-living and living, is instrumental. (It should be noted, by the way, that the notion of instrumentality is built into the definition of a resource.) We prefer a biocentric, or ecological, perspective, based on the understanding that human beings are part of an ecosystem. Do bees, or any other species, only have value because of the services they provide us?
- Assigning a value to any species assumes that we can understand the complex role it plays in the whole system of life on Earth, where life is interrelated in ways that scientists struggle to understand, let alone to price.

Green economists are disturbed by this process of pricing nature. They argue that it amounts to 'commodification' of something that they see as having intrinsic value, perhaps even sacred value. If we can cost the Amazon rainforest in terms of the daily resource it provides to people who live there, what can stop a logging company from paying the local people to destroy the rainforest? These economists argue that even putting prices on aspects of the natural world assumes and facilitates sale in the market.[5]

---

3. A trillion is 1,000,000,000,000 (a million million).
4. For an update analysis and an answer to their critics, see Costanza et al. 2014.
5. If you are interested in finding out more about the issues relating to valuing nature, we suggest consulting Pearce (1992) and Sullivan (2013).

THINKING QUESTIONS

If we cannot rely on money to measure the value of what is produced by a factory or a whole economy, how can we make an assessment about their relative success?

Can you explain the difference between the price of a good and its value?

How would you value a human life? Is this even possible? Does it matter if the person is from a developed or developing nation? Does it matter if the person is engaged in risky behaviour?

CLASS ACTIVITY

Construct a production function for the activities that occur in your classroom. What is the output? What are the inputs? What are the factors of production? How are they related? How could you measure each?

AREAS FOR RESEARCH

We can measure inflation by selecting a representative basket of goods and comparing their price changes over a period of time. Consider the main measure of inflation in your country: Is it characteristic of all consumers or just a few? Is the basket of goods representative of all consumers or just a few?

Conduct a critical and reflexive investigation on valuing non-market items. Depending on the context, these might be local environmental sites; threatened species that are an important part of their local bioregion; or social relationships, such as feelings for your best friend or relative. By extension, conduct surveys on other students, family members or members of the public to ascertain how they would carry out such a valuation. Focus on how the decisions and conclusions are reached.

UN SDG FOCUS

Goal #13 is: Take urgent action to combat climate change and its impacts.
Goal #14 is: Conserve and sustainably use the ocean, seas and marine resources.
Goal #15 is: Sustainably manage forests, combat desertification, halt and reverse land degradation, halt biodiversity loss.

These are formidable tasks. The first step is to decide how to take account or measure the existing situation. How would you start? How would you measure the 'impact' of climate change? Can everything be monetarised? How would you value biodiversity, forests and marine resources? How would you 'combat', 'halt' and 'reverse'?

FURTHER READING

Aldred, J. (2009) *The Skeptical Economist: Revealing the Ethics Inside Economics.* London: Earthscan.

Brown, J., Söderbaum, P. and Dereniowska, M. (2017) *Positional Analysis for Sustainable Development: Reconsidering Policy, Economics and Accounting.* London: Routledge.

Heinzerling, L. and Ackerman, F. (2002) *Pricing the Priceless: Cost-Benefit Analysis of Environmental Protection.* Washington: Georgetown University Law Center.

Pearce, D. (1992) *Economic Valuation and the Natural World.* Policy Research Working Paper Series 988, Washington: The World Bank.

Söderbaum, P. (2008) *Understanding Sustainability Economics: Towards Pluralism in Economics.* London: Earthscan.

Sullivan, S. (2013) 'Banking Nature? The Spectacular Financialisation of Environmental Conservation', *Antipode*, Vol. 45, No. 1, pp.198–217.

10
Firms, Industries and Markets

This is a chapter about economic organisation. If economies are about the provisioning of goods and services, then there will be organisations responsible for those tasks. In the previous chapter we noted that people can meet their needs directly from the natural world, and that livelihoods understood in this way have dominated human history and are widespread across the world today. However, in a capitalist economy, goods and services are bought and sold in the market, and this form of organisation is the focus of this chapter. So we will explore what is meant by a market system and ask if this is an efficient way of organising economic life. We will also examine the firm, the most common type of productive unit in a capitalist economy, and consider different ways that firms can be governed internally, and what this means for effectiveness and equity. What type of firm is most consistent with our core values of justice and sustainability? We will also explore the connection between economic efficiency and innovation.

10.1 WHAT IS A FIRM?

In capitalism, producers must organise their resources and their workers in order to transform them into products. Generally speaking, organisation of people in this way is defined as a 'firm'. While it is easy to say what a firm does (i.e. produce goods, employ workers, develop new technologies, etc.), defining it is more difficult. A definition that we like to use is: a **firm** is 'a focal point for a set of transactions amongst interested stakeholders in the production of goods and services'. But what does this mean? Let's examine the definition's key elements:

- 'Focal point' means crux or centre of attention.
- A **stakeholder** is an individual, group or community with an interest in the existence and institutional survival of the firm.
- 'Transactions' implies interaction (negotiating, selling, buying) among the stakeholders.
- 'Set' means that the transactions can be defined and delineated, and enlarged or contracted over time.

A firm can be organised and managed along many dimensions, including:

- size
- for-profit vs non-profit
- type: sole proprietorship, partnership, corporation
- cooperative vs non-cooperative
- sustainable vs non-sustainable.

In the remainder of this section we present a brief overview of the above dimensions, while later in this chapter and the next we discuss the corporation – the dominant type of firm in the twenty-first century – and the cooperative – the centrepiece of tomorrow's sustainable economy.

Let's look in more detail at two of the above dimensions for organising and managing a firm:

- **Size:** Firms can range from the very small (measured by a host of different metrics, such as profits, assets, number of employees) to the very large. What is the ideal size for a firm? And what firm size best comports with sustainability? Is a large firm able to produce more goods cheaper than a small firm? But if so, what does this imply for the power of the firm and how it is used vis-à-vis other stakeholders, especially the community in which it operates? Is it possible for a firm to become so large that it is unable to coordinate its activities? Economics cannot answer this question specifically – only with a 'it depends': it depends on the firm's relationship with its stakeholders, the technology used and the historical evolution of its industry.
- **For-profit** means that a firm is motivated primarily to make a profit (simply defined as total revenue minus total costs), and its modus operandi is defined by its profit-making activities. A **non-profit** firm is often legally designated by the state, requiring special tax status. A cooperative firm (discussed in the next chapter) can be either profit or non-profit.

10.2 DEFINING A CORPORATION

The word 'corporation' is derived from the Latin *corpus*, meaning 'body', from which we also derive the words incorporate, corset, corporal, corps, corpse, corporeal. A **corporation** is a group of people who pool their capital and risk according to a legal agreement and thus acquire particular rights, privileges and responsibility. It emerged during the sixteenth century in Europe as a socially constructed institution in order to minimise the liability of individual investors in risky ventures such as exploration. It is no accident that today's largest businesses are all corporations. Indeed, all large firms are corporations, but not all corporations are large.[1] In addition to minimising risk, the corporation facilitates and enables growth: in fact, without any upper limit, the corporation can grow as large as the total funds its investors are willing to supply.

Early corporations were issued a **charter**, which 'represented a grant from the crown that limited an investor's liability for losses . . . to the amount of his or her investment in it – a right not extended to individual citizens [setting] forth the specific rights and obligations . . .' (Korten, 1995: 55). The charter was issued for a specific time period, usually 20 years, and if during this time the corporation failed to meet its stipulated objectives, the charter would be revoked – a practice fairly typical until the 1860s. But as corporations grew, so did their power and their ability to influence governments that were supposed to regulate them. Due to this growing influence, charters were increasingly issued in perpetuity, effectively freeing corporations from oversight and renewal. In the US Supreme Court case Santa Clara County v. Southern Pacific Railroad (1886), the corporation was ruled a person, protecting it under the US Constitution, including the Bill of Rights and the First Amendment, effectively giving it the right to free speech. Thus, in the eyes of the Court, the corporation, an artificial institution constructed by people, is afforded the same protected rights as individual citizens.

Some early corporations were notorious for exploitation, greed and monopolisation of trade (e.g. the British East India Tea Company (1600–1874); the Dutch East India Company (1602–1799); and Standard Oil (1870–1911)). The latter was one of the few companies dismantled under US antitrust laws. In 1911 it was dismantled into 34 'little Standards', two of which, Standard Oil Company of New Jersey (eventually becoming Esso and then Exxon) and Standard Oil Company of New York (Socony) merged in 1999 to become the world's largest corporation, Exxon Mobil.

But not all corporations were (or are) bad. Indeed, the minimisation of risk enabled the corporation to greatly enlarge its scope and volume of production:

> represent[ing] an important institutional innovation [opening up] enormous new opportunities to advance the interests of human societies – so long as civil society held in check the potential abuse that the concentration of power made possible.
>
> Korten, Ibid: 54–5

But its open-endedness, effectively setting no upper limit on its size, enabled it to grow and increase its power vis-à-vis state and national governments: its

1. Of the ten largest corporations in the world, five are oil/gas companies: China National Petroleum, Sinopec, Royal Dutch Shell, Exxon Mobil and BP; two are car companies: Volkswagon and Toyota; and one is a utility, State Grid, albeit with a strong interest in renewable energy. If we wonder why in 15 years hence almost 80 per cent of our fuel consumption is predicted to be fossil fuels, this is a good reason. *Source:* Fortune Global 2017: http://beta.fortune.com/global500/

ostensible regulators. What began as an institution designed to further human interests devolved into a device to further corporate interest. Indeed, it is quite obvious that today, as Korten (Ibid.: 54) states, 'it is the corporate interest more than the human interest that defines the policy agendas of states and international bodies . . .' In his *Supercapitalism*, Robert Reich (2009), approaching the issue from a liberal perspective, similarly perceives over-powerful corporations to be threatening democracy.

Given its size and immense resources, the corporation has used its power vis-à-vis other stakeholders, especially workers, to shift production across the world. Marx and Engels wrote in *The Communist Manifesto* (1848 [1960]: 6), 'the need of a constantly expanding market for its products chases the bourgeoisie over the whole surface of the globe. It must nestle everywhere, settle everywhere, establish connections everywhere'.

We define a **multinational corporation** as a corporation with a national home base, doing business in more than country; and a **transnational corporation** as a corporation global in scope but rootless in national identification.

While the corporation's goals comport with the overall objectives of capitalism to accumulate capital and increase profits, the corporation does not comport with the overall goals of sustainability. How can it, when its modus vivendi is to ship goods across the world, relying on cheap oil, and more often than not shipping between its own subsidiaries? How can it be sustainable when it possesses and uses immense power vis-à-vis other stakeholders?

In many corporations, the managers and the owners, who may be shareholders or partners not directly involved in managing, are separated. Both are rewarded if the firm is successful – the shareholders will receive dividends and the managers will receive higher pay – but they may conflict over who gets what proportion of the surplus, and how the firm should be run. This is referred to as the '**principal–agent problem**', where the owner (as the principal) employs the manager (as the agent) to run the firm on her behalf. Clearly the managers have much more detailed information about what is happening within the firm, giving them considerable power, especially if they choose not to share this information with shareholders. Will the agent always act in the best interests of the principal? If not (as evidence suggests), how best to align the interests of principal and agent?

In recent years there have been a number of high-profile scandals where firm managers (agents) have deceived the company's owners (principals) and defrauded them of large amounts of money. This has led to questions about the nature of the firm and whether it is (or still can be) an ideal form of organisation of productive activity. In such a situation the 'principals', i.e. the shareholders, will seek to improve firm reporting, thus enhancing the audit process. They may also try to better align their objectives with those of the managers, e.g. creating a system whereby employees own some of the company stock. If managers know that they receive a dividend, reflecting good performance by the firm, rather than just their salary, this incentivises them to ensure that the value of the company is maximised. Shareholders might also insist that the board of directors includes people not employed by the firm, perhaps especially for tasks such as auditing and setting salary rates. The problem of the conflict between owners and employees, as we shall see in the next chapter, can be solved by the cooperative form of enterprise, where the employees actually own the firm.

In recent years corporations have focused on generating maximum value for shareholders, often with negative impacts for other stakeholders. There are

Box 10.1 Joseph Schumpeter on Innovation

Joseph Schumpeter (1883–1950) was born in Austria and later became a professor at Harvard. He was a highly creative economic thinker who contributed to a wide range of economic theory. Here we focus on his ideas about innovation in capitalism. Economists at the time were interested in 'business cycles', an explanation of the periodic 'booms' (rapid expansion) and 'busts' (when the expansion suddenly ends). Schumpeter followed Marx in portraying capitalism as highly dynamic but experiencing a series of crises. He used the Marxist term 'creative destruction' to describe this process, and has since become identified with that phrase. This challenged existing thinking that economies settle at an 'equilibrium' or stationary point, with resources used in the most efficient way to achieve maximum well-being. In contrast, Schumpeter argued that economies evolved through periods of radical and rapid change brought about by challenges to the existing technological or social system:

> the fundamental impulse that sets and keeps the capitalist engine in motion comes from the new consumers' goods, the new methods of production or transportation, the new markets, the new forms of industrial organisation that capitalist enterprise creates.
>
> Schumpeter, 1942: 83

Innovation provides the rationale for this process of **creative destruction** 'that incessantly revolutionises the economic structure from within, incessantly destroying the old one, incessantly creating a new one. This process of creative destruction is the crux of capitalism' (Ibid.; emphasis in original).

An important, almost heroic, role in Schumpeter's theory is played by the individual entrepreneur, whose innovations spur creative destruction, which in turn engenders economic growth. This aspect of the theory has proved popular with contemporary commentators who justify the major social dislocations that often accompany economic transformation, such as the movement from the land into urban areas of many people who live in today's developing economies.

The significant changes to the global economy thanks to the Internet exemplify the process of creative destruction through innovation. The ability of large corporations to maintain production in low-wage economies, while undertaking research and development globally, has greatly increased their profitability, at the same time reducing the prices of consumer goods. However, this process has also had negative impacts, such as the destruction of small retailers who cannot compete

▶

with online retailers, and the difficulties faced by smaller producers without access to the same global production systems.

Today's capitalism is based on unattractive social and ecological traits that threaten the human species. Capitalism, with its profit-driven firms, assumes citizens are competitive. This can have damaging social consequences, as countries compete with each other to reduce wages and employment standards, and consumers engage in consumption-based competition that threatens their psychological well-being. Capitalism also begets inequality, given that competition produces losers and winners. Perhaps most importantly, the very benefits claimed for market systems – their dynamism and compulsion to create innovation and economic growth – lead us to interpret progress in human terms but ignore the ecological limits and carrying capacity of our world.

Several important and highly relevant questions to today's capitalism are raised by Schumpeter's notion of creative destruction: If a firm, no matter what size, fails, should its existence be allowed to continue? Should the government bail it out? How does this comport with Schumpeter's thesis of creative destruction? Is there such a thing as 'too big to fail'? And should the government consider the ethical behaviour of a firm before it decides to invest public money supporting it?

Finally, as professional economists we should mention (and recommend) Schumpeter's *History of Economic Analysis* (1954), for its detailed discussion of the evolution of economics and economic thought.

myriad stakeholders impacted by a firm's activities and to whom the firm has a responsibility, and to whom it should, to some extent, be accountable for its activities we turn to this subject below.

10.3 WHAT IS AN INDUSTRY?

An **industry** is defined as a collection or grouping of firms producing a relatively similar product, such as healthcare, cigarettes, copper, oil, cars, etc.

One of the more interesting questions that all economists wrestle with is: How should an industry be structured? Specifically, should all firms be small; should some be large? Should there only be one firm? Or just a couple? Should the firms be of equal size? How easy should it be for a new firm to enter; or an established one to leave?

Economists have identified the following types of industry structure:

- **Monopoly**: One firm in the industry; in fact, the firm is the industry. **Entry barriers** (defined as economic conditions and/or institutions preventing an existing or potential firm from entering) are significant, due to ownership of key resources, copyrights and patents, giving the firm extensive power. In Western nations, monopolies are banned, given their relative power. A variation of a monopoly is a **cartel**: an agreement between producers to fix prices and output, so that each firm in a cartel acts as one, as if a monopoly.

- **Oligopoly:** A few, large firms within the industry. The keywords 'few' and 'large' are not defined, but their existence renders behaviour interdependent, i.e. one firm cannot act without anticipating the actions of its rivals. This interdependence has led economists to use game theory as a deductive tool to map out strategy.[2] Entry barriers are significant in oligopolies, usually due to economies of scale, mergers and acquisitions. Most of the world's large corporations operate in oligopolies, e.g. oil, nuclear, banking, cigarettes, personal computers, publishing, air travel, beer, solar power, wind power, etc.
- **Monopolistic competition:** Many small firms, each producing a similar product. While entry barriers are low, each possesses a relatively inelastic demand, giving the firm some staying power. Good examples are restaurants, laundry, hair styling, beauty parlours and most services. Given low entry barriers, such industries are attractive for immigrants.
- **Pure/perfect competition:** Small, numerous firms, each producing an identical product. Entry barriers are non-existent, allowing any firm to enter or exit with ease. This is mythical structure that has received undue attention from neoclassical economists (see Box 10.1).

10.4 IS THERE AN IDEAL INDUSTRY STRUCTURE?

This is one of the more interesting questions in economics. And, like most of our questions (especially the more interesting ones), the answer is: it depends. Actually our answer does depend on myriad factors and questions:

- Is the industry young or old? Often a newly established firm, producing a new product without any competitors, is by definition a monopoly, either protected by patents or otherwise. But a mature industry might monopolise in order to preserve the status quo. What might be an 'ideal' type at an early stage of industry development might be problematic at a later stage.

2. Game theory, as it name implies, is a theoretical game, offering theorising strategies rather than empirically based suggestions. Game theory is largely based on the assumptions of neoclassical economics: maximisation, rational behaviour and equilibrium. Although narrowly focused on the specific actions/reactions of the actors, it can still provide powerful insights, based of course on the validity of the underlying assumptions. To give one example: if firm A enters an industry with well-entrenched firms, say the automobile industry, how will the existing firms react? And how will the new entrant react to the initial reactions? In a way, game theory is like a chess game (although some variations involve simultaneous moves, for example, Pepsi and Coke deciding whether to enter ads in the Super Bowl, anticipating each other's reaction; and their reaction to initial reactions). Game theory also works backwards: if we look ahead to a undesirable outcome, what actions can we take now to prevent that, and ensure a favourable outcome?

Box 10.2 A Note on Perfect Competition

It is obvious that the theory of perfect competition describes a market ideal that does not exist in reality, or ever did for that matter. And, even if it existed, it would be highly unstable. Why? Think about this for a moment: What firm would be content with no entry barriers? Why would any firm produce a product identical to another?

The idealisation of perfect competition is a serious issue, since the theory carries considerable weight in discussions about any preferred industry structure. Thus, rather than help explain how an economy works, perfect competition ideologically rationalises what an economic system *should be* like. Paul Deising argued that all ideologies conceptualise an ideal – a utopia – with neoclassical economics locating its utopia in the distant past of the early nineteenth century. This is dangerous because 'Those perspectives whose utopias are in the past perform an ideological function . . . by the actual exercise of power and by idealising some existing institution projected into the past' (Deising, 1982: 327; original emphasis deleted).

The artificially constructed assumptions of identical firms and ease of entry guarantees that individual buyers and sellers will not have power. Thus the so-called 'theory' of perfect competition is proselytising rather than educating. So why even mention it? So you can beware of its mythical, ideological, utopian nature. It also forms the ideological basis of arguments against trade unions and the minimum wage: if we begin from the mythical world of perfect competition, and assume equilibrium, then any 'interference' such as a minimum wage or unionisation law will distort the wonderful workings of perfect competition.

Thus it is helpful to take an evolutionary perspective, as advocated by institutionalists.

- The start-up costs to get a business up and running. Are the initial costs significant, requiring an outlay of capital? An example might be an electrical utility, whereby generators must be built, or distribution lines laid, before production begins; but once the actual production begins, a unit of electricity can be produced cheaply, and the cost often declines as more output is produced. Such a firm is a **natural monopoly**, defined as a firm producing for the entire market and enjoying continuously decreasing costs per unit of production. Traditionally, most neoclassical economists assume that it would be wasteful to have competition (think of multiple, competing generators, and multiple competing lines of distribution); thus, it would be more efficient to award one firm a monopoly, with active government regulation, ensuring a fair price and a fair rate of return.[3]

3. For a critical perspective of natural monopoly, see DiLorenzo (1996). Jeremy Rifkin tells the interesting story of Theodore Vail, president of AT&T during the 1920s. (The telephone was invented in 1876 and AT&T was incorporated in 1885.) Intending to control the US national telephone service, but sensing growing popular demand for regulation, Vail struck 'a deal with Washington [calling] for regulation, hoping it would

- The million-dollar question is: From whose perspective are we to judge if a particular industry structure is ideal? The perspective of the community, financers, retailers, employees, etc.? And, if ideal from one perspective, is it ideal from another? Economics isn't able to answer this a priori; the best we can do is to set up the parameters for active, pluralist debate.
- Although this question is partly answered, it is also crucial to at least ask: By what criteria do we measure the ideal industry? Neoclassical economists idealise firms that use resources most efficiently, that is, produce the greatest output with the least cost. But, as other economists have emphasised (Fullbrook, 2009), this is only one conceptualisation of efficiency, heavily imbued in ideology, and a narrow one at that. Why should this definition be used, instead of, say, equating efficiency with sustainability; or taking efficiency to mean 'best utilising workers' talents in order that they reach their full potential'? Or even jettisoning the use of efficiency in favour of measures of sustainability?

In order to conceptualise these questions, we introduce several important definitions and concepts in the language of economics:

- **Fixed costs** include items like renting office space or staff, to be paid no matter how many products are made and sold.
- **Variable costs** include items like labour, or raw materials. Their quantity, and therefore the cost, is directly proportional to the quantity of output. In contrast, as output increases, fixed costs account for a smaller proportion of total cost.
- **Total cost (TC):** Fixed costs + variable costs.
- **Average total cost (ATC):** Total cost divided by output: TC ÷ Q (where Q = output).
- **Marginal cost (MC):** the additional cost of producing an additional unit: $MC = \Delta TC \div \Delta Q$
- **Economies of scale:** As output increases, even though total costs are increasing, the cost per unit, or the average total cost, decreases. This of course implies that profit per unit is increasing, all else being equal.
- **Diseconomies of scale:** As output increases, even though total costs are increasing, the cost per unit, or the average total cost, increases.
- **Constant returns to scale:** As output increases, the cost per unit, or the average total cost, remains the same.

make his own company the "natural monopoly" the government was looking for . . . As soon as the ink was dry on the contract, AT&T applied for significant rate increases . . . and received them . . . Within five and half months of being 'taken over' by the federal government, the company had secured a 20 per cent increase in its long-distance rates, a far greater return than it had enjoyed when still wrestling with the competitive free-enterprise marketplace' (Rifkin: 2014: 50–1).

Given economies of scale, a firm is often incentivised to expand, usually via: (1) a **horizontal merger** (between firms in the same industry, such as the formation of General Motors in 1908, and US Steel in 1901); (2) a **vertical merger** (between firms at different stages of the production process, as in steel companies such as Bethlehem Steel acquiring coal companies, or, as just recently announced, in 2017: Amazon acquiring Whole Foods; or (3) a **conglomerate merger** (expanding beyond the firm's traditional industry, usually in goods that might be complementary). While most mergers can be categorised into one of these three types, platform capitalism (see Chapter 6) is 'giving rise to a new merger and a new modus operandi, more like rhizomatic connections driven by a permanent effort to place themselves in key platform positions' (Srnicek, 2017: 103–4).

By merging, a firm can use its established position, technical knowledge and market connections to broaden its production range and hence its size and profitability. This in turn increases entry barriers and economic and political power vis-à-vis other stakeholders, while providing additional resources for further expansion. If two firms merge, resulting in a lower ATC, this sends a message to potential firms thinking of entering the industry: only do so if you can produce at a lower ATC. This was the motivation for the formation of General Electric (1891), US Steel (1901) and General Motors (1908), along with many others, as well as for ongoing consolidation in banking, energy and healthcare.

This tendency of firms to become larger, or to join up, in order to have more power in the market is known as **consolidation**, and it is a palpable aspect of today's global economy.

Consolidation in the global music industry, for example, has been intense in recent years, with the industry now dominated by the 'big four': Universal Music Group, Sony and Warner Music Group, together accounting for nearly 75 per cent of the global music market (Music & Copyright Annual Survey, 2017). This nicely illustrates Schumpeter's theory of creative destruction and the stubborn reluctance of firms to surrender their privileged positions as new technologies develop. Another example is the mining industry, which is also becoming highly consolidated, with a small number of multinational corporations – BHP Billiton, Vale and Rio Tinto – now owning most of the world's scarce mineral resources. And likewise with bituminous coal mining: as demand shrinks due to concern over global warming, the less efficient firms go bankrupt, with the remaining firms consolidating, thereby increasing their profitability.

10.5 *TECHNIQUE 8*: CONDUCTING A STAKEHOLDER ANALYSIS

Table 10.2 helps to conceptualise the meaning of 'stakeholders', and forms the basis for conducting a stakeholder analysis.

Perhaps it would be more realistic to present Table 10.2 in three dimensions, in order to depict the embeddedness and mutual dependencies amongst all the

Box 10.3 The Risks of Foreign Investment

One justification often given for the superiority of a globalised economy based on open markets is that capital can flow freely between countries, bringing together the optimal combination of human and material resources to achieve efficient production. But what is the empirical basis for this argument? How secure is foreign capital when it is invested in countries with different economic cultures and histories?

Since the dissolution of the USSR in 1991, Russia has become a highly attractive destination for foreign investment, especially because of its significant oil reserves. However, information from the US State Department suggests that investment conditions in Russia differ from investment conditions in the USA. In Russia, rapid growth in the market economy and a highly educated population are listed as advantages, but political conditions are not so favourable: Russian politicians are wont to investigate businesses that they believe are accumulating unjustifiable levels of profit or not operating in the national interest.

Global firms may also lose their investments when governments nationalise ownership and control of national resources. This is a popular strategy in Latin America. Following his re-election in 2006, for example, Venezuelan President Hugo Chávez nationalised his country's remaining private oil companies. In 2012, Argentina's President Cristina Fernández de Kirchner followed a similar policy, nationalising the oil assets of the Spanish company Repsol. In both cases compensation was paid, with the companies involved disputing the value of their assets, with subsequent legal action.

Perhaps the most well-recorded story of the failure of global investment is that of the Cochabamba Water Revolt. Cochabamba is Bolivia's third largest city, and by 2001 its rapidly growing population had exceeded half a million people. Bolivia is a poor country, where the average wage at the time was approximately US$70 per month. Due to its poverty it had also become indebted to the World Bank and was urgently in need of further loans. In February 1996 the World Bank made the privatisation of Cochabamba's water supply company a condition of a new, urgently needed US$14 million loan. In 1999, Bolivia privatised the country's water, including water that fell as rain. A 40-year contract was signed with a consortium of US corporations led by the engineering giant Bechtel. The US$2.5 billion contract meant that citizens now had to pay monthly water bills of around US$20. Since they could literally no longer afford to pay for water, this led to huge street protests throughout 1999 and 2000. Eventually the Bechtel executives left the country and the government cancelled the contract (Shultz and Draper, 2009).

stakeholders. For example, just as employees have a stake in the firm, the firm also has a stake in the employees. 'Having an interest in', however, is not the same as stating that one stakeholder can exercise power over the other. If we define power as 'the ability to influence outcomes' (see Chapter 4), it is clear that in some situations, one or more stakeholders can exercise power over another. Conceptualising different stakeholders allows both a static analysis (the situation at a moment in time) and a dynamic analysis (how it evolves over time), as the firm, the environment and the stakeholders evolve. A dynamic analysis is especially interesting, since it allows us to investigate how power allows for a changing configuration among stakeholders. This also comports with the historical evolution of Western economies and is a main focus of institutional economists. In addition, conducting a stakeholder analysis can shed some light on the ideal size of the firm (and from whose perspective).

Table 10.2 Stakeholders: A Classification

Classification of stakeholders	*Types of stakeholders involved*
Internal stakeholders	Employers, managers
Connected stakeholders	Customers, suppliers, financiers, distributors, shareholders
External stakeholders	Government, society, local communities, media

Source: Elaborated by the authors from the CIPS (Chartered Institute of Purchasing and Supply) Group (CIPS, 2014).

Conducting a stakeholder analysis successfully depends on being committed to knowing and genuinely working with all one's actual or potential partners/adversaries. For some companies, the idea is more to manage expectations and deflect potentially damaging criticism. However, responsible companies recognise social responsibility that goes beyond the confines of the firm itself. Manchester Metropolitan University (UK) has developed a useful toolkit to undertake a stakeholder analysis, from which the following three steps are taken.

Step 1: Identify the stakeholders

This can be very complex. It is best undertaken through a brainstorming exercise, following which company executives must decide the most important stakeholders and how they should be kept informed and allowed to participate in decisions.

Step 2: Prioritise the stakeholders

Sometimes a 'power grid' is used to assess potential stakeholders according to two elements: how interested they are in the activities of the firm, and their power in affecting the firm's operation and outcomes. From the point of view of the profit-driven firm, the most important stakeholders are those with a high degree of power who are also very interested in the firm's business. They need to be kept fully informed and aligned with company decision-making. Powerful stakeholders with a low level of interest also need to be given information, but not as much. The ethical behaviour of a firm can be judged by how it deals with its less powerful stakeholders. Companies whose commitment to corporate responsibility is superficial, or intended for marketing purposes, are likely to give interested but powerless stakeholders heavily slanted information, and to prevent them from discovering potentially damaging information about the firm. More ethical firms, however, may use such individuals or groups as useful sounding boards for potentially controversial new strategies or policies.

There are also interesting questions about how a company assesses a stakeholder's potential power. For example, any large corporation is likely to maintain friendly relations with politicians responsible for regulating their industry, but what about campaigners? Do they also constitute powerful stakeholders? Helen Steel and Dave Morris, for example, were two stakeholders heavily interested in the activities of the global fast-food giant McDonald's. McDonald's, in turn, judged them to have a low degree of power and so did not engage with them. As members of London Greenpeace they distributed leaflets outside company premises criticising its environmental record and food quality. In 1990 McDonald's sued the pair for libel, beginning the longest legal trial in England. The outcome resulted in quite negative publicity for McDonald's: The judge ruled that they produced misleading advertising that exploited children; that they paid low wages and were responsible for cruelty to animals. Steel and Morris were found guilty of libel on aspects of unsubstantiated claims, and were ordered to pay £60,000 in damages. In a later appeal, the Court of Appeal ruled that if one eats enough McDonald's food, one's diet may well become high in fat . . . with the very real risk of heart disease: a statement that was clearly damaging to McDonald's. Through poor management of stakeholders, its global reputation was undermined.

Step 3: Map your stakeholders

Key individuals and groups can be plotted onto a stakeholder map, allowing a visual conceptualisation. This will enable the firm to devise appropriate strategies to deal with them in terms of engagement, consultation, information and dealing with conflicts of objectives.

10.6 EXTERNALITIES

As we discussed in Chapter 1 of this textbook, neoclassical economics developed in the late nineteenth century, when little attention was directed to the environment. Back then, it was assumed by most (but certainly not all) that the firm should focus on producing a product, while anything else, especially the harmful dumping of wastes, was excused (and thereby justified) as secondary to its main objective. The capitalist firm received a carte blanche to pollute, sanctioned by neoclassical economics. Pollution became synonymous with economic progress.

Neoclassical economists refer to the harmful *ex-post* effects of market transactions as **negative externalities**: the unintended consequences of a market transaction on an innocent third party. Quite often these innocents are non-humans and the unborn of future generations.

While this nineteenth-century view is longer ethically tenable, it is surprising that neoclassical economists still advocate separating the harmful environmental effects of production from the actual process of production (especially the firm's relationship to the environment), focusing on the former while ignoring the latter. Rather than focus attention on developing new technologies *ex ante*, or new visions of production in which the firm produces within its ecological boundaries – becoming part of the environment rather than separate from it – or developing products that are much more amenable to multiple users rather than a quick fix for immediate consumption (Braungart and McDonough, 2009), neoclassical economists focus exclusively on fixing the externality.

Their suggested solution is simple yet highly misleading: force the culpable buyer and seller to internalize the externality. This is done via a two-step process of first recognising and measuring the negative externality; then imposing a tax (also known as a Pigovian tax, from the British economist Arthur Pigou's influential book *Economics of Welfare* (1920 [1986])) to the negative damage. Not only is the idea of a tax on environmental damage quaint and misleading, but it also assumes that all things have a price, and that resulting costs can be easily measured. Contemporary public policy, largely influenced by neoclassical economics, tries to redress environmental damage after the fact, often with Pigovian taxes, which reinforces the mindset that such polluting behaviour is OK, and that its after-effects can be solved with the proper nudging. This, as we discussed in Chapter 2, is a business-as-usual veneer of sustainability.

Our position, which we believe comports with justice, sustainability and the UN 17 SDGs, is not to slap taxes and regulations on businesses to solve negative externalities, for

> a regulation is a signal of design failure. In fact, it is what we call a *license to harm*: a permit issued by a government to an industry so that it may dispense sickness, destruction, and death at an 'acceptable' rate. But . . . good design can require no regulation at all.
>
> Braungart and McDonough, 2009: 61; emphasis in original

Rather, we agree with Braungart and McDonough (2009) that we must rethink *how* we design goods and services, how we produce goods and services, and how we conceptualise both the process of production and the process of consumption, by:

- Ensuring that the resources used are organic and non-polluting.
- Comporting the production process with the local environment so that the process and the firm become part of it.
- Reconceptualising the product so that it is amenable to sharing across many owners rather than one; maximising long-term usage rather than short-term growth.
- When the product's useful life is over, allowing its components and constituent parts to be recycled, used in other goods, or simply returned to the environment.

Putting these together, rather than redesign, let's reinvent. Take the car, for example:

> Instead of aiming to create cars with minimal or zero negative emissions, imagine cars designed to release *positive* emissions and generate other nutritious effects on the environment. [Imagine that] the car's engine is treated like a chemical plant modelled on natural systems. Everything the car emits is nutritious for nature or industries. As it burns fuel, the water vapour in its emissions could be captured, turned back into water, and made use of. (Currently the average car emits approximately four fifths of a gallon of water vapour into the air for every gallon of gas it burns.) . . . Develop the means to use nitrous oxide as a fertiliser and configure our car to make and store as much as possible while driving. Instead of releasing the carbon the car produces when burning gasoline as carbon dioxide, why not store it in black canisters that could be sold to rubber manufactures? Using fluid mechanics, tires could be designed to attract and capture harmful particles, thus cleaning the air instead of further dirtying it. And, of course, after the end of its useful life, all the car's materials go back to the biological or technical cycle.
>
> Ibid.: 179; emphasis in original

While capitalism, with its profit-maximising firm, is expected to overproduce negative externalities, it is also expected to under-produce **positive externalities**, defined as unintended beneficial effects on an innocent third party. An example of a positive externality is an inoculation against a specific disease or illness: the more people inoculated, the less likely the disease will spread. Thus all benefit, even those not inoculated. Another example is networks: when an additional individual joins a network, this benefits all, since it increases the potential information available and the number of buyers and sellers.

A suggested 'solution' for positive externalities is for the government to subsidise new or existing users; another solution is for the government to help construct the needed infrastructure. So for example, an additional person switching from fossil fuels to renewable energy engenders positive externalities on the rest of us, by reducing the pollutants and carcinogens in the air. Thus, a legitimate government activity is to encourage such behaviour by offering subsidies to the firm and/or the consumer.

10.7 CONCLUSION

Korten (1995: 324) suggests that 'the global institutions of money have only the power we yield to them. It is our power. We can reclaim it.' Very true, but easier said than done! But how to reclaim so that the firm, and especially the corporation, comport with sustainability? Perhaps start with the government: since the corporation is a creature of government, it should also be regulated by the government. But, at the same time, are corporations too large and powerful to be reined in (and controlled) by any government? Transforming the corporation to align it with human interest and sustainability must begin with you and I as individuals. We must coordinate our efforts and work at the local level to develop the appropriate institutions. This in turn is a function of education and of the ability and willingness of individuals to understand and construct institutions to serve the human interest at the local level. One of the lessons of this book is that *we* can construct our own institutions to take back our economy and to help us provision within an overall context of sustainability.

THINKING QUESTION

What value judgments are necessary for a different system to work, say one based on cooperation rather than competition? Which is more amenable for sustainability?

CLASS ACTIVITIES

Compare the income of the largest corporations with the income (GDP) of the largest nations. Combine the rankings. What are your findings?

Research the consolidation of different industries over the past 30 years. How many companies were powerful players in 1980 and how many today? What impact has this had on competition? What has been the role of technology?

AREAS FOR RESEARCH

What is the life expectancy of the typical firm? Does it differ by size or type of firm?

Select a company that you are familiar with. Undertake a complete stakeholder analysis.

UN SDG FOCUS

Obviously the firm is critical in any economic system. Which type of firm is most conducive to achieving the UN 17 SDGs? Which type of firm is the least conducive? Is there a new type of firm (not yet imagined) that might be most effective?

FURTHER READING

Birch, K., Peacock, M., Wellen, R., Hossein, C. S., Scott, S. and Salazar, A. (2017) *Business and Society: A Critical Introduction*. London: Zed Books.

Braungart, M. and McDonough, W. (2009) *Cradle to Cradle: Remaking the Way We Make Things*. London: Vintage.

Korten, D. (1995) *When Corporations Rule the World*. West Hartford, Connecticut: Kumarian Press.

Madden, B. J. (2016) *Value Creation Thinking*. Naperville, Illinois: LearningWhatWorks.

Shultz, J. and Draper, M. (2009) *Dignity and Defiance: Stories from Bolivia's Challenge to Globalization*. Berkeley: University of California Press.

Stout, L. (2012) *The Shareholder Value Myth*, San Francisco: Berrett-Koehler.

Even the Rain (2010) (the film of the Cochabamba water protests), www.eventherainmovie.com

11
Economic Democracy

Apart from the lucky few, most of us are born into the world owning very little. The resources enabling the creation of economic value – land, factories, stocks and shares, etc. – are already owned by others, and we will spend most of our lives working hard just to acquire a few personal assets such as a home and maybe a pension. Marx referred to capitalism as 'wage slavery' because unless you work for somebody who controls the system of production and pays you a wage, you will starve. This is also referred to as 'generalised market dependence' (Srnicek, 2017: 11), since one is no longer free to choose whether or not to work; and, conversely, in order to accrue the necessary items for survival, one must purchase them in the market. In this chapter we will question whether such an allocation of initial resources is morally justified and how we might think about resources owned in common rather than by individuals. We will also consider firms where, rather than a small number of people owning them and taking the value as profits, workers themselves own them and keep all the value of their work.

11.1 WHO OWNS THE ECONOMY?

Table 11.1 illustrates the formal ownership of stock in US companies, according to Gallup (see notes to table). The percentage has steadily decreased to 52 per cent in 2016, matching its historical low of 52 per cent in 2013 and considerably lower than its peak of 65 per cent in 2007, as McCarthy explains:

> recession and big market losses took their toll on Americans' sense of job security, confidence in the economy and financial means to invest, as well as their general confidence in stocks as a place to invest their money. [And] although Americans in all income groups are less likely to have stock investments than before the Great Recession, middle-class Americans have been the most likely to flee the market.
>
> McCarthy, 2016

In Chapter 3, we saw that resources are key to the working of any economy, and began to explore how resources are owned and used. Historically, many ways of considering who 'owns' the resources, and who has the right to use them, have developed. Many societies considered that the available resources, say the animals roaming the forests or the fish in the sea, belonged to all as a community, and they developed social systems for sharing those resources. This is still true of some communities today. We call these resources that people own on a shared basis the **commons**.

Table 11.1 Percentage of US Adults Who Own Stocks

Year (data closest to April of each year)	*Percentage of adults*
1999	60
2005	62
2007	65
2008	62
2010	56
2013	52
2016	52

Notes: (1) Percentage of adults responding positively to the question 'Do you, personally, or jointly with a spouse, have any money invested in the stock market right now – either in an individual stock, a stock mutual fund, or in a self-directed 401(k) or IRA? (2) Gallup first began collecting data on this issue in 1999.

Source: Elaborated by the authors; data from Gallup's Economics and Personal Finance Survey (various years): www.gallup.com/poll/162353/stock-ownership-stays-record-low.aspx

The growth of capitalism was mirrored by the decline of 'self-provisioning', i.e. using resources owned in common to provide for one's needs. For example, rather than buying food at the shop you grew it on an allotment; or rather than earning money to buy clothes or shoes you cut down a tree and made it into furniture to exchange for other needed items. If you wanted to move into your own home you could choose a piece of land and build a house on it. Increased density of population and the need to coordinate people's actions to avoid conflict have rendered self-provisioning no longer viable, in addition to ownership of land and resources becoming more concentrated.

From our perspective, these are important issues, since certain economic systems place a different emphasis on the right to private property relative to the right of access to commonly owned resources. Generally speaking, if societies focus more on private ownership, as in capitalism, access to shared resources becomes diminished, with greater reliance on the labour market and the sale of labour-power to guarantee individuals a contented life. In systems where assets are owned primarily by the state, as under socialism, livelihood depends on adherence to a set of politically determined values, and scope for collaborative economies based on solidarity is also radically diminished. However, there are different possible systems of organisation where access to productive assets, particularly land, is protected.

In countries where capitalism is less firmly entrenched, a large segment of the population has access to a small area of land on which they can produce food for their own consumption. In the Czech Republic these areas are known as *zahradky* ('little gardens'); in the Philippines they are the result of a recent process of land reform, with families claiming title to land to ensure that small plots are available to all families; in Brazil they result from claims made under the country's law that land not being used productively should be reallocated.

11.2 PUBLIC GOODS

A **public good** is defined as a good available to all, whereby use by one individual does not preclude use by another.

The classic example is a sunset, which is available to all, whereby one's enjoyment does not reduce another's enjoyment. To say that a public good is enjoyed by all means that it is **nonexclusive** (i.e. no one is excluded from enjoying the good); and to say that one person's use does not reduce the availability for others means that good is **non-rival**.

Contrast this with a typical **private good**, like an car, which is only available to the buyer, meaning that it is both excludable (the price excludes) and rival, since my purchase reduces the amount available for others. Since firms cannot capture all the benefits of producing a public good and make a profit, they will either under-produce or not produce them. Thus it is recommended that the government should produce public goods such as national defence, highway systems, and communication systems like the Internet and public radio.

While the difference between national defence as a public good and a car as a private good are distinct and clear, quite often the distinction has a lot of grey areas and overlaps. Is clean water a public good or private good? But if the former, why are some firms trying to monopolise and profit from its sale?

Negative externalities (see Chapter 10) can reduce the viability and amount of a public good. For example, air pollution due to the burning of coal in nineteenth-century London contributed to both killer fogs and less frequent visible sunsets.

11.3 ELINOR OSTROM AND MANAGING THE COMMONS

We welcomed Elinor Ostrom's receipt of the Bank of Sweden's Prize in Economics in 2009. Not only was she the first woman to win the Nobel Prize[1] but also her

1. Although often referred to as the Nobel Prize in Economics, it is officially known as the Sveriges Riksbank (Bank of Sweden) Prize in Economic Sciences in Memory of Alfred Nobel. It is awarded annually by the Royal Swedish Academy of Sciences. When Alfred Nobel died in 1895, he left in his will instructions to distribute annual prize money to physics, chemistry, literature, peace and medicine/physiology; economics was omitted. The Bank of Sweden initiated their annual prize in economics (in memory of Alfred Nobel) in 1969.

work suggests the importance of pluralism and moving beyond the traditional boundaries separating the social sciences. At the same time, Ostrom shares many values of neoclassical economics, as well as its proclivity to parry dissenting views. Nevertheless, her work on the commons represents an important stepping stone and perhaps a move towards more open dialogue and a greater understanding of the problems confronting our generation.

Ostrom urged active cooperation between and among the social sciences, and engaging in fieldwork (as opposed to deductive logic) from which we can learn the 'immense diversity of situations in which humans interact'. Such empirical investigations will indeed bring us far beyond the traditional dualistic thinking of state versus market (see below), so typical in neoclassical economics. This sounds like simplistic advice, but unfortunately neoclassical economics has often emphasised the opposite: begin with ahistorical assumptions taken as true, and then deductively demonstrate consequences.

But as we conceptualise the different possibilities of managing the commons, it is also imperative to explicitly recognise, conceptualise and investigate *power* in all its manifestations. Who has power will determine who benefits from existing institutional relationships. If, as Ostrom argues, effective communication is often a vehicle for articulating rights, this must occur with an explicit recognition of power in existing institutional relationships. How should we develop institutions to challenge abuse and exploitation inherent in any power relationship? If power is recognised and appropriate institutions conceptualised (and designed) then the 'inherent logic of the commons which assumes tragedy as inexorable' (Hardin, 1968: 1244) can be avoided.

In addition, it is just as important to investigate existing regimes of private property, which can often prevent transition to a sustainable society and prevent any counter-suggestion, especially since ownership of key resources, which should be common to all, can lead to overexploitation and ecological degradation. Indeed the private ownership of what should be common resources is often the cause of such degradation.

Ostrom outlined many types of social organisation of resources that actually exist in practice. This is refreshing, because economic theory tends to draw a simple but false dichotomy between private market systems labelled as 'capitalism', and state-ownership systems labelled as 'socialism'. The reality is that for most of human history neither has operated, and that in many places we find more socially embedded systems of asset management. Contemporary theorists are beginning to include this shared approach to assets and resources under the heading of 'commons'.

The word 'common' means something shared between a group of people, as in the 'commune' of the early Christians, who shared what they owned; or the communes of 1960s hippies, who took a similar approach to property. Gary Snyder described the commons as 'a curious and elegant social institution within which human beings once lived free political lives while weaving through natural systems' (Snyder, 1990: 40). Under economic systems based on the commons, one had a right to use resources that could support one's life, simply by virtue of being a member of the community rather than possessing a legal right or doing a certain amount of work. The use of common resources was socially organised, so that people's needs were met without individuals being allowed to over-exploit resources:

> the commoner could only turn out to common range as many head of cattle as he could feed over the winter in his own corrals. This meant that no one was allowed to increase his herd from outside with a cattle drive just for summer grazing. (This was known in Norman legal language as the rule of *levancy and couchancy*: you could only run the stock that you actually had 'standing and sleeping' within winter quarters.)
>
> Ibid.: 33

Rules protected the vulnerable, e.g. widows and their children were allowed to gather grain that had fallen during the harvest (a right known as 'gleaning'); people were allowed to gather wood for their fires, to graze their pigs in the woodland, and to gather nuts and berries. Although these may sound like marginal sources of food and fuel, Humphries (1990: 31) calculated that 'the annual income from the cow was often more than half the adult male labourer's wage, and an average-priced cow would pay for itself in about a year'.

11.4 COOPERATIVES AND WORKER-MANAGED FIRMS

Given the present-day crisis of confidence in corporations, there is considerable interest in enterprises that both share profits more widely with their employees and also enable participatory decision-making. The most widespread alternative form of ownership is the **cooperative**. According to the International Cooperative Alliance (founded in 1895), a cooperative is

> an autonomous association of persons united voluntarily to meet their common economic, social and cultural needs and aspirations through a jointly owned and democratically controlled enterprise.
>
> ICA, 2017

Cooperatives are usually divided into three types:

- **Worker cooperatives:** The employees who produce the product also manage the workplace.

- **Consumer cooperatives:** More like retail clubs, where people work together to buy goods or services of better quality at a lower price. Financial cooperatives such as building societies also fall into this category.
- **Cooperative consortia:** Family firms or small business share some services, and/or cooperate together to get a better price for their product. Many cooperative consortia are in the agriculture sector, such as dairy cooperatives.

Cooperatives serve the interests of either their employees or their customers rather than of external shareholders. Members actively decide the cooperative's direction and strategy. So, if you become a member of a retail cooperative, for example, you could vote to stop buying unfairly traded coffee; and as part of a worker cooperative you could vote to set your own rates of pay. This is not as liberating as it sounds, since you must (along with the other members) ensure the viability of the enterprise. So in a cooperative you have to take your responsibility as an owner very seriously.

Cooperatives represent a significant element of modern economies. As of 2016 there were 2.6 million cooperatives globally, with approximately 1 billion members. In the G20 countries, cooperative employment comprises approximately 12 per cent of employment. (ICA, 2017). In Africa, agricultural cooperatives help ensure that small producers receive a good price for their tea, coffee or cocoa crop; more than 40 per cent of the population of Africa belongs to a cooperative. Similarly, in India, much of the dairy and rural agriculture is organised through cooperatives, which underpin the livelihoods of two-thirds of the rural population.

People's decisions about purchasing may be based on strong moral or religious commitments, (e.g. the growth in the fair trade movement). We also argue that the division into producers and consumer is problematic: after all, most of us have jobs (or would like to have one) and we are also buyers. In fact, given the changing technology which enables buyers to produce and to make available (and to freely share), a new term has emerged: **prosumer** – consumers who have become their own producers (Rifkin, 2014: 4). The artificial and historically antiquated division between buyer and seller; and producer and consumer can become damaging (and exploitative) if pressure to reduce costs and seek the lowest price threatens our own employment conditions and our own livelihoods. Unfortunately, it already has.

The central theme in cooperative thought is the importance of sharing the benefits of labour between everyone involved in its production, and balancing their competing interests within the business. As Brown (2004: 24) writes:

> All enterprises need employees, customers and investors in order to function in a market economy. These stakeholders have competing economic interests

in the enterprise: employees want higher wages, customers want cheaper products and investors want bigger returns. The aim of cooperatives is to reconcile the competing interests of stakeholders by operating within an ethical code of values and principles, where interests are aligned in pursuit of a common social purpose. Cooperatives must also produce wealth that can be shared by all the stakeholders. The best measure of this wealth-creating ability is productivity not profitability. Higher productivity benefits all the stakeholders.

Cooperatives actively enforce and promulgate their own principles of governance. The following are the values of the International Co-operative Alliance (ICA, 2017), largely based on the principles of the original Rochdale Society (see Box 11.1):

- Voluntary membership – no discrimination.
- Democratically run and controlled, with each member enjoying a single vote.
- Members contribute to the capital of their organisation.
- Every cooperative is autonomous and independent.
- Each provides education and training for its members.
- Cooperation among cooperatives: members are served most effectively by broadening the network of cooperatives.
- Each cooperative works for the sustainable development of its members.

The most recent financial crisis showcased the resilience of the cooperative model, with cooperative banks and credit unions (financial cooperatives) much less subject to collapse than their market rivals. Rabobank, the Dutch Cooperative Bank, for example, increased its market share to 43 per cent; while building societies, a form of mutual savings institutions, also saw deposits increase. **Credit unions**, a sort of financial club where people lend and borrow from each other at different points in their lives, when they have more or less access to financial resources, are particularly popular in Canada, where one in three people are members.

Cooperatives can also be used to take back control of ownership, and sometimes the very soul, of our cities and towns. One example is a cooperative founded by Bar25 regulars in Berlin, who rented land on the River Spree in central Berlin to construct a 12,000 square-metre cooperative containing a nightclub, a studio for acrobats, a nursery, a children's theatre, and a canteen for the 300 people working on the site (Ottermann, 2017). Rather than letting such prime land go to the highest bidder for luxury residences, the cooperative took charge and developed a much more open and welcoming enterprise.

And finally, as changing technology forces the marginal cost of producing many goods and services to near-zero, and as more economic activity takes place in the commons, the obvious question becomes: Is the typical capitalist firm capable of helping us to provision? Or is a cooperative firm intrinsically more capable? Jeremy Rifkin (2014: 221) is quite clear:

> The capitalist mode of private ownership, in which each firm is an island unto itself and attempts to gather economic activity vertically under one roof to achieve economies of scale, is incapable, by dint of its very operational features, to manage activities that require the active collaboration of thousands of players in laterally scaled operations. [Such a] firm will attempt to optimize its own temporal flow at the expenses of others, leading only to greater congestion in the network and a loss of operability, affecting every company in the system and resulting in a tragedy that goes with an unmanaged commons.

And, even more direct and forthright, Rifkin writes (Ibid.: 214), 'Cooperatives are the only business model that will work in a near zero marginal cost society.'

Box 11.1 The History of the Cooperative Movement

The impulse for the growth of the cooperative movement arose from a critique of capitalist production suggesting that a significant amount of value created by labour was extracted by owners. This argument was hotly debated in the British parliament in the nineteenth century. Some liberal economists, including John Stuart Mill (1806–73), supported the right of working people to become entrepreneurs in their own right. They argued for a change in the law to enable working people to finance productive activity that they themselves owned. This eventually became the Industrial and Provident Societies Act of 1852, which still governs the operation of cooperatives in the UK today.

The cooperative idea is to remove external owners such that the employees themselves own the firm and/or control their own work; so that any surplus generated will either be reinvested in the firm or paid to employees as bonuses. Robert Owen (1771–1858), known as the 'father of the cooperative', argued that the capitalist system 'has made man ignorantly individually selfish; placed him in opposition to his fellows; engendered fraud and deceit; blindly urged him forward to create but deprived him of the wisdom to enjoy'. Owen rose rapidly during industrialisation to become the manager of one of the largest woollen mills in the country, at New Lanark in Scotland. He first tried to improve factory conditions for workers, but later went one step further, advocating that they should own their own factories and keep the total value of production.

In Britain, the cooperative movement began with consumers rather than producers. The rapid expansion of woollen and then cotton production sucked thousands of people into urban centres, such as the Lancashire town of Rochdale,

▶

away from working the land.[1] For the first time they had to buy most of their food from shops, which had a monopoly and often sold low-quality food at high prices. People became vulnerable to exploitation from dishonest shopkeepers who 'adulterated' food by adding chalk, dust and other impurities. In 1844 in Rochdale, a group of local people established a buying cooperative to prevent shop-owner exploitation. Known as the 'Rochdale Society of Equitable Pioneers', their cooperative is still a major player in the UK today.

This is often celebrated as the birth of the cooperative movement, but actually it was just the start of cooperative retail, rather than production. The Rochdale Pioneers were not the first to create a cooperative, but rather the first to work out a clear system for organising their cooperative, with a membership structure and clear rules of operation. The Pioneers operated according to principles of open membership, democratic control, political and religious neutrality, cash trading and the promotion of education. These principles form the basis of the values still followed by the International Co-operative Alliance (ICA, 2017), which we explained above in the text.

Cooperatives also developed as working people found ways to solve their economic problems by working jointly for the benefit of all, in strong contrast to the capitalist firm, where a person with assets creates a private solution which is then sold to individuals with wants, with profits accruing to the individual entrepreneur. After the success of the food cooperatives, the building society was created in order to enable working people to save money to buy their own homes, to avoid the profiteering of private landlords. This was followed by a whole range of other services, such as mutual insurance, funeral services, medical treatment, and financial support in times of vulnerability and dependence (Birchall, 2011).

The story of the cooperative movement is thus a story of working people coming together to meet their own needs when workplaces were exploitative and governments felt no obligation to provide what are now considered essential public services.

In Britain – the 'nation of shopkeepers' – the consumer cooperative was the main focus, whereas in continental Europe cooperatives focused more on the production side of the economy and grew into a movement known as **syndicalism**, which sought worker control of firms. In France it was the craft-workers or artisans who felt exploited and developed the idea of syndicalism, with skilled workers taking control of production. This model of cooperative production also spread to Spain and Italy. In Spain it was a major source of strength in the fight to maintain the left-wing democratic government in the face of fascist attacks led by Franco. In Italy it led to the establishment of networks of cooperative production and exchange, particularly in the region of Emilia-Romagna.

▶

1. 'The enclosure movement', as it became known, was instrumental in transforming and uprooting people from the land, laying the economic foundation for capitalism. The enclosures, centred in England, occurred in several waves during the period 1500–1800. Regarding causation, Rifkin notes (2014: 31), 'rising demand for food, occasioned by a burgeoning urban population, triggered an inflationary spiral, placing increasing hardships on feudal landlords whose land rents were fixed at preinflationary rates. At the same time, an incipient textile industry was forcing up the price of wool, making it more financially lucrative for landlords to enclose communal land and switch over to raising sheep.'

In the Basque country, in Spain, the Mondragon Corporation is the world's most successful producer cooperative and a beacon for worker-managed firms. The movement began when a local priest, José María Arizmendiarrieta, founded a technical school in the 1940s because of his conviction that knowledge was the key to economic success. In 1956, several of his students started the first producer cooperative, Fagor, which has grown to become a European leader in the production of domestic electrical goods. The Mondragon Corporation now consists of 67 industrial enterprises, eight involved in distribution and fifteen which serve the group as a whole, primarily in the educational field. It also has Eroski, the leading chain of hypermarkets in northern Spain and with outlets throughout the country, and Caja Laboral, the workers' bank, which provides reasonably priced investment capital to other businesses in the group. The harsh winds of globalisation have pressured the guiding vision of Mondragon, with production capacity now partly offshored and workers outside Spain not invited to join the cooperative. But as an organisation it still meets its core cooperative principles.

11.5 THE JOHN LEWIS PARTNERSHIP

The cooperative is not the only alternative to the standard firm. The John Lewis partnership in the UK is an interesting example of a hybrid firm with some characteristics of a cooperative. According to the company website:

> Spedan Lewis was committed to establishing 'a better form of business', and the challenge for Partners of today is to prove that a business which is not driven by the demands of outside shareholders and which sets high standards of behaviour can flourish in the competitive conditions of the third millennium. Indeed, we aim to demonstrate that adhering to these Principles and Rules enables us over the long term to outperform companies with conventional ownership structures.

The John Lewis Partnership is certainly a different kind of business. The company is named after the son of its founder, John Spedan Lewis, who undertook an 'experiment in industrial democracy' by trusting his workers to run their own company, and by signing away his personal ownership rights in the process when he effectively gave the company to its workers in 1929. The business is owned by a trust whose constitution states that its ultimate purpose is to ensure employees having a satisfying job in a successful business. Employees, known as 'partners', face entirely different motivations from conventional employees, since it is recognised that the success of the business is their responsibility. And if the business does well, they receive a share of the profits. Each year this dividend is announced as a percentage of each employee's salary. Although employees at John Lewis do not have the same power as members of a cooperative, they still have a role through their ability to elect one of the three main controlling bodies, in addition to electing five of the members of the partnership council, which is the main decision-making body.

Box 11.2 Reclaimed Companies (*Empresas Recuperadas*) in Argentina

The economic crisis in Argentina that began in December 2001 saw increased bankruptcies, foreclosures and poverty among the lower and middle classes. Banks were reluctant to lend, and entrepreneurs were afraid to invest, so workers took power into their own hands, taking over the factories where they had previously worked – a phenomenon that became known as ***empresas recuperadas*** or 'reclaimed companies'. It is now a social movement whose objective is to resume production in order to maintain workers' livelihoods. The emergence of the *empresas recuperadas* is closely linked to the evolution of social vulnerability that resulted from neoliberal economic policies. Since the 1970s, financial and trade liberalisation, stabilisation and privatisation negatively impacted the labour market. As a result, precarious work has significantly increased, along with the weakening of labour rights, such as the minimum wage and secure employment.

Most of the *empresas recuperadas* have an urban and industrial bias, with 70–80 per cent of such workers belonging to this sector; the remaining 20–30 per cent are in the service sector. As of 2013, in Argentina there were 350 *empresas recuperadas*, employing nearly 25,000 workers. The majority are located in urban conglomerates, with 80 per cent residing in Buenos Aires and its suburbs. They negotiate with company owners or the courts in order to achieve temporary expropriation by the state. 'Recuperation' implies a new legal structure in which workers take over responsibility for production and management. At the beginning of the recuperation process, there were numerous potential difficulties faced by the workers, relating to the legal status of the property, the lack of capital and limited access to credit, lack of qualifications, lack of information and cooperative education, debts to suppliers, commercialisation and technological problems.

Source: Howarth (2007).

11.6 A PARTICIPATORY ECONOMY

So far we have questioned how assets are owned in capitalism and considered firms organised along cooperative lines, while emphasising participation and equity. But what about the organisation of society as a whole? Can we, as citizens, become more involved in political decisions that affect our economic well-being? In many countries our involvement is limited to voting for representatives on the local council, or perhaps standing for election ourselves. But in Brazil there are exciting developments involving communities in deciding how their paid local taxes are used to improve their community. This process of inclusion and empowerment is known as **participatory budgeting**.

The process began in Porto Alegre, the capital of the Brazilian state of Rio Grande do Sul, a city of 1.3 million in the centre of a metropolitan region of 3 million inhabitants. Like many Brazilian cities, Porto Alegre had a very poor level of infrastructure and basic services. Many rural citizens had moved into the cities and built their own homes on pieces of land they did not own on the outskirts of the city. These communities are known as *favelas*.

In 1989 a radical government from the Partido dos Trabalhadores (PT) ('Workers' Party') took control of the council. Although its objective was to improve services for the poor, it faced a serious financial situation, with empty coffers and yet very high expectations. To accommodate, the government decided to involve the citizens in decisions about how the limited resources were spent. It also increased taxes on those who owned larger properties, to increase its available budget. The process of participatory budgeting involved organising a number of meetings in local communities, where people debated how the money should be spent. The budget was allocated through a participatory process, amounting to a total of US$700 million. The priorities for spending have been a clean water supply, improved sewerage systems, new and better-quality housing, and improved pavements.

After the first seven years, the number of people with access to a sewage system increased from 46 per cent to 74 per cent (Utzig, 1996). The number of children enrolled in school has doubled, and the number of local schools in the *favelas* has increased. But perhaps the most important achievement has been the re-engagement of the citizens of Porto Alegre in the decisions about spending their tax money and improving their communities.

Since the early days of experimentation in Porto Alegre, participatory budgeting has spread across Brazil, where 70 cities now have a similar process of deciding how some of their budget is spent. Across the country 60 per cent of the population understands the process, and millions have participated in local community meetings debating how the budget is spent. Across the world local communities are learning from this process and demanding their own right to have a say in developing their local budget.

11.7 THE SOLIDARITY ECONOMY IN LATIN AMERICA

The phrase **solidarity economy** is used, especially by theorists in Latin America, to describe an approach to economic organisation that emphasises social justice. It is particularly relevant in countries where many people do not have easy access to the basic necessities of life. An important theorist of the solidarity economy is the Austrian-born Brazilian economist Paul Singer, who proposed the Technological Incubators for Popular Cooperatives (*Incubadoras Tecnológicas de Cooperativas Populares*) (ITCP). The first ITCP was created in 1995 at the engineering postgraduate centre at the Federal University of Rio de Janeiro (COPPE). After

1996, this 'incubator' began to form cooperatives in Baixada Fluminense and the Rio slums. The ITCP not only provided assistance to solidarity ventures, helping local people build small businesses in poor communities, but also fostered the organisation of productive and marketing activities and the improvement of techniques used. Often these small businesses serve a social purpose, and they are frequently organised as cooperatives so that the profits of work are equally shared, along with investment decisions.

More recently, new ITCPs have developed at the Federal Universities of Paraná, Santa Catarina, Pará and Amazonas. Education is understood as necessary for the staff of the cooperatives and for supporting institutions. Indeed, research is indispensable for understanding and generating new theoretical propositions. This network of ITCPs currently involves more than 80 Brazilian universities which aim to place the services of the universities at the disposal of the workers and their class organisations.

The solidarity economy developed from a number of ostensibly incompatible intellectual sources: the social teaching of the Catholic Church, especially liberation theology; the communist commitment to a fully egalitarian ownership of economic assets; and the anarchist idea of self-managed work. The Catholic Church has long argued for the need for justice in economic life. In the medieval era, for example, it ruled against charging interest on money-lending (pejoratively called 'usury') and insisted that those who sold goods should do so for 'a just price' rather than charging whatever the market would bear. As capitalism developed, the Vatican issued an important encyclical (message to the faithful) on economic matters: *De Rerum Novarum* (1891), also known as 'Rights and Duties of Capital and Labour'. This was the Church's attempt to address the changes due to industrialisation and to oblige those who controlled capital to treat with justice those who sold their labour. The Church considered that the operation of the market should be constrained within moral limits. For example, it endorsed trade unions and the principle of a price floor for wages to improve the living standards of workers.

In line with much radical thought in the 1960s, Pope John XXIII examined how the Church dealt with social and economic change, and established the Second Vatican Council as a major exercise in consultation and debate. The Council established that the Church should operate as a community rather than a hierarchy of believers, and questioned the extreme levels of inequality on a global basis. This was taken up by bishops in Latin America, who established the Latin Conference in Medellin, Colombia in 1968. They created the concept of **institutionalised violence** to describe a situation where powerful forces, especially the state, use mechanisms such as the law and armed force to entrench power relationships, which lead to deprivation, disease and death for many citizens.

This thinking influenced a number of radical priests, who saw an inconsistency between Jesus' message of love and equality and the hierarchy and wealth of the Catholic church. For example, the Brazilian theologian Leonardo Boff called for the Church to follow instead 'the path of radical love', which he believed more accurately characterised Jesus' message. This approach became known as 'liberation theology' but might also be called 'the theology of the oppressed' or 'the option for the poor'.

Liberation theology developed an 'emancipatory praxis', that is, the idea that priests should abandon their wealthy congregations to work with the poor in their *barrios* and *favelas* ('urban slums' in Spanish and Portuguese). They established 'ecclesiastical-based communities', which relate closely to the solidarity economy 'incubators' (ITCPs) described above.

In the countries of the Global North, the idea of a socially focused economy is often discussed in terms of a 'social economy' rather than a 'solidarity economy'. Sometimes this is called the 'third sector' to contrast it with the 'first sector' of private-enterprise businesses and the 'second sector' of publicly owned enterprises.

THINKING QUESTIONS

If you had the choice of a secure job for life or access to enough land to provide for your own needs, which would you choose and why?

Can you think of any cooperatives in your own home community or local economy? How do you know that they are cooperatives?

CLASS ACTIVITY

Corporations have established a right to own the music of artists they sign, and downloading the music of these artists has been labelled as 'piracy' and is illegal under international copyright or 'intellectual property' law. But who really created the music? The blues, for example, is a fusion of music brought from Africa by slaves and the communities of poor workers from Europe who brought their own folk music. Without these basic rhythms and riffs we would not have rock and roll or everything that came later. How does music become a commodity that can be owned by a corporation? Who defines this process?

AREAS FOR RESEARCH

Obtain a budget from your city/town and investigate how the money is budgeted. Form groups and conduct a participatory budgeting exercise along the model presented in the text.

Select a number of diverse firms, e.g. cooperatively owned, owned by external shareholders, etc. Give a brief description of their ownership and management structure. Sketch a diagram illustrating the flows of value and the power structure within the firm. Describe the diagram to the class.

UN SDG FOCUS

SDG Goals #14 and #15 call for:

14. Conserve and sustainably use the ocean, seas and marine resources.
15. Sustainably manage forests, combat desertification, halt and reverse land degradation, halt biodiversity loss.

How does one 'conserve'? How does one 'combat'? What is meant by 'sustainably use' and 'sustainably manage'? Which type of property regime is most compatible with 'sustainably using' and 'sustainably managing'? Why is biodiversity so important? Research the UN's findings on Goals #14 and #15. How would you recommend implementation?

FURTHER READING

Boff, L. (1986) *Option for the Poor: Challenge to the Rich Countries.* Edinburgh: T&T Clark.

Davies, W. (2009) *Reinventing the Firm.* London: Demos.

Neeson, J. M. (1989) *Commoners: Common Right, Enclosure and Social Change in England, 1700–1820.* Cambridge, UK: Cambridge University Press.

Ostrom, E. (1990) *Governing the Commons: The Evolution of Institutions for Collective Action.* Cambridge, UK: Cambridge University Press.

12
Economic Governance

In the previous chapter we saw how, at the level of the individual enterprise, power can be shared between producers and consumers. In this chapter we will explore how national governments can create a framework within which economic activity can focus on the general good, rather than serving minority or elite interests. We believe that government plays a major role in the economic life of every country, whether maintaining basic infrastructure like roads and energy grids or providing basic needs like healthcare and housing. We discussed earlier how different economic systems make different decisions about the role of government. In this chapter we focus on the key roles of government in modern capitalism: providing the framework within which private and cooperative enterprises can flourish; offering a sense of the size and scope of the economy and how well it is meeting national objectives; and providing governance at the international level, dealing with the most significant problems facing the global community, especially climate change.

12.1 A MARKET WITHIN A SOCIAL AND ECOLOGICAL FRAMEWORK

We began this textbook by making clear that we see social justice and sustainability as key economic and political goals, suggesting a change of emphasis and a shift in the balance of power between society, the economy and the environment. We argue that sustainability is a principled recipe for general living, not something that characterises only part of our global community. We also challenge the suggestion that any part of the economy can exist apart from the environment, from which all resources are ultimately drawn. And we believe it is not possible to have an economy without society; without the people who provide the ideas and the labour-power to make the economy function.

The environment is all-important, since it is our fundamental life-support system and without it other sectors have no meaning. Society is embedded within the environment, that is to say, human communities exist within its limits, thus benefiting from the bounty of the natural world. Finally, we have the economy nested within society. Many neoclassical economists suggest that the market is the most powerful mechanism and that its laws will achieve the best for humankind with minimal intervention of social rules and controls.

As has been clear from previous chapters, we challenge this suggestion, while recognising that the economy serves social needs and is constrained by laws that serve society. Throughout this chapter we will explain the different ways in which social forces, at the level of regulation or political intervention, can be used to ensure that our economy works for the benefit of all, without destroying our environment.

Every society limits the extent of the market system. Under socialism, the market was effectively banished, although it existed via very limited retail activity combined with a 'black market' operating outside the legal framework. In today's mixed economies, politics decides which goods and services should be sold in the market, which should be made illegal, and which should be offered through the public sector. In the UK, for example, acute and chronic healthcare is still largely funded through the public sector, but it is not illegal to offer plastic surgery or even major operations in a private business. Laws about drugs vary widely between societies, with the sale of alcohol being illegal to those below the age of 21 in the USA, while cannabis can be sold legally in certain premises in the Netherlands. These decisions are deeply cultural.

Governments also need to ensure that markets work 'efficiently' and do not damage the interests of consumers. As a basic example, few would suggest that we do not need environmental health officers to ensure that restaurants meet 'acceptable' hygiene. We have already seen that some markets can become consolidated, such that a few or sometimes only one company can become very powerful and can control the market to enable it to maximise profits rather than to serve consumer interests. The legal cases against Microsoft by both the European Commission and the US Department of Justice are examples of a supranational body intervening in a market to prevent monopolistic practices. (The US antitrust laws are briefly discussed in the next section.)

Some might assume that our interests as consumers are best served when competitive businesses supply goods in a market where the price is determined by the interaction of demand and supply. However, this is not always the case. For example, between 1990 and 1997, the UK book trade operated under legislation called the Net Book Agreement. This meant that publishers, effectively the producers of books, fixed the price at which bookshops could sell them. Under lobbying from corporate publishers the UK repealed the legislation, allowing free competition in the book trade. The result was domination by large-scale publishers such as Amazon, who could buy in bulk and thus discount book prices, leading to the bankruptcy of many small bookshops. So, while customers pay lower prices, they have lost the quality of service provided by small retailers, and the power of corporate publishers and booksellers has been increased vis-à-vis authors and customers.

12.2 A QUICK LOOK AT US ANTITRUST LEGISLATION

The US offers an interesting example of the development of market power. As 'the land of the free' it was assumed that anyone could become a successful farmer or entrepreneur. However, over time certain businesses became so powerful that they undermined the opportunity for others to become successful. To prevent this, the US government implemented laws with the confusing name of 'antitrust legislation'. The 'trusts' were groups of business that operated to control the market: the Sugar Trust and the Steel Trust, for example. The most powerful trust was Standard Oil, owned by John D. Rockefeller. In 1910 Rockefeller's net worth was equal to nearly 2.5 per cent of the US economy, the equivalent of nearly $250 billion in today's terms, or at least twice as much as Bill Gates' private wealth.

The first significant piece of antitrust legislation was the Sherman Antitrust Act (1890), which aimed to curb the growth of monopolies. Any business that attempted to restrain commerce could be fined up to $5,000 and its operators could be jailed for up to a year. The Act is still in force, and penalties have continued to be severe: fines of up to $100 million for a corporation and $1 million for an individual, along with up to 10 years in prison.

The 1890 legislation was weak in practice and was followed by the Clayton Antitrust Act (1914), which forbade practices that could lead to the formation of a monopoly, especially price-fixing. For a market to work effectively, new companies need to compete on price: if existing firms control the price they can block new entrants and keep the whole market for themselves. Also in 1914 the Federal Trade Commission was established, to ensure free competition in the US market. It still exists (along with the Antitrust Division of the Justice Department) to enforce the Clayton and Sherman Acts, and to 'protect the process of competition for the benefit of consumers, making sure there are strong incentives for businesses to operate efficiently, keep prices down, and keep quality up'.

Since 1914 three significant laws were passed to update the Antitrust legislation.[1] The Robinson-Patman Act of 1936 was passed due to the lobbying of small neighbourhood businesses, worried that large national corporations would force them out of business. The law prohibits gratuitous differences in prices at the wholesale level, unrelated to cost. In 1950 the Celler-Kefauver Act was passed, which extended the government's purview in regulating mergers. Specifically, the 1890 Sherman Act had only allowed the federal government regulatory enforcement in **horizontal mergers**. The 1950 Celler-Kefauver Act allowed the federal government enforcement in **vertical mergers** and **conglomerate mergers** (i.e. between unrelated firms). In 1976 the Clayton Act was amended by the

1. For a helpful primer on US antitrust laws, see the Federal Trade Commission (1990) *Guide to Antitrust*, www.ftc.gov/tips-advice/competition-guidance/guide-antitrust-laws

Table 12.1 Practices Banned by US Antitrust Law, 1890 and 1914

Practice	*Description*
Monopolies 'in restraint of trade'	A single company controlling most, if not all, of the market can use its power to undermine competition.
Predatory pricing	A large company can set prices very low in the short term (below its average total cost) to drive out competitors and ensure it has a monopoly position, after which it is free to control prices.
Price-fixing	An agreement between producers in the same market to decide the price between themselves, rather than the market through competition; they can also agree to restrict output to drive prices up.
Illegal business practices	Restrictions on producers enforcing a fixed price on retailers.

Source: Authors.

Hart-Scott-Rodino Antitrust Improvements Act to 'require companies planning large mergers or acquisitions to notify the government of their plans in advance'.

The first significant test case for US antitrust legislation was against the oil trust Standard Oil, although initial lawsuits were first brought against trade unions during the 1890s. After a lengthy legal battle in 1911, the courts ruled that Standard Oil should be broken up, since it controlled almost 90 per cent of oil production, and deliberately engaged in predatory pricing, driving out competitors then acquiring their assets.

Since then, constituent remnants have merged: Chevron buying Gulf in 1984 (the largest corporate merger in US history up until then); and Exxon (formally called Esso), with an obvious play on Standard Oil, merging with Mobil, another part of the former Standard Oil trust in 1997. Together with BP Amoco (a merger between two former Standard Oil companies), Chevron and Exxon Mobil currently control almost as much of the market as Rockefeller did.

The main weakness of the antitrust legislation is that it is not actively enforced by federal agencies, but rather is left to courts to enforce, meaning that those who have a complaint must initiate legal action. Clearly this is expensive and risky, and legal interpretations have also tended to weaken enforcement, given the legislation provision that the Acts do not prohibit every restraint of trade but only those that are 'unreasonable in restraining competition'.

Furthermore, while one branch of the US government makes monopoly illegal in business structure, another branch legalises it in terms of advocating and enforcing intellectual property rights, which include:

- **Patents:** Granted by a government to the innovator/inventor of a product, the sole right to produce that product for a specified period of time, usually for at least 20 years.

- **Trademarks:** Protecting a name, symbol, or anything else identifying a product, and can last indefinitely.
- **Copyrights:** The legal right to exclusive publication, production, distribution and sale of a literary or artistic work, which lasts for the author's lifetime, plus an additional term (usually 70 years).

The pharmaceutical industry offers a clear example of corporate control over intellectual property to maximise profits, even when it means the loss of life in some of the world's poorest communities. In the late 1990s, with 25 per cent of its working age citizens HIV-positive, the South African government decided to ignore international law and import generic AIDS drugs from India. The price difference was staggering – US$350 for a year's supply compared with US$10,000 for the branded medicines – so a poor country like South Africa had little choice. Under the 1995 Trade-Related Aspects of Intellectual Property Rights (TRIPS), which sets minimum, binding standards for enforcement of intellectual property rights, South Africa was clearly able to justify its actions under clauses exempting countries facing public-health disasters, but its actions were legally challenged by the US trade representative, and action was taken against the government of South Africa by the Pharmaceutical Manufacturers' Association. The courage of the SA government was rewarded and the PMA eventually withdrew its case in 2001, agreeing to a deal over reasonable pricing and availability of AIDS drugs.

Even when they have innovative products to offer, new manufactures can find it hard to enter established (and entrenched) markets. Creating such a product already represents a significant investment in terms of research and development, which can operate as a 'barrier to entry' for those who cannot access capital. James Dyson has described such problems for innovative products such as his Dual Cyclone™ vacuum cleaner, which was rigorously opposed by existing manufacturers. According to the Dyson Company, the Dual Cyclone was almost not made, due to other manufacturers trying to keep Dyson out of the market. While developing his new product, James Dyson had to pay substantial patent fees while earning no income. Then, once the product was successful, the rival company Hoover tried to imitate the Dyson design and the company had to defend the patent in court. This is a clear example of unfair competition and of an established company trying to keep a newcomer out of the market (Mackay and Wilmshurst, 2002).

Indeed, Guy Standing (2016: 50) writes that intellectual property has proliferated since the TRIPS (1995), representing 'a political choice by governments around the world to grant monopolies over knowledge to private interests, allowing them to restrict public access to knowledge and to raise the price of obtaining it or of products and services embodying it.' Pertaining to patents, of which over 2.7 million were filed in 2014 alone (Ibid.: 51), Standing argues that they are used 'mainly for purposes other than rewarding or supporting innovation. Most patents are acquired to gain or protect a monopoly, acting as a deterrent, not a spur, to innovation' (Standing, 2016: 61).

12.3 MEASURING WHAT MATTERS

Before we can start introducing policies to change our economy we must understand what we are working with. Most governments have a vast amount of economic data at their fingertips, ranging from the prices of goods and services to the number of people employed, but the most basic measure that governments have traditionally used to measure our economy is **Gross Domestic Product (GDP)**, defined as the market value of all final goods and services produced within a nation's geographical borders in one year. GDP measures the market value of economic activity, or, in other words, the amount of stuff that an economy produces in one year. This is a rather strange measure to set at the heart of policy-making, since it excludes many things we value that are never bought and sold (most importantly the environment). The end result is quantitative – a single number reported in the nation's currency – rather than qualitative.

Key points about GDP

- The final goods and services considered in GDP are produced within the country, that is, within the country's geographical borders, irrespective of the nationality of the producer or of the firms' capital composition.
- Transactions in the informal economy, and goods and services produced by households for their own consumption, are excluded from GDP. So if I do all my housework, this work is not included in GDP, but if I contract these services out, it is.
- Only human-made capital (such as factories, computers, etc. is included in GDP. Environmental, human (intellectual) and social capital are excluded.
- Thus, **depreciation** (the normal wear and tear of a good over time) of only human-made capital is included in the calculation of GDP. Depreciation increases with the use of capital goods in the production of goods and services, and can also be influenced by technological innovation.
- Price changes can affect the monetary value of final goods and services produced and exchanged by a country in a specific period of time, without changes in the volume of such goods and services. Thus, it is essential to distinguish between 'nominal GDP' and 'real GDP', so as to exclude from the latter the effect of price variations. **Nominal GDP** uses current prices whereas **real GDP** uses constant prices at a selected base year; in other words, real GDP holds prices constant.

An important lesson of this book is that economic indicators are constructed to reflect the underlying contours of the economy, which in turn reflect existing institutions, often constructed to benefit existing vested interests. So rather than accept an indicator as sacrosanct we should analyse its original objective; asking specifically who benefits under the initial construction, and whether current conditions have sufficiently changed to warrant a revision. Not to do so is tantamount to either claiming ignorance of the original objectives, or assuming that underlying conditions do not change. Neither is acceptable. The following are criticisms of GDP as an economic indicator.

Criticisms of GDP

- GDP does not distinguish between beneficial and harmful activity. GDP focuses on total throughputs which are paid for, and so the negative aspects of life, such as fighting crime, are counted on the positive side of the balance sheet. An illustrative example often used by environmentalists is the running aground of an oil tanker. This generates a large amount of economic activity – cleaning beaches, repairing the tanker, treating the contaminated wildlife and compensating the affected people – all of which add to GDP. Critics argue that GDP does nothing to encourage (and measure) sustainable economic activity focusing on socially beneficial activities, and is not only misguided but also incompatible with the UN 17 SDGs.
- GDP focuses on flows rather than stocks of wealth. This means that economies that exploit their natural resources to turn them into products to be consumed appear to be richer, even though they have lost a great deal of their national and natural wealth, and the well-being it brought to citizens.
- The focus on market value means that activities not bought and sold in the market are not considered to have economic value. Much of this work, such as domestic and caring work, is primarily done by women, which diminishes their economic contribution; and this is particularly true in developing countries, in which, as we discussed in Chapter 5, women and girls devote a lot of time to gathering energy supplies and water.
- GDP is a total or average measure and does not give information about the distribution of wealth. Critics argue that measures which ignore how wealth is distributed encourage growth at the cost of inequality.
- GDP distorts and misleads, as Fioramonti (2013: 156–7) explains:

> GDP is built on a great lie. This lie says that markets are the only producers of wealth . . . Nature, the ultimate provider of all richness, is enslaved and devalued. GDP gives mankind the illusion that growth is about production, when it actually should be viewed as a transfer. Mankind does not produce anything. It simply turns natural wealth into money

> Price tags are the ultimate symbol of GDP. Continuous production and endless consumption are its underlying values. Durability, reusability, and self-production are its worst enemies... Things that we produce for ourselves are even worse, because they are not priced at all.

- In addition to simply measuring, GDP has become an arbiter of what is important: of what should be valued and, conversely, what should not be valued.

12.4 WHEN, WHY AND BY WHOM WAS GDP CONSTRUCTED?

The basic methodology for GDP was constructed during the 1930s by a Russian emigrant to the United States, Simon Kuznets, who was awarded the Bank of Sweden Prize in Economic Sciences (also known as the Nobel Prize in Economics) in 1971. The immediate motivation for GDP was obvious: during the Great Depression the US economy was in dire straits, so in order to improve the economic situation, an empirical measure of just how bad the economy was was needed. Indeed GDP proved helpful in conceptualising aggregate demand during the 1930s, and even more so in winning the Second World War:

> [GDP's] origin and development were deeply intertwined with the most fundamental political struggles of the past century. It was initially employed as [a] 'war machine' in the Second World War, allowing the US to assess the projected capacity of its economy and wage the war on two fronts without curtailing internal consumption. It was then used as a propaganda device during the bipolar rivalry between capitalism and the Soviet Empire.
>
> Ibid.: 153

GDP has since become entrenched as the world's most important economic indicator. Thanks to the insistence of the United Nations, every nation has adopted it. In 1999 the US Commerce Department declared GDP to be the most important invention of the twentieth century.

However, we need to remember that the conceptualisation, measurement and construction of GDP occurred in a completely different economic era (the 1930s) from the present day: when few nations traded with each other; unpaid work, especially raising families, was ignored and considered unimportant, since it was mostly undertaken by women; and the typical firm was large and industrial, making it somewhat easier to measure outputs and inputs, as opposed to a firm producing a service, which is much more difficult to measure. Add to this that only human-made capital is included, and GDP is severely handicapped as a measurement – and hopelessly inconsistent with sustainability.

Box 12.1 Digging Holes and Filling Them In

The economist J. M. Keynes joked that a capitalist economy could be run successfully on the basis of people undertaking pointless activities such as digging holes and filling them in, or other time-consuming activities such as building cathedrals or pyramids. Although ostensibly tongue-in-cheek, Keynes (1936 [2010]: 129; emphasis in original deleted) spoke an important truth about capitalist economies: they are about movement rather than balance. The passage from *The General Theory of Employment* is worth quoting in full:

> If the Treasury were to fill old bottles with banknotes, bury them at suitable depths in disused coal mines which are then filled up to the surface with town rubbish, and leave it to private enterprises on well-tried principles of laissez faire to dig up the notes again . . . there need be no more unemployment and, with the help of the repercussion, the real income of the community, and its capital wealth also, would probably become a good deal greater than it actually is. It would, indeed, be more sensible to build houses and the like; but if there are political and practical difficulties in the way of this, the above would be better than nothing.

The reasons for this are complex, best explained thus: when money circulates, profits can be made, and profit-maximising, rather than satisfaction or happiness, is the driving force of a capitalist economy. If this is true, then it makes achieving sustainability very difficult, and we should urgently consider which aspects of the structure of our economies need to change to enable us to be economically successful while also living in balance with the planet.

12.5 *TECHNIQUE 9*: CALCULATING GDP

Despite these pervasive and damning criticisms, traditional GDP is persistently (and perhaps stubbornly) used throughout the world. Therefore it is worthwhile to understand its calculation. To illustrate the underlying methodology, let's perform a simple mental exercise: assume your classroom is a self-contained economy, with consumers and firms and £500 of value initially circulating within the economy. One method of calculating GDP, known as the **expenditures approach**, is to estimate total spending on all goods and services bought (if not all goods produced are bought, then an adjustment must be made – investment in inventories – by adding this amount to total spending). A second method, known as the **Incomes approach**, is to calculate the income earned by all those engaged in producing the goods and services. A third approach is to calculate the **value added** – defined as the new value added at every stage of production. Theoretically, each approach yields the same answer; in reality, however, each method yields different answers, due to incomplete and faulty data.

The theoretical equivalence is due to the following basic macroeconomic identity (an identity is always true, by definition):

Incomes ≡ Expenditures

This means that the sum of all spending in an economy must equal the sum of all income received; in other words, income received does not disappear, but is either used to purchase the goods and services produced, pay taxes, or is saved.

Kuznets divided those who buy goods and services into four groups: consumers, firms, the government at all levels, and foreigners. Not coincidentally, these are also the constituent elements of **aggregate demand (AD)** as defined in Table 12.2.

Table 12.2 Components of Aggregate Demand (Total Expenditures)

Components	*Definition*
Consumption (C)	Spending on goods and services by consumers, e.g. cars, computers, education, food, etc.
Investment (I)	The sum of the purchases of capital assets by firms, including residential, non-residential and changes in inventories. Aggregate investment increases both the productive capacity of the economy and GDP.
Government expenditures (E)	Includes spending on goods and services at all levels of government.
Net exports (X – M)	The difference between the goods and services produced domestically but sold overseas – **exports** (X) – and purchases of goods and services produced abroad – **imports** (M).

Source: Elaborated by the authors from Kalecki (1954).

We can calculate the GDP of a country based on the expenditures approach with the following formula:

$$GDP = \Sigma p_i q_i,$$

where:

p_i = the price of a final good or service
q_i = the quantity produced of a final good or service.

If a particular good or service is deemed very important, it can be weighted more. The most difficult aspect of calculating GDP is collecting data: a process made less accurate since new products are, by definition, not known and thereby excluded.

12.6 ALTERNATIVES TO GDP

Sustainable development seeks the balance of the economic, environmental and social dimensions of development in a long-term and global perspective. In November 2007, the European Commission, the European Parliament, the Club of Rome, the World Wildlife Foundation and the Organisation for Economic Cooperation and Development organised the conference Beyond GDP. The Conference concluded that:

> GDP, the best-recognised measure of economic performance in the world, is often used as a generic indicator of progress. However, the relationship between economic growth as measured by GDP and other dimensions of societal progress is not straightforward. Effectively measuring progress, wealth and well-being requires indices that are as clear and appealing as GDP but more inclusive than GDP – ones that incorporate social and environmental issues. This is especially important given global challenges such as climate change, global poverty, pressure on resources and their potential impact on societies.

An early proponent of alternative economic indicators to GDP, Victor Anderson (1991), raised the following essential elements to be included in any alternative measure:

- What is the end result we want to measure? Economic activity? Socially beneficial activity? Happiness? Health?
- What goods are included?
- What bads are deducted?
- How can we handle things we can't measure easily?

Anderson suggested that a good economic indicator (as an alternative to GDP) would have the following characteristics:

- based on data readily available to all nations, to facilitate international comparisons.
- easy to understand, not based on abstruse maths.
- relate to something measurable, e.g. not 'loss of community'.
- measure something believed to be important in its own right, e.g. infant mortality is an indicator of general standard of health and living.
- be rapidly available, as an early-warning signal of potential trouble.

Some economists are concerned that the focus on a measurable indicator will reduce the emphasis on the immaterial aspects of life that are so important in terms of human happiness. The Himalayan kingdom of Bhutan has attracted international attention by focusing its economy on Gross National Happiness. Policy outcomes from this include the banning of plastic bags and the limiting of the ownership of any business by one person to 10 per cent of the total size of the firm. Bhutan also ended the export of timber, due to the social consequences of deforestation.

Similarly, but with more emphasis on measurement, the London-based think tank The New Economics Foundation (Thompson et al., 2007) derived the 'Happy Planet Index' (HPI), which uses survey data about a country's happiness and divides this by the amount of resources consumed to produce the level of well-being. The results demonstrate that Latin American nations are much more efficient at generating well-being than the countries of Europe or North America.

Table 12.3 compares two different additional indicators to GDP. We might think of these as different ways of looking at 'the wealth of nations' in more or less material terms. GDP per capita measures total economic activity (as described above) divided by the number of people in the country. Of course, we should remember that in reality the wealth may be very concentrated or more equally shared. The Human Development Index (HDI) is a UN measure of country performance on a range of social measures, including life expectancy and education, while also incorporating GDP, which can skew the index in favour of countries that are wealthy by conventional measures (this index is elaborated below). The third ranking is the Happy Planet Index (HPI).

Table 12.3 GDP, HDI and HPI Rankings for a Selection of Countries, 2014

Country	*GDP per capita in US$*	*GDP per capita ranking*	*HDI ranking*	*HPI ranking*
Luxembourg	107,206	1	26	10
Qatar	99,731	2	36	149
Norway	99,731	3	1	29
USA	49,922	11	3	105
United Kingdom	38,588	23	26	41
Russia	14,246	48	55	122
Brazil	12,078	58	85	21
Costa Rica	9,672	68	62	1
Thailand	5,678	93	103	20
China	6,075	87	101	60
Afghanistan	621	168	175	109

Note: For details on compiling the Happy Planet Index, see Mutert (2010).

Sources: International Monetary Fund (IMF, 2014); United Nations Development Programme (UNDP, 2013).

12.7 *TECHNIQUE 10*: CALCULATING GPI AND HDI

It is useful to be familiar with the calculation of the following two widely recognised alternative indexes of economic well-being, which we believe are both more amenable to working with the UN 17 SDGs.

The Genuine Progress Indicator (GPI)

Various researchers have attempted to measure economic progress in ways that compensate for the shortcomings of GDP. The New Economics Foundation calculated such an index for the UK, entitled the Index of Sustainable Economic Welfare (ISEW). A related measure of human progress, based on the ISEW, is the Genuine Progress Indicator (GPI). Here we offer a simplified version of just the first part of the calculation of the GPI – weighting income according to equality – to get some sense of the additional benefits and costs needed to provide a true measure of economic progress. The GPI is comprised of the following components:

$$GPI = A + B - C - D + I$$

Where:

A = income-weighted personal consumption
B = value of non-market services generating welfare
C = private defensive cost of natural deterioration
D = cost of deterioration of nature and natural resources
I = increase in capital stock and balance of international trade

Variable A, 'income-weighted personal consumption', weighs consumption according to how equally personal consumption is distributed. Thus, it tries to determine how well off the average person is, since if a small percentage of people are consuming most of the wealth then a generalised measure of economic production is not useful in determining welfare. The 'weighting' is according to the Gini Coefficient, which is an index that compares current income distribution with an ideal distribution, giving equal weight to all income levels by calculating the square root of the sum of the squared difference of each quintile from a 20 per cent share. (See also our discussion on the Gini Coefficient in Chapter 5.) As inequality grows, weighted personal consumption shrinks, thereby reducing well-being.

Consider for example the GPI for just the US state of Colorado. The Colorado GPI incorporates income inequality by discounting personal consumption expenditures by the amount of inequality in each year, using Gini and income distribution indices. We divide per-capita consumption levels by the inequality index for each year, and multiply by 100 to get a weighted personal consumption level. This is shown in Table 12.4.

Table 12.4 Impact of Income Inequality in Colorado

	X *Personal Consumption Per Capita ($)*	*Y* *Indexed Gini Coefficient*	*Z* *Weighted Personal Consumption Per Capita ($)*
2012	37,560	136	27,618
2011	36,909	135.1	27,329
2010	37,070	134.5	27,556
2009	36,293	133.3	27,217

Note: column Z equals column X divided by column Y multiplied by 100.

Source: Colorado Fiscal Institute (2013).

Now let's consider some of the other additions and subtractions (from the equation GPI = A + B - C – D + I) we need in order to get a clear sense of the true costs and benefits of a growing economy:

- **Variable B**, 'value of non-market services generating welfare', should include all caring activities, volunteering and other activities that make people happier but are not bought and sold.
- **Variable C**, 'private defensive cost of natural deterioration', should include all costs relating to pollution and social impacts of economic activity.
- **Variable D**, 'cost of deterioration of nature and natural resources', should include all costs resulting from the deterioration of natural ecosystems.
- **Variable I**, 'increase in capital stock and balance of international trade', attempts to balance the costs of net additions to the capital stock as contributions to well-being, and treats money borrowed from abroad as reductions.

The Human Development Index (HDI)

The Human Development Index introduces a new way of measuring development by combining indicators of life expectancy, educational attainment and income into a composite index. There are three components, or 'dimensions', of the HDI (hence it is termed 'the three-dimensional index'):

- **A long and healthy life:** Measured by life expectancy at birth.
- **Education:** Measured as a combination of mean years of schooling and expected years of schooling.

- **A decent standard of living:** Measured as Gross National Income (GNI) per capita. GNI begins with GDP, then adds income received from other nations, and subtracts income paid to other nations.

The HDI facilitates comparisons within and between countries.[2] It sets a minimum and a maximum for each dimension and then assigns a number for each dimension for each nation. For example, the first dimension (a long and healthy life) is 1 when life expectancy at birth is 85 and 0 when it is 20; and the third dimension, (a decent standard of living) is 1 when GNI per capita is US$75,000 and 0 when it is US$100. The second dimension is slightly more complicated: an education index is calculated by constructing a 'mean years of schooling' index (with 15 as the maximum) and an 'expected years of schooling' index (with 18 as the maximum, equivalent to a master's degree in most countries). The HDI is then taken as the geometric mean of the three dimensional indices.

The HDI emphasises that people and their capabilities are the main criteria for assessing development, and is based on the work of Amartya Sen (1999: 318–19, note #41). Economic growth alone does not reveal social developmental conditions. For example, countries with the same level of income per capita can present different human development outcomes. In the Bahamas, the income per capita is higher than in New Zealand, but its HDI is lower. Indeed, life expectancy at birth and schooling shows striking contrasts.

Table 12.5 Dimensions and Indicators of the Human Development Index (HDI)

Dimensions	A long and healthy life	Education	A decent standard of living
Indicators	Life expectancy at birth (years)	Mean years of schooling and expected years of schooling	Gross National Income per capita
HDI Dimensional Index	Life expectancy index	Education index	Gross National Income index

Source: Human Development Index (2017).

12.8 GOVERNMENT'S ROLE IN THE ECONOMY

The most recent global financial crisis caused a re-examination of the ideas of the free market, especially pertaining to old questions about the role of government in the economy: When is it appropriate for government to become involved in directing a national economy? When should investment decisions be left to the

2. This discussion of HDI methodology is heavily based on (Human Development Index, 2017).

market, to be decided on the basis of profit-maximisation? Which public goods should the government provide? What is the proper balance between market and commons? These questions tend to be answered differently depending on both the level of development of an economy (and hence the development of the institutions to support the market) and the degree of crisis. In countries where people die of starvation, or suffer from lack of basic sanitation, it is palpably evident that they are too poor to be able to find solutions to these problems though the market, since they cannot afford to pay for adequate food or clean water supplies. In such situations the government clearly has a role to play in supporting basic incomes or subsidising the price of food. But the catch-22 is where does the government get the requisite funds?

In economies where the majority of people have an adequate standard of living, then government involvement may be limited to organising the redistribution of cash to those who are in poverty, perhaps through a system of welfare payments, and maintaining the existing institutional structure of the economy. Sometimes, when the market for an essential product for human welfare reveals exploitation, or unmet needs, then the government can intervene to 'regulate' the market. An example is the introduction of rent control in New York City.[3] It may surprise you to read that in this heart of global capitalism the market for rented housing has been controlled by the local government since 1943.

Rent control, defined as a legal reduction of the rent, established below the market rate, was introduced originally to deal with the problem of 'slum landlords' who exploited the shortage caused by overpopulation to charge high rents for poor-quality apartments, particularly where they had subdivided existing apartments into smaller and smaller units to take rents from more families. The city of New York controls rents so that they are at a 'reasonable' level. Neoclassical economists argue that this causes inefficiency, since landlords will be less willing to rent their properties and/or renovate or build new ones. This seems a weak argument, since the problem with substandard accommodation was itself the shortage of housing, which was gratuitously assumed 'pre-intervention' to be in equilibrium. In cities such as New York and London, where rented housing is in short supply, the market will always be slanted in favour of the supplier of housing and the landlord, which justifies local government to intervene to protect the tenant.

Governments may also support new sectors that are not yet able to become viable in their own right. For example, in several European countries the government subsidises the renewable energy sector through a **Feed-in Tariff**,

3. Rent control in New York (including the NY metro, but also Albany and Buffalo) is the longest running such system in the USA. California, Maryland, New Jersey, and the District of Colombia has also enacted rent control. See http://www.landlord.com/rent_control_laws_by_state.htm

i.e. a high price paid to renewable energy producers to encourage use. This is a form of subsidy to transfer money from energy consumers to energy producers. Governments may also make decisions about where they site their own offices, which bring many jobs with them.

Taking into account these government actions, what is the role of **government planning**, (defined as a means of coordinating decentralised economic decisions) in the twenty-first century? Planning has been very important in Europe after the Second World War, since it had been part of the post-war effort to help nations recover from the war and the economic depression. In the former Soviet Union, government planning was devastating (since it could not fulfil its original expectations) and led to the more market-orientated experiments in Hungary and Yugoslavia. However, today, planning across the globe is based more on community organising, along with public debate about opportunities for sustainability. Sustainability issues cannot be dealt with in isolation but require an understanding of the complex and dynamic interrelationships between social, economic and ecological systems.

Economists differ widely on the accepted role for government in capitalism, so much so that it is difficult to offer agreed responsibilities beyond protecting property rights, providing public goods (especially national defence) and correcting *ex post* for externalities. Partly this disagreement is due to ideology: as we have discussed, neoclassical economists gratuitously assume that markets are stable, and thus that any disturbances will eventually return the economy to equilibrium; whereas most other economists believe that the economic system constantly evolves, and is essentially characterised by non-equilibrium.

As we mentioned at the start of this book, we see nothing wrong with disagreement: it is part and parcel of a vibrant intellectual discourse. Having said that, we feel that changes do not occur naturally (or inevitably); on the contrary, if we want to get from A to B, we first have to map out our terrain, understand the obstacles, and instead of waiting for change to magically happen, we have to actively take charge. If we want to transition from unsustainability to sustainability so that all can provision, we must first and foremost ascertain the factors blocking change and which institutions are needed to effectuate change. If the 17 UN SDGs are to become part of our daily living, we need to become economic activists, peacefully debating and dialoguing, and constructing an active agenda.

We prefer change at the local level, involving active, pluralist debate; after all, this is the essence of democracy. We also wholeheartedly endorse the recommendation from the former University of Manchester economics students to form citizen counsels in which citizens and (and, we would add, all concerned stakeholders) actively engage with each other and with economists to understand policy (Earle et al., 2017: 154–7). In the next section, we will discuss briefly fiscal and monetary policy: two government tools to stabilise the economy. Both are accepted by most (but certainly not all) economists.

12.9 FISCAL AND MONETARY POLICY

To illustrate how the tools of fiscal and monetary policy are used, let us assume a recession in which actual GDP is less the economy's potential, i.e. $GDP_t < GDP_p$. If the goal is to stimulate the economy,[4] then fiscal or monetary policy, or both, can be used to get it moving again and close the GDP gap. And, conversely, if the economy is overheating, where $GDP_t > GDP_p$, we can use either tool or both to slow it down.

Which tool is preferred? And what are the differences? While institutions, values and ideology differ significantly between countries (and even within countries over time, as the nation and its economic system evolves), we can offer the following generalisations:

- **Fiscal policy** is defined as deliberate changes in either tax policy or government spending in order to influence the GDP gap, i.e. to stabilize the economy. Specifically, if $GDP_t < GDP_p$, then tax rates will be reduced and/or government spending will be increased. Conversely, if $GDP_t > GDP_p$ then tax rates could be increased and/or government spending can be reduced.
- **Monetary policy** is defined as using monetary aggregates, such as the money supply and/or short-term interest rates, to either stimulate the economy by increasing the money supply and/or reducing short-term interest rates, if $GDP_t < GDP_p$; or slow the economy down by reducing the money supply and increasing short-term interest rates, if $GDP_t > GDP_p$.
- Monetary policy is conducted by central banks, whose leaders and members are seldom elected; whereas fiscal policy (in democracies) is conducted by elected officials, rendering fiscal policy accountable (at least in theory) to the electorate. An obvious problem, at least in democracies, is that because fiscal policy is conducted by elected officials, it is easier to reduce taxes and/or increase spending than the opposite. It is for this reason that democracies and prudent fiscal spending are argued to be incompatible (Buchanan and Wagner (1977 [1999]).
- Fiscal policy is based on underlying economic theory, especially consumption and investment theory as articulated by Keynes in *The General Theory*, and elaborated by Post-Keynesianists. Monetary policy is also based on underlying theory, especially by monetarists and Post-Keynesianists.

---

4. Such a goal dates only from the Great Depression; prior to this, it was assumed that the economy was self-equilibrating, so that given a shock or disturbance, the economy would eventually right itself. To give one example: during a recession, consumption falls and savings increase, which would reduce the interest rate, increasing investment equal to the initial reduction in consumption. The Great Depression, however, and the most recent financial crisis proved emphatically that the economy does not work like this.

- While governments tend to use both fiscal and monetary policies, today the latter is often preferred, for three reasons (Carlin and Soskice, 2015: 82): (1) fiscal policy involves lengthy debate, and there is no equivalent to the gradual adjustment of interest rate; (2) fiscal policy is inherently political, since it involves the use of tax revenue; and (3) monetary policy is viewed as more neutral, not obviously creating winners and losers, making it less contentious.

We will further discuss fiscal policy and its underlying theory in the next chapter; and likewise monetary policy will be discussed in Chapter 16. In Box 12.2 below we briefly discuss US deficits and debt from an historical perspective.

Box 12.2 US Budget Deficits and Debt: A Historical Perspective

In any given fiscal year, the federal government can run either a:

- **balanced budget**, defined as federal revenues = federal spending
- **budget deficit**, defined as federal revenues < federal spending
- **budget surplus**, defined as federal revenues > federal spending.

If a federal deficit is financed by borrowing funds from the public (as is done today in the USA, rather than printing money, which, all things being equal, can lead to inflation) then the public debt increases. The **public debt** is defined as the sum of outstanding liabilities owed by the government to the public in order to finance past deficits.

Budget deficits and the public debt have always figured into American politics. The USA was born with a significant debt, when it subsumed the individual debts of the 13 colonies in order to form a greater union, of approximately 34 per cent of its GDP: a significant sum in those days, forcing the USA to be fiscally conservative and mindful of its European creditors.[1] Nevertheless, the Washington administration ran deficits in four of its first eight years, for which President Washington himself was criticised.

Running a budget surplus or, at worst, a balanced budget was the concern of every administration from George Washington until the 1930s. No reason was given other than that the government should be no different from any individual balancing his or her budget. In fact, a central theme of the 1932 US presidential election (Herbert Hoover, the Republican incumbent, vs Franklin Roosevelt, the Democratic challenger and eventual winner) was how to best balance the budget.

Only war could justify borrowing and hence accruing an increased public debt. But during peacetime it was considered essential to run budget surpluses in order to reduce the debt, i.e. the government paying back its creditors. So for example in 1860, on the eve of the US Civil War, the public debt was $64 million; in 1866, one year after the Civil War ended, the public debt was $2.7 billion. From 1866 until 1893, the USA ran successive budget surpluses, reducing the public debt to $961

▶

1. All data in this paragraph are obtained from Gordon, 1998: 205–10. All data are in nominal terms, and in US dollars.

million. The period 1866–93 set a record for continuous budget surpluses. Given the sorry state of USA politics today, it is unlikely that this record will be soon broken. And similarly, during the First World War, the US debt increased from $1.2 billion to $25 billion, followed immediately by budget surpluses from 1920 to 1930 (the second-longest era of successive surpluses in American history), reducing the public debt to $16 billion.

While today the bulk of US federal revenue (approximately 92 per cent) comes from income taxes, social security, and corporate taxes; before the Second World War the major source of revenue was **tariffs** – taxes on imported goods. Tariffs then did double duty, not only providing the federal government's major source of revenue but also keeping out cheaper goods by making them more expensive, thus helping the US to industrialise. It was no coincidence that during the period 1866–93 the US was highly protectionist – amongst the most protectionist in the world.

We would be remiss for not mentioning Alexander Hamilton and Andrew Jackson, two prominent Americans who also figure into our deficit/debt story. Each graces a denomination of US currency: Alexander Hamilton the $10 bill; Andrew Jackson the $20 bill. Alexander Hamilton (1757–1804), co-author of *The Federalist Papers*, founding father of the USA and Treasury Secretary under the Washington administration[2] was instrumental in appeasing the financial markets (centred in Europe), assuaging their concerns to the effect that not only would they get their money back (in gold), but at a very of favourable interest rate. This allowed the US to borrow substantially in order to finance the Louisiana Purchase (1803), which effectively doubled geographically the size of the USA.

Andrew Jackson (1767–1845) was US president from 1829 to 1837, and was the only president to eliminate the public debt during his tenure, a feat which was 'unique in the history of modern nations and one that arose far more from the personality and history of Andrew Jackson than from economic theory. Indeed, it would contribute in no small way to [the] country's first great depression' (Gordon, 1998: 57). It is beyond our purview to delve into the intricacies of Jackson's life[3] other than to say that in addition to eliminating the debt he also did not renew the charter of the Bank of the United States (functioning as a central bank from 1816–36). Both of these events stemmed from a friend's bankruptcy during his youth, who had used promissory notes to purchase significant assets, making Jackson liable when his friend declared bankruptcy. This unfortunate event 'gave [Jackson] a lifelong horror of debt and the use of paper to finance, or even to facilitate, transactions' (Ibid.: 59).

Fast-forward to 1910, when a coterie had gathered on Jekyll Island off the coast of Georgia to plan a new central bank – the Federal Reserve. What better way to motivate long-term survival of the Fed than to grace the $20 bill with the man who deliberately ended the nation's previous central bank?

▶

2. While there is no shortage of biographies of Hamilton (or Jackson, for that matter), an informative source is Ellis (2000). Hamilton, of course, died in a duel with Aaron Burr, vice-president under Thomas Jefferson.

3. The best place to begin is Arthur Schlesinger's *The Age of Jackson* (1945), for which he won the Pulitzer Prize. Schlesinger adroitly captures the interdependency of early nineteenth-century America with Jackson's formative years and his presidency.

Thanks to the Great Depression and the Second World War, the US ran successive deficits from 1931 to 1946, increasing the debt from $16 billion (18 per cent of GDP) to $269 billion respectively (130 per cent of GDP – an all-time high). Also during this time there was a gradual acceptance by most economists (but certainly not all) of the beneficial role of deficits and debt in economic stabilisation.

The federal government ran successive budget surpluses from 1946–52, after which, however, as debt culture became more institutionalised, deficit spending became the norm, with budget surpluses increasingly rare. The federal government ran surpluses in 1956 and 1957, but not again until 1969. This was followed by a record-setting era of continuous budget deficits (1970–97). Needless to say, the federal debt increased from 1957, from $270 billion in that year to $909 billion in 1980, crossing the psychologically important trillion-dollar barrier in 1981.

Since 1980, the US has experienced only four budget surplus years (1998–2001), largely due to a tax increase in 1996 and relative peace without major war or recession. Since 2001 the USA has run a deficit every year and, thanks to the severe recession from 2007 to 2009 and significant stabilisation spending, federal deficits ballooned to over $1 trillion annually during each of the years 2009–12. The projected US deficit for fiscal year 2018 is $440 billion, with little prospect of a budget surplus anytime soon. Currently the US debt is $19.9 trillion,[4] which is approximately 104 per cent of USA GDP.

The large recent deficits and increasing debt have handicapped active fiscal policy[5] and prevented concerted effort in investment in renewable-energy infrastructure – a cornerstone of sustainability. Large deficits pressure politicians not to increase spending further, especially on investment. We are witnessing this now, especially in the European Union and the United States. And we believe this is one reason (albeit among many complicated and interrelated reasons) why the Trump administration announced that it would renege on the 2015 Paris Climate Treaty, and why the US is reluctant to invest significantly in renewable energy. This is not to say that we advocate blind reduction in federal deficits, but rather that the path toward sustainability is complex and involves active dialogue about spending priorities.

4. For an eye-watering experience of US deficits and debt increasing in real time, see the 'US Debt Clock' at www.usdebtclock.org

5. Phillips (2002) and many others argue, quite persuasively, that increasing debt, partisan politics and deficit spending is both cause and effect of declining superpowers, afflicting (at various times) Spain, the Netherlands , Great Britain, and the USA.

12.10 FINANCING FOR DEVELOPMENT: SMALL BUSINESS CHALLENGES

The UN Monterrey Consensus (2003) recognised the crucial role of finance and investment in the process of economic growth. The emphasis relies on strengthening international and domestic capital markets, in addition to creating/expanding domestic credit and capital markets to reach small firms and other excluded agents or economic sectors. In developing countries, small firms have generally poor innovation, low competitiveness and low participation in global export markets, with restricted access to credit and financial institutions. Indeed, small firms are unable to implement strategies to increase productivity.

The main barrier to the sustainability of small firms is the lack of capital for investment and the difficulty in obtaining financing. From the firms' perspective, bank loans remain expensive and bureaucratic. Aware of these demands, some governments in East Asia and Latin America have attempted to simplify credit access, along with enlargement of guarantees, improved agility in opening enterprises, financial cost reduction and expansion of access to online regulatory information. Nevertheless, strong asymmetries exist between small and big firms in terms of credit access.

What can be done? Credit-allocation policies could be combined with small firms' investment and employment targeting, and the central bank could shape asset-based reserve requirements to stimulate innovations in small firms (Epstein, 2007). Otherwise, central banks could give preferential access for financial institutions that invest in or lend to small firms, which may generate more and better jobs. It is also relevant to reassess the importance of industrial and regulatory policies to promote the expansion of the small business vis-à-vis the active, and sometimes hostile, presence of private-equity investments. This effort is crucial to the important task ahead for policy-makers in order to shape institutions toward sustainable and inclusive growth for future generations.

12.11 LIVELIHOODS AND FOOD SECURITY

Since the 1990s, agriculture modernisation in developing countries has increased productivity, while also increasing poverty, agribusiness and the exodus of small farmers. Between 1990 and 2007, the number of people suffering from hunger globally increased from 842 million to 923 million. The global increase in food prices since 2005 worsened conditions of the poor, since they spend a disproportionate portion of their income on food. Today, food prices remain well above levels reached before the recent financial crisis, and the extreme volatility in world food prices poses a global challenge (King et al., 2014). For example, in the next ten years, the prices of meat and dairy products are expected to increase relative to the prices of crops. And among crops, the price of coarse grains and oilseeds used for feed might rise relative to the prices of food staples. To explain this trend, causal factors include: (1) growth of the world's population by 2.24 billion, or 32 per cent by 2050 (UN forecast); and (2) growth of China's GDP and the urbanisation of China, with millions of people migrating from rural areas, exerting greater pressure on food supply in urban areas.

Underdeveloped countries' potential for food production has weakened due to lack of resources for investment and the poverty of local markets, which is exacerbated by a number of factors, including: low formal education and management capacity; lack of knowledge of market conditions; absence of economic feasibility studies; absence of economies of scale in commercialisation; lack of standardisation and quality; fragile farmers' organisation; lack of credit; deficient infrastructure; unfamiliar sanitary legislation and unproductive techniques.

Many governments (supported by international organisations) have implemented measures to strengthen the social protection of the poor and raise agricultural production through incentives to family agriculture. The UN FAO (Food and Agriculture Organization), for example, fosters the development of productive capacity of small farming and distributes agricultural inputs such as seeds. The Brazilian government supports family agriculture with programmes like Pronaf, which guarantees credit for investment and production. In Honduras, the agricultural inputs distribution programme with government seed has involved family farmers previously trained by FAO. Countries in Central America and the Caribbean are implementing actions to carry out joint purchases of agricultural inputs, e.g. fertilisers.

We suggest that, given its importance in long-term planning, the support of family farming requires new actors, including cooperatives, associations and other representatives of the rural sector; along with support in discussing, designing and implementing public policies; and strengthened public policy and regional investment.

12.12 DEVELOPING A GREEN ECONOMY

We must remember that 'GDP is not just a statistical metric. It represents a way of organising society' (Fioramonti, 2013: 153). So how do we want to organise society according to sustainability and justice? Let's start with how we measure and conceptualise economic activity, which in turn will tell us what is important.

One of the most powerful critics of GDP as a measure of economic success was the New Zealand feminist economist Marilyn Waring. In her book *If Women Counted* (Waring, 1988: 1) she criticised GDP for ignoring women's work caring for children, old people and households since they are not paid, and for failing to value the natural environment:

> I learned that the things that I value about life in my country – its pollution-free environment; its mountain streams with safe drinking water; the accessibility of national parks, walkways, beaches, lakes, kauri and beech forests; the absence of nuclear power and nuclear energy – all counted for nothing. They were not accounted for in private consumption expenditure, general government expenditure, or gross domestic capital formation. Yet these accounting systems were used to determine all public policy. Since the environment effectively counted for nothing, there could be no 'value' on policy measures that would ensure its preservation.

In response, some governments now collect data on resources as well as output. For example, Norway has been monitoring its fish stocks since the 1980s, enabling it to chart the decline of its two most important fish species: the spring-spawning herring and the northeast Arctic cod. Norway has also been monitoring emissions of air pollutants since the 1970s, enabling it to substantially reduce emissions of SO_2 and of lead to less than half the levels of the early 1970s.

Environmental accounting, also called **green accounting**, developed during the late 1990s, involving the active participation of multilateral institutions such as the United Nations, OECD (Organisation for Economic Co-operation and Development) and World Bank. Since the mid 2000s, the revised version of the System of Environmental and Economic Accounts (SEEA) has progressed towards the standardisation of concepts, definitions and methodologies, helping national and international institutions to compile the necessary information for elaborating environmental accounting. Indeed the idea of carefully assessing a company's impact on the environment is slowly taking root. Pavan Sukhdev (2013) argues that adoption of green accounting requires new global governance and corporate models. Environmental accounting assesses economic outcomes in terms of the spending reduction of water, energy and other resources; renewable or not.

Due to the recent economic and financial crisis and the need to support new sectors, many governments currently support (domestically) the growth of the green economy, as an alternative vision for growth and development. This effort is sometimes branded as the ***Green New Deal*** (echoing policies of US President Franklin Roosevelt in the 1930s, when the US and the rest of the capitalist world faced an extended period of economic depression).

One of the most dramatic examples of the expansion of green energy is that of Denmark. The country changed its energy policy in the 1970s after recognising that being 90-per-cent dependent on imported oil made it very vulnerable to geopolitical events. There was a fierce political debate during the 1980s between proponents of nuclear power and the Greens, who favoured transition to renewables. During the 1980s the Danish government funded 30 per cent of investments in wind turbines, so that by 2009, 28 per cent of Denmark's electricity came from renewable sources. While the economy grew by 78 per cent between 1980 and 2009, energy consumption has not increased, indicating significant advances in energy efficiency (Cumbers, 2012). The country's renewable generation also focused on local cooperative ownership, meaning that the local communities investing in the turbines also used the energy and gained the income. This reduced obstacles to the building of wind farms encountered in other countries due to local communities' landscape views being compromised without direct economic benefit. The most important lesson from the Danish case is that governments can facilitate rapid technological change, which is more likely if local people have a genuine ownership of the new technologies.

At the city government level, the introduction of a congestion charge on private vehicles entering central London significantly improved air quality, along with achieving a 40-per-cent reduction in traffic accidents, as traffic levels in the congestion charge zone declined by over 20 per cent in its first ten years of operation (Leape 2006). This raises the important question: To what extent does the promotion of a green economy require central, regional or local planning? And, which is the most appropriate and effective level?

Green economists favour localisation for reasons of accountability, power and control. According to the United Nations (UN, 2014b):

> **Localisation** refers to the process of defining, implementing and monitoring strategies at the local level for achieving global, national and subnational sustainable development goals and targets. This involves concrete mechanisms, tools, innovations, platforms and processes to effectively translate the development agenda into results at the local level. The concept should therefore be understood holistically, beyond the institutions of local governments, to include all local actors through a territorial approach that includes civil society, traditional leaders, religious organisations, academia, the private sector and others.

In localisation strategies, small firms are highlighted because of their contribution to job creation and income growth in the process of development. Small entrepreneurs emphasise the need for support for systematic innovation in products, processes and markets, including lower taxes, access to credit, consulting and commercialisation. In short, taxation and credit policies are crucial to promote productivity and competitiveness in small firms.

Actually, localisation planning is decisive to reduce small firms' vulnerability to economic shocks. And in that sense, there is good reason to keep and foster a policy environment oriented to small businesses that may contribute to sustainable economic growth and job creation. For example, access to finance, innovation and knowledge is important and provides new parameters for entrepreneurial behaviour and decision-making. Besides, alternative sectorial and regulatory policies could be adopted to promote the sustainability of the small-business sector to favour long-term investment. Policies and institutions certainly contribute to conventions and norms that could influence business expectations.

The new agenda should express the holistic approach to sustainable development (reducing inequalities, poverty, global warming, etc.). In creating this framework, the business environment could benefit society as a whole. The attempt to shape small-business policies and institutions toward sustainable growth for future generations is decisively worthy of our effort (Madi, 2015).

12.13 THE INFANT INDUSTRY ARGUMENT

It is interesting that once nations become economic superpowers they preach the gospel of free trade – but not before. The reason should be obvious: a superpower's firms require unrestricted access to global markets for cheap resources and as an outlet for finished goods. Great Britain was very protectionist during the late eighteenth century and early nineteenth, and it was not until Great Britain emerged as a superpower that it preached the virtues of free trade – for its own self-interest, particularly the interests of its firms. The newly formed United States in the nineteenth century argued vociferously against Britain's clarion call for free trade: the USA was a developing country, not wanting to be subjugated to the economic domination of a superpower. The USA was very protectionist from its birth until the mid-1940s, and especially during the late nineteenth century, when it rapidly industrialised and experienced its own industrial revolution.

The US founding father Alexander Hamilton (see Box 12.2 earlier) developed the idea of 'infant industries' to justify increasing tariffs against British imports. At the time, Britain was the world's strongest manufacturing economy (and also an enemy from which the USA had only recently become independent). The infant industry argument was later theorised by the German economist Friedrich List in his book *The National System of Political Economy* (1841). During its period of rapid technological expansion following the Second World War, Japan used this argument to justify imposing tariffs on imports.

Although there is a tendency in market economies to favour free competition, some economists argue that there are times when particular sectors are young and vulnerable, like children or infants, and in need of protection from the harsh winds of competitive trade. Examples of such policies include trade barriers and tariffs, limiting the level of imports, charging a tax on imports, or providing subsidies to producers. (We will discuss these issues in Chapter 16). China has been artificially holding down its currency, thereby making its exports cheaper to allow it to build up its industries and compete with other countries. The infant industry argument also justifies subsidies for important new industries, as has been discussed recently in the case of the renewable energy, in theory (Mityakov and Portnykh, 2012) and in practice.

As noted above, the rejection of free trade is common to developing nations. An historical example can be drawn from examining infant industries and import-substitution policies in Latin America. Since the end of the nineteenth century until the Great Depression, the debate on economic development related to the problem of overcoming the shortage of factors of production and absence of technology. The reigning neoclassical ideology, based on the division of labour, postulated a role for each country based on its relative scarcity of the factors of production. Growth inequalities between countries were explained by the absence of free movement of goods, services and capital.

Adopted in many Latin American countries between the 1930s and the 1980s, import-substitution had its theoretical genesis in the works of Raúl Prebisch (1949), Celso Furtado (1969) and other Latin American structural economists. It was adopted in some Asian and African countries from the 1950s. In 1948, the United Nations Economic Commission for Latin America and the Caribbean (ECLAC) was formed, led by Prebisch, an Argentine economist, who argued that the process of capitalist accumulation within the international system generated a particular dynamic between centre and periphery, reflected in the international division of labour. The periphery would suffer from large cyclical swings in export prices, mainly in agricultural commodities, leading to a deterioration of the terms of trade between the agricultural products of the periphery and the industrialised products from the Centre. In this sense, underdevelopment constituted a condition of international capitalist accumulation, with capital expansion deepening the asymmetries between the centre and periphery. Import-substitution policies were intended to reduce the foreign exchange demand, given the restrictions caused by the deterioration of the terms of trade (for an expanded discussion of trade, see Chapter 16).

In the 1950s, ECLAC argued that industrialisation of the periphery required deliberate political action via economic planning in order to achieve the necessary conditions for a qualitative structural transformation. Thus, during Latin America's industrialisation, the growth of public spending, particularly in state enterprises, should be understood in the context of a particular arrangement between the state and private companies. The expansion of the state productive sector arose from the economic and financial restructuring required to ensure the *jump to industrialisation*. However, with import substitution, the incorporation of the central countries' technology by the periphery reproduced and reinforced structural heterogeneity as a characteristic of underdevelopment.

Thus, with import-substitution policies, government interventions favour the replacement of industrial imports in order to encourage local production, rather than producing for export markets. Import substitution involves trade policy issues in order to protect the infant industry by limiting competing imports. Indeed, infant industry protection occurs when a tariff in one period causes an increase in output sufficient to allow the firm to survive, whereas otherwise it would not. In the 1980s, critics of import-substitution industrialisation emphasised the costs involved: complex, time-consuming regulations; high tariff rates for consumers and also for firms needing to buy imported inputs for their products.

Today, the global consensus toward economic growth is essentially one enabling free trade for global corporations. Indeed, according to the United Nations Conference on Trade and Development (UNCTAD, 2013) the global economy is characterised by global value chains (GVCs) where intermediate goods and services are traded in fragmented and internationally dispersed production processes. These GVCs are coordinated by transnational corporations (TNCs) within their networks of affiliates, contractual partners and suppliers, accounting for approximately 80 per cent of global trade.

Considering the current links between trade and growth, trade agreements highlight the role of global corporations. One recent example was the proposed Transatlantic Trade and Investment Partnership (TTIP), a proposed trade agreement between the European Union and the United States. Besides investment, the TTIP was expected to include reciprocal market openings in goods and services, and to foster the compatibility of regulatory and protection standards. As a bilateral agreement, TTIP aims to reduce the regulatory barriers to trade for big business, such as food safety laws, environmental legislation, health services and banking regulations. It is this perceived bias that led to the Treaty's defeat after Donald Trump was elected US president. We would argue that the TTIP and the current system of global trade is not sustainable; more specifically, it does not comport with the UN 17 SDGs, and represents a major obstacle for their implementation.

THINKING QUESTIONS

In what situations might a monopoly comport with the interests of consumers?

What are the advantages and disadvantages of having only one company providing computer software?

In what ways might it be necessary to pay for care of the elderly in order for caring work to be properly valued?

CLASS ACTIVITY

Is climate change a serious enough crisis to justify government intervention in the market? Or is the market capable of resolving this on its own? Is an 'either/ or' the best way to phrase this question?

AREAS FOR RESEARCH

How have antitrust laws been enforced in the USA? Are the existing laws just? Do we need a new set of antitrust laws to comport with the UN SDGs?

UN SDG FOCUS

Goal #3 is: 'Ensure healthy lives and promote well-being for all at all ages.' How can this be ensured? And how can 'well-being' be defined and measured?

FURTHER READING

Leape, J. (2006) 'The London Congestion Charge'. *Journal of Economic Perspectives*, Vol. 20, No. 4, pp.157–76.

13
Consumption, Investment and Savings

Given the central role of consumption in contemporary global capitalism, this chapter explores the economic concepts of consumption, investment and savings, while explaining how finance currently dominates decisions about consumption and investment. To understand the contemporary challenges to sustainable investment, the recent history of private investment and the flow of finance between countries will also be analysed. Our discussion will draw on the contributions of John Maynard Keynes and Michał Kalecki. Both articulated a different view of the relationship between finance and economic development from neoclassical economists; each emphasised the importance of 'effective demand' to understand the dynamics of the capitalist system.

13.1 HOUSEHOLD CONSUMPTION

As we have seen previously, livelihoods, work and consumption are central to understanding economics as the provisioning of human needs. In contemporary capitalism, and especially in the United States, consumption is the engine of economic growth, comprising approximately 70 per cent of US GDP. As the scale of consumption increases, the sheer volume of production of material goods pressures the ecosystems on which we depend. So while ecological sustainability requires us to recognise the existence of biophysical limits, the need to keep aggregate demand (i.e. the sum total of a nation's demand for goods and services made by consumers, firms, government at all levels, and foreigners) at sufficiently high levels means that we have to maintain current consumption: in other words, if we do not follow a path of increasing consumption we will condemn the economy to recession. From another angle, consumption is no longer just about meeting our everyday needs but establishes our identity and becomes a substitute for face-to-face human relationships.

Household consumption (C) is the portion of disposable income (Y) spent by consumers on goods and services for the satisfaction of immediate needs. And **personal savings** (S) is that portion of disposable income not immediately consumed.

Keynes argued that consumption is stable and positively related to income; that is, as income increases, so does consumption. In addition to income, Keynes argued that consumption depends on both objective (relatively easily measured and thereby controlled) and subjective (whimsical and differing amongst individuals) factors (Keynes, (2010 [1936]: 89–131). Included among the objective factors affecting consumption are:

- **Fiscal policy:** Tax burden and benefits received from the state, such as unemployment compensation.
- **Credit availability:** Both in terms of the amount available and the interest rate. This also includes access to bank loans, credit cards and other financial products.
- **Expectations of future income:** Expecting more income in the future will increase consumption now, and vice versa.
- **Valuation of financial market assets**, also known as the 'wealth effect': Consumption increases if your assets (such as stocks and bonds) increase in value.

And the following subjective factors affecting consumption include:

- **Caution:** Using savings as a buffer to cope with unforeseen contingencies.
- **Calculation:** Considering the benefit gained from equity in the financial market.
- **Independence:** Keeping money in reserve for a rainy day.
- **Initiative:** The wish to hold money back in case a money-making opportunity arises.
- **Pride:** The desire to bequeath a fortune.
- **Avarice:** Intrinsic desire to hold money rather than spend it.
- **Pension planning:** Establishing a reserve to cover old age, to pay for education of children or to care for dependents.

13.2 THE MARGINAL PROPENSITY TO CONSUME

As Keynes noted, income and consumption are positively related: as income increases (or decreases), consumption increases (or decreases), but by not as much. The specific relationship between change in consumption and change in income is the **marginal propensity to consume** (MPC), defined as:

$$\text{MPC} = \frac{\text{change in consumption}}{\text{change in income}}$$

A simple example: If the government gives every citizen an extra £100 (change in income), and if one citizen, Jane, for example, spends £90 on consumption (change in consumption), then her MPC is 0.90. Interpreted slightly differently, given an MPC of 0.90, then 90 per cent of extra income goes toward consumption.

Since the alternative to consumption is savings, assuming that income is either saved or consumed, we can introduce the **marginal propensity to save** (MPS):

$$\text{MPS} = \frac{\text{change in savings}}{\text{change in income}}$$

In the above example, Jane's MPS is 0.10.

As a general rule MPC + MPS = 1. Furthermore, the MPC will differ between individuals, and for each individual over time. Specifically, wealthier individuals have a higher MPS, while the poor have a very high MPC, close to 1. Younger people and older tend to have a higher MPC, while middle-aged people tend to have a higher MPS.

13.3 CONSUMPTION AND CREDIT IN BRAZIL

In the first decade of the twenty-first century, the opening up of formal financial services and the fast growth of credit strongly influenced Brazil's consumption. According to Febraban (the Brazilian Federation of Banks), between 2002 and 2012 the number of people with access to financial services increased from 28 million to 54 million. This has, not surprisingly, changed consumption patterns. Since 2004, 2.2 million Brazilian households in income classes D and E have introduced new products into their consumption 'basket'. This income category refers to those who, since 2004/5, have a monthly income of less than US$600, while households in class C have a monthly income between US$600 and US$1,150. These low-income and new middle-class-income families have not only diversified in the food products they buy but also bought cars, mobile phones and other electronic devices (Madi and Gonçalves, 2007).

Tables 13.1 and 13.2 indicate that rates of growth of consumer loans increased sharply and that this was the main driver of consumption. In all regions of Brazil, between 2004 and 2010, the highest rates of borrowing (almost 60 per cent of total consumer credit) was for personal loans, credit cards and cars. Even after the financial crisis of 2007–08, the number of individual borrowers increased from 17.9 million to 30.2 million and the total amount of credit as a percentage of GDP (households plus corporations) was 52.8 per cent in 2015. However, since 2014 consumer credit has negatively suffered from economic instability. The lower consumer confidence, combined with inflation, higher interest rates and high levels of household indebtedness led to a weak demand for credit and restricted credit from banks.

Table 13.1 Brazil: Credit Indicators, 2005–2010

Year	*Total credit as a percentage of GDP (households plus corporations)*	*Consumer credit loans: annual average rate of growth (in percentage)*	*Number of borrowers registered at the central bank, in millions*
2005	28.3	21.5	10,580
2006	30.9	21.1	12,509
2007	35.2	24.7	15,146
2008	40.5	19.9	17,927
2009	44.4	15.2	22,233
2010	46.4	17.0	30,159

Source: Banco Central do Brasil (2011).

Table 13.2 Brazil: Macroeconomic Indicators (in Percentage)

Indicator	*2016*	*2018**	*2020**
Real GDP (annual rate of growth)	−3.3	5.1	0.2
Lending rates	32.6	31.7	29.8
Sovereign debt (annual interest rate)	14.3	13.2	11.0
Unemployment rate	11.8	10.9	10.1
Inflation	7.2	4.8	4.5

Note: * = projections.

Sources: International Monetary Fund (IMF, 2016); Banco Central do Brasil (2017).

13.4 LINKING INVESTMENT AND CONSUMPTION: INTRODUCING THE SPENDING MULTIPLIER

Have you ever stood on the shore of a lake or river and thrown a stone into the water, watching the initial plop, then the rippling in every direction? This mental picture can help you to understand the multiplier, an important concept in economics. Think of the initial plop as additional spending, perhaps investment, which then creates a ripple effect, extending through the economy. The multiplier in effect measures the economic rippling, and we use it to ask a very important question: What is the total effect of increased spending?

The **spending multiplier** (M) measures the magnified change in aggregate income (GDP) resulting from a change in spending; more specifically, M is defined as the amount income changes when spending increases by one unit. The MPC, discussed above, affects the multiplier process, along with the magnitude of the induced consumption.

Let's look at an example. Say you get a gift of £500. Your income immediately increases by £500. Then you decide to take your whole economics class (and your professor!) out to lunch. The proprietor of the restaurant is happy for the added business – her income has now increased by £500 thanks to you. Let's say she then uses all of the £500 to fix a leak in the roof. She calls the roofer immediately; the roofer obliges, and is now £500 richer. Now assume the roofer spends the £500 on office supplies, increasing the supplier's income by £500.

How long can this process continue and when will it end? Just like throwing a rock into the water, the ripple generates a forward motion which runs into the resistance of the water – an opposing force that slows the motion down. The larger the initial plop, the larger the ripple, but eventually, given the resistance of the water, it must stop. The same applies to your £500: it eventually must stop, given any 'leakages', i.e. money that is not consumed, or money that is saved. Say for example that instead of spending your initial £500, you put it under your mattress. There is an initial plop, yes – your income has now increased, but there is no ripple. Only you have become richer and no one else.

Spending all of the £500 or none of it are two extremes; in reality, you are more likely to spend or save some. Or would you? Say you only spend £200 but still spend it on taking your fellow students to lunch (and of course your professor). Now what happens? Of course the restaurant owner's income has increased, thanks to you, but only by £200, so perhaps she cannot fix the roof, so let's say she uses the money to repair a refrigerator, but also keeps £50 for her daughter's birthday. The repair person is now £150 better off, but what does he do with the money? Let's say he pays back taxes of £100 and buys a new coat with the remainder. The clothing store owner is now £50 richer.

Obviously the more each person saves, the less money (added income) others will have to spend, and the less total income will increase. Money taken out of the circuit of spending is called a **leakage**, and leakages can occur either due to government tax or a decision to save. If everyone decided to save all of their money in a local bank, and no one went out to lunch, how would the restaurant owner, roofer and fridge repair person be affected? Would they still act in the same way? Why, or why not?

The initial increased income results in increased spending, resulting in additional production, which generates more income, which induces more consumption. This next round of consumption also triggers an increase in production, which generates more income, and induces more consumption. And on it goes. The end result is a magnified, multiplied change in aggregate production, initially triggered by the change in spending but amplified by the change in consumption. The MPC enters into the process because it determines how much additional consumption is induced with each change in production and income.

Keynes believed that the marginal propensity to consume for a given society is relatively stable in a given period of time, so a society's income fluctuations and the level of employment depend mainly on additional (especially investment) spending and consumption.

But just like a stone doesn't drop out of heaven, (usually) a change in spending (such as investment) doesn't just happen but rather is consciously engineered as an active decision.

13.5 *TECHNIQUE 11*: CALCULATING THE MULTIPLIER

You might wonder what is the cumulative effect of the spending decisions on total (or aggregate) income. The multiplier is designed to measure this. The initial spending results in increased aggregate income, which induces additional consumption; which increases aggregate income; which induces additional consumption, and so on. Theoretically, this could go on for ever. Fortunately, we can approximate the total spending with the following simple (relatively) mathematical process:

$$\Delta Y = (1 + MPC_1 + MPC_2 + MPC_3 + MPC_4 + \ldots MPC_n) \text{ x } \Delta I$$

where:

ΔY = change in disposable income
ΔI = initial change in spending
MPC_i = the marginal propensity to consume for each individual during a specified time period; where $0 < MPC < 1$.

The first term is 1 because if the MPC is 0, then the ΔY is simply the ΔI.

The expression in parenthesis $(1 + MPC_1 + MPC_2 + MPC_3 + MPC_4 + \ldots MPC_{n)}$ is in the form of an infinite geometric series. Thankfully, we know from the work of mathematicians that if the first term is 1, and the common ratio is MPC, the sum of the series is:

$$(1/1\text{–}MPC)$$

Substitute (1/1–MPC) for the parenthetical expressions above, and we have:

$$\Delta Y = [(1/1\text{–}MPC)] \text{ x } \Delta I$$

Then divide left and right by ΔI to obtain:

$$\Delta Y/\Delta I = (1/1\text{–}MPC)$$

The expression on the left is the change in total spending given the initial spending, which is the definition of multiplier. It equals the expression on the right, which is our mathematical expression of the multiplier. And remember that MPC + MPS = 1; and thus: 1 – MPC = MPS, the spending multiplier can also be written as:

$$\Delta Y/\Delta I = (1/MPS)$$

If the MPC is 0 (i.e. MPS = 1) then **M** = 1, (using our analogy above, there is only a plop and no ripple); whereas if MPC = 1 (there is no leakage, and hence no resistance), **M** is theoretically infinite and the process never stops. And, for example, a MPC of 0.75 results in a multiplier of 4; and a MPC of 0.8 results in a larger multiplier of 5. The greater the multiplier, the greater effect of initial spending on total income.

13.6 INVESTMENT

Investment is the most volatile component of GDP, and it is independent of previous levels of national income; that is to say, investment is an autonomous form of spending. It is determined by interest rates, business confidence, taxes and capacity utilisation. If firms are confident of the future, they will invest more, all else being equal; and, conversely, uncertainty about the future will reduce investment.

Total (or gross) investment spending is composed of:

- spending on capital goods, i.e. the purchase of machinery and equipment either to replace existing capacity that is wearing out or to increase capacity (also called 'fixed capital formation')
- inventories that firms hold to satisfy miscalculated demand on the final goods they produce.

Because capital goods are used in the production of other goods and services, they will wear out or depreciate. For example, a nuclear power plant, thanks to the intensive energy of the fission process, lasts approximately 40 years and then will have to be discarded and replaced. This wear and tear from normal use, i.e. **depreciation**, can be calculated either all at once or, more usually, pro-rated each year.

Consumption and investment are invariably linked. A change in investment spending, such as building a nuclear power plant, changes income, which then changes consumption and savings. The exact mix depends on the MPC and MPS.

13.7 A BRIEF NOTE ON FRIEDRICH VON HAYEK (1899–1992)

A fundamental problem in economics, according to the Austrian economist Friedrich von Hayek, is coordinating the plans of many individuals. The main advantage of a competitive economic order, in Hayek's view, is that rational individuals respond to price signals, which convey the relevant information available in markets for the purpose of economic calculus. In his view, competition, through the price market system, leads to such coordination (Hayek, 1944).

In truth, Hayek was one of the strongest critics of Keynes' effort to transform the discipline of economics.[1] Hayek argued that for the Keynesian income expenditure model to work, the economist must know the aggregate level of current consumption, investment and public spending; the full employment level of output; and the multiplier effect. Which, of course, presupposes that detailed knowledge of economic life is available and that the outcomes of each policy intervention will have precise effects on economic activity. In lieu of such specific information, Hayek advocated a decentralised market system as the best way to disseminate, gather and coordinate knowledge. Assessing the practical superiority of the free market vis-à-vis government, Hayek believed that no government could know enough to effectively plan the future path of the economy; and, likewise, that central banks do not have the relevant information to correctly manage the money supply.

Hayek criticised arbitrary interventions by the state in *The Road to Serfdom* (1944). He critiqued the redefinition of the state's legitimacy and stressed the need to defeat growing state intrusion. He emphasised the values that shape the interrelations of individuals in a free society, such as the inviolability of human beings, individual freedom and justice.

Hayek restated the relevance of concepts and ideas proposed by classical philosophy in order to apprehend contemporary threats to individuals. He rebuilt the foundations of constitutional governments given contemporary institutional decay in modern societies. He proposed the abolition of the government's monopoly over the issue of fiat money in order to prevent price instability. His argument for privatising the money supply was due to his disappointment with central banks' management, which, in his opinion, had been highly influenced by party politics. Hayek also argued that political interference over monetary policy and price stability are inherently incompatible. He advocated denationalisation of money so that only bank currencies guaranteeing a stable purchasing power would survive. He felt that employment and price stability do not necessarily conflict, but that priority resides with monetary stability. Aware of price stability

1. For an interesting discussion of both Keynes and Hayek, and how each has been betrayed by their disciples in specific reference to the recent Greek financial crisis (beginning in late 2009), see Varoufakis (2012).

challenges, Hayek strongly highlighted the dangers arising from government monetary financing. He strongly recommended dissolving 'the unholy marriage' between monetary and fiscal policy that had formally consecrated the victory of 'Keynesian' economics after the Second World War.

13.8 KEYNES AND KALECKI ON EFFECTIVE DEMAND

The Great Depression was a clear case of reality severely challenging neoclassical economics. Keynes proposed instead the importance of 'effective demand', which in turn heavily depended on investment and consumption. In *The General Theory of Employment, Interest and Money* (1936), Keynes was mainly concerned with entrepreneurs' decisions about production and investment, along with the unstable nature of investment. His 'general theory' asserts that the primary logic of the market is on the demand side and at its heart is the principle of effective demand.

Working independently, the Polish economist Michał Kalecki (1889–1970) arrived at basically the same conclusion in his 'Essay on the Business Cycle Theory', first published in 1933. Kalecki (1933 [1971]) argued that in the absence of effective demand, inventories rise and output declines, leading to a vicious cycle of unemployment as the entrepreneur restrains from investing and employing labour and other factors of production. Kalecki's contribution adds relevant insights to how income distribution effects the evolution of aggregate consumption and investment. Like Keynes, a need arises for government intervention to ensure the restoration of effective demand and thus the continued functioning of the economic system.

Indeed, it is often claimed that Kalecki developed many of the same ideas as Keynes before Keynes himself. Both Keynes and Kalecki were critical of Say's law, which dominated economic thinking at the time. Say's Law assumed that for every excess supply (glut) of goods in one market, a corresponding excess demand (shortage) existed, so that a general excess can never be accompanied by inadequate demand for products on a macroeconomic level. Whereas Kalecki developed his economic ideas from a Marxist perspective that emphasised the significance of social relationships in production, and the critical understanding of the relationship between the capitalist state and the capitalist class, Keynes ideologically supported capitalism, which he sought to stabilise so that it would function more efficiently.

13.9 *TECHNIQUE 12*: A KALECKIAN APPROACH TO CONSUMPTION, INVESTMENT AND INCOME DISTRIBUTION

Michał Kalecki developed a model, in accordance with Marxian class analysis, to explain the basic workings of capitalism, and in particular how the capitalist class maintains profits during business cycles and during times of economic crisis, while strengthening its power relative to labour. Whereas Keynes did not differentiate on the basis of class, Kalecki introduced a dimension of class struggle, and the importance of income distribution especially on workers' consumption.

Like all models, Kalecki highly simplified in order to focus on underlying relationships. Key assumptions include:

(1) There are three sectors of the economy, producing capital goods, consumer goods for capitalists, and consumer goods for workers.
(2) There are two social classes (capitalists and workers).
(3) There are two categories of income (wages and profits).
(4) Workers do not save.
(5) The economy is closed, with no government activity.
(6) No stocks of finished products remain unsold.
(7) Production in each sector is vertically integrated (i.e. retailers merge with suppliers).

Kalecki's theory of effective demand focuses on the relationship between spending, production, prices and income distribution. He splits the capitalist economy into three sectors (which he termed 'departments'), producing: capital goods (D1), consumer goods for capitalists (D2), and consumer goods for workers (D3). The value of output in each department is split into profits (P1, P2 and P3) and wages (W1, W2 and W3).

The key elements of his model are shown in Table 13.3.

Kalecki postulated that given the income distribution in each department, aggregate production and aggregate profits are determined by the level of investment (I) and capitalists' consumption (Ck). Indeed, the more capitalists spend on investment and consumption, the greater their profits. As a result, workers' aggregate consumption is subordinated to the consumption and investment decisions of the capitalist class.

Table 13.3 Kalecki's Economic Model

Aggregate profits, wages, income	*Economic sectors*		
	Department of capital goods: D1	*Department of consumer goods for capitalists: D2*	*Department of consumer goods for workers: D3*
Aggregate profits: P = P1 + P2 + P3 = I + Ck	Profits earned in D1: P1	Profits earned in D2: P2	Profits earned in D3: P3
Aggregate wages: W = W1 + W2 + W3 = Cw	Wages paid in D1: W1	Wages paid in D2: W2	Wages paid in D3: W3
Aggregate income: Y = I + Ck + Cw	Investment: I	Capitalist consumption: Ck	Workers' consumption: Cw

Source: Authors, based on Kalecki (1954).

More specifically:

- Aggregate profits depend on the level of spending by the capitalist class.
- Aggregate workers' consumption depends on the level of workers' income.

Kalecki argued that income distribution is affected by:

- the degree of monopoly (the extent of market competition)
- costs of raw materials and labour
- industry structure
- the strength of trade unions

Prices depend on the market power of firms to fix prices above direct costs (wages and raw materials). A firm facing limited competition is much freer to vary its product price than one facing substantial competitive pressure.

Considering the relations between wages, prices and employment, Kalecki highlighted that

1. A reduction of nominal wages is generally not associated with expansion but with employment decline in D3, the department that produces consumer goods for workers.
2. Trade union strength, which increases the level of nominal wages and reduces mark-up levels, could obtain higher employment and real wages; and conversely, during recessions, if unions accept nominal wage cuts, this could deepen unemployment, and thus the decline in effective demand.
3. The reaction of workers to inflation could further pressure nominal wages, leading to higher prices as capitalists increase the mark-up to maintain their profit margin. As a result, real wages and the levels of worker's consumption decreases.

Kalecki's analysis (1954) of increased oligopolisation in contemporary capitalism sheds light on income distribution. The role of mark-up prices and real wages introduces the class struggle, not just between capitalists and workers but also between capitalists competing for market share.

13.10 THE FINANCIAL CONCEPTION OF INVESTMENT

Keynes emphasised that investment takes place within a context of uncertainty. This is unlike **risk**, which refers to a situation in which all outcomes are known, as well as the probability of each outcome, like flipping a coin. Ordinary statistics can be used to analyse decision-making. Whereas with **uncertainty**, all possible outcomes cannot be ascertained, so we cannot calculate the risk of each outcome, rendering ordinary statistical decision-making ineffective.

Box 13.1 The Paradox of Thrift

Commenting on the horrifying consequences of the Depression of the 1930s, Keynes noticed that people's natural response to be cautious in times of crisis could actually make the problem worse. While saving at the individual level may be entirely practical and praiseworthy, at the level of the economy, and especially one with insufficient demand, it can be devastating. Let's explore this in more detail.

The paradox of thrift indicates that consumers' desires to initially increase savings (S) reduces spending (Y), and ultimately, while consumers save more of their income, S/Y increases not because S increased but because Y decreased. Indeed, Keynes did not believe it was legitimate to hold income constant when analysing aggregate saving, as in neoclassical theory. And he also disagreed with the neoclassical belief that saving is primarily a function of the rate of interest.

In order to understand the interrelations between consumption, investment and savings, it is worth remembering that investment (I) has two components, capital goods and inventories:

I = capital goods + inventories

If individuals consume less, consumption falls and, at first, firms accumulate inventories of unbought goods. This situation cannot continue, as firms will lose money; thus they will reduce their output and incomes will fall, consumption may fall further, and savings will also fall, reducing the initial increase in savings. The process ends when firms stop accumulating inventories. Each time firms reduce their output to match lower demand, incomes and savings fall. Eventually the initial rise in savings is reversed, because total income has fallen. In particular, if output is falling, firms may be reluctant in the future to add to their capital stock.

In short, the paradox of thrift is rooted in the two-sided nature of spending and saving, arising from a view of the economy as a complex system rather than from the perspective of an individual producer or consumer. Looking only at an individual firm or household, we don't see the impact that our actions have on other participants in the economy. So, while for any one individual it might be beneficial to save more for the future, for the economy as a whole it could exacerbate an incipient recession.

Add to this the preponderant role played by finance, and we have a powerful conceptualisation of the determinants of investment in contemporary capitalism. Hyman Minsky (1919–96) incorporated Keynes' basic ideas while expanding them to formulate his **demand price of investment**, defined as the maximum price that the entrepreneur will pay for an additional unit of capital assets. The demand price refers to the present value of the flow of expected returns discounted at the appropriate interest rate, which depends on future expectations, and is strongly influenced by central banks' actions and banks' strategies. Expectations from the entrepreneur about firm costs and revenues determines a flow of expected returns during the useful life of capital assets. Based on Minsky's (2008) insights, we specify the demand price of investment as:

$$P_d = f(A, F_i, F_m)$$

Where:

P_d = demand price of investment
A = valuation of capital assets
F_i = financing available from internal funds
F_m = financing available from financial markets

The **supply price of investment** is related to the production of new capital assets. It represents the minimum price needed for the capitalist to produce a new additional unit of capital assets, given her short-term expectations. It is specified as follows:

$$P_s = f(p_k)$$

where, P_s is the supply price of investment, which in turn is a function of the market price p_k.

Higher liquidity preference may lead to a continuous decrease of the demand price of investment. When the speculative demand for money or other financial assets increases, due to an increase in uncertainty about the future or expectations about returns, firms will reduce the demand of capital goods. As a result, higher liquidity preference leads to a collapse of investment, profits and income.

13.11 FINANCE, FUNDING AND INVESTMENT

According to Keynes, investment decisions are highly dependent on credit and capital markets. The expansion of finance (short-term financing) and funding (long-term financing) depend on banks' and investors' expectations and decisions. A firm's decision to expand productive capacity is strongly based on expected net returns on sales, and not limited by the previous amount of savings. As Keynes argued, investment is affected by expected net returns on sales and also by expectations about future interest rates, each of which is clouded by uncertainty. In a famous passage in *The General Theory*, Keynes (1936 [2010]: 161) wrote:

> Most, probably, of our decisions to do something positive, the full consequences of which will be drawn out over many days to come, can only be taken as a result of animal spirits – of a spontaneous urge to action rather than inaction, and not as the outcome of a weighted average of quantitative benefits multiplied by quantitative probabilities.

Contrast this with the staid and unrealistic neoclassical model, in which rational firms coolly calculate the costs and benefits of respective actions (see Chapter 9).

When firms expect the future rate of profit to be higher than the return on alternative assets, then investment is worthwhile. They would seek financing externally if internal savings do not equal the requisite needed funds. Firms largely depend on short-term finance and long-term funding, and are very mindful of future rates of interest, the growth rate of the economy and their own debt and equity. Because of the financial implications and long-term nature of investment spending, the firm cannot rely on short-term finance but must obtain funding from capital markets. Until such time that capital markets are able to sufficiently meet the long-term funding needs of entrepreneurs, entrepreneurs' short-term financial requirements could be met by banks. As commercial banks create short-term credit (finance), the flow of additional investment could start. If such short-term loans were profitable, banks will manage risk conditions and offer liquidity to lend to entrepreneurs. As a result, firms expand the flow of investments after the initial expansion of finance.

In the process of income expansion, there is an interrelation between the economic sectors that produce capital goods and consumption goods, since the increase in employee wages in the capital-goods sector pressures the production of consumption goods. Workers' marginal propensity to consume plays an important role in the intensity of this process. Capital markets could provide long-term funds through sales of equities and bonds, which could be purchased from savings. According to Keynes, business confidence increases trading in capital markets, which could favour funding investment. However, lack of funding for investment could occur, due to the uncertainty of future interest rates. In other words, prospective investors might not be interested in bonds and shares being traded and, therefore, could constrict the funding required for sustainable investments. When expected returns on bonds and equities are too low for investors, they prefer to hold cash instead of buying long-term debt instruments. If investors feel that holding money today is better than holding other assets, this creates a problem for funding investment; and with high liquidity preference, they will not commit resources to buying bonds or equities.

13.12 GOVERNMENT EXPENDITURE: CONSUMPTION, INVESTMENT AND THE BUDGET CYCLE

Governments can finance public investment either by taxes or debt. A **tax** is a financial charge or other levy imposed upon an individual or legal entity by the state. **Debt** – borrowed funds that must be paid back with interest – can be issued in the form of money or public bonds negotiated in the financial market. All expenses and sources of funding are part of the government budget.

Box 13.2 Composition of Aggregate Demand in India Before and During the Global Crisis, 2002–2015

During India's Tenth Five Year Plan period (2002–07), the rate of gross capital formation in both the public and private sectors was extremely important in explaining increases in economic growth. **Gross capital formation** consists of additions to the fixed assets of the economy plus net changes in the level of inventories. **Fixed assets** include plant, machinery and equipment purchases; the construction of roads, railways, schools, offices, hospitals and private residential, commercial and industrial buildings; and land improvements, such as fences, ditches and drains.

Much of the increase in gross capital formation was attributable to increased investment by the corporate sector, resulting from a positive business environment and the optimistic outlook for the Indian economy. Up until 2007, the rate of growth of gross capital formation increased in mining and quarrying, transport storage, communication, financing, insurance, real estate and business services, and community personal and social services. However, the growth rate of gross capital formation fell abruptly soon after the global financial crisis, due to the performance of agriculture, manufacturing, electricity, gas and water supply, construction, trade, hotels and restaurants.

As indicated in Tables 13.3 and 13.4, Indian GDP growth was determined by the growth rate of private consumption, mainly in food, beverages and tobacco, clothing and footwear. The evolution of government consumption also fostered expansion of aggregate demand and helped cushion the fall in gross capital formation and worsening net exports. India's economic growth was indeed deeply affected by the global recession.

Table 13.4 Demand-Side Growth in Indian GDP: Growth Contribution (Percentage)

Growth contribution	*2009–2010*	*2015–2016*
Consumption, private sector	78.2	48.3
Consumption, government	33.6	4.5
Gross capital formation	–29.6	n/a
Gross fixed capital formation	25.8	22.4
Net exports	–36.2	1.2

Sources: Government of India (2011); Government of India (2017).

Table 13.5 India: Main Economic Indicators

Indicator	*2012–2013*	*2015–2016*
GDP growth (annual percentage)	5.6	7.6
Inflation, CPI (annual percentage)	7.4	4.9*
Index of Industrial Production (growth)	1.1	3.1**
Export growth (US$)	–1.8	–17.6*

Notes: * April–January 2015–2016; ** April–December 2015–2016.
Source: Government of India (2017).

The budget is important because it reveals what the government is doing or intends to do. It reflects, in financial terms, actions and planned expenditures with respect to expected tax collection and proposed borrowing operations. It transforms development plans and priorities into flows of spending.

The **budget cycle** generally includes the following steps:

- budget formulation by the executive
- budget enactment by the finance minister, who generally submits the budget to parliamentary debate and approval
- budget execution by government agencies and departments that implement programmes and spend the money
- auditing and assessment by national audit institutions. The Treasury, central bank, ministry of finance, politicians, donors and international financial institutions, legislatures and the private sector are all actors in the budget cycle; however, they have different degrees of power.

Historically, many states have reached a stage where they cannot 'service' their debts, given that the interest owed becomes unsustainable. Indeed, many governments have defaulted repeatedly, including economically developed ones. Table 13.6 highlights some defaulters since the Napoleonic Wars.

Table 13.6 Sovereign Debt Defaults 1824–2017

1824–1837	*1868–1890*	*1932–1945*	*1998–2004*	*2005–2017*
Argentina	Austria	Austria	Argentina	Argentina
Brazil	Argentina	Brazil	Ecuador	Greece
Chile	Bolivia	China	North Korea	Ireland
Columbia	Chile	Columbia	Russia	Portugal
Ecuador	Columbia	Germany	Ukraine	
Greece	Mexico	Greece		
Guatemala	Peru	Hungary		
Mexico	Turkey	Italy		
Portugal	Uruguay	Japan		
Spain	Venezuela	Turkey		
Venezuela				

Source: Frenkel (2012) and authors.

Taking into account the possibility of default, the main concern with debt is the composition and level of government spending. What *is* counted in government spending on goods and services? Government spending comprises two categories: current spending on goods and services, and investment spending. The former is composed largely of income transfers from taxpayers to assist the needy, i.e. the elderly, the unemployed and the poor, but also includes social security, healthcare services, education, defence spending and interest payments. Investment spending covers long-term spending on infrastructure such as highways, airports, railways, water and sewage systems.

Any purchase by the government, such as new weapons or highway construction, can increase aggregate demand. A declaration of war (or its threat) can also increase aggregate demand, because of government contracts for weapons and military vehicles; unless the declaration results in increased uncertainty, which could very well reduce investment. Other side-effects of increased government spending occurs on income, employment, and consumption via the multiplier effect described earlier in this chapter. However, given import levels it is conceivable that much of this spending can 'leak' out of the national economy, to be enjoyed by other economies.

Keynes favoured counter-cyclical fiscal stimulus (by the federal government) during recessions, and fiscal contraction during boom periods, to prevent overheating:

> Just as it was advisable for the Government to incur debt during the slump, so for the same reasons it is now advisable that they should incline to the opposite policy . . . The boom, not the slump, is the right time for austerity at the Treasury.
>
> Keynes, 1937: 390

There is an ongoing debate about the extent to which government policies can affect aggregate demand. Table 13.7 shows a range of government actions with the aim of increasing or reducing aggregate demand. Post-Keynesians suggest that increasing government spending and decreasing tax rates will stimulate aggregate demand (AD), which, given the multiplier, will further expand income and hence AD. This policy can be used in times of recession or low economic activity in order to move the economy toward full employment. To promote this policy, governments usually increase their deficits by borrowing money, which will increase the future debt of taxpayers. Conversely, the government can increase the budget surplus, by reducing government spending and thereby increase public saving.

Table 13.7 Government Actions and Changes in Aggregate Demand

Objective	*Actions*			
Increase in aggregate demand.	Purchasing more goods and services.	Increasing individual income.	Reducing taxes.	Increasing income transfers.
Reduction of aggregate demand.	Imposing limits to debt in the federal budget.	Reducing individual income.	Increasing taxes.	Reducing income transfers.

Source: Authors.

13.13 THEORETICAL SUMMARY OF CONSUMPTION AND INVESTMENT FROM A SUSTAINABLE PERSPECTIVE

An important question that most of you will debate and help resolve is: What role should the government play in transitioning to a sustainable society? Such transitions do not just happen, but are implemented and engineered by conscious and deliberate decision making. What should be the role of the government vis-à-vis that of the individual?

Consumption

Consumption is one of the most important economic variables. Not only does it proxy for well-being and for increasing welfare, but it is also the nexus between the present and the future, i.e. the more we consume now, the less we can consume in the future. Likewise, consumption also is an important linkage with saving and investment: without present savings, we cannot consume in the future.

Patterns of present consumption are grossly inequitable: too few people have too little access to the world's resources. How we make the world sustainable and how we implement the UN 17 SDGs will crucially depend on how we reconceptualise consumption and investment so that all can benefit. In Chapter 16 we will address the issue of global imbalances, and will see some economists advocating reducing the consumption/GDP ratio in the US (among the highest in the world, at 70 per cent) while increasing that of China (one of the lowest in the world, at around 45 per cent). However, what does this mean for sustainability? If we reduce this ratio in the US, what, if anything, will take its place? And if we increase the ratio in China, what does this mean for resource use and the environment?

Here we would like to summarise briefly what we know about the theory of consumption:

- Empirically, it is central in many lives and in many economies.
- We know how to increase/decrease consumption, as evident by the following function:

$$C = f(Y_d, Yd^e, W, r, \theta)$$

Where:

C = Consumption

Y_d = **Disposable income**, equal to personal income minus taxation, plus welfare benefits

Yd^e = Expected disposable income

W = Wealth
r = The real interest rate
θ = Credit constraints, i.e. aside from the real interest rate, how easy/difficult is it to borrow money

- We also know the expected causation of each of the independent variables on the dependent variable in the above equation. Specifically, if we want to increase consumption we can increase personal disposable income, reduce taxes or increase welfare. We can increase expected disposable income by increasing employment (all else equal, since that increases disposable income). Increasing (or decreasing) wealth will increase (or decrease) consumption. Decreasing the real interest rate will increase our demand for more big-ticket items, for which we have to borrow money, for example, housing, cars, computer systems, etc.

Note that in the above consumption function and the investment function below, we do not assume that the independent variables only linearly affect the dependent variable (i.e. that they only affect the dependent variable separately without combining with the other independent variables). On the contrary, we expect non-linear effects (i.e. two or more variables combining to produce an added effect). And we also expect causation to run both ways, i.e. consumption affects expected disposable income, for example, by contributing to climate change and increasing uncertainty. In the above, we simply list the variables for expositional convenience.

- We can also encapsulate the essence of consumption in the simple equation:

$$C = C_o + (MPC)(Y_d)$$

Where:

C = Consumption
Y_d = Disposable income, equal to personal income minus taxation, plus welfare benefits.
C_o = **Autonomous consumption**, i.e. the consumption that occurs when disposable income equals zero
MPC = The marginal propensity to consume, which significantly differs between individuals, and over the lifespan of the same individual.

And we know that increasing/decreasing either C_o, the MPC or Y_d (all else being equal) will directly increase/decrease consumption.

The above equation discusses consumption from a given point in time; missing of course is how consumption changes over time, both for the individual and the nation. Thanks to the work of Thorstein Veblen (1857–1929), we know that a lot of consumption is conspicuous, merely to flatter and persuade; and that a lot of consumption is compulsory, merely to keep pace with one's neighbours or one's peers (Veblen, 1973 [1999]). Suffice to say that most consumption is unnecessary, fruitless waste, and unsustainable. While some economists posit a permanent theory of consumption, i.e. that one's annual consumption is a function of one's estimated permanent income (plus wealth) over one's lifetime, we feel that given pervasive uncertainty a better explanation of dynamic consumption is Veblen's. The former theory posits a robotic rationality to calculation, whereas the latter posits a subjective and emotional fixation.

The million-dollar question is of course how to transit from our current unsustainable situation to one more sustainable without unfairly discriminating or punishing the world's poor, who have not effectively participated in current consumption. The neoclassical and Keynesian theory of consumption was developed (and is still practised) in an age devoid of the concept of sustainability. Arthur Dahl (1996: 70) suggested that 'it may help in considering the renewal of economics to explore some basic economic concepts and mechanisms from the perspective of equivalent biological systems', i.e. the basic concepts of growth, interest, etc. To this we add the urgent necessity of reconceptualising the concepts of consumption and investment. The current theory ignores important questions such as: By increasing disposable income, and thereby increasing consumption, what goods will be purchased, and how will they affect sustainability? How will this depend on the specific MPCs? We desperately need empirically based models, along the lines of Kalecki, and Sraffa (1960), which detail the interrelated effects of consumption, the MPCs and other variables within the context of sustainability. If our goal is to become more sustainable then we must begin with a reconceptualisation of consumption, both empirically and theoretically.

Investment

Thanks to Keynes, Kalecki and Minsky, we understand how investment occurs within a context of uncertainty.

- Their contributions can be captured in the following equation:

$$I = f(S, Yd, Yd^e, r, \Psi, \varnothing, \theta, D_c)$$

Where:

I = Investment
S = Savings

Yd = Disposable income, equal to personal income minus taxation, plus welfare benefits.
Yd^e = Expected disposable income, which loosely translates into expected sales.
r = The real interest rate
Ψ = Business optimism, which is a mixed function of 'animal spirits' and uncertainty.
Ø = MEC, the marginal efficiency of capital (MEC), defined as the difference between an investment's present value of expected returns and the interest rate.[2]
θ = credit constraints, i.e. the availability of credit and whether (and how) it is rationed
D_c = current degree of utilisation of capacity

- And we know the direction of causation: so, for example, increased business optimism should, all else being equal, increase investment; while increases in the marginal efficiency of capital should increase investment. And, as with consumption, we know that the direction of causation runs both ways: increased investment in, say, new roads or a steel plant, will increase global warming gases, which could decrease business optimism (as is currently occurring in China). Or increased investment in renewable energy could increase the MEC of related capital.

Similarly to consumption theory, much of the theoretical work on investment has been formulated without reference to sustainability. What is much needed for sustainable living is a global refocus on the cause/effects of investing in renewable-energy infrastructure. How will this be financed? And what government policy is necessary to nudge us forward?

THINKING QUESTIONS

What is the current impact of credit availability on consumption?

How do citizens in your country view debt? Is it culturally acceptable to increase debt?

Does the view on debt depend on the specific motivation? In what ways might financial education be effective in reducing the misuse of credit?

2. Keynes defined the MEC as 'equal to that rate of discount which would make the present value of the series of annuities given by the returns expected from the capital-asset during its life just equal to its supply price' (Keynes (1936 [2010]: 135).

CLASS ACTIVITIES

Analyse the investment data for a specific country over time. How would you interpret it? Is it stable or volatile?

With your colleagues, discuss and then decide upon the kind of interventions required in the federal/national budget process to address the following problems:

(1) Procured medicines are ineffective in treating the low-income population for whom they are dispensed.
(2) You have received a report on poor financial management of the department of education.
(3) Half of the money allocated to district hospitals was not spent during the financial year.
(4) The private company the government contracted to run its prisons has been found guilty of fraud.

AREAS FOR RESEARCH

Who are the key power holders in the formulation and execution of the budget in your country? Who benefits? Who pays?

How can ordinary citizens influence the budget process?

UN SDG FOCUS

Goals #9 and #12 call for:

9. Build resilient infrastructure, promote sustainable industrialisation and foster innovation.
12. Ensure sustainable consumption and production patterns.

What is meant by 'sustainable consumption and production'? What does 'resilient' mean? How would you conceptualise, define and measure it? How would you 'ensure' and 'promote'? Research the UN's findings on Goals #9 and #12. How would you recommend implementation?

FURTHER READING

Minsky, H. P. (1982) *Can 'it' Happen Again?: Essays on Instability and Finance.* New York: Routledge.

14
Recessions and Financial Crises

All economies go through cycles of boom and bust, otherwise known as 'the business cycle'. This chapter will investigate whether the business cycle is inevitable or is a consequence of how the economy is structured. Are there institutional adjustments that can prevent or ameliorate it? We will first define the business cycle, then discuss how recessions are defined and measured. We then ask about the causes and origins of financial crises – a specific type of recession that most of us are now familiar with. We will then look to the global picture and ask: What is the proper role of global financial architecture? And what are alternative economic policies for sustainable economic growth?

14.1 SETTING THE SCENE: WHAT IS A BUSINESS CYCLE?

A **business cycle** refers to the ups (expansions) and downs (recessions) of the economy. Perhaps the term 'business cycle' is misleading, since it affects everyone rather than just businesses; and the word 'cycle' implies circularity; that what goes around comes around. But no two business cycles are alike: they differ in terms of severity, causation and length. Likewise, no two recessions are alike, for they differ in length and severity; and no two expansions are alike, also differing in length and vigour.

A business cycle is a short-term phenomenon, to be distinguished from long-term economic swings. Throughout the business cycle there are alternating increases and decreases in the level of economic activity, of varying amplitude and length. A conventional business cycle contains the following phases:

- a beginning or recovery
- an expansion phase, in which the economy grows
- a peak, at which the expansion reaches a relative maximum
- a contraction (recession), in which the level of economic activity declines
- a trough, in which the economy reaches a relative low point. After the trough, the economy recovers, and we begin the next cycle.

Empirical analysis on business cycles began with Clement Juglar in the mid nineteenth century (Juglar, 1856). From data on the French economy he noted that cycles of economic activity averaged seven years, with a range from three to eighteen years; and for the UK, a similar analysis indicated a period of six years

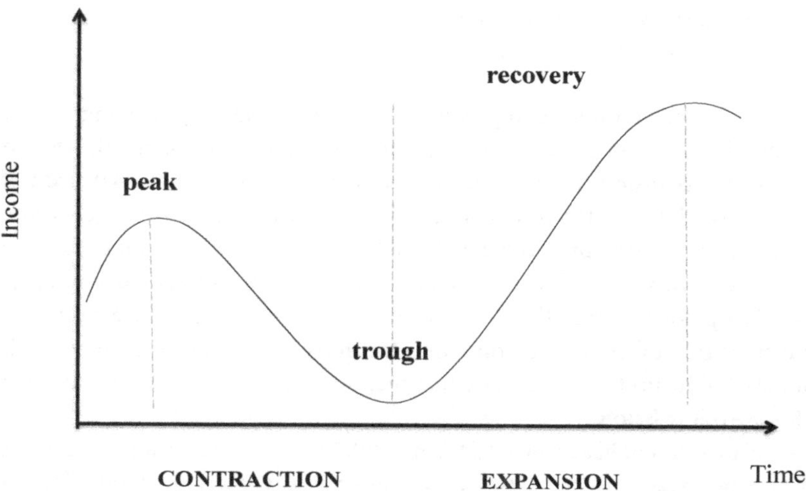

Figure 14.1 The Business Cycle

Source: Authors.

with a range from two to ten years. Based on the data, Juglar believed that cycles were roughly synchronous in France, the UK and the USA.

In 1933, Michał Kalecki presented his business cycle theory, based on his analysis presented in the previous chapter. For Kalecki, investment is cyclical primarily as a result of its 'gestation period', which causes two delays, or 'lags': (1) between investment orders and actual expenditures of investment; and (2) between investment orders and equipment deliveries. More specifically, three stages must be distinguished in the investment process:

- investment orders
- the production of investment goods
- the deliveries of equipment (investment outlays).

Increasing levels of investment entails rising profits and a higher stock of capital. Higher investment will increase demand and profits and encourage more investment. However, the rising stock of capital will tend to reduce the current profit rate and negatively affect future investment decisions. It is the interplay of these two opposing forces that precipitates the cyclical movement in investment. Thus, instability inherent in investment, all else being equal, will self-generate four distinct movements in the business cycle:

- expansion will lead to recession
- recession will lead to depression (if severe enough: it certainly was during the 1930s)

- depression will lead to recovery
- recovery will lead to expansion.

The increased capital stock dampens the expansion, eventually bringing it to an end and, if severe enough, causing an eventual recession. Consequently, we can say that the expansion contains the seeds of recession. The additional stock of capital accrued during the recession will be underutilised during the recession, becoming productive only during the subsequent expansion. Likewise, the recession contains the seeds of the expansion. But as we shall see, there is nothing magical or preordained in these 'seeds'. So, on the one hand, all recessions and expansions result from active, conscious decisions; but on the other hand, both Marxists and institutionalists argue that recessions are intrinsic to capitalism: a topic we explore below.

While investment has received a lot of publicity, given its volatility, recessions can also be caused by *any* significant change in aggregate demand. Thus, a significant decrease in consumption could precipitate a recession. Given the preponderance of consumption in US GDP (70 per cent of the total), a significant consumption decrease could plunge the economy into recession. Potential precipitating factors include increased interest rates, constricted credit, attempts to balance the budget, a decrease in either nominal or real wages, etc. Likewise, given the preponderance of consumption in the American economy, an *increase* in consumption (based on consumption theory) is the quickest tonic for recession, which raises questions about the long-term compatibility between economic growth, a consumption-based economy and sustainability.

The crucial questions are: Are such changes intrinsic to the system (thus possibly leading to instability)? Or are they external to the system, and caused chiefly by unanticipated 'shocks'? Marx, Keynes and Minsky advocated the former position, whereas neoclassical economists advocate the latter. We agree with the former, since the causal factors identified are self-enforcing and do not tend to equilibrium, and can only be rectified with external solutions. It is also clear that in two historical examples, the Great Depression and the 2007 global financial crisis, attempts at laissez faire were unsuccessful.

Friedman and Schwartz (1963: 53) conclude that changes in money income and prices are accompanied by a mutual change in the rate of growth of the money stock:

> There seems to us, accordingly, to be an extraordinarily strong case for the propositions that (1) appreciable changes in the rate of growth of the stock of money are a necessary and sufficient condition for appreciable changes in the rate of growth of money income; and that (2) this is true both for long secular changes and also for changes over periods roughly the length of business cycles.

Indeed, in a later paper, Friedman (1968) argued that at the root of the economic cycles, central banks actively increase the money supply in order to maintain short-term domestic income level higher than its non-inflationary level. In other words, monetary and financial crises are caused by misguided government policies that provoke long-run distortions in investment, consumption and prices. Thus, the solution to ending inflation should be restrictive monetary policy to stabilise prices and income in the long term. In short, Friedman and his followers, unlike Marx, Keynes and Minsky, argue that the free market economy is inherently stable.

Although we understand the causes of the business cycle, we cannot predict when recessions will begin. If we could predict, we could prevent. Perhaps this is due to our limitations on understanding how the human brain works and how people act in groups – or how group behaviour can sometimes turn into a herd mentality and even a frenzy. Perhaps our inability is due to arrogant thinking that we have control over a situation, when in reality we do not.

While the field of economic forecasting is littered with misdiagnosis, no better example stands out than Irving Fisher's speech on 17 October 1929. He boasted that the business cycle had been solved, and that the country was embarked on a permanent plateau of endless prosperity. Less than two weeks later, the stock market crashed, plunging the USA into depression. (Unbeknownst to Mr Fisher, the recession had already begun in August 1929.) In his defence, sophisticated models did not then exist, computers were not invented, and most available data were shoddy and incomplete. Yet just a decade ago neoclassical economists, even with sophisticated models, were not able to predict the most severe recession since the Great Depression.

14.2 HOW ARE RECESSIONS DEFINED AND MEASURED IN THE USA?

The United States has had 42 recessions since 1856.[1]

- The longest was from 1873 to 1877.
- The shortest was for only six months, in 1980.
- The most severe was from 1929 to 1933 (as measured by the unemployment rate).

1. While prior data exists, after 1856 it became a lot more detailed and trustworthy; nevertheless, we can say with some degree of accuracy that every US administration experienced a recession prior to 1856. And after 1856, only three US presidents did not have a recession during their watch: (1) James Garfield, elected in 1880 and assassinated after one year; (2) Lyndon Baines Johnson, assuming office in 1963 after JFK was assassinated and remaining until 1968; (3) Bill Clinton, in office 1992–2000. LBJ presided over the third-longest expansion in US history, while Clinton presided over the longest.

- While a consensus does not exist on the 'mildest' recession (if we can even use such a word) the eight-month 1990–91 recession is a leading candidate.

An important lesson that you should take from reading this book is that all economic systems are built on institutions, which in turned are constructed by human beings in historical and cultural settings. Thus, if we don't like a particular aspect of the economic system, or if we feel it is not benefiting all, we can change it. Moreover, it should come as no surprise that how we measure the economy, and what aspects are emphasised, are also built on institutions, subject to discretion. So, if we feel that a specific measurement is inadequate, we can change it. Indeed, as an economic system evolves, so should our conceptualisation of how to measure its performance.

Having said that, let's consider how a recession is defined in the United States. Earlier in this chapter we briefly defined the business cycle as 'the ups and downs of the economy'. The 'downs' refer to a recession – one phase of the business cycle – while the 'ups' refer to an expansion. Policy-makers, however, if they are to ameliorate a recession, need a more specific definition. In the United States, the National Bureau of Economic Research (NBER), founded in 1920, is responsible for conceptualising, defining and measuring a recession. Despite the word 'national', the NBER is a private organisation, separate and distinct from the government. (If the government decided itself when a recession occurred, there would be a palpable conflict of interest.) According to its website, the NBER

> is a private, non-profit, nonpartisan research organisation dedicated to promoting a greater understanding of how the economy works. The NBER is committed to undertaking and disseminating unbiased economic research in a scientific manner, and without policy recommendations, among public policy-makers, business professionals, and the academic community.

The NBER officially defines a **recession** as

> a significant decline in economic activity spread across the economy, lasting more than a few months, normally visible in real GDP, real income, employment, industrial production, and wholesale-retail sales.

Before the mid-1980s, the NBER used an ostensibly much simpler definition of a recession: 'a decline in two consecutive quarters of real GDP'. In switching to the current definition, the NBER argued that the former definition was too simple and that the new one is more comprehensive.

While you might think this definition strenuously objective, it is not; on the contrary, it exudes subjectivity. 'Subjective' means that any two people could interpret the data differently, with neither right or wrong. Consider the following subjective words and phrases in the above definition: 'significant'; 'spread across the economy'; 'lasting more than a few months'; 'normally visible'.

Noticeably absent are the terms 'poverty', 'inequality' and 'underemployment', or 'the incapability to provision'.

The official definition of an **expansion**, referring to the 'ups' of the economy, differs in just one word from that of recession: substitute the word 'increase' for the word 'decline', and we get the official definition of an expansion, which is equally subjective. Even more subjective is the definition of a **depression**, defined as a 'severe' recession. But what exactly does 'severe' mean? Unfortunately, an objective, mutually agreeable definition of a depression does not exist.

Who decides whether the US economy is in recession? All citizens? Or a selected group, much like a jury decides a criminal case? Neither. This important question is decided by a committee of about seven expert economists, none of whom, presumably, has ever worried about experiencing unemployment or poverty. After analysing the data, the committee decides when a recession begins, when it ends, and if it is severe enough to merit the label of depression. Thus, not only is the definition rife with subjectivity but deciding when (and if) the definition is met is also subjective. Is there any way around this? Is it quixotic to think that a 100-per-cent objective definition can be constructed? Or that those most affected by the problem can help in its conceptualisation?

14.3 THE BUSINESS CYCLE AND FINANCIAL CRISES

Finance is not just related to management techniques, procedures or product phenomena but also involves institutions, behaviours and policies. It is central to capitalism since it fosters and enables capital accumulation.

How do financial crises differ from ordinary crises? Neoclassical economists argue that financial crises result from misguided economic policies, particularly over-spending/under-regulation by governments, while ignoring the active role of money, financial institutions and the destabilising effects of speculative activity. Neoclassical economists assume (based on deductive logic rather than empirical investigation) that financial markets transfer funds efficiently to maximise income; thus, they argue that financial deregulation is necessary to increase the efficient allocation of funds.

But as Keynes argued in *The General Theory*, stock markets foster the risk of speculation and instability, since these markets are mostly based upon conventions whose precariousness affects the rhythm of investment. Writing from within the Keynesian tradition, Hyman Minsky considered the role of finance in the business cycle and developed the **financial instability hypothesis**, which states that financial crises are inherent to the capitalist economy. While considering the factors that determine investment, Minsky argued that weak financial regulation and supervision induces financial fragility. Indeed, financial stability requires political authorities to shape the behaviour of financial institutions and the path of sustainable investment.

Minsky argued that banks play a crucial role in determining the path of economic growth since investment decisions are affected by available finance. In particular, he added some important concepts to economists' lexicon (Minsky, 2008: 230–33). Each of the following terms represents a consumer's situation concerning the ability to repay a debt, which ranges from relatively easy (the debt is manageable, i.e. hedge-financing) to impossible (the debt is unmanageable, i.e. Ponzi-financing):

- **Hedge-financing:** firms or households can make debt payments, covering interest and principal loan, from current cash flows from revenues.
- **Speculative-financing:** the current cash flow can service the debt, i.e. cover the interest due, but the firm or household must regularly roll over, or re-borrow, the principal loan.
- **Ponzi-financing:** firms or households cannot make sufficient payments on interest or the principal loan with current cash flow.

The individual borrows believing that his or her appreciating asset(s) will be sufficient to refinance the debt. The collapse of Ponzi-financing will, however, bring down even debtors engaged in hedge-financing, unable to find loans as banks restrict lending on behalf of the expected decrease of economic activity (and profits and wages) and the expected increase of credit risk.

During the expansion phase of the business cycle, increasing demand for investment increases the demand for finance and funding. The supply of short-term finance depends on bankers' expectations about future incomes. During the expansion, entrepreneurs borrow from banks and accumulate debts. Euphoria seeps in and some firms speculate, while becoming over-optimistic in their short-term expectations. Minsky referred to such activity as 'Ponzi-financing' because income flows fall short of debt repayment plans. Because of fear of losses, banks are unwilling to lend money to such individuals.

The lack of new loans increases uncertainty and pessimism in the economy, decreasing investment. Consequently, through the multiplier process, employment, income and consumption fall, leading to a recession. If the crisis also leads to a sharp decline in prices, **debt deflation**, in which asset prices fall, can occur. Thus Minsky warned, 'The greater the weight of speculative and Ponzi finance, the smaller the overall margins of safety in the economy and the greater the fragility of the financial structure' (Ibid.: 233). Minsky suggested that the only possible antidote to this credit crunch is the role of the central bank as a 'lender of last resort', making enough credit available for the economy and enabling higher spending by the government.

Box 14.1 Who Was Charles Ponzi?

A Ponzi scheme is named for Charles Ponzi (1882–1949), born in Parma, Italy. He was not the first and certainly will not be the last conman. Ponzi payed out returns with other investors' money. His specific asset was an international return coupon, which allowed individuals to mail letters to recipients in different countries. Given that the prices often differed, the opportunity for **arbitrage** (from the Latin *arbiter*, meaning 'judge') arose, that is, buying low and selling high and pocketing the difference. He earned millions and lived luxuriously.

In the short term he sustained his scheme by attracting new investors who paid up-front; he then used these funds to pay returns to existing investors. Obviously, in the long term such a scheme was not sustainable, since it did not produce a value-added product. Eventually, thanks to persistent news reporting (including from Charles Barron, one of the founders of the Dow Jones Company and publisher of Barron's) along with public scrutiny, his scheme was exposed; angry investors demanded their money, causing him to eventually go bankrupt. Owing an estimated US$7 million, Ponzi spent 14 years in prison. He died in 1949, in Rio de Janeiro. Perhaps he is gloating in his grave right now, having his name forever memorialised. Nevertheless, it raises the question of whether such schemes can be prevented in the future.

Source: Charles Ponzi (2017).

14.4 FINANCIAL CRISIS AND SOCIAL COSTS IN EMERGING COUNTRIES: INDONESIA IN THE LATE 1990S

During the late 1990s, the South Asian countries suffered a financial and economic crisis. Their free-market agenda deepened financial instability as Indonesian corporations were highly leveraged in foreign currencies, which unfortunately were not supported by adequate domestic financial regulation and supervision. The Indonesian solvency and currency crisis followed the crisis in Thailand. The lack of credibility reduced incoming capital inflows, forcing the Indonesian central bank to depreciate the exchange rate as assets left the country (see Chapter 16 for a discussion of exchange rates). Among the impacts of the crisis were higher unemployment rates followed by a sharp increase in poverty, from 18 per cent in 1996 to 24 per cent in 1999. The deterioration of Indonesia's human development index (HDI) underscored the overall impact of the crisis (UNDP, 2001).

Indonesian economic policy remained under the International Monetary Fund watch until 2003. The search for international help, led by the IMF, was based on the understanding that a bailout would enable Indonesia to regain credibility from foreign banks and investors. The conditions of international help included, among other measures, market deregulation, removal of subsidies and closure of 16 banks without any deposit insurance in place. However, as the IMF rescue package was dispersed, these conditions exacerbated market scepticism that Indonesia could really overcome its problems.

In 2004, the government changed its policy orientation, instead accelerating economic growth, job creation and poverty reduction. Proactive policies, government expenditures on education and health, and investment in infrastructure were implemented. Even though changes in the competitive regulatory regime have been implemented, the Indonesian business environment is still considered costly by investors.

From 2000 until 2005, economic growth averaged 4.5 per cent, in contrast to the 7.3 per cent during the six-year pre-crisis period. In spite of significant strides in reducing poverty since the 1997 crisis, half the population still lives on less than US$2 a day. And in 2010 more than 13 per cent of the population, about 30 million people, were living on less than US$1.25 a day. The GDP in Indonesia was worth US$878 billion in 2012, representing 1.4 per cent of global GDP (World Bank, 2009).

14.5 BANKING: A SIMPLIFIED BALANCE SHEET

In this section we describe how a typical bank operates. We present a simplified commercial bank balance sheet, composed of:

- **Assets** (things banks own): Short-term assets (up to one year) include: cash on hand, liquid financial assets, loans to other banks, foreign currency, and loans to consumers and firms. Long-term assets include: loans to consumers and firms, financial assets, equipment (e.g. furniture, computers) and real estate.
- **Liabilities** (things banks owe): Short-term liabilities (up to one year) include: deposits, loans from other banks, bonds issued by the bank. Long-term liabilities include: deposits, bonds issued by the bank. Plus **Equity** (shares owned by bank shareholders/owners).

Note: Equity, sometimes referred to as net assets or net worth, equals assets minus liabilities. Equity is a liability because a bank owes money to its shareholders if and when they decide to sell.

Thus:

Assets = Liabilities + Equity

Here is a simple example:

Let's say our bank has $2,000 in cash, $20,000 in liquid financial assets, $30,000 in real estate, $20,000 in long-term loans (housing loans). On the liability side the bank has $5,000 in short-term deposits, $20,000 in short-term interbank loans, $22,000 in long-term deposits and $25,000 in equity.

Balance sheet:

Assets (short-term):	
Cash	$2,000
Liquid financial assets	$20,000
Assets (long-term):	
Housing loans	$20,000
Real estate	$30,000
Total assets:	**$72,000**
Liabilities (short-term):	
Deposits	$5,000
Interbank loans	$20,000
Liabilities (long-term):	
Deposits	$22,000
Equity	$25,000
Total liabilities:	**$72,000**

If we decide to include short-term loans to the value of $20,000 and issue long-term bonds to the same value, our new balance sheet will look like this:

Balance sheet:

Assets (short-term):	
Cash	$2,000
Liquid financial assets	$20,000
Loans	$20,000
Assets (long-term):	
Housing loans	$20,000
Real estate	$30,000
Total assets:	**$92,000**
Liabilities (short-term):	
Deposits	$5,000
Interbank loans	$20,000
Liabilities (long-term):	
Deposits	$22,000
Equity	$25,000
Bonds	$20,000
Total liabilities	**$92,000**

While money is needed in any economic system, different possibilities exist to inject money. A common way in capitalist economies is for money to be created whenever a loan is established. As economic conditions improve, more loans will be demanded, and more money created. Also known as the endogenous view of money creation, this assumes that money creation is positively related to the business cycle. So our typical bank, once it approves a loan, automatically increases the money supply.

14.6 FINANCIAL INNOVATIONS AND LIABILITY MANAGEMENT: THE ACTIVE ROLE OF BANKS

Commercial banks (depository banks) have a set of liabilities with a variety of maturities, risks and regulatory requirements. These banks, with complex portfolios, acquire funds through attracting deposits from individuals and companies, along with other funds from domestic and foreign markets. Financial innovations are not just techniques or product phenomena but also involve changes in banks' practices. Indeed, **liability management**, as a financial innovation, relates to banks' active management of net funds already available for lending and investment, as well as the search for additional funds. Its aim is to collect sufficient funds to meet the bank's asset growth and earning targets at acceptable levels of risk (Saunders, 1994). Liability management involves strategies to refinance their positions without threatening their financial stability. This stability could be challenged by a longer maturity of assets than liabilities, changes in regulation, and market price volatility, among other factors.

Looking back, commercial banks began to actively manage liabilities in the 1960s, with the issuance of **negotiable certificates of deposit**, which could be sold in the interbank market, prior to maturity, so banks could raise additional funds. This financial innovation, which aimed to increase banks' non-deposit fundraising, configured new financial products such as the Fed funds market. Since the 1990s, commercial banks have adopted an integrated approach called **asset-and-liability management (ALM)** to coordinate assets and liabilities to mitigate financial risks. For example, banks might implement asset securitisation in order to enhance credit and liquidity risk management. Banks could change the maturity of their deposits when expectations of interest rates significantly change. In this case, accounting methods, such as gap analysis or duration analysis, could also maintain a controlled gap between the maturities of assets and liabilities. ALM is also used to analyse currency and other trading-related risks that could cause potential losses. As a result, financial innovations could include off-balance-sheet banking and hedging techniques, such as derivatives, currency futures and swaps, to control balance sheet exposures.

14.7 THE AMERICAN HOUSING CRISIS AND THE BANKING SECTOR

Analysing the recent crisis in terms of Minsky's analysis described earlier in this chapter, it is clear that it is financial. The financial industry encouraged speculation dependent on future house prices, the future price of securitised assets, the renewal of lending operations and the role of credit-rating agencies. This was sustainable until housing prices began falling. Then bank profits fell; and marginal home buyers, who had invested in speculative mortgages (subprime lending) could not pay and lost their homes, since the asset value was less than what they owed. Here are some key concepts you need to be aware of:[2]

- **Subprime lending:** Lending to borrowers of high credit risk. Interest rates for these borrowers are usually higher.
- **Credit crunch:** When banks stop lending money and, as a result, many people cannot pay back the mortgage loans from their current cash flows of revenues. It is characterised by a lack of liquidity, especially in the interbank market, which could lead to failure of financial institutions if central banks do not intervene.
- **Securitisation:** Transforming mortgages and other credit contracts into collateralised debt obligations (CDO) and mortgage-backed securities (MBS). The objective is to transfer to third-party investors the credit and mortgage payments, and the resulting related credit and default risk. Simply put: bankers reassembled various mortgages with differing degrees of risk into one asset, then charged an interest rate.
- **Credit rating agencies:** Non-financial institutions that rate securities based on expectations on different types of risk (sovereign, credit and liquidity, among others).

Minsky's theory, along with Keynes' insights, elucidates the causes of the crisis and why the Federal Reserve System (the US central bank) intervened as it did. Since 1981, 30-year fixed mortgage rates had declined, reaching record lows in 2003. Housing prices, however, increased steadily from 1991 to 2005. In other words, the cost of financing was decreasing, while the housing asset price was increasing; thus, increasing profit expectations in the housing market encouraged more investment, more speculation, and more Ponzi-financing.

Lending requirements were liberalised and banks managed the capital requirements adjusted to risk by means of enhancing further securitisation operations. Banks were interested in selling credit so as to enhance credit and liquidity risk management within a new profit pattern, where they stopped

2. For an enhanced discussion, see Carlin and Soskice, 2015: 223–60.

requiring income, assets or even job verification, i.e. lending more to people who could not pay (subprime), justifying that risk on the basis of the value of the asset held as collateral – the house. The banking system was, in a sense, encouraging speculative and Ponzi portfolios. As profits in the housing industry began decreasing in 2006, homeowners who invested in Ponzi and speculative mortgages could not pay their debts, and the ensuing credit crunch led to an epidemic of foreclosures (see Figure 14.2).

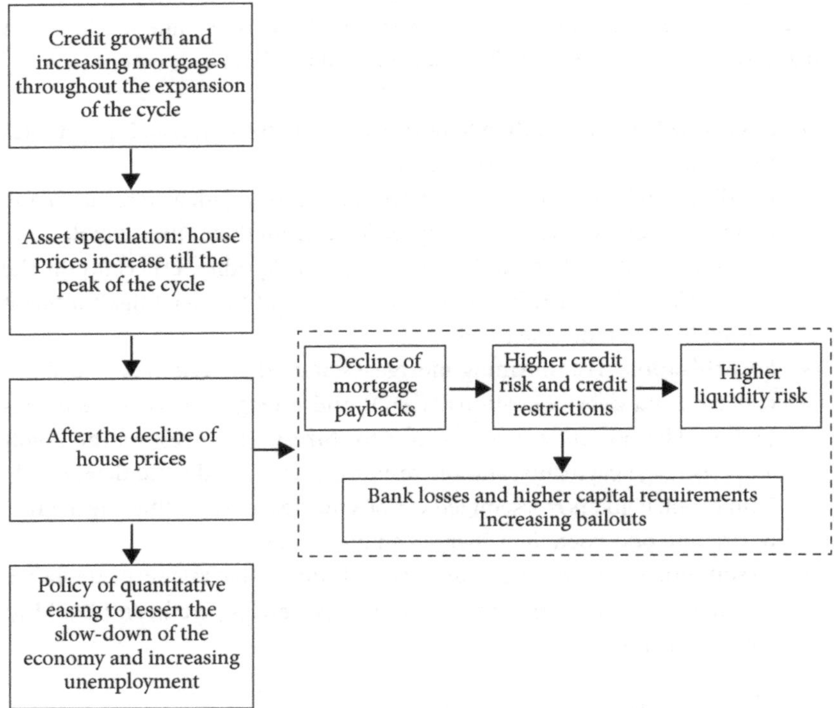

Figure 14.2 Financial Instability and the Subprime Crisis: Causes and Outcomes

Source: Adapted and elaborated by authors from Bernanke (2007); Roubinil (2008).

As asset prices and bank profits declined, the credit crunch deepened bank instability. In this context, the so-called 'shadow banking system' deepened the financial crisis. The **shadow banking system** represents financial institutions not subject to the same Federal Reserve regulatory controls as depository banks. As these institutions borrowed short-term in liquid markets to purchase long-term, non-liquid and risky assets, any disruption in financial markets could subject them to rapid deleveraging, selling their long-term assets at depressed prices. Thus, speculative strategies and the narrow interconnections between the operations in credit and stock markets explain the recent crisis.

14.8 FINANCIAL LIBERALISATION AND SYSTEMIC RISK

Financial crises are major disruptions in financial markets characterised by a sharp credit crunch, declines in asset prices, and financial and non-financial firm failures. They are certainly not new. One complete financial cycle is much longer than the typical business cycle (often peaking before the peak of the business cycle). Since the early 1990s, global liquidity has fostered the expansion of private capital flows and banking activities, stimulated by the evolution of American monetary policy and market deregulation (see Chapter 16).

In 1988, the global but voluntary Basel Capital Accord (named after the Swiss city where the Accord took place) introduced an 8-per-cent capital requirement on the risk-weighted value of a bank's assets. It was designed to avoid systemic risk: the simple thinking being that additional capital in and of itself would be enough to prevent a financial crisis. In 2004, a new Capital Accord, Basel II, was established, which reinforced the requirement of added capital, the need of supervision by monetary and financial authorities, and the importance of transparency. After the financial crisis, additional regulations were introduced, including liquidity requirements and rates of leverage. The recent crisis underscored the persistent vulnerability of banks (and non-bank financial institutions) to both individual and systemic risk (i.e. risk to the whole system). Indeed, Basel II did not prevent the financial crisis from happening. In response, a Basel III was signed, emphasising higher capital ratios, liquidity requirements and leverage constraints within an overall context of prudential regulation. The effectiveness of Basel III remains to be seen. Table 14.1 shows the spread of banking systemic crises around the world after the crisis.

Currently, there remains a lack of supervision of global financial risk, which could at least theoretically dampen speculative strategies of financial institutions. In spite of Basel I, II and III, the expansion of global universal banks and of stock markets, abetted by the World Trade Organization's liberalisation of financial services, has increased financial instability (see Chapter 16). Indeed, the global nature of banks reveals the inefficacy of the segmentation of supervision. Another significant challenge is the absence of a shared objective among countries to achieve stable financial flows (Griffith-Jones, 2002). Finally, the lack of representation of developing countries in multilateral agencies such as the IMF, World Bank, and the Bank of International Settlements makes the challenges even greater and the possibilities of change more difficult and remote.

14.9 THE GOVERNMENT AND THE BUSINESS CYCLE: ALTERNATIVE ECONOMIC POLICIES

The 2007–08 financial crisis, originating in the United States, soon spread to other national economies and led to the most severe recession since the

Table 14.1 Systemic Banking Crises: Main Features by Country

Country	*Start of the crisis*	*Date when the crisis became systemic*	*Extensive liquidity support by central banks*	*Significant restructuring costs*	*Significant asset purchases by central banks*	*Significant nationalisations of banks*
Austria	2008	2008	X	X		X
Belgium	2008	2008	X	X		X
Denmark	2008	2009	X			X
Germany	2008	2009	X			X
Greece	2008	2009	X	X		
Iceland	2008	2012	X	X		X
Ireland	2008	2011	X	X	X	X
Latvia	2008	2008	X			X
Luxembourg	2008	2008	X	X		X
Mongolia	2008	2009	X	X		X
Netherlands	2008	2008	X	X		X
Nigeria	2008	2011	X	X	X	X
Portugal	2016	2017	x	X		
Spain	2008	2012	X	X		
Ukraine	2008	2009	X	X		X
United Kingdom	2007	2008	X	X	X	X
United States	2007	2008	X	X	X	X
Venezuela	2009	2010				X

Note: Systemic banking crises occur when at least three of the listed interventions took place, whereas borderline cases are those with just two.

Source: Elaborated by the authors from Laeven and Valencia (2012).

Great Depression of the 1930s. The immediate impacts of the global crisis lessened expectations, causing a fall in the level of production, investment and employment; and an increase in liquidity constraints on credit and capital markets. This led to economic policy responses in order to support the growth of the domestic market.

Paul Krugman, in his book *End This Depression Now!* (2013), argued that the economic downturn is due to the lack of demand. Less spending on the part of consumers translates to less output by producers and less work for workers. In his opinion, printing money and lowering interest rates will not eliminate the lack of demand and, therefore, these policies will no longer revive the economy since we are currently in a **liquidity trap**, that is to say, interest rates nearly at zero does not provide enough incentive to increase spending and borrowing. In his opinion, austerity is not the answer. We agree.

Nevertheless, the implementation of austerity policies in the European Union, prompted by the **Troika** (European Commission, European Central Bank and the IMF) reinforced a spiral of economic contractions. Following the Troika's recommendations, Greece, as well as Portugal and Spain, among other nations, must undergo painful adjustments in government budgets and external competitiveness, mainly through deflationary policies and the reduction of wages.

In the Greek rescue package, aimed to provide additional funding until 2014, the commitment to a fiscal and structural reform (privatisation) agenda is highlighted in order to reduce the Greek public debt / GDP to 120.5 per cent by 2020. Similarly, Spain has recently revised its deficit objective in order to assess the strength of the new fiscal governance regime.

A downward trend of nominal wages has also been pursued to increase competitiveness. However, nominal wage cuts are not effective, not only socially and politically but also economically, as they quickly translate into falling domestic demand. Indeed, the negative effects of reduced domestic demand will affect future economic growth. With fiscal policy reducing domestic demand, the economic and social crisis can only be intensified.

The debates about austerity versus further fiscal stimuli in Europe and the US are symptoms of the weakening of a global system which is now unsustainable and imbalanced (Varoufakis, 2015). Actually, the recent financial crisis revealed the urgency of exhaustively reviewing the international financial architecture. The dismantling of regulations since the 1970s, and the lack of new ones, has contributed to reduced control of national authorities on policy-making (Kiciloff, 2015).

A number of economists have discussed the impact of globalisation on the public sector in both developing and developed countries. It is interesting to ponder whether fiscal and monetary policies can withstand the adverse impact of shocks. In the short term it can if monetary policy could maintain necessary liquidity to meet the increasing money demand for transactions that result from higher levels of demand for goods and services. This is the principle of **monetary easing.**

According to Keynesian theory, the money supply affects prices and output through the nominal interest rate. Increasing the money supply reduces the interest rate, which in turn stimulates output and spending. The short-term nominal interest rate, *normally*, however, cannot be less than zero, based on a basic arbitrage argument: no one will lend £100 unless she gets at least £100 back. This is often referred to as the **zero bound** on the short-term nominal interest rate. Hence, once the money supply has been increased to a level where the short-term interest rate is zero, there will be no further effect on either output or prices, no matter how much money supply is increased; in other words, traditional monetary policy is rendered ineffective.

The use of combined fiscal and monetary policies enhances the ability to expand income and employment. Minsky suggested that when investors and entrepreneurs no longer have confidence in the economy and investments are declining because of lack of finance and funding, central banks must intervene and increase liquidity. Increased money supply to commercial banks will enable banks to restart lending to businesses. Central banks should also ensure that interest rates and exchange rates are kept low and stable. The government should, via fiscal policy, increase domestic spending and reduce tax rates. Quantitative easing would foster economic recovery, with a cooperative fiscal policy reducing interest rates and encouraging growth and stability. Economic policy decisions should be dynamic to ensure prudent and manageable situations. Thus, a mix of good fiscal and monetary policy could promote expansion, with systematic intervention in monetary and fiscal policy and an active regulatory system to guide the economy.

But would such a system comport with sustainability? Yes, if decisions on how to use the money are decided democratically, rather than by privately owned banks; and the investment funds are used to implement the 17 UN SDGs, rather than to increase consumption. We must adopt credit policies that contribute to sustainable growth. Monetary policy should redirect credit flows to where they are most needed for sustainable and humane policies. For example, credit policies could be combined with small business investment and employment targeting. Money should be thought of as a public good to create a new convention of trust based on financial regulation. Central banks' actions should be subordinated to meeting the 17 SDGs. Such regulation should express a holistic approach to finance and sustainable development (inequalities, poverty, global warming, etc.). Economic integration in the global order does not guarantee sustainable growth: countries must deliberately adopt selective measures. This understanding is crucial for the task ahead: policy-makers need to rethink institutions and instruments toward sustainable and inclusive growth for future generations.

Social and political tensions reflect the subordination of society to the bailout of the financial system and austerity programmes, which unduly burden those least able to afford it. Macroeconomic adjustment fostering fiscal austerity and real-wage flexibility can be costly, both socially and politically. Currently, in the European Union, the attempt to achieve higher real incomes, while subject to the constrictive demands of banks, investors and speculators, is challenging. The apprehension of this political and social reality can enhance alternative government responses focusing on investment and job-creation policies. This attempt is crucial to refocus the policy agenda toward sustainable finance and inclusive growth for future generations.

The central question related to the policy-making process is: *Who will benefit?* (Minsky, 1991). The global financial crisis has revealed a deep interconnection between the government and the financial system, with the preponderant benefits flowing to the latter.

14.10 A THEORETICAL NOTE ON LONG-TERM ECONOMIC CYCLES

Around the time of the First World War, the idea of long cycles, or 'long waves', in capitalism emerged, prompted by the work of Nikolai Kondratieff (1892–1938)

Box 14.2 US Supremacy in the Age of Finance: Expansion and Crisis

In the post-war boom between 1945 and 1971, the US recycled part of its surplus via foreign direct investment – mainly into Western Europe and Japan, in order to rebuild the war-ravaged nations. The US exported goods to the rest of the world and also financed these purchases, thereby stimulating export demand of foreign countries. After the 1970s, this global flow of funds reversed, with the US twin deficits (government budget and the balance of trade) now playing a crucial role in the new global economic order, as the engine of global growth. Currently, global surpluses flow to the US to provide the funds for the insatiable US twin deficits, what Yanis Varoufakis (2015) calls the 'Global Minotaur' (see Chapters 16 and 17).

The Minotaur, in Greek mythology, is half bull, half man. To make a long (but interesting) story short, Poseidon, god of the sea, obliged King Minos with a fine bull as a sign of divine endorsement, demanding, however, that it be sacrificed. When the King refused, Poseidon, angered by the King's defiance, enraptured the King's wife with a lust for the bull. After the bull's offspring was born, the disgusted King Minos instructed the renowned architect Daedalus to build a labyrinth from which escape was impossible, to imprison the Minotaur.[1] The Minotaur could only feast on human flesh, requiring a steady diet of slaves and prisoners of war.

Indeed, Varoufakis' Global Minotaur was supported by the close collaboration of the expansion of finance and the political power of economic neoliberalism. As a result, the global surplus recycling mechanism reversed the flow of global trade and capital flows: the United States provided sufficient demand for manufacturing in foreign countries – mainly China – in return for capital inflows. Between 1971 and 2008, the era of high finance supported the expansion of global trade at the cost of financial bubbles, corporate mega-profits and increasing social inequalities, supported by neoclassical economics.

However, according to Varoufakis (2015), the Global Minotaur has a crucial weakness: just like the mythical beast, the maintenance of US supremacy atop a precarious global infrastructure requires permanent unbalances. Consequently, since the fundamental structural flaws in the global economy have not been addressed (especially the global imbalances) since the recent financial crisis, there are serious concerns that a new global economic crisis of unprecedented magnitude might very well occur.

1. This was the same labyrinth from which Daedalus and his son Icarus tried to escape with hand-made wings, with Icarus flying too close to the sun, plunging to his death.

and Joseph Schumpeter (1883–1950).[3] Kondratieff was a Russian economist and director of the Business Cycle Research Institute in Moscow. Unfortunately, he was convicted of anti-Soviet crimes and executed in prison at the age of 46. But, as Mason (2015: 32–3) notes, the charges were fabricated, and his real crime was thinking 'the unthinkable about capitalism: that instead of collapsing under crisis [as predicted by Marx] capitalism generally adapts and mutates'. Kondratieff researched several developed nations during the period 1790–1920,

3. This section draws heavily from the work of Mason (2015: 32–48).

tracking interest rates, wages, foreign trade, commodity prices, and coal and iron production. Kondratieff (Mason, 2015: 33) found evidence of three distinct long waves, each characterised by

> an upswing lasting about twenty-five years, fuelled by the development of new technologies and high capital investment; then a downswing of about the same length, usually ending with a depression. In the 'up' phase recessions are rare; in the 'down' phase they are frequent. In the up phase, capital flows to productive industries; in the down phase it gets trapped in the financial system.

More specifically, for Kondratieff, a long wave begins

> because large amounts of cheap capital have been accumulated, centralized, and mobilized in the financial system, usually accompanied by a rise in the supply of money, which is needed to fund the investment boom. Grandiose investments are begun – canals and factories in the late eighteenth century, railways and urban infrastructures in the mid-nineteenth century. New technology is deployed and new business models created . . .
>
> Ibid.: 37–8

And a long wave ends because

> more capital [is] accumulated than can be invested in productive industries, so it tends to get stored inside the finance sector, depressing interest rates because the ample supply of credit depresses the price of borrowing. Recessions get worse and become more frequent. Wage and prices collapse, and finally a depression sets in.
>
> Ibid.: 36

Based on his analysis, Kondratieff identified three long waves in the period he had researched. Mason extended Kondratieff's analysis to add a fourth wave and a fifth, underway now, coinciding with the decline of the fourth.

Whereas Kondratieff assumed that the dynamics of capital investment were the primary cause of the long wave, Joseph Schumpeter argued that technology is the primary cause, driven by the innovator and entrepreneur (Mason, 2015: 38 & 45). In his 1912 book *The Theory of Economic Development*, Schumpeter argued that economic development depends on entrepreneurs and innovative activities:

> The characterisation of the entrepreneur type by expressions such as 'initiative' and 'foresight' shows the relevance of this economic actor as the one who carries out 'new combinations' by introducing new products or processes.
>
> Schumpeter, 1912 [1934]: 75

Table 14.2 Kondratieff's Long-wave Cycles

	Rise (causal factor)	*Decline*
First Long Wave	1780s–1817 (Factory system)	1817–1849
Second Long Wave	1849–1873 (railways, telegraph, ocean-going steamers, machine-produced machinery)	1873–1896
Third Long Wave	1890–1914 (telephone, scientific management, mass production)	1914–1945
Fourth Long Wave	Late 1940s–2008 (transistors, nuclear power, automatic computing power, mass consumer goods)	2008–?
Fifth Long Wave	Late 1990s–? (information goods, network technology, global mobile technology)	

Source: Mason (2015: 32–48).

Indeed, for Schumpeter, the entrepreneur destroys old traditions and habits with innovations. He viewed the entrepreneur as creating new industries, precipitating major structural changes in the economy. Old industries are rendered obsolete by a process of 'creative destruction'. One side effect of innovative investment is the modification of market structures, since the innovations increase competition between firms at least initially (Schumpeter, 1939 [2006]).

THINKING QUESTIONS

Imagine yourself an entrepreneur planning investments in the food sector. What might influence your decision to expand the productive capacity (stock of capital)? How do you envision the process? And what about possible obstacles? What about the role of uncertainty?

Why have financial crises been so prevalent throughout history? Why are financial crises followed by severe contractions in economic activity and employment levels?

How would you define a recession, based on what you have learned in the text? Is this definition adequate? Should we differentiate between a 'normal' recession and a recession caused by financial mismanagement?

While we understand the genesis of recessions and how to end them once they occur, we are not able to predict their occurrence. Perhaps some time in the future we might; but how would we use such information?

CLASS ACTIVITES

Play around with the concepts that relate to a bank's balance sheet. Apply them to the following situations:

(1) The bank increases short-term loan contracts in foreign currency to exporters and issues short-term bonds to increase the funding of its operations. Amount US$15,000.
(2) The bank increases loans and increases interbank operations to fund the operation. Amount US$7,000.
(3) The bank decides to sell US$10,000 from housing loans. How will this affect the composition of assets and liabilities?

AREA FOR RESEARCH

Why did the recent financial crisis occur? How did this differ from previous recessions?

UN SDG FOCUS

Since its inception, capitalism has been prone to recessions, depressions and financial crises. How will this affect the ability to implement the UN 17 SDGs?

FURTHER READING

Krugman, P. (2013) *End this Depression Now!* New York: Norton.
Stiglitz, J. (2013) *The Price of Inequality.* London: Penguin.
Varoufakis, Y. (2015) *The Global Minotaur: America, Europe and the Future of the Global Economy*. London: Zed Books.

15
Justice, Political Economy, Global Development and Governance

A central theme of this book is justice. How can we use economics to ensure all citizens, especially citizens of the Global South, reach their full capabilities within a sustainable world? But what is justice? How do we distinguish between just and unjust? Neoclassical economists wash their hands of the need to discuss justice by assuming prima facie and gratuitously that market outcomes are just. But, as Hobsbawm (2007: 104) noted:

> Market sovereignty is an alternative to any kind of politics, since it denies the need for political decisions, which are precisely decisions about common or group interests as distinct from the sum of choices, rational or otherwise, of individuals pursuing their private preferences. . . Participation in the market replaces participation in politics; the consumer takes the place of the citizen.

Justice requires pluralist dialogue – the two are intrinsically linked – and a hands-on, active approach. The promotion of justice in order to implement the 17 UN SDGs requires new forms of governance, amidst an active, global and pluralist dialogue.

An important lesson of history is that global superpowers get to write the rules of the game. And, not surprisingly, such rules reflect the superpower's interests and objectives, with potentially adverse effects on the rest of the world. This chapter will discuss the emergence of the United States as a global superpower during the Second World War (1939–45), overtaking Great Britain, which had previously dominated the world during the 'Pax Britannica' (1815–1914: the period of relative peace in Europe during which the British Empire ruled as global superpower). History also teaches us that the rise and fall of superpowers is not accidental, but the result of deliberate and conscious policy. In the context of the 'Pax Americana' (1945–?) we will also discuss today's dominant global institutions – the International Monetary Fund, the World Bank and the World Trade Organization. It should be no surprise that the developing nations are criticising these institutions for ignoring their interests. Of special interest is the rise of the BRICS nations (the five major emerging national economies: Brazil,

Russia, India, China and South Africa). The chapter will conclude by asking if it is time to conceptualise a new set of global institutions.

15.1 JUSTICE AND INJUSTICE

In Chapter 1 we discussed the concept of justice, and the fact that, given its subjectivity, it might be difficult for all to agree on what exactly a just society is. Two broad categorisations throughout human history have been offered to conceptualise and hence develop just societies. One outlines an ideal 'just' society that exists only in the imagination or as a theoretical exercise, like Rawls' 'original position', More's 'Utopia' and Rousseau's 'social contract'. While these exercises are indeed mentally stimulating, they offer an ultimately elusive ideal. Nevertheless, we can seek to act pragmatically in accordance with some key principles of justice, and in the process create, through our actions and relationships, a socially, economically and environmentally just world.

The second approach, what Amartya Sen (2010: 7) calls a 'realisation-focused comparison', begins, as its name implies, not with an ideal but with existing conditions in the real world. Here perhaps we could recognise more easily the absence of justice rather than justice itself, and thus focus on palpable injustice, since after all 'the identification of redressable injustice . . . animates us to think about justice and injustice . . .' (Ibid.: vii). Someone living on the street, someone without adequate healthcare, without means to obtain an education, and without the ability to provision are obvious examples of injustice. We prefer Sen's approach.

While the literature on justice is prodigious, we must now turn our attention to injustice in economics, which, given our definition of economics, can be identified as the failure of an individual, group or economy to provision. Rather than identify an ideal situation in which everyone can provision, we suggest identifying the obstacles to *preventing* provisioning in contemporary society. In order to redress palpable injustice, it is necessary to engage in a substantive dialogue with all interested stakeholders, which is the essence of democracy.

> Particular importance has to be attached to the role of public discussion and interactions in the emergence of shared values and commitments. Our ideas of what is just and what is not may respond to the arguments that are presented for public discussion, and we tend to react to one another's views sometimes with a compromise or even a deal, and at other times with relentless inflexibility and stubbornness.
>
> Sen 2009: 253

And, given our focus of sustainability, it is important to give active consideration to future generations. Hence the term 'intergenerational justice'.

15.2 THE POLITICAL ECONOMY OF DEVELOPMENT AND THE PURSUIT OF JUSTICE

The uneven expansion of capitalism in the world economy means we must understand the challenges of particular historical trajectories of national economies. Indeed, underdeveloped economies cannot be understood in isolation but only in relation to the global system of which they are an integral part. Celso Furtado (1920–2004), a Brazilian intellectual, author and government minister, argued that development and underdevelopment are part of the same process of capitalism's global expansion. Thus, the study of underdevelopment requires consideration of the historical formation of underdeveloped economies in their regional framework in order to apprehend the dynamics between them and advanced, developed economies.

While you might assume that development lessens underdevelopment, Furtado (1987) and many Latin American social scientists argue that the two are concomitant: one begets the other. But how can a global system that produces underdevelopment and development be just?

Among the structural problems associated with modernisation, especially in agriculture, is that the coexistence of capitalist production with non-capitalist production (subsistence agriculture) fosters dependency of the latter on the former. More specifically, the surplus created in the capitalist sector depends on conditions in the non-capitalist sector. Indeed, sustainable economic growth depends on the creation of a positive feedback among flows of production, wages and consumption in all economic sectors. The duality of the economic structure – modern and archaic sectors – precipitated Furtado's agrarian reforms to reinforce the supply of food and the sustainability of economic growth. His proposal, however, has never been adopted in Latin America.

Development occurs if all citizens benefit. If not, they become subordinated to capital dynamics in a process of modernisation that enhances dehumanisation. Today, we have a 'new dependency' in which financial capital dominates economic systems and reinforces poverty, illiteracy and concentration of income, wealth and land, while subordinating society to financial interests. Achieving some degree of autonomy of macroeconomic policy could occur with capital controls and exchange-rate centralisation; however, the challenges and possibilities of 'national policies' is more complex in an interdependent global structure, and made more difficult with the high indebtedness of the public sector. Furtado teaches us that existing underdevelopment can be changed once we understand the dynamics of capitalism as a worldwide system in the context of imperialism.[1]

To help us understand imperialism, let us turn again to Schumpeter, whose ideas were introduced in the last chapter. In *The Sociology of Imperialism* (1919),

1. For a good introductory background, see Birch et al., 2017: 26–41.

Schumpeter focused on groups and classes as the real agents of change in global capitalism, reinforced within the analysis of imperialism in history. In *Capitalism, Socialism and Democracy* (1942), Schumpeter presented the sociological foundations of imperialism, arguing that imperialism, as an expression of national objectives, serves specific interests within the nation state: the state is viewed as an instrument of power of capitalists in order to guarantee monopoly profits. On the other hand, the capitalists serve the state, which increases tensions between classes. Who benefits and loses from imperialism, and can it ever be just?

In the context of current globalisation, Joseph Stiglitz (2013) suggested rethinking the foundations of wealth and income inequality. All recent changes in wealth are very closely linked with the credit system. Through deregulation and lax standards, banks increased lending, but not for creating new business nor for capital goods; instead for increasing the value of land and other fixed resources (buildings, real estate, etc.), which accrue disproportionately to the rich. While that is a major part of the increase in wealth, the workers, who have little wealth, don't benefit. The ratio of wages to productivity is decreasing, while the ratio of CEO pay to worker pay has increased, suggesting increased exploitation founded on increased market power.

Amartya Sen (2010) argued that globalisation has deepened social differences and increased polarisation between groups. Also drawing on Sen's insights, we surmise that different historical legacies shape development; indeed, colonialism and its aftermath powerfully impact on social capabilities. Low literacy rates, poor health, weak governance and institutions, and the lack of infrastructure all hinder economic and social development.

Concerns with inequality extend well beyond issues of justice and fairness, since the degree of economic inequality also affects social cohesion and political stability, and can negatively affect economic growth and sustainability.

15.3 GLOBAL GOVERNANCE: FROM PAX BRITANNICA TO BRETTON WOODS

In the nineteenth century, Britain dominated the world economically and politically:

- London was the financial, economic and political capital of the world, thanks to the growing power of the British Empire and trade relationships.
- The British currency – the pound sterling – became the global currency. A superpower carries a lot of advantages, especially that its home currency becomes the global currency, which in turn allows the country to enjoy persistent trade deficits, i.e. importing more than exporting – thereby living beyond its means. (More on this in the next chapter.)

- Given the global nature of the British Empire, standardisation, uniformity and predictability were considered virtues, especially with exchange rates and prices. The former were fixed to the price of gold, which, because of its scarcity, depressed prices, thereby preventing inflation. Standardisation of prices reduced uncertainty, which in turn increased investment, and low inflation benefited British banks.
- Finally, Great Britain became adamant in preaching the doctrine of free trade, which would obviously benefit British firms by enabling access to resources and markets.

Thus, any country wanting to trade with Great Britain, or to participate in the global economic system (which for all practical purposes was the same thing), had to abide by Great Britain's rules. Not everyone accepted this arrangement. A central theme of this book is that the manifestation and exercise of power sets in motion measures to attenuate it. Germany and the United States were both determined to dislodge Great Britain. Germany flexed its economic and military might during the 1930s, only to be destroyed during the Second World War, after which the US emerged as the lone global superpower.

The scene for this transition (the UK descending and the US ascending) is the 'global' conference held at Bretton Woods, New Hampshire in July 1944. Bretton Woods is a beautiful resort with a splendid view of Mount Washington, the highest peak in the northeastern US at 1,916.6 metres; and, thanks to the confluence of continental wind patterns, it is home to very inhospitable weather, claiming until very recently the world's highest wind gust.

By 1944, it was clear to all that Germany would lose the war in Europe. Delegates from 44 Allied nations gathered in Bretton Woods to map out a global strategy for reconstruction.

Specifically, to map out a post-war international system that would ostensibly ensure prosperity – while, at least from the US perspective, guaranteeing its economic supremacy and that of its corporations.

It is very interesting to read the transcripts of the Bretton Woods Conference, especially negotiations between Great Britain (represented ably by J. M. Keynes), the declining global superpower, and the US, the emerging superpower. US delegates were brash, rude, overly confident and highly dismissive of Great Britain's suggestions. Of the three institutions created during this conference – the World Bank, the International Monetary Fund (IMF) and the General Agreement on Tariffs and Trade (GATT) – the first two were located in the US (right in the nation's capital, Washington DC, where Roosevelt, it was said, could keep an active eye on them), while the GATT was located in a neutral country: Switzerland. (The United Nations was conceptualised during a later conference in San Francisco in 1948, to be headquartered in New York.) Thus, three of the 'big four' institutions were located in the very corridors of political and economic power of the newly emerging superpower. And, not surprisingly, each institution embodied and implemented the interests of the United States.

Box 15.1 Keynes' Proposal to Reorganise the International Order

In his seminal work, *The Great Transformation* (1944), Karl Polanyi argued that the severity of the economic crisis of the interwar years (between the First and Second World Wars) was due to a mistaken attempt to restore the liberal international economic order of the nineteenth century: a set of policies based on the fallacious construct of the self-regulating market.

During the 1930s Keynes argued that deflationary national policies decreased aggregate demand and world trade, while increasing mass unemployment. In Keynes' opinion, the business environment is conditioned by monetary, fiscal and exchange-rate policies. For Keynes, the priority of the state was to stimulate employment and growth; employment is not only a social good in itself but also the main driver of economic growth, as it increases consumption and thus aggregate demand. Increasing a society's 'marginal propensity to consume' leads to greater 'expectations' of demand for employers. This in turn triggers greater investment in expanding productive capacity and therefore more employment.

Keynes' vision, presented at Bretton Woods, was a managed international regime to enhance stable flows of trade and finance, economic stability and prosperity. Keynes pointed out the need of a system of international currency that might only work by means of a 'wide measure of agreement', i.e. a new international convention incorporating an international currency, stable exchange rates, redistribution of international reserves from surplus to deficit nations, macro stabilising mechanisms, and international sources of liquidity. As uncertainty is inherent in all economic decisions, Keynes relied on credibility and confidence:

> more generally, we need a means of reassurance to a troubled world, by which any country whose own affairs are conducted with due prudence is relieved of anxiety, for causes which are not of its own making, concerning its ability to meet its international liabilities; and which will, therefore, make unnecessary those methods of restriction and discrimination which countries have adopted hitherto, not on their merits, but as measures of self-protection from disruptive outside forces.
>
> Keynes, 1969: 21

Keynes' proposed currency was the Bancor, to be issued by a global central bank, the International Clearing House. The Bancor would be available to all countries in proportion to their trade volume. This innovative and potentially effective idea was dismissed by the delegates of the United States, partly due to disdain that this suggestion came from a British citizen, but also due to insistence by the US on constructing a global system based on the hegemony of the US dollar; and of course for the very practical reason that Keynes' proposed funding for the Bancor was to tax nations with trade surpluses, the US being the paramount example (Akyüz, 2013: 19).

15.4 PAX AMERICANA (1945–?)

One of the more interesting questions social scientists ask is, why do nations rise and fall? The research is prodigious, and, based on the work of Phillips (2002), Chua (2007) and Landes (1999), we believe that both a nation's rise and its fall is enabled by conscious decisions, aided and abetted by the construction of appropriate institutions (or lack thereof). The rise is deliberate, with active decisions to increase investment, aggregate demand, new technologies, health, education and welfare, enabling the nation to take advantage of unique circumstances such as resources, access to cheap energy, land mass, etc. Interestingly, the advent of every global superpower's rise is characterised by strict protectionism, with vociferous opposition to free trade. And, according to Phillips (Ibid.), the fall of every superpower is characterised by: crippling debt, overextension, increasing inequality, reduced living standards, lack of pluralism, a paralysed and ineffectual government, a decreased manufacturing base, and increased religious fundamentalism. These factors combine to produce impotency and a failure to act until it is too late.

The United States emerged as the only superpower in the aftermath of the Second World War: partly due to being relatively unscathed during the war, unlike Britain, France, Russia, Germany and Japan; but also as a result of deliberate economic policies dating from the late nineteenth century. Back then, the US was the most protectionist in its history, and one of the most protectionist countries in the world, yet determined to overtake Great Britain.

With Bretton Woods, the US emerged as a global superpower, exercising its global hegemony, with an overextended and debt-crippled UK unable to oppose. The following are key elements of the Pax Americana:

- Washington became the global political capital, and New York the economic capital. Power and money would flow outward from these two centres across the globe.
- The dollar became the global currency, affording the US the luxury and ability to run persistent trade deficits, allowing it to literally live beyond its means.
- A gold standard was linked to fixed and convertible global exchange rates (see the next chapter for a discussion of exchange rates).
- A quid pro quo emerged between the largest US corporations and organised labour to achieve labour peace (no strikes by labour and management shares the profits), enabling the US to penetrate global markets. This labour peace began with the Treaty of Detroit signed between the United Auto Workers and General Motors, promising workers a greater share of profits (in the form of wages, pensions and medical insurance) in exchange for

renouncing strikes and other militant action (Standing, 2016: 7). Although, as Standing notes (2016: 7), 'this accord was copied across US industry, and to a large extent, in other industrialized countries', not all corporations acquiesced – a notable exception was General Electric.

- The US became a strident believer in free trade, which would benefit US firms and consumers.
- To protect US interests abroad, and to combat its perceived existential threat – socialism – the US became increasingly militarised.
- Construction of a global architecture enabled the rise of US interests, anchored by the IMF, the World Bank and the GATT, with the dollar as the global currency. It is to these institutions that we now turn.

15.5 THE GLOBAL INSTITUTIONS OF PAX AMERICANA

(1) The International Monetary Fund (IMF)

The International Monetary Fund was conceived during the 1944 Bretton Woods Conference and officially established in 1945. It is still in existence. Its preponderant objectives are: to promote international monetary cooperation, to enhance exchange-rate stability, and to provide temporary financial assistance to countries with balance-of-payment difficulties. Specifically, the IMF provides:

- **Surveillance:** An assessment of economic and financial developments which provides a framework facilitating the exchange of goods, services and capital among countries, mainly to promote external stability.
- **Lending:** This enables countries to manage their international reserves and stabilise their currencies.
- **Technical assistance:** The IMF helps member countries to manage their economic policy and financial affairs.

Since the 1990s the IMF has emphasised reduced government interventionism, liberalisation of markets and macroeconomic stability, basically to encourage financial capital flows. The IMF's basic modus operandi is: first, price stabilisation to achieve real interest rate stability and financial sector growth; second, only after obtaining some degree of financial deepening, including the development of non-bank activities in capital markets, it is possible to deregulate the banking system.

The IMF argues that the long-term benefits of financialisation include a better allocation of global saving, and in addition: (1) reduced cost of domestic credit, as domestic saving is complemented by foreign savings; (2) the possibility of diversifying risk by acquiring assets not available in domestic markets; (3) the possibility of supplementing residents' investments with foreign investments, enabling access to new technologies and new markets; (4) offering more efficient and complete financial services for residents in a new environment characterised by competition between domestic and foreign players.

However, the IMF policies have not been very effective:

- Evidence suggests that the liberalisation of capital flows enhances macroeconomic instability, increases social vulnerability and unemployment, and decreases real incomes.
- The IMF agenda has favoured global economic integration and price stabilisation, rather than competitiveness, employment and growth.
- Global financial markets have not supported the composition and amount of investment necessary to encourage sustainable development.
- Deregulated finance has increased the volatility of capital flows, along with the volatility of stock prices and the systemic risk to banks (Akyüz, 2013).
- Deregulated finance increases currency speculation and the volatility of exchange rates, since domestic currencies compete with other financial assets.
- The efficacy of domestic monetary policy to prevent capital outflows and currency speculation has been restricted.

In the aftermath of the recent global crisis, however, capital controls were 'blessed' by the International Monetary Fund. **Capital controls**, i.e. explicit government controls regulating the financial assets entering a nation, have increased in many countries (e.g. South Korea, Taiwan, Turkey and Brazil) due to threats to macroeconomic instability. Table 15.1 presents an overview of African nations that prevented significant private capital inflows prior to the crisis. Although the policy challenges associated with private capital inflows have been similar, the responses vary, depending on institutional factors.

It is expected that central banks would improve monitoring of short-term capital flows and financial prices, to avoid propagation mechanisms for contagion effects, namely in the currency and stock markets. Indeed, capital controls are used by many African nations to redesign their capital accounts. Thus, further institutional and financial policies should be required to affect the composition of inflows.

Indeed, since the crisis, the growing volume of capital inflows to African and other emerging economies has raised several concerns. Foreign inflows are appreciating some currencies (see Chapter 16), making it harder for local exporters to compete in global markets. The real problem is the short-term capital inflow: the so called 'hot money'. Capital inflows threaten to create asset bubbles in real estate and stock markets. From a sustainability perspective, are such inflows beneficial? And, beneficial for whom? What are the funds used for?

Table 15.1 Type of Controls on Portfolio Investment and Foreign Direct Investment in African Countries (1990–2006)

Country	*Debt (bonds)*	*Equity (shares)*	*Foreign Direct Investment (FDI)*
Cameroon	No controls.	Control on issuing foreign securities above certain amounts.	Controls above certain amounts.
Nigeria	No controls.	No controls.	No controls, only registration of FDI inflows.
South Africa	Controls on resident sale or issue abroad.	Controls on resident sale or issue abroad; limits on resident purchasing abroad.	No controls.
Uganda	No controls.	No controls.	No controls.
Zambia	No controls.	No controls.	No controls.

Source: Elaborated by the authors from International Monetary Fund (IMF, 2009b), Table A3; Murinde (2009).

(2) The World Bank

Also created during the 1944 Bretton Woods Conference was the International Bank for Reconstruction and Development, known as the World Bank. Initially the Bank's main objective was to assist in the reconstruction of post-war Europe, then its focus shifted to providing development loans. Currently, the World Bank's preponderant objective is to reduce poverty by financing and assisting in healthcare, education, infrastructure and communications, among others, through its various institutions:

- **International Bank for Reconstruction and Development** (1946): Attempts to reduce poverty in middle- and low-income countries.
- **International Development Association** (1960): Promotes interest-free loans and grants.
- **International Finance Corporation** (1956): The private-sector arm of the World Bank.
- **Multilateral Investment Guarantee Agency** (1988): Promotes foreign direct investment in developing countries.
- **International Centre for Settlement of Investment Disputes** (1966): Facilitates settlement of investment disputes between governments and foreign investors.

Today the World Bank provides aid in order to reduce poverty in countries with sound economic management and robust government institutions, i.e. open trade, secure private property rights, absence of corruption, respect for the rule of law, social safety nets, and sound macroeconomic and financial policies. In this setting, the importance of current aid policies spills over to the importance of achieving (and increasing) foreign investment. Indeed, every dollar of foreign aid attracts more dollars of investment, because aid increases the confidence of the private sector and helps to provide public services that investors need, such as education and infrastructure. In countries that lack the policies and institutions to make good use of large financial flows, World Bank aid policies can foster a climate for successful reform without offering large-scale financial assistance, for example, by providing advice and sponsoring forums in which government officials can learn from other countries.

Official development assistance (ODA) is defined as government aid designed to promote the economic development and welfare of developing countries. Aid may be provided from donor to recipient or channelled through a multilateral agency (OECD, 2016). The total amount of ODA to developing countries has increased after the global crisis from US$154.3 billion in 2008 to US$181 billion in 2014, with most flows bilateral. In 2014, the four largest donors by volume were: the United States, the United Kingdom, Germany and France.

Since 2003, most ODA flows (46.7 per cent of the total) have been concentrated to lower-income countries. In 2003 lower-middle-income countries received 29.1 per cent of the total, increasing to 31.5 per cent in 2014; aid to upper-middle-income countries decreased from 24.6 per cent of the total in 2003 to 17.4 per cent in 2014.

(3) The World Trade Organization (WTO)

Between the First and Second World Wars, most countries were protectionist, assuming that restricting cheap imports was the best means to increase domestic growth. Although perhaps effective if done by a few countries, this becomes problematic when done by most, since if most nations reduce their imports, it also means (by definition) that most nations reduce their exports. In 1930 the US enacted the Smoot-Hawley Act (SHA), which significantly increased tariffs on imported goods. And, predictably, after the SHA other nations retaliated against the US, so that by 1939 very few nations were trading with each other. Although the immediate causes of the Second World War were political, it is well known that tensions over trade during the 1930s contributed to the hostility, making war inevitable.

Thus, one deliberate outcome of Bretton Woods was the construction of a framework for a new global body reducing protectionism and encouraging free trade: the General Agreement on Tariffs and Trade (GATT). Its preponderant focus on reducing tariffs was subsequently enlarged to include other non-tariff barriers such as quotas.

In 1995 the GATT was replaced with the World Trade Organization (WTO), which placed less emphasis on the avoidance of conflict and more on the promulgation of free trade. The WTO 'does not adopt a neutral stance on trade policy. Indeed, it is passionately against protectionism and just as profoundly for trade liberalisation' (Peet, 2009: 193).

Box 15.2 Key Concepts in International Trade

- **Free trade:** Countries will not limit the products of other countries coming into their domestic markets, even if this might undermine their own productive sectors and reduce unemployment within their economies, and unfortunately, reduce sustainability. The traditional methods used to limit such imports are: **quotas** (a quantity limit on the amount of a imported good); and **tariffs:** the imposition of a tax on either imports or exports, making either more expensive. Pertaining to the latter, the law of demand predicts that as tariffs increase the price of imports, less will be demanded; and the higher price will protect and encourage domestic production.
- **Protectionism:** The implementation of tariffs or quotas which restrict free trade.
- **Beggar thy neighbour:** A trading policy based on currency devaluations and protective barriers which alleviate a nation's economic difficulties at the expense of others.
- **Dumping:** When a nation sets a good's export price at less than its sale price in its domestic market.

The WTO has currently focused on anti-dumping policies, while at the same time, due to globalisation, countries are searching for ways to protect their own production. Thus it should not be surprising that the number of anti-dumping cases has increased, especially in metal, chemical, plastic, textiles, machinery and equipment, agriculture and food. Anti-dumping law will remain a protectionist tool for members to protect import-competing industries.

In its mission to liberalise trade, the WTO has undertaken a series of global negotiations (rounds) to persuade countries to reduce their trade barriers. At times this has brought the organisation into conflict with the social and environmental priorities of citizens, e.g. countries cannot limit the import of products that are produced in ways that damage the environment, say rainforest timber, or, to use the same example, because the import of this timber might damage their own forestry industry. By agreeing to become members of the WTO, nations accept that they will suffer this damage in return for the benefits of trade, especially lower prices for domestic citizens and the ability to export to the other nations according to similar rules. Such a system is archaic and narrowly focused.

However, in recent years many developing nations have challenged this system of trade, arguing that the rules of the WTO benefit the rich nations of the Global North, while undermining the growing economies of the Global South. It is worth noting that many nations of today did not exist as independent states in 1944 and so were not part of the Bretton Woods negotiations. Many nations at the time suffered the oppression of colonisation, which explains why today they enjoy fewer benefits from the international trading system vis-à-vis countries present at the negotiations, especially the powerful economic and political players of the West.

The most recent round of trade negotiations, which began in Doha in 2001, struggled in an atmosphere of intensifying acrimony before collapsing in June 2008. As a result, the international trading system established in 1944 has effectively broken down. The reality is that developed countries impose terms on developing nations requiring them to accept competition from much more powerful and technologically sophisticated producers, while they subsidise their own agricultural products, which effectively undermines production in the countries of the South. Many developing countries have decided that the trade game is biased against them and are refusing to play. In the place of the global trading system we now have a patchwork of bilateral and regional trade agreements.

15.6 THE BANK FOR INTERNATIONAL SETTLEMENTS (BIS) AND THE GLOBAL BANKING CAPITALISATION RULES

The mission of the Bank for International Settlements (BIS), located in Basel, Switzerland, is to serve central banks (discussed in the next chapter) in their pursuit of monetary and financial stability, to foster international cooperation, and to act as a bank for central banks. While not created during Bretton Woods – it was created on 17 May 1930, making it the oldest international financial organisation – it remains a crucial institution of the current global framework. And, incidentally, the BIS is distinguished by several of its economists calling attention to low and stable inflation . . . coincid[ing] with the build up of private sector debt that sowed the seeds for future banking crises (Carlin and Soskice, 2015: 224).

The BIS has implemented capital requirements to promote safe banking risk management and higher levels of capitalisation as essential to stability. These measures aimed to overcome **asymmetric information** (defined as the buyer and seller to a transaction possessing different information), and were supposed to foster financial stability. However, banks developed financial innovations, such as off-balance-sheet assets and SIVs (structured investment vehicles), excessively leveraged in US and European banks. This was certainly a main cause of the recent global financial crisis.

The recent crisis underscored the fact that global trade and financial integration promoted by the IMF, World Bank and WTO has increased exposure (and even caused) global macroeconomic instability. Although domestic banking regulation can induce better practices, it cannot eliminate the impacts of global crashes. In the future, global action is necessary, with coordination and coherence of the main international agencies, and perhaps some new ones as well.

15.7 THE BRICS AND THE EVOLUTION OF GLOBAL GOVERNANCE

Coined in 2001 by Jim O'Neil, a Goldman Sachs investment banker, BRIC united four countries with little in common except for their phenomenal growth rates: Brazil, Russia, India and China. Indeed, it is interesting and ironic that these countries would adopt a term created by a US financial institution to define themselves. In 2011, South Africa was added to the BRIC, resulting in BRICS.

It is predicted that by 2030 the combined economies of the BRICS nations will overtake the G7 (the 'Group of Seven' major advanced economies), and that China will become the world's largest economy (Beattie, 2010). If these predictions come true, the consequences for global consumption, investment, resource allocation and the environment will be profound. Is economics (and economics education) able to meet the challenge? How does this comport with 17 UN SDGs?

The BRICS nations represent almost half of the world's population and about a fifth of the Earth's surface, with a combined GDP comparable to the EU or the US. Despite similarities, there are significant political, cultural and social differences between the five BRICS nations. Table 15.2 indicates some of their main characteristics.

From 2000 to 2008 the world experienced one of the greatest commodity and credit booms in history, stimulated by US expansionary monetary policy, which flooded the world with cheap financing, especially benefiting the BRICS nations. Currently, growth rates have fallen and current account balances have deteriorated. Brazil and Russia have been adversely affected by declining commodity prices. India's inflation is too high and its macroeconomic instability might jeopardise its budget deficit, public debt and current account deficit. Although the BRICS have accumulated large foreign reserves, they have not significantly invested in the necessary infrastructure. China's over-leveraged banking system raises concern. South Africa faces a number of long-standing economic problems that, in part, still reflect the harmful legacy of apartheid.

Table 15.2 BRICS Main Indicators, 2014

Indicators	*Member countries: Brazil, Russia, India, China, and South Africa*
GDP	US$15.76 trillion
Share of world GDP	19.8%
Population	2.998 billion
Share of world population	41.6%
Total exports (2012)	US$3.19 trillion
Share of global exports	17.7%
Total imports (2012)	US$2.95 trillion
Share of global imports	16.1%
Total trade (2012)	US$6.14 trillion
Share of world trade	16.9%
Trade balance (2012)	US$244 billion

Sources: International Monetary Fund (IMF, 2014); United Nations Conference on Trade and Development (UNCTAD, 2014).

The BRICS have vociferously argued for a new international economic order, arguing that the current global structure is 'asymmetric in which certain countries and people benefit from globalisation, while others do not' (Birch et al., 2017: 125). In other words, at least from the BRICS nations' perspective, we need a new global governance.

Governance is an increasingly used word today. We like and will use the following definition:

> Often compared with the concept of 'government' – which refers to the formal political system and formal authority – the term 'governance' is used to conceptualise the coordination of the political-economic system across an array of social actors and institutions (e.g. government, business, civil society, etc.). Increasingly, governance is associated with the growing role and importance of private actors in political-economic decision-making, especially at the global scale.
>
> Birch et al., 2017:117

And **global governance** means 'the systematic and collective attempt to organise and coordinate global activities in the pursuit of common global goals, which would be beyond the capacity of any individual country to undertake' (Ibid.). The BRICS are figuring out how to use their combined clout to affect the institutions of the global economy, and establish a new global governance. Perhaps the formation of a formal group within the framework of the UN Assembly; or through partnerships in discussions with the IMF and the World Bank; or perhaps we need a new Bretton Woods, considered within a context of pluralist sustainability.

15.8 TIME FOR A NEW BRETTON WOODS?

In the context of this crucial question, three specific questions must be addressed: (1) Is there a need for a global conference that is representative, and focuses on the key themes of justice and sustainability? (2) What is the most appropriate unit of participation – the nation state, the region, or the individual; or some other grouping? (3) What should be the objectives of the conference: to tweak the existing institutions or to develop a radical new order?

Following Van der Berg (2012), we believe that these three questions are among the most important you will confront. We don't claim to have all the answers, nor do we claim that our suggestions are original. But we believe it necessary to think and to engage in dialogue in an open and friendly manner.

Pertaining to the first question: yes, we feel it is time for a new Bretton Woods Conference, for all nations to meet and discuss a new global architecture: Active participation by all nations is needed, from developed and developing; North and South. While the Mount Washington Hotel has been recently refurbished with room for all, we recommend choosing a site that is environmentally vulnerable, in order to hammer home the message that our task is urgent: perhaps a Pacific Island such as Vanuatu, whose future is threatened by rising sea levels. But, as Van den Berg laments (2012: 494), 'who would play the role of Keynes? Is there someone today of his stature – the elder statesman? . . . And if there is a person of Keynes' stature today, would he [sic] be invited to take a prominent seat at the table of a new Bretton Woods conference?'

Pertaining to the second question, perhaps we take for granted that the nation is best to advocate the interests of its citizens, but this has not always been the case. Additionally, as Robert Nelson (2012: 328–9) reminds us, the nation states, far more than markets and corporations, have been responsible for significant environmental damage, including the UK in the nineteenth century, the US in the twentieth and of course the USSR. And today the biggest environmental despoilers are the US and China; one capitalist and one socialist.

But as recent climate negotiations have revealed, nation states, theoretically representing the interests of their own members and no one else, are impotent in resolving complex global issues – which in turn can undermine the existing global system, as Philip Bobbitt (2002: 468) cautions: 'the legitimacy of the society of nation-states will not long outlast the delegitimating acts of its leading members'.

In order for justice and sustainability to be addressed we must go beyond our narrow, parochial interests, since 'assessment of justice demands engagement with the "eyes of mankind"' (Sen 2010: 130). Sen expands:

> We identify with people of the same religion, same language group, same race, same gender, same political beliefs, or same profession. These multiple identities cut across national boundaries, and people indeed do things that they feel they really 'must' do, rather than virtuously accept to do.
>
> Ibid.: 129

And nothing is more important from a perspective of justice than limiting our effects on the environment, attenuating climate change, and hence adopting the UN SDGs. So, are other institutional arrangements more effective in reaching agreement than the traditional nation state?

The third question at the start of this section is perhaps the most difficult: Should we keep the existing system as is, or radically reconstruct it? There are two options: (1) Do nothing, with some tweaking around the edges; (2) Make a radical change. The rationale for each is as follows.

Do nothing:

- We have in place the IMF, the World Bank and the WTO, each with a specific objective. This is enough and perhaps we can tweak the existing systems to make them better and more accountable. Why should we have to reinvent the wheel?
- Markets work; the problem is too much government. And, likewise, globalisation and markets benefit all, with each necessary for solutions.
- Trade has dramatically increased since 1945. Isn't this the goal of Bretton Woods, specifically that of the GATT/WTO? So in this sense, isn't the system a success?
- Although poverty still persists, extreme poverty has been dramatically reduced. Is not this the objective of the IMF and World Bank? While the world has significantly changed since 1944, poverty could be a lot worse.
- With the exception of the recent financial crisis there has not been a systematic breakdown of the global order, like we had during the 1930s. There has not been a global war, and the nations of Europe have integrated economically and to an extent politically. Thus, a preponderant objective of Bretton Woods has been met. While the World Bank and the IMF in particular have received a lot of criticism for the recent crisis, it was caused by poor decision-making and not by faulty institutions.

Radical change:

- Where do we start? Although the objective of Bretton Woods was not to solve poverty and global inequality, both have persisted and have increased significantly since the crisis – a crisis, by the way, which the IMF did not anticipate.
- The track record is abysmal. Frequent and severe crises: Russia, Argentina, Turkey, the United States, to name just a few. Perhaps one or two is excusable, but certainly not on a regular and recurring basis.
- A main problem is ideological: the existing institutions are suffused with neoclassical economic theory, with no toleration for dissenting or heterodox views. For many years, a litmus test for being hired at the IMF or World Bank was belief in the neoclassical orthodoxy. This is also a problem with economics in general – a lack of pluralism. A long-running, persistent criticism is that the IMF is ideological: conditioning its aid on the client's acceptance of neoclassical policies, especially reduced budget deficits, reduced safety nets and reduced government regulation.
- Social cohesion and justice have deteriorated, accompanied by threats to individual freedom, control on individuals and insecurity in social interrelations. This raises the important question: Who has really benefited from the Bretton Woods institutions?
- It is unacceptable to continue with the dollar as the global currency: this floods the world with dollars, while allowing the US to run persistent trade deficits, which is a fundamental cause of global imbalances. Nor should any one nation's currency be used. We need to implement Keynes' idea of the Bancor, along with an International Clearing House.
- Although the number of international wars between sovereign states has declined since the mid 1960s, the number of conflicts within states has increased.
- To make matters worse, it is predicted that climate change will exacerbate conflict and violence. Specifically, it is claimed that 'for each one standard deviation change in climate toward warmer temperatures or more extreme rainfall, there is a 14 per cent increase in conflict between groups and a 4 per cent increase in conflict between individuals' (Burke et al., 2013: 12). With a projected increase in global temperature of at least 3.6°C by 2100, it is predicted that 'group conflict like civil wars could increase by 50 per cent, if nothing is done' (Ibid.). In the United States, drought conditions are extremely severe in many states west of the Mississippi River, especially in Nevada, Arizona and California (the latter home to 10 per cent of the US population and a $47 billion agriculture industry).This is indeed scary, suggesting that not only will climate change worsen and drought conditions intensify, increasing violence, but also that all will coalesce to reduce the ability of individuals to

provision. The Bretton Woods institutions have failed and are ill-equipped to deal with these problems.

- In summary, the existing global architecture is poorly positioned to implement the UN 17 SDGs.

15.9 ELEMENTS OF A NEW GLOBAL ORDER

Perhaps we need a new global order, as both of the options described above have some good and bad points, and neither by itself seems satisfactory. Here are our suggestions for a new global order:

- Global institutions need to be conceptualised, implemented, and run by all, not just by the elites of the rich, northern nations. A global perspective is needed since the main thread uniting each of our problems is sustainability, which can only be solved globally.
- We need recognition that the ability to provision, financial stability and sustainability are global public goods. We need new thinking beyond the simplistic and outmoded duality between state and market.
- We need a new global currency. Possibly the Bancor.
- Real wages have fallen relative to capital around the world, largely due to financialisation and neoliberalism. We need to reverse this by increasing wages, labour income, employment and growth within a sustainable modus operandi. Difficult but not impossible. Tackling this problem should attract the best and brightest of our students.
- The IMF needs a fundamental makeover in its corporate governance, specifically separating its functions of surveillance and policy implementation.
- Africa, perhaps with the exception of Egypt in the north and South Africa in the south, is a forgotten continent and requires urgent attention.
- Neoliberalism, the Washington Consensus, and the post-Washington consensus have not worked, only benefiting the few. Each is impotent in offering solutions for our current problems. Rather than needing a new ideology, we need to debate and discuss, while respecting the legitimacy of competing views – in other words, we need a global debate within the context of pluralism.
- Rather than assume away uncertainty and non-equilibrium, each must be the foundation of our dialogue and new models. Given our limited knowledge and lack of ability to see into the future, we can still plan for the impossible, conceptualise all possible outcomes and be prepared to quickly revise our ideas when outcomes do not match predictions.
- Focus attention on global capital movements: their genesis, their travel and their effects.

- Focus attention on debt of all kinds: why it is increasing and what to do about it.

15.10 THE EUROPEAN UNION AND ECONOMIC AND POLITICAL INTEGRATION

One of the earliest advocates for free trade between nations was David Hume (1711–76), a Scottish contemporary of Adam Smith. Hume argued that trade between nations is one way (but certainly not foolproof) to foster peace. Indeed there is some truth in this: nations integrated economically care, at the very least, for the other's institutional survival, and are less likely to go to war.

This was a principal motivation in developing the European Union (EU). After two devastating world wars, with approximately 70 million dead, the groundwork was laid almost immediately for economic integration, partly to ensure that a Europe-based war would never happen again, and partly as an attempt to economically supersede the United States.

The EU traces its roots to 1950 with the founding of the European Coal and Steel Community; its founding members were Belgium, France, Germany, Italy, Luxembourg and the Netherlands. The EU was officially born with the signing of the Maastricht Treaty in 1993, which set the stage for the eventual adoption of the Euro as a common currency, while coordinating foreign policy and limiting domestic deficits and debt. With the signing of the Maastricht Treaty the name 'European Union' officially replaced 'European Community'.

Of the 28 current EU members, 19 use the Euro as the common currency, which effectively means they have relinquished control over domestic monetary policy and the nominal exchange rate. While independent nations are able to use both monetary and fiscal policy to end a recession and stimulate economic growth (unless they choose otherwise, on the basis of the Triffin Paradox, as explained in the next chapter), EU members using the Euro can only use fiscal policy. Many have argued that this has increased both interest rates and the level of debt, especially in Greece, Ireland and Spain, and is largely responsible for the resulting severe economic dislocation. The UK voted to leave the EU in a referendum on 23 June 2016, although, as this textbook goes to press, it is still officially a member, and it has never used the Euro. How the EU will react and respond to Brexit remains uncertain at this point.

Countries can integrate both politically and economically, with the extent of integration ranging from a regional trade agreement to a full-scale economic and political union. An example of the former is the North American Free Trade Agreement (NAFTA) (1994), which significantly reduced tariffs, and in many cases eliminated them, between the US, Canada and Mexico, each the other's largest trading partner. Unlike the EU, the NAFTA is not an economic union and the three nations retain their sovereignty over political and economic issues, especially fiscal and monetary policy.

A problem with free trade areas (which typifies the entire global architecture established by Bretton Woods) is that economic objectives, i.e. reduced prices and access to markets, tends to supersede environmental issues, and capital mobility is given precedence over labour mobility. A problem in terms of sustainability is that large corporations, especially in agriculture, can produce at a much lower average total cost than smaller firms, resulting in further consolidation, internal and external migration as displaced agricultural workers seek work elsewhere; and further intensification of already marginal land, especially in Mexico, thanks to the NAFTA. The latter is an important point and deserves elaboration:

> Larger commercial farms will displace smaller farmers who lack good access to export markets. This will increase pressure on the marginal farmlands . . . Hill slopes, forest margins, and arid lands are especially vulnerable to the kind of environmental degradation that results when displaced people move to whatever land is available. We see the effects of this throughout much of Africa, Latin America, and Asia.
>
> Harris and Roach, 2018: 446

At the other extreme of integration is a full-scale economic and political union in which nations cooperate and fully share fiscal and monetary policy. An example is the 50 states of the United States. Each state cedes direct control over most economic and political issues, yet (at least theoretically) each state has some input in their effective utilisation and any redress needed. This is missing in the EU.

As this textbook goes to press, there is a deep-felt reaction against globalisation. This is evident in Donald Trump winning the 2016 presidential election. Trump attracted many (economically) disenfranchised voters, who felt alienated from the present system; angry that the so-called benefits of globalisation bypassed them. This reaction against globalisation is also evident in the Brexit vote, in which many older voters, especially outside London and in more depressed areas, voted to exit the EU, frustrated with elitist control of global institutions. The reaction against globalisation is also evident in the rise of many far-right parties in Europe. They share with the Trump presidency and the Brexit campaign a turning inward, a dislike of elites, a preference for increased political and economic barriers, an anti-immigration and anti-globalisation stance. In 2002, Phillip Bobbitt wrote presciently:

> As the nation-state increasingly loses its definition, the sharp cultural borders that, for example, made the Danes different from the Dutch, are losing legal and strategic significance. . . As Martin Wolf put it, globalisation

> has undermined the collective values represented by the nation-state and turned attention to the benefit of individuals. Governments of nation-states are faced with the prospect of asserting national cultural identities against a fragmenting populace that takes its various identities from associational but largely non-national sensibilities. Indeed the nation-state may come to be seen as a kind of enemy of its people.
>
> Bobbitt, 2002: 469

A common theme of this book is that the formation of global institutions has never been democratic or sustainable; rather they have been constructed by economic superpowers. They have to be reconceptualised, but not in a bitter, belligerent, backward-looking, partisan spirit as is happening now. Perhaps we are naive in hoping for democratic and forward-looking participation, but the pressing issue of climate change and the imperative of sustainability leave us no choice.

Having said this, it is worth asking if the nation state is the best entity to achieve sustainability. There are 196 nations in the world today, each with its own political and economic interests. Is the nation state too myopically concerned with its own interests, or, perhaps more accurately, only concerned with the interests of its most political and economically influential citizens? Perhaps the nation state isn't the most effective medium to achieve sustainability? Perhaps what is needed is more active cooperation on a decentralised basis?

THINKING QUESTIONS

Amartya Sen (2009: 414, emphasis in original) wrote: 'The pursuit of a theory of justice has something to do with a similar question: *what is it like to be a human being*?' What is it about human nature that causes us to care about justice, across all societies and cultures? How can we define and describe justice? Can we construct a universal definition of justice acceptable to all cultures?

How can we reconcile environmental sustainability with economic development?

Can trade ever be free?

CLASS ACTIVITIES

Divide the class into two groups: delegates from developed nations and delegates from developing nations. Try your best to simulate a meeting about the next Bretton Woods Conference. Begin with where it should be held. You will need to do a little preparation. Try to understand the attendant power conflicts and emotions when considering these elements:

- Global capital flows have grown much faster than GDP and trade.
- While the share of relatively more stable foreign direct investment has increased since the 1990s, private capital flows have been highly cyclical and spectacularly unstable.
- Financial integration and openness of developing countries continue to increase, both in terms of capital flows and cross-border holdings.
- The nature of capital flows also changed in the last decade. Debt flows played a key role. Investors continued to buy significant amounts of US treasury bonds. Foreign purchases of US corporate bonds, particularly from European financial institutions, also increased sharply.
- Despite widely improved external positions, developing countries were vulnerable in the recent global crisis because of financial greater integration and interconnectedness.

Source: United Nations Conference on Trade and Development (UNCTAD, 2013).

AREAS FOR RESEARCH

Research one or more of the following topics associated with the political economy of development:

- The role of the state in promoting or hampering development.
- The role of markets in generating incentives, information, positive and negative externalities, instability and inequality.
- How states and markets help or hinder each other.
- The capacity of political institutions to alleviate or exacerbate state and market failures.
- How external actors (aid donors, lending institutions, foreign powers) encourage or discourage development.

UN SDG FOCUS

Is this chapter helpful in understanding how the UN 17 SDGs can be implemented based on a perspective of justice? After reading this chapter, how would you recommend implementing UN SDG #17: 'Revitalise the global partnership for sustainable development.' Do we need a new Bretton Woods?

FURTHER READING

Akyüz, Y. (2013) *The Financial Crisis and the Global South.* London: Pluto.
Arrighi, G. (1994 [2010]) *The Long Twentieth Century.* London: Verso.

Chua, A. (2007) *Day of Empire: How Hyperpowers Rise to Global Dominance – and Why They Fall.* New York: Doubleday.

Landes, D. (1999) *The Wealth and Poverty of Nations.* New York: Doubleday.

Nelson, R. (2010) *The New Holy Wars: Economic Religion Versus Environmental Religion in Contemporary America.* University Park: The University of Pennsylvania Press.

16
Trade, Exchange Rates and the Balance of Payments

Most contemporary discussions of trade assume that its purpose is to ensure economic growth and to enable companies to make greater profits, and that international trade is the requisite foundation to improve the lives of the world's citizens. But surprisingly (then again, perhaps we should not be surprised), the impact of trade on the global environment is barely considered. By now you should probably realise that in this chapter we will discuss this important subject from a very different perspective, getting right to the point of whether trade is just and sustainable: Are the gains from trade shared equitably within countries and between countries? Is trade itself a root cause of global inequality? If trade is beneficial, then does it help us provision more sustainably than localised systems? If not, should trade play a more limited role in the sustainable economy of the future? Is international trade consistent with the UN 17 SDGs? Before addressing these questions we will begin with a very basic question: Why trade?

16.1 WHY TRADE?

In the novel *World Made by Hand*, James Howard Kunstler depicts a post-apocalyptic world without oil, without travel, without trade, where everything is made by hand. While reading the novel you can taste the home-made beer, the whopping plates of eggs and omelettes, and feel the sweat after physically working all day. But this is a world not chosen, but imposed on all. The novel's chilling message is clear: if we don't act now, this will be our world in the very near future. No oil. No trade.

But trade is essential to successful provisioning. Isn't it? Why should we trade, and on what basis?

Arguments in favour of trade:

- Trade enlarges the panoply of choice. Rather than restrict consumer choice to goods and services that are produced locally and limited by climate, resources or other factors of production, trade allows us to purchase goods from elsewhere.

- Trade reduces the cost of goods and services, thus increasing relative incomes.
- Trade allows nations to specialise, producing what one does best.
- Free trade increases the wages and profits of workers and firms respectively, who produce the nation's specialization.
- Trade integrates nations economically and thus reduces their chances of going to war, e.g., the EU.

Arguments against trade:

- Unless the trading nations are relatively equal in terms of wealth and income, trade can ossify existing patterns and prevent poor nations from developing. If nations are relatively unequal in terms of wealth and income, then the terms of trade will favour the more powerful. This explains why the US, during the nineteenth century, rejected Great Britain's clarion call for free trade.
- Unrestricted trade can reduce or prevent the development of critical industries that comport with individual wealth or the national interest. Known as the infant industry argument, this was explained in Chapter 12.
- Free trade can reduce incomes and profits of workers and firms in industries not producing products in which the nation specialises.
- Free trade is not necessarily fair trade.
- Free trade relies on cheap energy, which is inherently unsustainable.
- Producing what we need (rather than what we want) locally is more democratic, equitable and sustainable. Local trade forces capital to be rooted and local, rather than carefree and global.
- Corporations unduly influence what and how we trade: our current patterns of trade favour and reflect the corporate interest rather than the human interest.

Adam Smith assumed that humans are by nature creatures of commerce, writing in *The Wealth of Nations* of 'a certain propensity in human nature . . . to truck, barter, and exchange one thing for another' (Smith, 1776 [1976], Vol. 1, Bk. 1, Ch. 2, p.17) – a quotation that has been used to justify an economy based on production for exchange.

Of course, others disagreed with Smith, citing greed, power and lust as justification for production and also trade. Karl Polanyi (1944), who, unlike most economists and even to an extent Adam Smith, engaged in actual field research to learn how societies function and how people live and work, argued that trade has a different role, distinguishing between 'internal', or local trade, and 'external' trade:

> Local trade is limited to the goods of the region, which do *not* bear carrying because they are too heavy, bulky or perishable. Thus both external trade and

> local trade are relative to geographical distance, the one being confined to the goods which cannot overcome it, the other to such only as can.
>
> Polanyi, 1944: 63

Smith said the same thing, emphasising the locality of trade, while gratuitously assuming that our nature begets trade. Smith was concerned with local trade and production as the best means to ensure adequate provisioning. This is a pragmatic view of trade: how far goods will be transported depends on their availability, perishability and weight. Today, when goods such as heavy machinery and apples are routinely transported halfway around the world, owing to cheap energy and instant communication, these factors are no longer important.

Much trade today is swapping of the same goods, which pass each other on a country's roads or on the world's oceans. Trade is now used to make deals and profits, to benefit the corporate rather than the human interest, including a whole range of 'derivatives' or gambles taken on how the price of a given commodity's price might rise or fall. When such trade produces carbon emissions we need to ask whether this is just, and who benefits and who loses.

The original motivation for trade was to augment the availability of goods, so that countries imported what they could not produce themselves. Today the motivation for trade is for large corporations to reduce costs and increase profits. This is done by dividing production between different nations, so that only a limited amount of skilled design and development work is undertaken in countries where wages are high, and the bulk of the production is done in countries where environmental standards, say limitations on pollution, are lower, along with wages. Sometimes called 'the international division of labour' it reinforces the existing inequalities between different national economies.

This directly contravenes (and stifles) the interests of citizens, which should take precedence. After all, aren't we provisioning for people and not corporations? Trade also carries a heavy environmental cost because components are transported across the world several times before the final product is sold, burning scarce fossil-fuel energy and producing unnecessary carbon emissions.

Let's look at the personal computer to illustrate how trade is driven by the search for cheaper labour and lower environmental and social standards, facilitating a race toward the bottom and enhancing corporate profits, rather than enhancing human interests and our ability to provision. Since the 1990s the global production of high-tech goods has been dominated by the economies of East Asia, first by Japan, later by South Korea and now predominantly by China. Japan used technological advantage (deliberately fostered by the state) to dominate the global market, but it was outcompeted by South Korea and later China on the basis of cheap labour.

Producing a computer is done in stages, with the sophisticated components made in Japan and Taiwan and then shipped to China for assembly in factories with low conditions of employment and poor wages, before the product is exported to the wealthy countries of the Global North. The computer industry, however, includes not only the computer hardware but also the computer software. Indeed, the IT (information technology) services companies include software publishers, suppliers of custom computer programming services and computer systems design firms. The United States is a market leader in computer power, big data and fintechs (Table 16.1). In this digital environment, new technologies – such as advanced analytics, block chains and big data, in addition to the use of robotics, artificial intelligence, and new forms of encryption and biometrics – have enabled changes in shopping patterns, marketing, advertisement and the provision of financial products and services – such as bitcoins.

In global markets, and the IT market is not an exemption, the original motivation for trade was to augment the availability of goods.

Table 16.1 Computer power, Big Data and Fintech

Main feature	*Outcomes*	*Examples*
Computer power	Increasing amounts of data that can be stored, processed, and analyzed.	Web browsing history, shopping patterns, internet of things.
Big Data and the development of analytics	All possible data is collected in order to search for any patterns that might emerge	Marketing and advertisement
FinTech		

16.2 EXCHANGE RATES: DEFINITION AND GLOBAL IMPORTANCE

If every nation in the world used the same currency, or, for that matter, if there was only one nation in the world – neither of which is very likely, or desirable – then the topic of exchange rates would be irrelevant. However, given that there are many nations and many currencies, and that these nations would like to trade with each other, the topic of exchange rates must be discussed.

Let us define an **exchange rate** as: the price of one currency in terms of another.[1] From this it is clear that this relationship is reciprocal, since one currency is always measured in relation to another, i.e. rather than say that the US dollar, for example, increased in value, we must say that the value of the dollar increased in relation to a specific currency, such as the European euro or the Japanese yen. And, since we measure one currency in terms of another, if one decreases in value, the other by definition increases.

1. For a listing of the world's exchange rates see: http://money.cnn.com/data/currencies/

In July 2015, 1 British pound was worth US$1.56. This means that if you had visited the US with 1 pound in your pocket you could exchange it for US$1.56; and, given the reciprocal nature of the exchange rate, we know that 1 US dollar in July 2015 was worth 0.64 pounds: 1/1.56. One year later, in July 2016, 1 British pound was worth US$1.32. This means that the same tourist visiting the US with one pound could exchange it for US$1.32. And, conversely, 1 US dollar in July 2016 was worth 0.76 pounds. The pound in one year depreciated by 18 per cent: (1.56–1.32)/1.32 x 100 = 18 per cent. In other words, the same pound could buy fewer dollars; and, equivalently, the US dollar appreciated by 18 per cent, i.e. it could buy more pounds.

If one currency is decreasing/increasing relative to another, what exactly does this mean? Think for a moment about the price of land. If the price of a hectare of land is increasing, this means you need more money to purchase it; or, alternatively, for a given sum of money you can buy less land. And conversely, if the price of land is decreasing, this means you need less money to purchase it; or, alternatively, a given sum of money will buy more land.

When one currency has cheapened relative to the other, we say that it has **depreciated** or weakened; likewise, when one currency has become more expensive relative to another, we say it has **appreciated**, or strengthened.

As the pound decreased in value relative to the US dollar, a UK firm exporting from the UK finds that its product is cheaper, not because of lower production costs but because US buyers will now have to exchange less of their own money in order to buy it. Likewise, anyone from the US investing in British assets, or securities, will find that the total cost of the asset is cheaper.

But since the relationship between exchange rates is reciprocal, as the British pound depreciates relative to the US dollar, and the US dollar appreciates relative to the British pound, imports from the US to the UK are now more expensive, not because it is more expensive to produce them, but because British firms and citizens must now exchange more pounds in order to buy the US product. Likewise, any British citizen purchasing US assets, stocks, bonds, US Treasury debt will now pay more to purchase the asset.

With a cheaper exchange rate of the British pound in terms of dollars, won't this bode well for British manufacturing? The reason for the precipitous decline of the pound in July 2016 was Britain's vote in the referendum to leave the EU (23 June 2016). Investors feared that without close ties to the EU, global industry, especially financial services, will leave the UK and migrate elsewhere. On the other hand, some analysts argue that the sharp decrease in the value of the British pound will provide the momentum for an export-led recovery. But this provokes the question: With a manufacturing sector of only 10 per cent of GDP (it was 20 per cent in 1995), how can exports lead an expansion (Duke 2016)?

There are two types of exchange rates:

- **Fixed exchange rate:** A country's exchange rate is fixed (pegged) in relation to another nation's currency, or to some asset, such as gold.
- **Floating exchange rate:** A country's exchange rate depends on the market forces of supply and demand.

To understand the difference, let's return to our land example. To fix a price for a piece of land means that that price is fixed *regardless of market demand*. So even if very few people want the land (or even if everyone does), the price does not fluctuate. But if the price of land is determined by market forces, then it will fluctuate depending on how many people want it, i.e. as demand and supply change. To return to the exchange rate, if, all else being equal, demand for US dollars increases relative to the British pound, and supply of dollars remains the same, then the price of the dollar relative to the pound increases.

But there is one important difference. If the price of land is artificially held high, for example (by the owners' decree), then this simply means that the owner foregoes a sale. But holding a currency artificially high (or low) means that the central bank must intervene, by buying (or selling) units of the currency while selling (or buying) another asset in order to obtain the necessary funds. Thus an opportunity cost exists for fixing an exchange rate; and such behaviour cannot continue indefinitely.

A number of factors will determine a nation's preferences for a fixed or flexible exchange rate, including: the nation's preponderance of imports and exports relative to its GDP, its relationship to the global superpower, and which of two objectives it chooses within the 'impossible trinity'. This, also known as the Triffin Paradox (Triffin, 1960), states that a nation can only select two of the following; it cannot select all three:

- independent control of domestic monetary policy
- fixed exchange rates
- free flows of capital between other nations.

Looking at the US, for example, which insists on a strong Federal Reserve in order to control domestic monetary policy, and, in addition, free flows of capital to satisfy its twin deficits, it cannot fix its exchange rates. In contrast, a small country like Ecuador, choosing to adopt and follow US monetary policy (i.e. foregoing independent monetary policy), is able to implement restrictions on capital flows if it so chooses.

It seems that a preponderant fact of life in the exchange markets is speculation. Keynes himself speculated (rather successfully) in the stock market, and, as chief bursar at King's College London, was instrumental in tripling its endowment. Nevertheless, he warned with good reason that 'speculators may do no harm as bubbles on a steady stream of enterprise. But the position is serious when enterprise becomes the bubble on a whirlwind of speculation' (Keynes, 1936 [2010]: 159). Surely this is the situation in today's foreign exchange markets? How does this current 'whirlwind of speculation' comport with the goals of sustainability?

We would expect that as trade increases then so would foreign exchange transactions, and that the two would change in tandem. To an extent this has happened, but a lot more is going on. Consider this statistic: in 2015 global GDP was approximately US$80 trillion. Divide this number by 365 (days in year) to obtain US$22 billion per day, which is the approximate amount of currency needed to purchase global output. But the actual value of currency traded per day is far greater: US$5.3 trillion dollars![2] And even more staggering, this amount increased from US$590 billion in 1989, far more than warranted by either increases in global trade or global GDP. This clearly suggests that something else is happening in the foreign exchange markets in addition to purchasing goods and services.

It should be no surprise that the dollar is the preponderant currency traded today, accounting for 87 per cent of total foreign exchange transactions; followed by the European euro (33 per cent), the Japanese yen (23 per cent), the UK pound (12 per cent) and the Australian dollar (9 per cent). (Note: the sum total of all currencies is 200 per cent, since every transaction is two-sided.) And, not surprisingly, 71 per cent of global currency exchange occurs in London, New York, Singapore and Tokyo.

16.3 BALANCE OF PAYMENTS AND THE BALANCE OF TRADE

The balance of payments and the balance of trade are two distinct concepts and should not be confused. Each will now be discussed.

The balance of payments (BoP) is a statistical statement that summarises for a specific period (usually a year) the economic transactions of an economy with the rest of the world. These transactions are summarised both in the **current account** and in the **capital account**.

The **current account** summarises all goods, services, net factor income (i.e. earnings from foreign investment received by domestic residents minus earnings from domestic investment paid to foreign investors) and transfers that an economy receives from or provides to the rest of the world in a period of time. Its balance:

- Indicates the net balance between the volume of exports and imports of goods and services, plus the cost of servicing international debt, and net transfer payments.
- Reflects the relationship between domestic saving and investment.

2. The statistics in this paragraph were obtained from the Bank for International Settlements (2015).

- Shows the relationship between total domestic demand (absorption) and output (domestic supply).
- Reflects the relationship between the net external demand for, and supply of, a country's financial assets.

A nation runs a **current account surplus** if, all things being equal:

- it exports more goods than it imports
- it exports more services than it imports
- the factor incomes received by its workers residing overseas are greater than the factor incomes paid to foreign citizens within the country.

A nation runs a **current account deficit** if, all things being equal:

- it imports more goods than it exports
- it imports more services than it exports
- the factor incomes paid to foreign workers within the country are greater than the factor incomes received by its citizens overseas.

The **capital account** summarises all the capital transfers (claims or inflows and liabilities or outflows) that an economy receives from or provides to the rest of the world in a period of time. Note: capital account liberalisation refers to the removal of controls on international inflows and/or outflows.

The balance of trade (BoT) is the difference between a country's imports and exports. The BoT is the largest component of a country's BoP. Debit items include imports, foreign aid, domestic spending and domestic investments abroad. Credit items include exports, foreign spending in the domestic economy, and foreign investments in the domestic economy. A country has a **trade deficit** if it imports more than it exports; it has a **trade surplus** if it exports more than it imports.

If a country runs a current account deficit, it will obtain money from other countries, banks, investors, corporations, or even official development flows to finance it. The resulting capital inflows will be registered in the capital account. If the country obtains money from banks or investors, this will increase the sovereign debt of the country in terms of bank credit or assets (bonds). In the future, the country will have to pay back this debt.

On the surplus side, China is the largest trade surplus country in the world, passing Japan after 2005. Surpluses also exist in Germany and other Central and Northern European countries. The US is the largest deficit nation. According to the IMF, the preponderant factor was the decline in US saving, given the large budget deficits, forcing the US to borrow from abroad reflecting a deep deterioration in public saving. The deficit is also affected by each citizen's economic and financial asset choices: do we buy from home or abroad? Locally or globally?

16.4 THE LINK BETWEEN MONETARISM AND EXCHANGE RATES

According to monetarism,[3] it is assumed that the demand for money is stable, and is an increasing function of income; specifically, as income increases we demand more money in order to finance more transactions. Monetarism also assumes that the aggregate money supply is the most important economic variable, directly affecting the level of output and employment. Putting these two statements together: if the economy is at full employment, then increasing the supply of money will only increase the nation's price level, with no effect on output. This important relationship is known as the **quantity theory of money** and can be expressed as:

$$MV \equiv PQ$$

Where:

M = the nation's money supply
V = the **velocity of money**, defined as the number of transactions per given unit of money
P = the nominal price level
Q = the level of output

The assumption of full employment is crucial, since by definition all resources are fully utilised, so output cannot increase. The equation states that the amount of money multiplied by the number of transactions (velocity) equals the market value of the goods and services produced, i.e. nominal GDP, which equals the level of output multiplied by the price level. This relationship was first noticed in the sixteenth century during Spain's global rule, when a sharp influx of gold and silver from the New World resulted in significant price increases in domestic goods.

3. Monetarism, advocated by Milton Friedman, is founded on empirical evidence of a close correlation between changes in money supply and nominal aggregate income. It assumes that inflation is always a monetary phenomenon. Monetarism achieved some fame and popularity during the early years of Margaret Thatcher's tenure as UK prime minister (1979–90). Thatcher focused on monetary aggregates in order to reduce inflation and increase economic growth. By all accounts monetarism failed, and has since largely been discredited, with Milton Friedman himself admitting so in 2003 (Carlin and Soskice, 2015: 472). Nonetheless, vestiges of monetarism continue, especially the European Central Bank's focus on the growth of the money supply. For an expanded discussion of monetarism, see Carlin and Soskice, 2015: 470–73. The failure of monetarism explains contemporary central banks' emphasis on short-term interest rates as a policy target, which we will soon explain.

But if the economy is not at full employment, then an increase in the money supply need not directly affect prices, since it can also affect output (Q). Also, the direction of causation can run in reverse: an increase in the money supply can affect the price level, leaving Q and/or velocity (V) untouched.

Velocity is a very crucial variable and needs to be further explained. Let's begin with an analogy: say a business established an output target of X amount per year. With employees not very productive (say below the industry average), the firm will need more employees in order to reach its target; conversely, with very productive employees the firm may not need as many. Likewise, if a central bank sets a target for the money supply, and each unit of currency is not that productive, i.e. its velocity is low, then the central bank requires more currency in order to achieve its target; conversely, if each currency unit is very productive then the central bank requires fewer units.

Money's productivity is measured by the number of transactions it makes: its velocity. If a dollar bill, for example, sits under a mattress and doesn't do anything, its productivity is essentially zero. But if that same dollar bill is used to make numerous daily transactions, then its productivity, or velocity, is quite high. What causes velocity to change (or remain the same)? In one sense we can answer directly from the following equation. Rearranging the terms from the equation above, we find:

$$V \equiv PQ/M$$

which states that velocity (i.e. money's productivity) always equals nominal GDP divided by the money supply.

But in another sense, velocity changes when individuals (or individuals acting collectively) decide to change their money holdings. Should we hold more or less money? Quite often this is due to future expectations, and also technology. For example, the invention of automated teller machines (ATMs)[4] reduced the need to carry a lot of cash, and hence increased the velocity of money. Uncertainty at the beginning of a recession can increase the desire to hold cash, thus reducing velocity.

One of the major debates in economics is over the stability of velocity. Neoclassical economists tend to assume that it is stable, especially in the long run, whereas other schools of thought in economics assume that velocity is unstable. We believe that, due to inherent and pervasive uncertainty, velocity is unpredictable and unstable both in the short and long run.

Returning to monetarism, assuming a stable demand for money and hence velocity, then expanding the money supply directly affects aggregate demand (assuming current output is less than potential output) and, consequently, the

4. The ATM was developed during the late 1960s in Europe. For a fascinating history see Bátiz-Lazo (2015).

domestic price level. Specifically, if the money supply increases and all else is equal, domestic prices will increase, which in turn will increase the price of exports and, as the law of demand predicts, will reduce the quantity demanded of the nation's exports.

Monetarism also assumes that markets, without state intervention, are inherently stable. As a result, external disequilibrium is determined by economic policy: specifically, the financing of fiscal deficits by additional money. Monetarists believe that changes in current prices are the result of central bank monetary policy. Additional money to finance an output gap (where actual GDP is less than potential GDP) increases prices, which all else being equal, reduces the demand for that nation's exports, causing (or increasing) a balance of payments deficit. On the other hand, reducing credit expansion will, all else being equal, increase the domestic interest rate, and dampen domestic investment and the domestic price level, while also increasing exports and decreasing the demand for imports. Thus, at full employment, money supply expansion, all else being equal, increases the trade deficit, while money supply contraction decreases it.

Milton Friedman (1912–2006) a neoclassical economist who was awarded the 'Nobel Prize'[5] in 1976 for his work on consumption theory and monetary policy, was a tireless critic of Keynesian economics and an avid supporter of free markets.[6] As an early advocate of monetarism he assumed that given independent monetary policy, flexible exchange rates will determine relative currency prices, and in the long run the domestic price level and the money supply will equilibrate. Thus, exchange-rate flexibility is advocated in order to rescue the autonomy of monetary policy and thus surmount the 'impossible trinity'. For Friedman, adopting flexible exchange rates permits the economy to achieve equilibrium since free exchange rates allowed domestic prices to equilibrate with costs, thereby stimulating trade. Equilibrium would result from rational choices of economic agents, and each country would take care of its monetary policy, letting the market determine exchange rates. His argument is based on the following assumptions:

- Money demand is a stable function of nominal income.
- An expansion of money supply directly affects aggregate demand (for a given level of product) and thus the domestic price level.
- Increasing domestic prices will increase imports and trade deficits.
- Exchange-rate markets, without state intervention, are inherently stable.

Madi (2004) argued that choosing between fixed and flexible exchange-rate regimes relates to the choices between rules, or discretionary actions, to conduct

5. As we have noted previously, the correct title for the prize is actually the Bank of Sweden Prize in Economic Sciences.

6. For a good introduction to his philosophy, we recommend *Free to Choose* (Friedman and Friedman, 1990), an easy-to read book co-authored with his wife, Rose.

monetary policy. Under the rubric of good global governance, however, this, according to Madi, ignores the key problem: integration in the international currency hierarchy. Central banks try to influence the price of domestic credit through the management of interest rates; however, domestic interest rates depend not only on the management of domestic currency in exchange rate markets but also on international finance and global capital flows seeking high returns and low inflation. As Birch et al. note (2017: 121): 'the system of floating rates also paved the way for financial globalisation, whereby foreign currencies can be acquired without limit on currency markets'.

The focus between fixed or flexible exchange-rates underscores the essence of the problem, that is, the unstable outcomes of increasing capital mobility and the loss of autonomy of monetary policy. It is impossible to conceptualise an independent monetary policy in a context of capital-account openness, in spite of the exchange-rate regime chosen: the autonomy of monetary policy is limited by capital flows and speculation.

16.5 MILTON FRIEDMAN AND THE CASE FOR FLEXIBLE EXCHANGE RATES

During the economic crises of the 1970s, in which many developed nations suffered **stagflation** (inflation and unemployment occurring together) and global growth slowed, active economic policy to stimulate economic growth was questioned. Milton Friedman's (1968) emphasis on the importance of self-regulated markets dominated economic policy debate in the US as an alternative to active state intervention. Friedman argued that flexible markets, and the elimination of restrictions both at the international and the microeconomic level, would guarantee stability and equilibrium. He developed and spread a new macroeconomic consensus that became the foundation of neoliberalism.

The emergence of a new international consensus around flexible exchange rates was followed by a domestic counter-revolution that resulted in the adoption of monetary targeting. As a result, undue monetary expansion fosters trade deficits and the loss of international reserves. Friedman believed that exchange rate flexibility would rescue the autonomy of monetary policy and allow achievement of monetary rules. In the monetarist view, discretionary monetary policy explains short-run cyclical fluctuations. Disequilibrium results from the wrong economic policy, and it is a monetary phenomenon: central banks maintain expansionary monetary policies in order to stimulate higher levels of domestic income vis-à-vis its non-inflationary level.

16.6 *TECHNIQUE 13*: CALCULATING THE TERMS OF TRADE

The **terms of trade** (ToT) is the ratio of a nation's export prices to import prices (multiplied by 100) during a specific period. Since the units in the numerator and denominator cancel, we are left with a pure number. When the ToT is less than 100, the nation buys less imports for any given level of exports; when the ToT is greater than 100, the nation can buy more imports for any given level of exports. Thus, the terms of trade measures a nation's buying power abroad. Table 16.2 shows changes in the ToT of country groups over a 20-year period.

Table 16.2 Changes in the Terms of Trade of Country Groups, 1980–1982 to 2001–2003

Group	*Annual average 1980–1982*	*Annual average 2001–2003*	*Percentage change*
Developed economies	95.7	103.3	+7.9
Developing economies	117.3	97.7	−16.7
Developing economics: Africa	131.7	100	−24.1
Least-developed countries	144	93.3	−35.2
Landlocked countries	114.7	96.3	−16
Sub-Saharan Africa	124	98.3	−20.7

Source: United Nations Conference on Trade and Development (UNCTAD, 2013); calculations in Lines (2008).

Given that Brazil exports soybeans to China and imports manufactured goods from Germany, a decline in Brazil's ToT means the price of exported soybeans falls relative to imported manufactured goods, implying that Brazil will have to export relatively more soybeans to get the same quantity of manufactured goods. In this case, Brazil's ToT has deteriorated. Conversely, an improvement in Brazil's ToT means the price of soybeans is increasing faster than the import prices of manufactured goods. This means that Brazil will have to export relatively fewer soybeans to get the same quantity of manufactured goods. Brazil's ToT have improved.

Using real data we will calculate the terms of trade for a hypothetical nation. We simplify by assuming only two goods for this nation: coffee (export) and wheat (import). In reality, given that nations export and import a lot of goods, an index for exports and imports must be constructed.[7] Table 16.3 indicates the prices of these two goods in 2000 and 2012.

Table 16.3 Relative Prices of Two Commodities

Commodity	*Price (US$) in 2000*	*Price (US$) in 2012*
Coffee (export)	192	411.1
Wheat (import)	127.7	261.2

Source: World Bank (various years), Commodity Price Data.

7. For more examples see the handy sites provided by the World Bank: http://data.worldbank.org/indicator/TT.PRI.MRCH.XD.WD; and http://data.worldbank.org/data-catalog/commodity-price-data

To calculate the terms of trade for exports (coffee) relative to wheat (import) in 2000, we obtain the ratio of the two (2000) prices:

ToT 2000 = 192/127.7 = 1.5

Then to find the terms of trade for the same commodities for 2012, we use the same procedure with data for that year:

ToT 2012 = 411.1/261.2 = 1.57

So the terms of trade have improved slightly for coffee relative to wheat; thus, this nation has slightly improved its trade position.

Because we are calculating changes in ratios, the absolute values of the commodities themselves is not important: it is the relative changes in their values that matter. Often these terms of trade are calculated in terms of average price indices.

16.7 THE THEORY OF COMPARATIVE ADVANTAGE

Classical and, later, neoclassical economists rationalised free trade with the 'theory of comparative advantage', first published by the English economist David Ricardo in 1817. 'Comparative advantage' extends the theory of 'absolute advantage' first offered by Adam Smith. The latter is intuitively obvious and states that each country should specialise in producing a product in which it has an absolute advantage and then trade the surplus. So given two countries, Spain and England, for example, if the former can produce more units of steel and the latter more beef, then Spain should focus on producing steel and England focus on beef.

But what if Spain can produce more steel *and* more beef than England? Should England withdraw from trading altogether? Not necessarily, according to Ricardo. Even if one country produces everything less efficiently than its neighbour, it is still best to concentrate on the good it produces *relatively more efficiently* and trade for other goods with its neighbours. The key to understanding 'relatively more efficiently' is opportunity cost: if Spain can produce one unit of steel with *fewer* units of input than England, while England can produce one unit of beef with *fewer* units of input than Spain, then Spain should produce steel, and England beef, even though Spain has an absolute advantage in producing both goods. Based on comparative advantage, each country should produce enough of their respective products to develop a surplus, then trade it for the surplus of the other country.

One theme throughout this chapter is that the global trade system is much about power. The derivation of the seminal theory of comparative advantage

Box 16.1 Adam Smith and Islamic Scholars

Before we move on, it is interesting that much of what is taken as 'free-market economics' was originally conceived by Muslim scholars between the eighth and eleventh centuries (Graeber, 2012: 278–82), especially by Ghazali (1058–1111) and Tusi (1200–74). In an important new book, *History of Islamic Economic Thought* (2014), Professor Abdul Azim Islahi argues that practically all topics in a typical textbook on the principles of economics: price, supply and demand, marginal utility, debt, rent control, wages, profits, minimum wage, economic growth, the division of labour, inflation, distribution, public finance, even sustainability, were conceptualised, debated and discussed by Islamic scholars during a fruitful period between the eighth and eleventh centuries. This in turn influenced Adam Smith, who perhaps borrowed more than he should have without attribution. Concepts that figure very prominently in *The Wealth of Nations* – like the invisible hand; the assumption that human beings possess a natural propensity to truck, barter and trade; and even the use of the pin factory to illustrate the beneficial aspects of the division of labour – were first developed by Islamic scholars.

Whereas Smith and the classical economists (and the neoclassical economists who followed) logically connected the ideas of the invisible hand, the 'natural' propensity to trade and the necessity for division of labour, to conclude that markets based on *competition* can best increase the wealth of the nation; the Islamist theorists reached a very different conclusion: markets based on *cooperation* can best promote human welfare. It is well worth quoting a passage from Tusi:

> But when men [sic] render aid to each other, each one performing one of these important tasks that are beyond the measure of his own capacity, and observing the law of justice in transactions by giving greatly and receiving in exchange of the labour of others, then the means of livelihood are realised, and the succession of the individual and the survival of the species are assured.
>
> Graeber, 2012: 279–80

In this view, although some competition is good to an extent, an excessive emphasis on competition as a modus vivendi is inconsistent with a sustainable society. Tusi and the early Islamic scholars suggest different possibilities for constructing a market system, which are not necessarily wedded to competition. So perhaps as we debate the contours of a sustainable society we should become familiar with the writings of these Islamic scholars. Islahi's book provides the means to do so.

Source: Graeber (2012, 280–82); Islahi (2014). Also see a two-part series in the *International Journal of Pluralism and Economics Education* (IJPEE) discussing Islamic economics, IJPEE Vol. 6(4) and IJPEE Vol. 7(3).

itself had such an origin, and it is important to understand its genesis within an historical context. So let's examine the specific elements: Ricardo's theory illustrates two countries (although the results are generally applicable), Portugal and the UK; and two goods, wine and woollen cloth. The first oddity is that Ricardo chose two goods for which each country would have been expected to have an absolute advantage, given their very different climates. On closer examination, however, Ricardo's choice is clear: Portugal had entered into a trade deal with Britain some 50 years earlier in exchange for the protection of the British navy against Portugal's neighbour and rival, Spain. Britain offered military protection under the Methuen Treaty (1703), but in exchange Portugal had to agree to import subsidised UK cloth, undercutting domestic production and putting thousands of textile workers out of work. So Ricardo's example in fact underscores the fact that trade is often about politics rather than free markets – a reality that remains true today.

Neoclassical economists accept the theory of comparative advantage as sacrosanct, disparaging anyone daring to question it. This is so despite its highly restrictive and unrealistic assumptions, which Ricardo himself acknowledged (Ricardo, 1817 [2004]: 77–93): (1) the two countries are relatively equal in wealth; (2) perfect competition exists in each country; (3) full employment; (4) movement of capital is unrestricted; and (5) constant rather than increasing returns to scale (meaning that small countries can produce as efficiently as large ones).

In addition, Ricardo was ideologically motivated to ensconce Great Britain's role as the industrial global superpower while subjugating developing countries (Portugal in particular) to an inferior status. It is also pertinent to remember that during Ricardo's day the dialogue focused on the national interest, hence 'the wealth of nations'. Thus the theory of comparative advantage assumes that countries trade with each other, whereas in reality it is firms and entrepreneurs trading, motivated not by what is in the best interest of the nation but by how best to increase profits. This is an important point and deserves elaboration:

> As nation-states emerged during the late middle ages, it was no accident that the earliest conceptualisation of international trade – mercantilism – was nationalist in focus, with the nation as the unit of analysis. This nationalist outlook was bequeathed to the classical school, which unfortunately hindered, stunted and precluded the development of a more realistic and accurate portrayal of international trade... From the trader's point of view, comparative advantage has little relevance ... because traders do not even know the concept or the comparative cost ratios.
>
> Yu, 2009: 22 & 24

When discussing the benefits of trade, and in fact providing mathematical calculations in many cases, the theory of comparative advantage relies on relative values of products (the terms of trade) that are fixed, whereas, as we saw in Technique 13, differences in the values are the basis of who gains from trade. And this in turn is influenced by relative power. This was understood by Ricardo, and offered his assumption that countries must be equal in wealth; otherwise the richer nation will negotiate more favourable terms of trade.

In summary, there is no reason to automatically accept the theory of comparative advantage as applicable today; indeed, to do so is to recklessly abandon any attempt at understanding its basic assumptions or original motivation. Douglas Dowd (2004: 31) writes that it is 'difficult to comprehend . . . why a theory enunciated so long ago would remain virtually intact today, in both form and content, in a world so utterly different'. Alas, this is a fundamental criticism of neoclassical economics.[8] And, from the perspective of sustainability, the theory was developed in a world without concern for environmental limits.

In the 1930s, Eli Heckscher and Bertil Ohlin developed their eponymous theorem in order to explain why nations are motivated to trade. Specifically, a country tends to export goods produced with its most abundant, and hence relatively cheapest, resource. For most developing countries this means unskilled labour, and, as competition between such countries reduces the prices of their exports, the wages of the unskilled will be reduced by more than the wages of more highly skilled workers less exposed to foreign competition. All workers in sectors exposed to international competition may therefore see their wages fall as markets open up, but those most exposed will fare the worst.

The Heckscher–Ohlin theorem took the radical step of introducing into the theory the different factors of production, i.e. land and labour. Doing so immediately demonstrated that unregulated global trade would lead to the continuation of low wages for labour. There is ongoing debate as to whether wage rates will converge over time between countries. This is highly unlikely unless the two countries are relatively equal to begin with, which in turn begs the question.

16.8 MAKING POVERTY HISTORY

No doubt trade has helped many economies expand their productive capacity and increase living standards – Japan, for example, in the post-war period, and recently China – but smaller countries can often lose as much as they gain through trade. One explanation for this is that many economies compete with each other to produce the same good – perhaps coffee or textiles – so that expanded production creates a global surplus, decreasing the product price. Given that developing countries often concentrate production on raw materials or basic commodities, this also makes it difficult to gain an advantage, since the prices for these goods are subject to pressure through commodities markets and often fluctuate wildly.

A report from the World Bank found that the impact of trade on poverty is mixed at best. It usually strengthens the economic power of elites in poorer countries and increases inequality across those societies. A study reviewing

8. For an extended critique of the theory of comparative advantage, see Hill and Myatt, 2010: 224–30.

household income data for 88 developing countries between 1985 and 1997 concluded that the average income of the poorest 10 per cent of people decreased from 30.7 per cent to 24.8 per cent of the average income. By contrast, the income of the richest 10 per cent increased from 273 per cent to 293 per cent of the average (Lundberg and Squire, 2003).

16.9 FROM UNFAIR TRADE TO LOCAL SELF-RELIANCE

There is a lingering concern in many countries that opening up to trade in even the most basic commodities can leave one vulnerable. In the words of Gandhi, 'Any country that exposes itself to unlimited foreign competition can be reduced to starvation and, therefore, subjection if the foreigners desire it.' What Polanyi (1944: 28) refers to as the 'incubus of self-sufficiency' is still a powerful influence in many countries, as it was for every economic superpower while it was ascending (including, as we saw in earlier chapters, Great Britain in the early nineteenth century, and the US in the late nineteenth century).

These concerns are exacerbated by the realities of climate change. Most likely we will face increasingly unpredictable weather patterns and extreme weather events that might disrupt temporarily or permanently the transport routes and infrastructure which we now depend upon (and take for granted) for some of our most basic commodities. Boasting of our interconnectedness, Parag Khanna writes in his influential book *Connectography*:

> The global connectivity revolution has begun. Already we have installed a far greater volume of lines connecting people than dividing them: Our infrastructural matrix today includes approximately 64 million kilometers of highways, 2 million kilometers of pipelines, 1.2 million kilometers of railways, and 750,000 kilometers of undersea Internet cables that connect our many key population and economic centers. By contrast we have only 250,000 kilometers of international borders. *By some estimates, mankind will build more infrastructures in the next forty years alone than it has in the past four thousand.*
>
> Khanna, 2016: 11; emphasis added

But this same infrastructure that connects us, the infrastructure of the Third Industrial Revolution – our connectography – is increasingly vulnerable to climate change:

> Climate change will have no less of a dramatic impact on human infrastructure . . . The power grid, transportation arteries, telecommunications, and water and sewage systems that were never designed to withstand the fury of a runaway hydrological cycle are being crippled in regions around the world. The energy infrastructure is particularly vulnerable . . . Droughts are

> increasingly threatening the supply of cooling water to power stations . . . Extreme storms are also damaging power and transmission lines . . . [which] has a cascading effect on other parts of the infrastructure since electricity is needed . . . High-intensity water-related events also damage roads, bringing freight and commuter traffic to a standstill, with severe impacts on the economy . . . Extreme wind and storms are also increasingly shutting down airports and backing up air traffic . . . Seaports and inland waterways are likewise experiencing downtime from an increase in floods, more droughts, and even more dense fog.
>
> Rifkin, 2014: 289–91

Our window of opportunity to do something positive now, to at least prevent the worst effects of climate change and to preserve our world for us and for future generations, is narrowing. Our world is changing – fast. To give just one example: in 2007 the Intergovernmental Panel on Climate Change predicted a 0.35-metre rise in sea levels by the end of the twenty-first century. However, just two years later, the speed of melting of Antarctic and Greenland ice caps caused scientists to revise their forecasts, declaring that sea-level rise was occurring at a much faster rate.

These effects, happening with quickening intensity, suggest that we should begin provisioning within a system of self-reliant national or regional economies. But unfortunately our current economic system and global trading architecture is heavily biased against this. We agree with Rifkin (2014: 291) that 'It's simply foolish to believe that we can get ahead of the extreme weather and effectively arrest its escalating assaults by patching up a carbon-based regime.'

16.10 WHAT IS THE MOST APPROPRIATE ORGANISATIONAL FORM TO ENGAGE IN TRADE?

Today, the global consensus for economic growth essentially advocates and enables free trade for multinational corporations, based on cheap energy. According to the United Nations Conference on Trade and Development (UNCTAD, 2013), the economy is characterised by global value chains (GVCs), where intermediate goods and services are traded in fragmented and internationally dispersed production processes. These GVCs are coordinated by transnational corporations (TNCs) within their networks of affiliates, contractual partners and suppliers; and they account for some 80 per cent of global trade.

A major concern of this book is the appropriate basic unit for the firm: for producing goods and services, for managing the economy, for tackling global issues, and for achieving sustainability. We don't advocate a position of autarky (self-sufficiency; from the Greek 'autarkeia'); nor do we advocate a continuation of the status quo. Rather, we believe that our answers, and hence any such decision, should be made by everyone affected – past, present and future – and in the interests of people, not of corporations. We agree with Korten (1995: 272) that 'the purpose of the human economy is to meet the needs of people – not of money, nor of corporations, nor of governments' .

On the one hand, global consciousness is necessary to tackle global problems such as climate change and systemic poverty, and to become sustainable. We cannot effect change if we insist on acting as isolated individuals; yet, at the same time, economic decision-making should reside as close as possible to the household – a far cry from the situation now. We like Korten's (Ibid.: 273–4) suggestion that

> The appropriate organisational form for the ecological era is likely to be a multilevel system of nested economies with the household as the most basic economic unit, up through successive geographical aggregations to localities, districts, nations, and regions. Embodying the principle of intrinsic responsibility, each level would seek to function, to the extent that it is reasonably able, as an integrated self-reliant, self-managing political, economic, and ecological community. Starting from the base unit, each system level would seek to achieve the optimal feasible ecological self-reliance, especially in meeting basic needs.

Korten advocates that each unit engage in trade with other units within its clusters: households with households, districts with districts, etc. The goal is to produce locally, to have capital rooted locally, to increase self-reliance, and to minimise the need for long-haul transportation, in order to reduce negative effects on the environment. This means developing and then adopting principles and preferences to define fair trade for a sustainable society, as Cato (2009) writes:

- Trade should be fair, with attention paid to the prices of basic commodities.
- Production should occur locally, with trade between basic units.
- Goods should be purchased as close to production as possible.
- Managed trade, if it serves the interests of all, is acceptable.
- Self-reliance is preferred.

But are we locked into our current system? How much freedom of manoeuvrability to make such a transition do we currently have? And what about the resistance of corporations and other vested interests? Won't they fight to preserve their privileged interests? While it is easy to state our goals, and even to recognise the formidable obstacles, it is difficult to recommend specific policies to achieve them. Nevertheless, it is clear that to continue on our present course is not only unsustainable but morally untenable.

Box 16.2 Mohandas Gandhi (1869–1948) and *Swadeshi*

Although Gandhi's reputation has shifted in the decades following Indian independence in 1947, for many he nevertheless well deserves the sobriquet of 'Mahatma' (a Hindu term, derived from the Sanskrit, meaning 'great soul'). A quintessential Indian, Gandhi, a pluralist and deeply spiritual human being, is much admired for how he galvanised and empowered the ordinary Indian during India's struggle for independence from the British.

For us, Gandhi's most relevant contribution is the concept of ***swadeshi***, or self-reliance, which offers a prototype for the localisation of the economy. Gandhi called for a self-sufficient economy based on a system of production and consumption of goods that was locally based and human-focused rather than dominated by the market. His salt marches and campaign for homespun cloth, or *khadi*, were designed to achieve not just national independence but also local and personal independence.

In addition to its meaning of using what one produces, *swadeshi* has a deeper, more profound meaning: 'reliance on our own strength', meaning the strength of our body, our mind and our soul. Gandhi's call for self-reliance clearly inspired the self-sufficiency movement in Europe and the US from the 1960s onwards, with its impetus to move back to the land and provide for one's own needs. Gandhi's message is still inspiring emancipatory activity in the poorer countries of the Global South.[1]

1. India, as the world's most populous democracy, has a rich history of pluralism and toleration of dissent. It is also expected to bear the brunt of future temperature changes. For a compelling history see Sen (2005); Guha (2008).

THINKING QUESTIONS

Does capitalism overemphasise competition and underemphasise cooperation?

Does either foster the wrong values for a sustainable society?

CLASS ACTIVITY

Each student chooses a firm. What is the firm's most appropriate form in the sustainable era? Would your answer change if there was no danger from climate change? Construct a list of firms that are currently sustainable. In what industries do they operate and why did they become sustainable?

AREAS FOR RESEARCH

Investigate the data for terms of trade for a range of countries over various time periods.

Identify the origins of the food you eat during a typical day. With the aid of a world map, link the products to the countries of origin and calculate the distances travelled, as well as the energy used. Are there some products that might be produced closer to home? Are there acceptable substitutes?

UN SDG FOCUS

Goals #16 and #17 call for:

16. Promote just, peaceful and inclusive societies.
17. Revitalise the global partnership for sustainable development.

What is meant by 'just', 'peaceful' and 'inclusive'? Is your society currently 'just, peaceful and inclusive'? Why, or why not? Is a 'global partnership' necessary for sustainable development? What form should it take? Research the UN's findings on Goals #16 and #17. How would you recommend implementation?

FURTHER READING

Cato, M. S. (2009) *Green Economics*. London: Earthscan.

Dowd, D. (2004) *Capitalism and its Economics: A Critical History* (2nd edn). London: Pluto Press.

Graeber, D. (2012) *Debt: The First 5,000 Years*. New York: Melville House.

Islahi, A. A. (2014) *History of Islamic Economic Thought: Contributions of Muslim Scholars to Economic Thought and Analysis*, Cheltenham, UK: Edward Elgar.

Khanna, P. (2016) *Connectography: Mapping the Future of Global Civilization*. New York: Random House.

17
Contemporary Global Economic and Financial Trends

This chapter discusses the causes of the current global imbalance between debtor and creditor nations, especially between the US and China. Which way forward? How can this relationship be improved to comport with sustainability? Debt, low wages, income inequality and their relationship to sustainability are all important topics. This chapter will also ask if national governments have any manoeuvrability to implement economic policies. We will also discuss the evolution of central bank policies, the role of central banks and the challenges to financial regulation after the global crisis.

17.1 THE SIGNIFICANCE OF GLOBAL IMBALANCES

Global imbalances between debtor and creditor nations represent a significant economic threat to the world's continued growth and stability. **Global imbalances** in this sense refers to some nations (e.g. the US) persistently running large trade deficits while other nations (e.g. China, Japan and Germany) persistently run trade surpluses. A brief characterisation of recent imbalances finds that:

- Imbalances reflect both domestic and international distortions.
- A variety of factors are required to apprehend and explain the evolution of imbalances over time.
- Factors such as high commodity prices, huge savings of oil exporters, high and rising savings rates in China, and investment booms foster imbalances over time.

There are clearly interrelations between these factors. For example, the recent rise in commodity prices is partly due to China's rapid growth, along with other emerging markets.

The main countries or country groups running surpluses or deficits are shown in Tables 17.1 and 17.2. Japan was the main counterpart to US deficits during the 1990s, with China's surpluses becoming preponderant after 2005.

Much of the current Asian foreign reserves, accumulated via current-account surpluses, have been used to purchase US government debt: as of March 2016,

Table 17.1 Current account Balance of Top Five Trade Surplus Countries, December 2015 (US$ billions)

China	347.8
Germany	286.3
Japan	124.3
South Korea	98.4
Taiwan	76.2

Source: Central intelligence Agency (CIA, 2016).

Table 17.2 Current account Balance of Top Five Trade Deficit Countries, December 2015 (US$ billions)

United States	460.6
United Kingdom	135.8
Brazil	72.8
Australia	49.9
Canada	45.8

Source: Central intelligence Agency (CIA, 2016).

the Chinese government was the largest holder of US debt (US$1,244.6 billion); Japan the second-largest (US$1,137.1 billion); followed by the Cayman Islands (US$265.0 billion); Brazil (US$264.3 billion); and Switzerland (US$230.0 billions) (*Source:* US Department of the Treasury, 2017).

17.2 GLOBAL IMBALANCES AND DEVELOPING COUNTRIES

Over the past three decades, rich countries have imposed trade and financial liberalisation requirements on many developing countries via the IMF, World Bank and the World Trade Organization. Indeed, despite adopting supposedly 'good' policies – based on global integration, market liberalisation and price stabilisation – many developing countries have not succeeded in achieving sustainable economic and social development. This has been particularly noticeable in Latin America and Africa.

Global imbalances have, for example, shaped the evolution of the Real, the Brazilian currency. In the aftermath of the Asian financial crisis of 1997, the Brazilian central bank depreciated the Brazilian currency, because the loss of international reserves reduced its ability to manage it. As a result of increasing capital outflows that put further downward pressure on the Real, the Brazilian central bank negotiated sovereign debt bonds indexed to the dollar, which dampened speculation against the Real. Indeed, currency speculation shaped the decisions of the central bank in a context where global economic imbalances favoured current-account deficits in Brazil. In the context of asset and wealth reallocation after the Asian crisis, global investors' flight to higher and better returns reduced the access of Brazilian corporations and banks to global credit markets.

Indeed, global markets have grown quickly. There is concern about the unfairness of global rules and their asymmetric effects on developed and developing poor countries. As in the framework of global trade discussed in the previous chapter, financial issues have predominated over social ones.

17.3 GLOBAL IMBALANCES: US–CHINA

Over the last decades the US has been consuming more than it is producing, sustained by borrowing from abroad to finance domestic consumption. Globalisation means rapid expansion of trade relative to domestic production, while fostering deep integration of global financial markets. Indeed, global liquidity and expansion of private capital flows are the direct result of American monetary policy and financial market deregulation. Globalisation has also resulted in a shift of manufacturing to several Asian nations, with attendant shifting in the balance of trade. In the US, high budget deficits and low savings rates are part of the global imbalances. Meanwhile, the Chinese current account surplus results from low wages and high profits, but is also due to the management of the Chinese currency (the renminbi; also called the yuan) to avoid significant appreciation relative to the dollar.

The globalisation of production and trade enables US capital flows of foreign direct investment into Asia to finance production of goods for sale in the US. Consequently, US dollars have flowed to Asia to pay for products consumed on behalf of expanding household debt. Then, US dollars return to the US in exchange for US debt. As a result, US consumption is financed with US debt purchased by Asian governments.

The global imbalances reveal asymmetries between the US and China, which are unsustainable in the long run. 2016 data from the People's Bank of China show that foreign reserves rose to US$3.2 trillion.[1] A stronger renminbi has alleviated the need for the central bank to sell foreign cash to support the domestic currency's value, and thus has helped ease the decline in China's reserves. A stronger renminbi also decreases the chances of capital flight, and enables companies and households to sell Chinese assets and firms to repay their dollar debts. Although the exact composition of China's foreign reserves is not publicly known, the diversification of China's financial assets will certainly affect the power of US financial markets, given that China is the most important holder of US government debt.

1. Source: www.pbc.gov.cn

17.4 CENTRAL BANKS

A central bank is responsible for issuing money, conducting monetary policy, maintaining currency stability and overseeing the nation's banking system, while acting as a lender of last resort. The two oldest central banks are the Swedish Riksbank (1668) and the Bank of England (1694). In the US, the Federal Reserve System, considered by many to be the world's most important central bank, was created in 1913, as a result of several bank panics and an over-reliance on federal government borrowing from private citizens. The European Central Bank (ECB) and European System of Central Banks (ESCB) were created in 1999, and have not yet challenged the global role of the Fed.

Central banks influence economic growth (and credit markets) by changing costs and availability of banks' demand for liquidity (reserves). Today, central banks manage the short-term interest rate as the preferred monetary policy instrument. Other policy tools include:

- the **discount rate** – the rate of interest charged to member banks for the privilege of a short-term loan.
- the **federal funds rate** – a short-term interest rate that one bank charges another.
- **open market operations** – the buying and selling of government debt in order to influence the money supply.
- the **required reserve ratio** – the percentage of deposits that must be kept at the bank.

Central features of contemporary central banks, on which there is surprising universal agreement, at least among central bankers, should be: autonomy (free from political interference); commitment, especially to an inflation level of 2 per cent (anything less than this might engender deflation, since the methodology of measuring inflation often overstates it); transparency; communication and trust (Carlin and Soskice, 2015: 135).

However, risk (along with crises) can destroy trust, as Walter Bagehot, a British journalist, warned in his seminal 1873 book *Lombard Street*:

> the peculiar essence of our banking system is an unprecedented trust between man and man [sic]: and when that trust is much weakened by hidden causes, a small accident may greatly hurt it, and a great accident for a moment may almost destroy it.
>
> Bagehot, 1873 [1922]: 151–2

Bagehot also critiqued the expectation that a central bank act as a lender of last resort (LLR). The LLR function is to provide liquidity for banks to accommodate sudden sharp changes in the demand for money. He believed that the LLR exists not to prevent shocks but to minimise their impacts. The LLR is not to prevent failure at all costs, but rather to confine the impact of such failure to unsound institutions and to prevent failures from spreading to sound ones. Bagehot warned against undue reliance on the LLR. He stressed the need to strengthen individual banks since, in his view, the LLR is not a substitute for prudent bank practices. As a defender of free markets, Bagehot argued that the basic strength of the banking system should not rest on the availability of last-resort accommodation but on the capital soundness of individual banks. Good advice! Too bad that it is often unheeded. And also easier said than done.

The LLR walks a fine line between protecting the public and engendering **moral hazard** (Carlin and Soskice, 2015: 166). Moral hazard occurs when incentives to prevent risk are reduced because of protections against it. So the LLR creates incentives for banks to avoid taking due care in their loan provisions and, more broadly, in their prudential behaviour; and it also reduces the incentives for households to be prudent (Ibid.: 166).

Today, with open capital accounts the autonomy of monetary policy subordinates fiscal policy and requires flexible exchange rates or managed floating exchange rates. Since the recent global crisis, evidence indicates that central banks cannot control the complexity of global, innovative and speculative financial markets, since the increased clout of the financial industry results in favourable legislation and systematically influences consumer preferences. And, given the importance of global debt, any individual central bank is ineffective in finding solutions, which must be done, as Keynes suggested, via democratic international cooperation.

The Federal Reserve System was created in 1913 with the passage of the Federal Reserve Act, largely due to the perceived shortcomings of the previous two central banks, and also to the 1907 financial crisis, which found the US in the unenviable position of borrowing from its own citizens. While both previous US central banks were well run and financially sound, their main shortcoming was in the eyes of the public: they were stingy with loans and, each based in Philadelphia, largely focused on the interests of the eastern US.

In Chapter 12 we mentioned Alexander Hamilton (co-author of *The Federalist Papers* and Treasury Secretary under George Washington) and Andrew Jackson (US Army general and seventh president of the US, 1828–36), whose respective portraits are on the US $10 and $20 bills. While each played a crucial role in the nation's federal debt, likewise each played a role in the first two central banks. Alexander Hamilton proposed, constructed and defended the Bank of the United States (1791–1811). And Andrew Jackson pledged that if he were elected US president he would not renew the charter of the Second Bank of the United States, which was established in 1816 and due to expire in 1836.

To compensate for the overtly regional interests of the first two central banks, in 1913 twelve Federal Reserve Banks were created across the United States, each united into the Federal Reserve System. At the time, it was reasoned that different areas have different economic interests/needs and should have a locally responsive bank. A seven-member **Board of Directors** (BOD) oversees the twelve banks, along with establishing a common monetary policy for the United States. Each BOD member is nominated by the US president and confirmed by the US Senate. Day-to-day monetary policy is by the **Federal Open Market Committee (FOMC)**, comprised of all seven members of the Board of Governors and five members selected on a rotating basis from the presidents of the twelve central banks that comprise the Fed. The Fed is quasi-independent from the federal government: the Fed is self-financing, deciding and implementing monetary policy on its own; yet each BOD member must be confirmed by US Senate. Based on Article I, Section 8 of the US Constitution, the US Congress can abolish, amend or rescind the Federal Reserve Act of 1913.

17.5 CONTEMPORARY CENTRAL BANKING: INTEREST-RATE MANAGEMENT AND INFLATION TARGETING

The early 1980s was a transition period for monetary policy, with central bankers moving away from focusing on monetary aggregates (the amount of money) and towards the short-term interest rate as the principal instrument of monetary policy. The remainder of this section will discuss monetary policy as conducted by the Federal Reserve System, which largely follows the Taylor Rule. It was developed by Stanford economist John Taylor (1993), and offers guidance (based on the actual experience of the US economy) how a central bank, such as the Federal Reserve (Fed), should set short-term interest rates in order to achieve long-term price stability and economic growth.

Specifically, the Taylor Rule is:

$$r_t = r_s + \beta_1(\pi - \pi^*) + \beta_2(y_t - y_e)$$

Where:

r_t = The short-term interest rate used as a policy option, e.g. the federal funds rate in the US.

r_s = The short-term interest rate when the economy is at equilibrium, i.e. with neither an inflation gap $(\pi - \pi^*)$ nor an output gap $(y_t - y_e)$.

π = The current rate of inflation

π^* = The targeted rate of inflation

y_t = The current rate of unemployment

y_e = The actual rate of unemployment

β_1 and β_2 = subjective weights respectively for the inflation and output gaps. Specifically, if the central bank is unconcerned about unemployment then $\beta_2 = 0$; if the central bank is more concerned about unemployment than inflation then $\beta_2 > \beta_1$. In his 1993 article, Taylor set β_2 and β_1 to 0.5, since this best matched US historical data. Such numbers imply that the Fed is equally concerned about both inflation and unemployment.

Implicit (and explicit) in the Taylor Rule is that interest rates, rather than monetary aggregates best affect the economy.

Suppose the Fed chooses an inflation target π^* and uses the federal funds rate (a short-term interest rate that one bank charges another) as its main instrument. The FOMC sets a target (equilibrium) level for the federal funds rate. The Taylor Rule then suggests the following reasons why it should be changed: (1) inflation moves away from its target; and/or (2) real GDP moves away from trend (potential). Thus the Fed responds to output gaps and inflation:

a) If the output gap increases, the Fed will reduce the federal funds rate.
b) If inflation increases, the Fed will increase the federal funds rate.

Simply put, if actual GDP is less than potential GDP, a lower interest rate can help stimulate the economy by making borrowing cheaper, which in turn will increase both consumption and investment; and conversely, a higher interest rate is hypothesized to slow down the economy by making borrowing more expensive.

Example: Suppose that the federal funds rate is 2%; that $\pi^* = 2\%$ and $\pi = 3\%$, leading to a positive inflation gap of $\pi - \pi^* = 1\%$ (= 3% – 2%). Also assume that real GDP is 1% above its potential, resulting in a positive output gap of 1%.

The Taylor rule suggests that the federal funds should be set at:

$$r = 2\% + \tfrac{1}{2}\,(1\%\text{ inflation gap}) + \tfrac{1}{2}\,(1\%\text{ output gap}) = 3\%$$

Notice in the above example that if we change the weight, we change the end results.

The output gap in the Taylor rule indicates future π as stipulated in the standard short-run Phillips curve, which demonstrated a reputed inverse relationship between inflation and unemployment.[2] The short-run Phillips

2. As Keen argues, this empirical regularity has since degenerated into rigid neoclassical policy: attempts to reduce unemployment below its 'natural' level (the rate of unemployment consistent with targeted inflation). This reductionism was contrary to Phillips' argument that the economy was characterized by non-linear, non-equilibrium,

curve indicates that a change in inflation is influenced by current economic activity relative to potential GDP, which in turn is a function of the natural rate of unemployment. A related concept is the NAIRU: the non-accelerating inflation rate of unemployment, which is the unemployment rate u at which $\pi = 0$.

When u > NAIRU, with current GDP < potential GDP, π will decrease.
When u < NAIRU, with current GDP > potential GDP, π will increase.

17.6 CHALLENGES TO ECONOMIC POLICY MANAGEMENT AFTER THE GLOBAL CRISIS: BAILOUTS AND AUSTERITY PROGRAMMES

The long-term process of financial expansion means *financialisation* of the capitalist economy, where finance capital has increasingly depended on credit and financial bubbles (Foster, 2009). In Chesnais' words (1998: 51; translated by authors):

> a pattern of high financial return was universally imposed by financial markets, with local variations, depending on the influence of financial arbitrages on domestic monetary policies. Financialisation has influenced the evolution of domestic currencies in exchange markets as well as the practices of central banks.

Minsky (2008: 50) argued that 'economic instability since the late 1960s is the result of the fragile financial system that emerged from the cumulative changes in financial relations and institutions following World War II'. Economic contradictions and tensions in the political and social spheres are created by globalisation; and clearly financialisation is not consistent with the UN 17 SDGs. Given that financialisation requires monetary stability, low and stable inflation is widely recognised as the preponderant objective of macroeconomic policies. The side effects reveal the loss of autonomy of national economic policies to stimulate investment and job creation.

We need to look beyond the dynamics of globalisation in order to account for political factors: the interplay of the two crucially shapes the economy and society. In this context, the scope of domestic policies to prevent and manage crisis is limited, in spite of the adoption of **good governance practices** (which in actuality refers to sound macroeconomic policies, both fiscal and monetary,

highly dynamic relations. Keen writes: 'Unfortunately, Phillips' noble intentions resulted in a backfire: far from helping wean economists off their dependency on static methods, the misinterpretation of his simple empirical research allowed the rebirth of neoclassical economics and its equilibrium methodology – and ultimately, the reduction of macroeconomics to applied microeconomics' (Keen, 2012: 202; and see pp.195–202).

and prudential financial regulation in the context of unrestricted market flexibilisation process). Thus, Latin American nations, for example, tend to support stable capital flows instead of increasing the levels of employment.

Soon after the global financial crisis, central banks tried to save financial markets from collapsing. The immediate intervention of the European Central Bank, for example, reassured the euro area ('the Eurozone') that its policy framework was robust in the face of global instability (Pisani-Ferry and Sapir, 2009). However, national bailouts revealed the challenges where no coordinated response was implemented, and nations experienced huge increases in public debt (ECB, 2009). In the European Union, for instance, social tensions have increased due to banks speculating against the risk of default of public debt securities, mainly issued by Greece, Portugal and Spain, after being rescued. In Greece, a downward trend of nominal wages has been pursued: wage cuts have been devastating, not only socially and politically but also economically, as they quickly translate into falling domestic demand, which in turn exacerbates the budget deficit.

The negative effects of reduced domestic demand also affect future sustainable growth. If fiscal policy reduces domestic demand, the economic and social crisis can only be intensified. The Greek rescue package, for example, commits to a fiscal and structural reform (privatisation) agenda to reduce the Greek public debt as a percentage of GDP to 120.5 per cent in 2020, which by definition can only be achieved by cutting spending or increasing taxes, either of which constricts growth.

In order to confront mounting public debt, the pursuit of macroeconomic austerity and sustainable capital inflows has overwhelmed the European Union policy options. Central banks' and Treasuries' actions have not been independent from private and public pressures: governments must intervene to prevent the global financial system from collapsing; thus, banking sectors, to a large extent, have depended on massive government support. Undoubtedly, the role of banks in the credit crunch and the cost of the financial sector bailout have undermined the financial efficiency of self-regulated markets. As the crisis generated a higher global risk aversion, banks and their governments have lost credibility. The inability to respond to financial shocks triggered a loss of confidence in the capital markets, increasing interest rates and thereby aggravating fundamental imbalances.

In the aftermath of the crisis, the distinction between private and public debt has become blurred. As Keynes (1936 [2010]) argued, there is a contradiction in money as a public good and a private good that overwhelms the central banks' actions. For example, during the recent crisis, governments were faced with choosing between austerity programmes and supporting investors' portfolios. Many governments have disappointed their citizens. Governments now face hard decisions in order to deal with the impacts of the debt overhang: less social spending, low growth, and increasing social inequalities.

Policies currently emphasise deflation, with low and stable inflation as the main target of macroeconomic policies. At the pragmatic level, fiscal policy subordinates the political decision-making process: policies to generate a surplus, such as tax increases and expenditure cuts, have been emphasised, with governments forced to assume, or to guarantee, the private debt. Governments, under global investor pressure, should meet budgetary targets and pursue further structural reforms. The financial challenges influence the risk premium and hence the capital inflows.

But how long can liquidity-driven policies last and influence investors' strategies and decisions? And how can such policies that clearly contradict the 17 UN SDGs be fostered and encouraged? Fiscal austerity engenders tighter fiscal policy (since public revenues decrease), resulting in even weaker economic growth and higher debt/GDP rates (Chesnais, 1998). The continuation of present austerity will certainly affect day-to-day life, especially the labour market, which is now subservient to the goals of financialisation, emphasising cost reductions, labour flexibility, longer working hours, loss of rights, etc. This has enhanced the vulnerability of workers, mainly young people, which has now become a global systemic problem. And, as Keynes warned, as uncertainty increases, entrepreneurs reduce the demand for capital goods. Thus, the expansion of productive capacity, especially producing renewable energy, will be postponed.

17.7 FINANCIAL REGULATION AFTER THE GLOBAL CRISIS

Among the lessons learned, the recent global crisis showed that the scope of domestic policies to prevent and manage crisis is limited. Indeed, financial regulation can induce better practices but cannot eliminate the possibility of a banking crisis. The universal nature of financial institutions reveals the challenges to financial supervision and fiscalisation. In this scenario, as we saw in Chapter 14, the Basel Capital Accords were founded on expectations about private risks (credit, market, operational) without regarding systemic risks that could decisively affect growth, unemployment and inequalities.

While global regulators try to implement tougher rules after the recent financial crisis, banks play governments against each other, threatening to move to other countries given too much regulatory burden. The European banks threatened to move to the US while the American banks threatened to move to Europe (Onaran, 2012). This should not be unexpected: the main objective of financialisation is to become big enough to influence the rules of the game. Another challenge to achieving global financial stability is the absence of a common project to ensure, among other objectives, the adequate provision of liquidity, stable financial flows to developing countries, and a concern for sustainability. The lack of representation of developing countries in multilateral agencies (IMF, World Bank and WTO) make the challenges even greater.

To counter the power of financialisation and to stabilise and reform the economy, Minsky (2008: 327–70) advocated a holistic set of policies including strong labour demand by the government; an industrial policy to promote growth and stem monopolistic power; a taxation policy to redistribute income to foster equitable employment and inclusive growth. Globalisation, with its attendant financialisation, has not achieved growth, stability or sustainability (Stiglitz, 2013). It is clear that investment, employment and finance cannot be left to free markets. Implementing Minksy's policies is a strong start for sustainable growth.

THINKING QUESTIONS

Does the recent global financial crisis change the rationale for the global role of the US dollar?

How do US–China relations affect the world's strategic future?

CLASS ACTIVITY

Each student chooses a country. What is its current youth unemployment? Why? Can you consolidate the reasons into a general statement about what works and what does not?

AREAS FOR RESEARCH

The recent crisis has redefined some of the most basic questions of political economy and global politics. Undertake group research and seek a collective view on the following questions:

- Is the goal of economic openness, especially financial openness, appropriate for most nations?
- Does the recent crisis demonstrate convincingly the failures of free-market capitalism?
- Can nations devise new forms of cooperation to manage the future of the globalisation of markets in a sustainable way?
- What new guidelines and practices of governance and regulation are needed?

UN SDG FOCUS

Goals #10 and #11 call for:

10. Reduce inequalities within and among countries.
11. Make cities inclusive, safe, resilient and sustainable.

What is meant by 'inequality?' How can redressing global imbalances reduce global inequalities? Can the redress of global imbalances be used to 'make cities inclusive, safe, resilient and sustainable'? Research the UN's findings on Goals #10 and #11: how would you recommend implementation?

FURTHER READING

Krugman, P. (2013) *End this Depression Now!* New York: Norton.
Onaran, Y. (2012) *Zombie Banks*. US: Bloomberg News.
Stiglitz, J. (2013) *The Price of Inequality*. London: Penguin.

18
Which Way Forward?

18.1 STUDENTS CHALLENGING THEIR PROFESSORS

Economists have been extensively criticised in recent years, and rightfully so, given their inability to predict and conceptualise the most recent financial crisis. And, not surprisingly, universities, national governments, the institutions that govern the content of economics curricula, and students have systematically criticised neoclassical economics for not adequately preparing them to understand twenty-first-century capitalism. One striking example: on 2 November 2011, students walked out of the class of one of the world's best-known economists, Nicholas Gregory Mankiw. They addressed an open letter to him ('An Open Letter to Greg Mankiw', 2011):

> As Harvard undergraduates, we enrolled in Economics 10 hoping to gain a broad and introductory foundation of economic theory that would assist us in our various intellectual pursuits and diverse disciplines, which range from Economics to Government, to Environmental Sciences and Public Policy, and beyond. Instead, we found a course that espouses a specific – and limited – view of economics that we believe perpetuates problematic and inefficient systems of economic inequality in our society today.
>
> A legitimate academic study of economics must include a critical discussion of both the benefits and flaws of different economic simplifying models. As your class does not include primary sources and rarely features articles from academic journals, we have very little access to alternative approaches to economics. There is no justification for presenting Adam Smith's economic theories as more fundamental or basic than, for example, Keynesian theory.

This criticism was not an isolated incident, but has occurred in a sea change of student-led movements to reconceptualise and rethink economics, ranging from Paris 2001 to Manchester 2017, spearheaded by the global, student-led network Rethinking Economics. Government officials and policy-makers are listening, and the discipline of economics is changing.[1] We hope that our textbook contributes to the reconceptualisation of economics.

1. For a perceptive and inside account of the genesis of the student-led criticisms, see Earle et al., 2017: 102–10.

Unlike most other disciplines outside theology, economics as a system of education at the time of the recent global crisis was monist, not pluralist. Orthodoxy was encouraged and heterodoxy actively discouraged. And, like most religions, neoclassical economics proselytised and trained, rather than educated. Its success is evidenced by the very narrow content of most economics textbooks.[2] Consequently, when the crisis hit there was only one tool in the toolbox, and it is quite obvious that the tool has failed.

As a result of this colonisation of economics education by just one idea – the idea of the competitive market,[3] populated by rational, utility-maximising individuals – it has fallen to students to call for more diverse, not to mention more interesting, curricula. With the Post-Autistic Economics Movement, the heterodox economists in Cambridge and the aforementioned Rethinking Economics network, the inheritors of the Hayekian tradition at last have a battle on their hands. We can only hope that future generations of students will have more opportunity to discuss a variety of economic theories and models, within a context of sustainability.

In the UK, the Royal Economic Society considered the skills needed by today's economists, according to potential employers and by teaching economists. A summary of the most important skills is reproduced in the box below. Their conclusion was that many courses were so narrowly focused on models and maths that they did not give students the practical skills they needed to work as economists: a crucial point which has been re-affirmed by Earle et al. (2017). Most economics students will currently achieve a degree without any knowledge of economic history and with very little requirement for critical thought concerning the problems of the neoclassical ideology that dominates their education.

Box 18.1 Skills Economists Need, According to the Royal Economic Society

- Greater awareness of economic history and current real-world context.
- Better practical data-handling skills.
- Greater ability to communicate economics to non-specialists.
- More understanding of the limitations of modelling and current economic methodology.
- A more pluralistic approach to economics.
- A combination of deductive and inductive reasoning.

Source: O'Doherty et al. (2007).

---

2. For an expansion of this thesis see Lee (2009), who documents with historical precision the visceral hostility of neoclassical economics towards pluralism and heterodoxy.
3. For a well-documented argument on a similar note, that neoclassical economics has colonised the other social sciences, see Fine and Milonakis (2009).

Steve Keen (2011: 458–9) provides helpful advice to students:

> New students of economics can also do their bit. Don't let lecturers get away with teaching the same old stuff. . . Challenge them. . . Make a nuisance of yourself – and organise with your fellow students to get a voice in designing the curriculum. . . Go beyond the standard curriculum too, to learn the skills you will need to be a twenty-first-century economist, rather than a not-yet-extinct fossil from the nineteenth century. Do basic courses in mathematics (calculus, algebra and differential equations), computer programming, history and sociology . . .

Organising with fellow students is a powerful technique not only for redesigning the curriculum but also for learning and empowering yourself with knowledge. Dan et al. (2009: 28) write of their experience at the University of Notre Dame:

> We supplemented our traditional economics training with an out-of-class discussion group. . . These gatherings were centred on articles chosen by the group in advance to be dissected, discussed, and debated. We relished the chance to talk about interesting and relevant topics in ways [that] were not possible in most of our economics classes. We could engage each problem in a dialogue with orthodoxy and its many alternatives. Here we could question assumptions, interrogate generalities, and ask about the morality of it all.

We would be remiss in our role as educators if we did not mention a disturbing new book by Rod Hill and Tony Myatt, *The Economics Anti-Textbook: A Critical Thinker's Guide to Microeconomics* (2010). Its title is self-explanatory. Sadly, we know of no other subject in which such a book has been published. The reasons for publication echo concerns made by the student-led groups: that economics and especially neoclassical economics, as the dominant economic paradigm, is anti-pluralist, ahistorical, deductive and largely ineffective in understanding our current economy. Not only does the book critique every aspect of traditional microeconomics but the authors also provide over 100 'Questions for your Professor' to help expedite the rethinking of economics currently under way.

This book was followed by an equally disturbing book by John Komlos, *What Every Economics Student Needs to Know and Doesn't Get in the Usual Principles Text* (2014). He explains that:

> most textbooks are not really suitable for understanding the essentials of the *real existing* capitalism in the globalized world of the twenty-first century. Rather, they present a caricature of the economy at a level of abstraction that distorts the student's vision . . .
>
> Komlos, 2014: 7; emphasis in original

Wow! We couldn't imagine a more damning criticism.

Your authors are committed pluralists, actively involved with Rethinking Economics, and we largely agree with the criticism of the various student-led movements and the criticisms of Hill and Myatt, Keen, Komlos and many others. Although we have done our best to inform and educate you, and to provide a strong foundation for further learning, sadly you are likely to take future economics courses to which existing criticisms of economics (and economic pedagogy) are still highly relevant. It is for this reason that student empowerment and student-led initiatives are most important.

18.2 IS CAPITALISM INEVITABLE? DOES IT COMPORT WITH SUSTAINABILITY?

Unless you are a music aficionado you probably would not be familiar with the 1960s pop band Zager and Evans, and their hit 'In the year 2525', in which they speculate whether humans would still be alive then and, if so, what we would be like. While most of us are caught up in our daily routines, often not thinking beyond the end of the day or the end of the week, sometimes it is helpful to peer into the future. What would it be like in 2150? Would humans still be in existence? Would we still 'rule' the planet?

One of our obligations as social scientists is to contemplate our present situation; to try to understand which institutions work and which do not. And specifically as economists we are duty-bound to devise the best economic system to help all people provision. But at the same time, we feel it is interesting and ethical – not to mention entertaining – to think of the future, and ask whether capitalism is up to the task, particularly that of achieving sustainability. If we improve our economy's ability to provision, will this come at the expense of future generations? Is there something we can do now at relatively little cost to improve the situation for all, especially those not yet born?

One of our main motivations for writing this book is that we believe that capitalism, with its intrinsic profit motive, is on a collision course with sustainability. As will have been clear throughout this book, we believe it is urgent to reconceptualise capitalism so that it is sustainable and capable of provisioning for all. If this is not possible, then we need to think about devising a new economic system. Perhaps an equally intriguing question to that posed by Zagar and Evans is to ask: In the year 2525, will capitalism still exist? Many citizens of the wealthiest countries might baulk at such a question: If people are still alive, wouldn't capitalism still exist almost by definition? Don't the two go together? Don't human beings, as Adam Smith assumed, have a natural proclivity to 'truck, barter and trade'?

Thinking about the future of capitalism forces us to understand its strengths and weaknesses, and consider how we can construct a better alternative, capable of meeting our social, environmental and ecological challenges. While some economists look at the small picture, asking if we can develop this or that policy, to tweak this or that outcome, it is also necessary to ask whether the overall system is working.

Certainly capitalism scores high for producing immense wealth and an abundance of material goods – a stellar achievement noted by two of capitalism's harshest critics, Marx and Engels (1848 [1960]): 7–8):

> The bourgeoisie, during its rule of scarce one hundred years, has created more massive and more colossal productive forces than have all the preceding generations together. Subjection of Nature's forces to man, machinery, application of chemistry to industry and agriculture, steam-navigation, railways, electric telegraphs, clearing of whole continents for cultivation, canalisation of rivers, whole populations conjured out of the ground – what earlier century had even a presentiment that such productive forces slumbered in the lap of social labour?

Nevertheless, poverty still exists amidst plenty – a regression interspersed with progress. Over 120 years ago, Henry George (1879 [1948]: 5 & 9) noted that:

> discovery upon discovery, and invention after invention, have neither lessened the toil of those who most need respite, nor brought plenty to the poor [. . .] that widespread destitution is found in the midst of the greatest abundance . . . it may clearly be seen that material progress does not merely fail to relieve poverty – it actually produces it.

And, despite spectacular increases in overall wealth, as Sen (1999: xi) writes:

> We live in a world of unprecedented opulence, of a kind that would have been hard even to imagine a century or two ago . . . And yet we also live in a world with remarkable deprivation, destitution and oppression . . . Overcoming these problems is a central part of the exercise of development.

Many critics of capitalism agree with George that a systemic reason exists for the production of poverty amidst plenty, 'as though an immense wedge were being forced, not underneath society, but through society. Those who are above the point of separation are elevated, but those who are below are crushed down' (George, 1879 [1948]: 9). For Marx, of course, the 'wedge' was caused by the separation of classes into workers and capitalists and the drive to accumulate, leading to exploitation and the creation of surplus value.

But why does capitalism continue to produce both progress *and* poverty? And why, after 150 years, does this 'wedge' persist? Given capitalism's failure to solve this pressing problem, is it unreasonable to doubt capitalism's ability to solve the looming environmental crisis? Is capitalism capable of rectifying itself, or will its inner logic of inexorable capital accumulation doom it (and us) to an ecological collision? We feel that this current 'wedge' is due to an absence of sustainability, and once recognised and consciously planned, perhaps we might be able to ensure adequate living standards for all within a context of sustainability.

For the first time in human history we are facing human-induced, catastrophic and irreversible climate change, indicating 'the inherent limitations of modern capitalism and the market system' (Larson, 2012: 17). Of course capitalism is not the only economic system guilty of environmental destruction. Phillip Bobbitt (2002: xxxii) wrote optimistically about our ability to change our institutions for the better:

> There are times when the present breaks the shackle of the past to create the future – the Long War of the twentieth century, now past, was one of those. But there are also times, such as the Renaissance – when the first modern states emerged – and our own coming twenty-first century, when it is the past that creates the future, by breaking the shackles of the present.

We agree that we are shackled to the present, and we must break these chains in order to fully grasp the wisdom of the past so we can conceptualise and plan a sustainable future. While renewable energy will form the basis of this sustainable future, we can still look to the past and take an important lesson from our coal-fired, nineteenth-century Industrial Revolution: the enthusiastic imagination of building a new world with a new source of energy:

> In imagining possible futures, it's important to factor in one last critical energy source: excitement. There was a time when coal was actually fun – not the mining, which was never fun, but the building of a powerful new coal-fired world, which inspired distinct bursts of imagination, enthusiasm, and daring at various historical moments.
>
> Freese, 2003: 246

Surely we can summon this enthusiasm to unshackle our present and start building a new sustainable world based on renewable energy!

While capitalism has a rich history of reinventing itself and adapting to new trends and technologies, three current developments suggest that capitalism might now be up against its final roadblock, suggesting either a reinvention from top to bottom or a new political economic system specifically designed to meet these challenges. Each has been discussed earlier in this textbook, but they deserve mention again:

- Capitalism's very success has significantly increased productivity, while reducing the marginal cost of producing many goods to near zero; a situation which will only intensify in the near future (Rifkin, 2014: *passim*).
- The combination of 3D printing and automation are changing the very concepts of firm, consumer, industry and the meaning of work.
- The above two developments are making the commons more important vis-à-vis the market, resulting in greater expectations for sharing (the modus operandi for the commons) rather than exchange (the modus operandi for markets). Rifkin (2014: 19) explains: 'Markets are beginning to give way to networks, ownership is becoming less important than access, the pursuit of self-interest is being tempered by the pull of collaborative interests, and the traditional dream of rags to riches is being supplanted by a new dream of a sustainable quality of life.'

And finally, capitalism's modus operandi – profit, growth and expansion – has been instrumental in causing climate change, which suggests that it would be very difficult to look within capitalism for adequate solutions to the problem. Capitalism and the environment, unless the former radically changes, are on a collision course.

No matter if our economic system is socialist, capitalist or some as-yet-unknown, 'we need big thinkers, worldly philosophers, if you will, in the likes of Smith, Marx and Keynes, who can think in terms of the big picture' (Backhouse and Bateman, 2011). Perhaps our vocation as educators and authors gives us more optimism: after all, we believe in the power of ideas to motivate, change and influence. We believe that we can effectively design an economic system so it provisions for all, not just for today but also for tomorrow. This is the essence of sustainability, and this is the obligation of the educated – a quid pro quo to help make the world a better place.

We hope this book educates and inspires you, enabling you to solve the problems of our generation, which includes presenting to the future a better world than the one we see today. We hope our book will empower you with knowledge and an understanding of how economic systems work and how they evolve. We urge you to question existing models; to identify, understand and critically analyse underlying assumptions; to explore and to read widely. Never take any institution for granted, including capitalism itself. Just because it currently exists does not guarantee that it will in the future – after all, it has only existed for the last 200 years.

Having read this book, you are now part of the economics community. Congratulations! We welcome your participation.

THINKING QUESTION

Please read again carefully the 17 UN SDGs. What are your specific thoughts? Do they fit well together? Are there ambiguous words? Do some of the goals contradict each other? What should be the initial steps in implementing these goals? Do you have any specific recommendations?

FURTHER READING

Kuhn, T. (1962 [2012]) *The Structure of Scientific Revolutions*. Chicago: The University of Chicago Press.

Larson, R. (2012) *Bleakonomics*. London: Pluto Press.

Dahl, A. (1996) *The Eco Principle – Ecology and Economics in Symbiosis*. London: Zed Books.

Mason, Paul (2015) *Postcapitalism: A Guide to our Future*, New York: Farrar, Straus and Giroux.

McManners, P. (2008) *Adapt and Thrive – The Sustainable Revolution*. Cornwall: MPG Books.

Bibliography

All websites last accessed October 1, 2017.

Acemoglu, D. and Robinson, J. (2012) *Why Nations Fail: The Origins of Power, Prosperity, and Poverty*. New York: Crown Publishers.

Akyüz, Y. (2006) *From Liberalization to Investment and Jobs: Lost in Translation*. UNCTAD Working Papers. Available at International Development Economics Associates (IDEAs): www.networkideas.org/featart/feb2006/fa28_Lost_in_Translation.htm

Akyüz, Y. (2013) *The Financial Crisis and the Global South*. London: Pluto Press.

Aldred, J. (2009) *The Skeptical Economist: Revealing the Ethics Inside Economics*. London: Earthscan.

Anderson, V. (1991) *Alternative Economic Indicators*. London: Routledge.

Anker, R. (2011) *Estimating a Living Wage: A Methodological Review*, Conditions of Work and Employment Series No. 29. Geneva: International Labour Office.

Anker, R., Chernyshev, I., Egger, P., Mehran, F. and Ritter, J. (2002) *Measuring Decent Work with Statistical Indicators*, Working Paper No. 2. Geneva: Policy Integration Department Statistical Development and Analysis Group, International Labour Office. http://natlex.ilo.ch/wcmsp5/groups/public/---dgreports/---integration/documents/publication/wcms_079089.pdf

Arrighi, G. (1994 [2010]) *The Long Twentieth Century*. London: Verso.

Backhouse, R. and Bateman, B. (2011) 'Wanted: Worldly Philosophers'. *The New York Times*, 16 September, 2013.

Bagehot, W. (1873 [1922]) *Lombard Street: A Description of the Money Market*. London: John Murray.

Banco Central do Brasil (2017) Política Monetária e Operações de Crédito do SFN. Notas econômico-financeiras para a imprensa. Brasília.

Banco Central do Brasil (2011) Notas Econômico-financeiras para a Imprensa. Brasília. www.bcb.gov.br/pt-br/#!/n/ecoimprensa.

Bank for International Settlements (2015) 'Survey of Foreign Exchange'. http://www.bis.org/statistics/

Bátiz-Lazo, B. (2015) 'A Brief History of the ATM'. *The Atlantic Monthly*, 26 March 2015. www.theatlantic.com/technology/archive/2015/03/a-brief-history-of-the-atm/388547/

Baum, L. F. (1900 [1998]) *The Wonderful World of Oz: The Wizard of Oz; The Emerald City of Oz; Glinda of Oz*. London: Penguin.

Baur, T. K. (2004) 'High Performance Workplace Practices and Job Satisfaction: Evidence from Europe'. DP No. 1265. Bonn: Institute of Labor Economics (IZA).

Baxandall, P. (2004) *Constructing Unemployment: The Politics of Joblessness in East and West*. Aldershot: Ashgate.

Bayón, M. C. (2006) 'Social Precarity in Mexico and Argentina: Trends, Manifestations and National Trajectories'. *Cepal Review*, Vol. 88, pp.125–43.

Benn, S. (1967a) 'Power'. In: Edwards, P. (ed.) *The Encyclopedia of Philosophy*, Vol. 5. New York: MacMillan, pp.424–6.

Benn, S. (1967b) 'Justice'. In: Edwards, P. (ed.) *The Encyclopedia of Philosophy*, Vol. 3–4. New York: MacMillan, pp.298–302.

Bentham, J. (1780 [2007]) *Introduction to the Principles of Morals and Legislation*. Mineola, NY: Dover Publications.

Bernanke, B. S. (2007) 'The Recent Financial Turmoil and its Economic and Policy Consequences' (Speech, 15 October 2007, New York). www.federalreserve.gov/newsevents/speech/ bernanke20071015a.htm.

Birch, K., Peacock, M., Wellen, R., Hossein, C. S., Scott, S. and Salazar, A. (2017) *Business and Society: A Critical Introduction*. London, Zed Books.

Birchall, J. (2011), *People-centred Businesses: Co-operatives, Mutuals and the Idea of Membership*, London: Sage.

Blewitt, J. (2014) *Understanding Sustainable Development*. London: Earthscan.

Bobbitt, P. (2002) *The Shield of Achilles: War, Peace, and the Course of History*. New York: Anchor Books.

Bodanis, D. (2000) *E = MC²: A Biography of the World's Most Famous Equation*. New York: Berkeley Books.

Boff, L. (1986) *Option for the Poor: Challenge to the Rich Countries*. Edinburgh: T&T Clark.

Boorstin, D. (1993) *The Discovers*. New York: Random House.

Boorstin, D. (1998) *The Seekers: The Story of Man's Continuing Quest to Understand his World*. New York: Vintage Books.

Borras, S. M., Hall, R., Scoones, I., White, B. and Wolford, W. (2011) 'Towards a Better Understanding of Global Land Grabbing: An Editorial Introduction'. *Journal of Peasant Studies*, Vol. 38, No.2, pp.209–16.

Bowles, S., Edwards, R. and Roosevelt, F. (2005) *Understanding Capitalism: Competition, Command and Change*. New York: Oxford University Press.

Boyd, G. and Reardon, J. (forthcoming) *Picasso and Einstein: You, Your Workplace and Our Economy*.

Bratton, J., Callinan, M., Forshaw, C. and Sawchuk, P. (2010) *Work and Organizational Behaviour: Understanding the Workplace*. London: Palgrave Macmillan.

Braungart, M. and McDonough, W. (2009) *Cradle to Cradle: Remaking the Way We Make Things*. London: Vintage.

British Petroleum (2017) *Energy Outlook: 2017*. www.bp.com/content/dam/bp/pdf/energy-economics/energy-outlook-2017/bp-energy-outlook-2017.pdf.l

Broswimmer, F. (2002) *Ecocide*, London: Pluto Press.

Brown, J. (2004) *Co-operative Capital: A New Approach to Investment in Co-operatives*. Manchester: Co-operative Action.

Brown, J., Söderbaum, P. and Dereniowska, M. (2017) *Positional Analysis for Sustainable Development: Reconsidering Policy, Economics and Accounting*. London: Routledge.

Buchanan, J. and Wagner, R. (1977 [1999]) *Democracy in Deficit: The Political Legacy of Lord Keynes*. Indianapolis: Liberty Fund.

Buchner, B., Stadelmann, M., Wilkinson, J., Mazza, F., Rosenberg, A. and Abramskiehn, D. (2014) *The Global Landscape of Climate Finance 2014*. San Francisco and London: Climate Policy Initiative. https://climatepolicyinitiative.org/wp-content/uploads/2014/11/The-Global-Landscape-of-Climate-Finance-2014.pdf

Burke, M., Hsiang, S. and Migeul, E. (2013) 'Weather and Violence'. *The New York Times*, 1 September 2013.

Carlin, W. and Soskice, D. (2015) *Macroeconomics: Institutions, Instability, and the Financial System*. Oxford, UK: Oxford University Press.

Cato, M. S. (2009) *Green Economics*. London: Earthscan.

Cato, M. S. (2011) *Environment and Economy*. London: Routledge.

Cato, M. S. (2012a) *The Bioregional Economy*. London: Earthscan.

Cato, M. S. (2012b) *Local Liquidity*. Weymouth: Green House.

Chakrabarty, B. (2005) *The Social and Political Thought of Mahatma Gandhi*. London: Routledge.

Chami, R. and Fullenkamp, C. (2013) 'Beyond the Household'. *Finance & Development*, Vol. 50, No. 3, pp.1–25.

Chang, H-J. (2007) 'Protecting the Global Poor'. *Prospect Magazine*, Issue 136.

Charles Ponzi (2017), entry in *Wikipedia, The Free Encyclopedia*. https://en.wikipedia.org/w/index.php?title=Charles_Ponzi&oldid=793669139

Chen, M. (2007) Rethinking the Informal Economy: Linkages with the Formal Economy and the Formal Regulatory Environment. DESA Working Paper No. 46, ST/ESA/2007/DWP/46. New York: United Nations Department of Economic and Social Affairs. www.un.org/esa/desa/papers/2007/wp46_2007.pdf

Chesnais, F. (1998) *La Mondialisation Financière: Genèse, Coût et Enjeux*. Paris: Syros.

Chua, A. (2007) *Days of Empire*. New York: Doubleday.

Chu, A. (2007) *How Hyperpowers Rise to Global Dominance – And Why They Fail*. New York: Doubleday.

CIA (Central Intelligence Agency) (2016) *World Factbook: Country Comparison: Distribution of family income – Gini index*. www.cia.gov/library/publications/the-world-factbook/rankorder/2172rank.html

CIPS (Chartered Institute of Purchasing and Supply) Group (2014) *Internal, Connected and External Stakeholders*. CIPS Knowledge Report. www.cips.org/Documents/Knowledge/Procurement-Topics-and-Skills/2-Procurement-Organisation/Stakeholders/Stakeholders.pdf

Cohen, A. J. and Harcourt, G. C. (2003) 'Whatever Happened to the Cambridge Capital Theory Controversies?' *Journal of Economic Perspectives*, Vol. 17, No. 1, pp.199–214.

Colorado Fiscal Institute (2013) *The Impact of Income Inequality on Colorado's GPI*. www.coloradofscal.org.

Commons, J. R. (1990 [1934]) *Institutional Economics: Its Place in Political Economy*. New Brunswick, NJ: Transaction Publishers.

Connell, J. (2010) *Migration and the Globalization of Health Care: The Health Care Exodus?* Cheltenham, UK: Edward Elgar.

Cordova, C. (2015) *Climate Finance as a Catalyst for Leveraging Private Sector Financing in the Energy Sector: Examples in Latin America*. Presentation at UNFCCC LAC Regional Workshop on NAMAs (Nationally Appropriate Mitigation Actions). Santiago, Chile: World Bank Group.

Costanza, R., Arge, R., de Groot, R., Farber, S., Grasso, M., Hannon, B., Limburg, K., Naeem, S., O'Neill, R. V., Paruelo, J., Raskin, R. G., Sutton, P. and van den Belt, M. (1997) 'The Value of the World's Ecosystem Services and Natural Capital'. *Nature*, Vol. 387, pp.253–60.

Cumbers, A. (2012) 'Making Space for Economic Democracy: Decentred Public Ownership and the Danish Wind Power Revolution'. In: Cumbers, A. (ed.) *Reclaiming Public Ownership: Making Space for Economic Democracy*. London: Zed Books.

Dahl, A. L. (1996) *The Eco Principle: Ecology and Economics in Symbiosis*. London: Zed Books.

Dan, N., Houpt, N., Mallin, S. and Witchger, P. (2009) 'A Revolution from the Margin: A Student Perspective'. In: Reardon, J. (ed.) *The Handbook of Pluralist Economics Education*. London: Routledge, pp.24–31.

Davidson, P. (1978) *Money and the Real World*. London: Macmillan.

Davies, W. (2009). *Reinventing the Firm*. London: Demos.

De Schutter, O. (2011) 'How Not to Think of Land-Grabbing: Three Critiques of Large-Scale Investments in Farmland'. *Journal of Peasant Studies*, Vol. 38, pp.249–79.

DEFRA (Department for Environment, Food & Rural Affairs) (2006) *Food Security and the UK: An Evidence and Analysis Paper*. London: The Stationery Office.

DEFRA (2011) *Costs and Benefits of the Thames Tunnel*. www.gov.uk/government/uploads/system/uploads/attachment_data/file/471839/pb13677a-thamestunnel-costsbenefits.pdf

Deininger, K. and Byerlee, D. (2010) *Rising Global Interest in Farmland: Can it Yield Sustainable and Equitable Benefits?* Washington DC: World Bank. worldbank.org/DEC/Resources/Rising-Global-Interest-in-Farmland.pdf

Devine, P. (2010) *Democracy and Economic Planning*. London: Wiley.

Diamond, J. (2005) *Collapse*. New York: Penguin.

Diesing, P. (1982) *Science and Ideology in the Social Sciences*. New York: Aldine.

DiLorenzo, T. (1996) 'The Myth of Natural Monopoly'. *The Review of Austrian Economics*, Vol. 9, No. 1, pp.43–58.

DIEESE (Departamento Intersindical de Estatística e Estudos Socioeconômicos) (2011) *Anuário das Mulheres Brasileiras*. São Paulo: DIEESE.

Djankov et al. (2002) *Innovative Policies for the Urban Informal Economy*. UN-Habitat, Kenya: United Nations Human Settlements Programme.

Dobbs, R., Oppenheim, J., Thompson, F., Brinkman, M. and Zornes, M. (2011) *Resource Revolution: Meeting the World's Energy, Materials, Food and Water Needs*. Chicago: McKinsey and Company.

Docherty, P., Forslin, J. and Shani, A. B. (2002) *Creating Sustainable Work Systems: Emerging Perspectives and Practice*. London: Routledge.

Domhoff, G. W. (2012) *Wealth, Income, and Power*. http://whorulesamerica.net/power/wealth.html (first posted September 2005; most recently updated October 2012).

Dow, S. C. (2012) *Foundations for New Economic Thinking: A Collection of Essays*. London: Palgrave.

Dowd, D. (2004) *Capitalism and its Economics*, 2nd edn. London: Pluto Press.

Duke, S. (2016) 'Cheap Pound Won't Sustain March of the Makers for Long'. *The Sunday Times (Scotland)*, Section 3, p.4, 10 July 2016.

Earle, J., Moran, C. and Ward-Perkins, Z. (2017) *The Econocracy: The Perils of Leaving Economics to the Experts*. Manchester, UK: University of Manchester Press.

ECB (European Central Bank) (2009) Financial Stability Review. Frankfurt: European Central Bank. www.ecb.europa.eu/pub/pdf/other/financialstabilityreview200906en.pdf?80524324b2777945e406ac541792fc72

The Economist (2007) 'Indecent Exposure'. Online Extra, 5 August 2007. www.economist.com/node/9609521

The Economist (2012) 'A Clouded Future'. 13 March 2012. www.economist.com/node/16116919

ECLAC (Economic Commission for Latin America and the Caribbean) (2015) *Social Panorama of Latin America 2014*. ECLAC: Santiago, Chile.

Ellis, J. (2000) *The Founding Brothers: The Revolutionary Generation*. New York: Vintage.

Elson, D. (2007) 'Macroeconomic Policy, Employment, Unemployment and Gender Equality'. In: Ocampo, J. A. and Jomo, K. S. (Eds.) *Towards Full and Decent Employment*. London: Zed Books.

Epstein, G. (2007) 'Central Banks, Inflation Targeting and Employment Creation', *Economic and Labour Market Papers* No. 2. Geneva: International Labour Office.

FAO (Food and Agricultural Organization of the United Nations) (2009) *The State of the World's Land and Water Resources for Food and Agriculture Use: Managing Systems at Risk*. http://www.fao.org/nr/water/docs/SOLAW_EX_SUMM_WEB_EN.pdf

FAO (2016) *Coping with Water Scarcity in Agriculture: A Global Framework for Action in a Changing Climate*. COP 22. Report. Marrakech: United Nations.

Federal Bank of St Louis (2016) Economic Research. Economic Data. https://research.stlouisfed.org/fred2/series/GFDEGDQ188S#

Federal Trade Commission (1990) *Guide to Antitrust Laws*. www.ftc.gov/tips-advice/competition-guidance/guide-antitrust-laws

Fine, B. and Milonakis, D. (2009) *From Economics Imperialism to Freakonomics: The Shifting Boundaries Between Economics and the Other Social Sciences*. London: Routledge.

Fioramonti, L. (2013) *Gross Domestic Problem: The Politics Behind the World's Most Powerful Number*. London: Zed Books.

Folkman, P., Froud, J., Johal, S. and Williams, K. (2007) 'Working for Themselves: Capital Market Intermediaries and Present Day Capitalism'. *Business History*, Vol. 49, No. 4, pp.552–72.

Foster, J. B. (2009) 'A Failed System: the World Crisis of Capitalist Globalization and Its Impact on China'. *Monthly Review*, March, 60 (10). http://monthlyreview.org/2009/03/01/a-failed-system-the-world-crisis-of-capitalist-globalization-and-its-impact-on-china/

Freese, B. (2003) *Coal – A Human History*, Cambridge, MA: Perseus.

Freire, P. (1998) *Pedagogy of Freedom: Ethics, Democracy, and Civic Courage*. Lanham, MD: Rowman and Littlefield.

Fremstad, S. (2013) *Poverty Bites: New Census Numbers Make it Official: 2000–2010 Was a Lost Economic Decade*. Center for Economic and Policy Research. www.cepr.net/data-bytes/poverty-bytes/new-census-numbers-make-it-official-2000-2010-was-lost-economic-decade

Frenkel, J. (2012) *Sovereign Debt Panel, Institute for Global Law & Policy*. Boston: Harvard Law School.

Friedman, M. (1968) 'The Role of Monetary Policy'. *American Economic Review*, Vol. 58, No.1, pp.1–17.

Friedman, M. (1969) *The Optimum Quantity of Money*. London: Macmillan.

Friedman, M. and Friedman, R. (1990) *Free to Choose: A Personal Statement*, New York: Houghton Mifflin Harcourt.

Friedman, M. and Schwartz, A. J. (1963) *Money and Business Cycles*. Princeton: Princeton University Press.

Frisby, D. (ed.) (1990) *The Philosophy of Money – Georg Simmel*. London: Routledge.

Froud, J., Sukhdev J., Leaver, A. and Williams, K. (2006) *Financialization and Strategy: Narrative and Numbers*. London: Routledge.

Fullbrook, E. (ed.) (2004) *A Guide to What's Wrong with Economics*, London: Anthem.

Fullbrook, E. (2009) 'The Meltdown and Economics Textbooks'. In: Reardon, J. (ed.) *The Handbook of Pluralist Economics Education*. London: Routledge, pp.17–23.

Furtado, C. (1969) Formação econômica da América Latina. Rio de Janeiro: Lia Editôra.

Furtado, C. (1987) 'Underdevelopment: to Conform or Reform'. In: Meier, G. M. (ed.) *Pioneers in development*. New York: Oxford University Press.

GEF (Green European Foundation) (2009) *A Green New Deal for Europe: Towards Green Modernization in the Face of Crisis*. Brussels: GEF.

George, H. (1879 [1948]) *Progress and Poverty*. New York: Robert Schalkenbach Foundation.

GHF (Global Humanitarian Forum) (2009) *Human Impact Report*. Geneva: GHF.

Ghosh, J. (2003) 'Exporting Jobs or Watching Them Disappear? Relocation, Employment and Accumulation in the World Economy', in: Ghosh, J. and Chandrasekhar, C. P. (eds.) *Work and Well-Being in The Age of Finance*. New Delhi: Muttukadu Press, pp.99–119.

Goethe, J. (1999) *Faust: A Tragedy in Two Parts, with the Urfaust*. (Translated, with an introduction and notes by John R. Williams). London: Wordsworth Classics of World Literature.

Gonçalves, J. R. B. and Madi, M. A. C. (2009) 'Globalisation, Democracy and Terrorism, by Eric Hobsbawm'. *International Journal of Green Economics*, Vol. 3, No.1, pp.103–6.

Gordon, J. S. (1998) *Hamilton's Blessing: The Extraordinary Life and Times of Our National Debt*. New York: Penguin.

Gorz, A. (1982) *Farewell to the Working Class: An Essay on Post-Industrial Socialism*. London: Pluto Press.

Government of India (2011) *Economic Survey 2009–2010*. Ministry of Finance Report. http://indiabudget.nic.in/es2009-10/chapt2010/chapter01.pdf

Government of India (2017) *State of the Economy: An Overview in Economic Survey 2015–16*. Ministry of Finance Report. http://indiabudget.nic.in/es2015-16/echapvol2-01.pdf

Graeber, D. (2012) *Debt: The First 5,000 Years*. New York: Melville House.

Greenbaum, J. (2004) *Windows on the Workplace: Technology, Jobs, and the Organisation of Office Work*. New York: Monthly Review Press.

Griffith-Jones, S. (2002) Uma nova arquitetura financeira internacional como bem público global. In: Fendt, R. and Tedesco Lins, M. A. (Eds.) Arquitetura Assimétrica. Rio de Janeiro: Fundação Konrad Adenauer. Série Debates.

Groves, S. (2012) 'Remittances Hit $534 Billion in 2012, Setting New Record'. International Diaspora Engagement Alliance (IdEA), 26 November 2012. http://diasporaalliance.org/remittances-hit-a-record-high-of-534-billion-in-2012/

Guha, R. (2008) *India after Gandhi – The History of the World's Largest Democracy*. London: Picador.

Hallegatte, S., Bangalore, M., Bonzanigo, L., Fay, M., Kane, T., Narloch, U., Rozenberg, J., Treguer, D. and Vogt-Schilb, A. (Eds.) (2016) *Shock Waves: Managing the Impacts of Climate Change on Poverty*. Climate Change and Development Series. Washington, DC: World Bank. https://openknowledge.worldbank.org/handle/10986/22787

Hardin, G. (1968) 'The Tragedy of the Commons', *Nature*, Vol. 162, pp.1243–8.

Harrington, M. (1962 [1997]) *The Other America*. New York: Simon and Schuster.

Harris, J. and Roach, B. (2018) *Environmental and Natural Resource Economics – A Contemporary Approach*, 4th ed., London: Routledge.

Hart, M. (1992) *The 100: A Ranking of the Most Influential Persons in History*. New York: Kensington Publishing Co.

Harvard Political Review (2011) An Open Letter to Greg Mankiw', 2 November 2011. http://harvardpolitics.com/harvard/an-open-letter-to-greg-mankiw/

Harvey, D. (2010) *The Enigma of Capital and the Crises of Capitalism*. London: Profile Books.

Harvey, J. (2015) *Contending Perspectives in Economics: A Guide to Contemporary Schools of Thought*. Cheltenham, UK: Edward Elgar.

Hayek, F. A. (1944) *The Road to Serfdom*. Chicago: University of Chicago Press.

Heinzerling, L. and Ackerman, F. (2002) *Pricing the Priceless: Cost-Benefit Analysis of Environmental Protection*. Washington: Georgetown University Law Center.

Heise, A. (2017) 'Defining economic pluralism: ethical norm or scientific imperative'. *International Journal of Pluralism and Economics Education*, Vol. 8, No. 1, pp.18–41.

Hermann, A. (2015) *The Systemic Nature of the Economic Crisis: The Perspective of Heterodox Economics and Psychoanalysis*. London: Routledge.

Hill, R. and Myatt, T. (2010) *The Economics Anti-Textbook: A Critical Thinker's Guide to Microeconomics*. London: Zed Books.

Hobsbawm, E. (2007) *Globalisation, Democracy and Terrorism*. London: Abacus.

Hochschild, A. R. (1979) 'Emotion work, feeling rules, and social structure', *The American Journal of Sociology*, Vol. 85, No. 3, pp.551–75.

Hodgson, G. (1999) *Evolution and Institutions*. Cheltenham, UK: Edward Elgar.

Howarth, M. (2007) 'Worker Co-Operatives and the Phenomenon of Empresas Recuperadas in Argentina: An Analysis of Their Potential for Replication'. Co-operative College Paper 11. Co-operative College and ILO. www.ilo.org/empent/Publications/WCMS_110457/lang--en/index.htm

Howe, J. (2006) 'Crowdsourcing: How the Power of the Crowd is Driving the Future of Business'. *Wired Magazine*, 14 (6), pp.1–4.

Human Development Index (2017) entry in *Wikipedia, The Free Encyclopedia*. https://en.wikipedia.org/w/index.php?title=Human_Development_Index&oldid=792849875

Human Rights Watch (2015) 'Bangladesh: 2 Years After Rana Plaza, Workers Denied Rights'. 22 April 2015. www.hrw.org/news/2015/04/22/bangladesh-2-years-after-rana-plaza-workers-denied-rights

Hume, D. (1955) *David Hume's Writings on Economics*, E. Rotvein (ed.). London: Nelson.

Humphries, J. (1990) 'Common Rights, and Women: The Proletarianization of Families in the Late Eighteenth and Early Nineteenth Centuries'. *The Journal of Economic History*, Vol. 50, No. 1, pp.17–42.

Hunt, E. K. and Lautzenheiser, M. (2011) *History of Thought: A Critical Perspective*. New York: M.E. Sharpe.

Hussen, A. M. (2000) *Principles of Environmental Economics: Economics, Ecology and Public Policy*. London: Earthscan.

ICA (International Co-operative Alliance) (2017) 'What is a Cooperative?' www.ica.coop/en

ILO (International Labour Organization) (1998) *Declaration on Fundamental Principles and Rights at Work*. Geneva: International Labour Office.

ILO (2008a) *Global Employment Trends*. Geneva: International Labour Office.

ILO (2008b) *Measurement of Decent Work*. Geneva: International Labour Office

ILO (2009) *Global Employment Trends*. Geneva: International Labour Office. www.ilo.org/wcmsp5/groups/public/@dgreports/@dcomm/documents/publication/wcms_101461.pdf

ILO (2012) Statistical Update on Employment in the Informal Economy. Geneva: International Labour Office. http://laborsta.ilo.org/applv8/data/INFORMAL_ECONOMY/2012-06-Statistical%20update%20-%20v2.pdf

ILO (2015) Global Employment Trends for Youth 2015: Scaling up Investments in Decent Jobs for Youth. Geneva: International Labour Office. www.ilo.org/global/research/global-reports/youth/2015/WCMS_412015/lang--en/index.htm

ILO (2015b) *Key Indicators of the Labour Market*. Geneva: International Labour Office.

ILO (2016) *Women at Work: Trends 2016*. Geneva: International Labour Office. www.ilo.org/wcmsp5/groups/public/---dgreports/---dcomm/---publ/documents/publication/wcms_457086.pdf

IMF (International Monetary Fund) (2009a) *Global Imbalances: In Midstream?* Prepared by Olivier Blanchard and Gian Maria Milesi-Ferretti, Research Department. Washington, DC: IMF.

IMF (2009b) *Impact of the Global Financial Crisis on Sub-Saharan Africa*. Washington, DC: IMF.

IMF (2014) World Economic and Financial Surveys, World Economic Outlook Database, April 2014. www.imf.org/external/pubs/ft/weo/2017/01/weodata/index.aspx

IMF (2016) *Brazil, Country Report No. 16/349*. www.imf.org/external/pubs/ft/scr/2016/cr16349.pdf

IPCC (Intergovernmental Panel on Climate Change) (2013) *Fifth Assessment Report*. www.ipcc.ch

Ipeirotis, P. (2012)*The (Unofficial) NIST Definition of Crowdsourcing*. www.behind-the-enemy-lines.com/search?q=cloudmechanical-turk-demographics.html

Islahi, A. A. (2014) *History of Islamic Economic Thought*. Cheltenham, UK: Edward Elgar.

IWMI (International Water Management Institute) (2009) *Water For Food, Water for Life: Insights from the Comprehensive Assessment of Water Management*. Colombo, Sri Lanka: IWMI. http://thewaterproject.org/world_water_week.pdf

Jackson, T. (2009) *Prosperity Without Growth: Economics for a Finite Planet*. London: Earthscan.

Jessop, B. (1992) 'Fordism and Post-Fordism: a Critical Reformulation'. In: Scott, A. J. and Storper, M. J. (Eds.) *Pathways to Regionalism and Industrial Development*. London: Routledge, pp.43–65.

Jevons, W. (1865 [2008]) *The Coal Question: An Inquiry Concerning the Progress of the Nation, and the Probable Exhaustion of Our Coal-Mines*, London: Macmillan.

Jevons, W. (1871 [1931]) *The Theory of Political Economy*. London: MacMillan.

Johnson, D. (2016) 'Not Since the Tudors Have We Seen So Many Powerful Women, and They're Going to Change Our World'. *The Sunday Times (Scotland)*, 10 July 2016, pp.28–9.

Juglar, C.(1856) 'Des crises commerciales en France de l'an VIII à 1855', *Annuaire de Léconomie Politique et de la Statistique*, Tome 13. Paris: Guillaumin, pp.555–81.

Kalecki, M. (1933 [1971]) 'An Essay on the Business Cycle Theory'. In: *Selected Essays on the Dynamics of the Capitalist Economy 1933-1970*. Cambridge, UK: Cambridge University Press, pp.1–14.

Kalecki, M. (1954) *Theory of Economic Dynamics*. London: Allen, Unwin.

Kalecki, M. (1990) *Collected Works*, Vol. I, and Vol. II. Oxford, UK: Clarendon Press.

Keen, S. (2012) *Debunking Economics*. London: Zed Books.

Kelley, J. and Zagorski, K. (2003) *Economic Change and the Legitimation of Inequality: the Transition From Socialism to the Free Market in Central-East Europe*. Melbourne Institute of Applied Economic and Social Research, University of Melbourne; CBOS (Public Opinion Research Center), Warsaw and Institute of Political Studies, Polish Academy of Sciences. www.international-survey.org/Kelley_Zagorski_RSSM_MS.pdf

Kennet, M. (2007) 'Editorial: Progress in Green Economics: Ontology, Concepts and Philosophy. Civilisation and the Lost Factor of Reality in Social and Environmental Justice'. *International Journal of Green Economics*, Vol. 1, No. 3–4, pp.225–49.

Kennet, M. and Heinemann, V. (2006) 'Green Economics: Setting the Scene. Aims, Context, and Philosophical Underpinning of the Distinctive New Solutions Offered by Green Economics'. *International Journal of Green Economics,* Vol. 1, No. 1–2, pp.68–102.

Keynes, J. M. (1937) 'How to Avoid a Slump'. In: Moggridge, D. (ed.) *Collected Writings of John Maynard Keynes, vol. XXI, Activities 1931-1939*. Cambridge, UK: Cambridge University Press.

Keynes, J. M. (1936 [2010]) *The General Theory of Employment, Interest, and Money.* Mansfield Center, Connecticut: Martino Publishing.

Keynes, J. M. (1969) 'Proposal for an International Clearing Union'. In: Horsefield, J. K. (ed.) *The International Monetary Fund 1945-1965*. Washington, DC: International Monetary Fund.

Khanna, P. (2016) *Connectography: Mapping the Future of Global Civilization*. New York: Random House.

Kiciloff, A. (2015) 'Preface'. In: Ugarteche, O., Puyana, A. and Madi, M. A. (Eds.) *Ideas Towards a New International Financial Architecture?* Bristol, UK: WEA Books.

Kindleberger, C. and Aliber, J. (2005) *Manias, Panics and Crashes: A History of Financial Crises*, 5th edn. London: John Willey & Sons.

King, R., Delbert, A., Chisholm, N. and Hossain, N. (2014) *Help Yourself! Food Rights and Responsibilities: Year 2, Findings from Life in a Time of Food Price Volatility.* Oxford, UK: Oxfam. http://policy-practice.oxfam.org.uk/our-work/food-livelihoods/food-price-bvolatility-research#5dc1a02e-a23f-458c-9be6-32f0093642d0

Klavins, M., Filho, W. and Zaloksnis, J. (2010) *Environment and Sustainable Development.* Riga, Latvia: Academic Press, University of Latvia.

Komlos, J. (2014) *What Every Economics Student Needs to Know and Doesn't Get in the Usual Principles Text.* New York: M.E. Sharpe.

Korten, D. (1995) *When Corporations Rule the World.* West Hartford, CT: Kumarian Press.

Krugman, P. (2013) *End this Depression Now!* New York: Norton.

Kuhn T. (2012) *The Structure of Scientific Revolutions*. Chicago: The University of Chicago Press.

Kunstler, H. (2008) *The World Made By Hand*. New York: Atlantic Monthly Press.

Laeven, L. and Valencia, F. (2012) *Systemic Banking Crises Database: An Update.* IMF Working Paper, WP/12/163. Washington, DC: International Monetary Fund.

Landes, D. (1999) *The Wealth and Poverty of Nations*. New York: Doubleday.

Larson, R. (2012) *Bleakonomics*. London: Pluto Press.

Lapavitsas, C. (2013) *Profiting Without Producing: How Finance Exploits Us All*. London: Verso.

Leape, J. (2006) 'The London Congestion Charge'. *Journal of Economic Perspectives*, Vol. 20, No. 4, pp.157–76.

Lee, F. (2009) *A History of Heterodox Economics: Challenging the Mainstream in the Twentieth Century.* London: Routledge.

Leeson, R. (2003) *Ideology and the International Economy: The Decline and Fall of Bretton Woods*. New York: Palgrave Macmillan.

Lines, T. (2008) *Making Poverty: A History.* London: Zed Books.

List, F. (1841 [2011]) *The National System of Political Economy*. New York: Cosimo Classics.

Lovelock, J. (1979 [2000]) *Gaia: A New Look at Life on Earth*. Oxford, UK: Oxford University Press.

Lundberg, M. and Squire, L. (2003) 'The Simultaneous Evolution of Growth and Inequality'. *The Economic Journal*, Vol.113, No. 487, pp.326–44.

McCarthy, J. (2016) 'Just Over Half of Americans Own Stocks, Matching Record Low'. Gallup poll. www.gallup.com/poll/1900883/half-ar

McManners, P. (2008) *Adapt and Thrive – The Sustainable Revolution*. Cornwall: MPG Books.

McManners, P. (2012) *Fly and Be Damned: What Now For Aviation and Climate Change?* London: Zed Books.

McNeil, J. R. (2000) *Something New Under the Sun: An Environmental History of the Twentieth-century World*. New York: Norton.

Machiavelli, Niccolo. (1532 [1988]) *The Prince*. Cambridge, UK: Cambridge University Press.

Mackay, A. and Wilmshurst, J. (2002) *Fundamentals and Practice of Marketing*. London: Butterworth-Heinemann.

Madden, B. J. (2016) *Value Creation Thinking*. Naperville, IL: LearningWhatWorks.

Maddison, A. (1991) *Dynamic Forces in Capitalist Development*. Oxford, UK: Oxford University Press.

Madi, M. A. C. and Gonçalves, J. R. B. (2007) 'Corporate Social Responsibility and Market Society: Credit and Social Exclusion in Contemporary Brazil'. In: Bugra, A. and Agartan, K. (Eds.) *Reading Karl Polanyi for the Twenty-First Century: Market Economy as a Political Project*. New York: Palgrave Macmillan.

Madi, M. A. C and Gonçalves, J. R. B. (2013) 'Entrepreneurship and Micro-credit: Social Challenges in the Context of the Productive Reconfiguration'. In: Chichilnisky, G., Madi, M. A. C., Yee, C. F., Kennet, M. and de Oliveira, M. G., *The Greening of Global Finance*. Reading, UK: The Green Economics Institute. pp.239–48.

Madi, M. A. C. (2015) *Small Business in Brazil: Competitive Global Challenges*, New York: Nova Publishers.

Madi, M. A. C. (2016) 'Canonical Debates on Exchange Rates'. WEA Pedagogy Blog. Bristol, UK: World Economics Association. https://weapedagogy.wordpress.com/2016/08/09/canonical-debates-on-exchange-rates/

Maes, J. and Reed, L. (2012) *State of the Microcredit Summit Campaign Report*. Washington, DC: Microcredit Summit Campaign.

Malthus, T. (1798 [1992] *Essay on the Principle of Population*. Cambridge, UK: Cambridge University Press.

Mamen, K., Gorelick, S., Norberg-Hodge, H. and Deumling, D. (2004) *Ripe for Change: Rethinking California's Food Economy*. International Society for Ecology and Culture. www.localfutures.org/wp-content/uploads/ripeforchange.pdf

Marshall, A. (1890) [1946] *Principles of Economics*. London: Macmillan.

Marx, K. (1867 [1967]) *Capital*, Vol. 1., New York: International Publishers.

Marx, K. and Engels, F. (1848 [1992]) *The Communist Manifesto*. Oxford, UK: Oxford University Press.

Mason, P. (2015) *Postcapitalism: A Guide to our Future*. New York: Farrar, Straus and Giroux.

Max-Neef, M. (1991) *Human-Scale Development: Conception, Application and Further Reflection*. London: Apex Press.

Meadows, D. H., Meadows, D. L., Randers, J. and Behrens III, W. W. (1972) *The Limits to Growth: A Report to The Club of Rome*. New York: Universe Books.

Mellor, M. (2006) 'Ecofeminist Political Economy', *International Journal of Green Economics*, Vol. 1, No. 1–2, pp.139–50.

Mellor, M. (2010) *The Future of Money*. London: Pluto Press.

Mellor, M. (2012) 'The World Financial Crisis and Money Systems from a Green Perspective'. In: *UNESCO's Encyclopedia of Life Support Systems* (Ref 6:29:32).

Meyer, B and Moors, A. (Eds.) (2006) *Religion, Media and the Public Sphere*. Bloomington & Indianapolis: Indiana University Press.

Microcredit Summit Campaign (2016), State of the Summit Report 2015. https://stateofthecampaign.org/data-reported/

Minsky, H. P. (1982) *Can 'it' Happen Again?: Essays on Instability and Finance*. New York: Routledge.

Minsky, H. P. (1991) *Financial Crises: Systemic or Idiosyncratic*, Working Paper No. 51. Annandale-on-Hudson, New York: Levy Economics Institute of Bard College.

Minsky, H. P. (2008) *Stabilizing an Unstable Economy*. New York: McGraw Hill.

Mityakov, S. and Portnykh, M. (2012) *The Infant Industry Argument and Renewable Energy Production*. Arlington, TX: The Marshall Institute.

More, T. (1516 [1965]) *Utopia*, New York: Penguin.

Murinde, V. (2009) 'Capital Flows and Capital Account Liberalisation in the Post-Financial Crisis Era: Challenges, Opportunities & Policy Responses'. Presentation, University of Birmingham Business School, Birmingham, UK.

Music & Copyright Annual Survey (2017). London: Ovum. https://musicandcopyright.wordpress.com/

Mutert, E. (2010) *Alternative Indicator: The Happy Planet Index*. www.marketplace.org/2010/10/07/business/economy-40/alternative-indicator-happy-planet-index

Neeson, J. M. (1989) *Commoners: Common Right, Enclosure and Social Change in England, 1700-1820*. Cambridge, UK: Cambridge University Press.

Nelson, J. (2008) 'Feminist Economics'. In: Durlauf, S. N. and Blume, L. E. (Eds.)*The New Palgrave Dictionary of Economics*, 2nd edn. London: Palgrave Macmillan.

Nelson, J. (2009) 'The Principles Course'. In: Reardon, J. (ed.) *The Handbook for Pluralist Economics Education*. London: Routledge, pp.57–68.

Nelson, R. (2010) *The New Holy Wars: Economic Religion versus Environmental Religion*. University Park: The University of Pennsylvania Press.

Newton, I. (1687 [1995]) *The Principia*. New York: Prometheus Books.

North, P. (2010) *Local Money: How to Make it Happen in your Community*. Totnes: Green Books.

Obeng-Odoom (2016) *Reconstructing Urban Economics: Towards a Political Economy of the Built Environment*, London: Zed Books.

OBIG (Observatório Brasil da Igualdade de Gênero) (2011). *A crise econômica internacional e os (possíveis) impactos sobre a vida das mulheres*. Nota Técnica. www.ipea.gov.br/sites/000/2/boletim_mercado_de_trabalho/mt40/04_NT_crise.pdf

Ocampo, J. and Martin, J. (Eds.) (2003) *Globalization and Development: A Latin American and Caribbean Perspective*. Stanford: Stanford University Press.

O'Doherty, R., Street, D. and Webber, C. (2007) 'Findings of a survey conducted on behalf of the Royal Economic Society and the Economics Network'. www.economicsnetwork.ac.uk/projects/employability2007full.pdf

OECD (The Organisation for Economic Co-operation and Development) (1996) The Role of Trade Unions in Local Development. Paris: OECD.

OECD (2013) *Water and Climate Change/Adaptation: Policies to Navigate Uncharted Waters*. OECD Studies on Water. OECD. www.keepeek.com/Digital-Asset-Management/oecd/environment/water-and-climate-change-adaptation_9789264200449-en#page1

OECD (2016) Official Development Assistance Database. Distribution of net ODA (indicator). https://data.oecd.org/oda/net-oda.htm

Ofcom (The UK's communications regulator) (2016) *The International Communications Market, International Report*. www.ofcom.org.uk/data/assets/pdf_file/0026/95642/ICMR-Full.pdf

O'Hara, M. and Leicester, G. (2012) *Dancing at the Edge: Competence, Culture and Organization in the 21st Century*. Devon, UK: Triarchy Press.

Onaran, Y. (2012) *Zombie Banks*. US: Bloomberg News.

Onishi, N. and Wollan, M. (2014) 'Severe Drought Grows Worse in California'. *The New York Times*, p.A1 and p.A13, 14 January 2014.

Ostrom, E. (1990) *Governing the Commons: The Evolution of Institutions for Collective Action*. Cambridge, UK: Cambridge University Press.

Otobe, N. (2014) *Resource Guide on Gender Issues in Employment and Labour Market Policies*. Geneva: International Labour Office.

Ottermann, P. (2017) 'The Party city grows up: how Berlin's clubbers built their own urban village'. *The Guardian*, 1 May 2017.

Panayotakis, C. (2011) *Remaking Scarcity: From Capitalist Inefficiency to Economic Democracy*. London: Pluto Press.

Panayotakis, C. (2012) 'Scarcity, capitalism and the promise of economic democracy'. *International Journal of Pluralism and Economics Education*, Vol. 3, No.1, pp.104–11.

Parkin, S. (2010) *The Positive Deviant: Sustainability Leadership in a Perverse World*. London: Routledge.

Pearce, D. (1992) *Economic Valuation and the Natural World*. Policy Research Working Paper Series 988. Washington: The World Bank.

Piketty, T. (2014) *Capital in the Twenty-First Century*. Cambridge, MA: Harvard University Press.

Pigou, A. (1920 [1986]) *The Economics of Welfare*. New Brunswick, NJ: Transaction Books.

Pigou, A. (1933 [1968]) *The Theory of Unemployment*. London: Routledge.

Pisani-Ferry, J. and Sapir, A. (2009) 'Euro Area: Ready for the storm?' In: Pisani-Ferry, J. and Posen, A. S. (Eds.), The Euro at Ten: The Next Global Currency? Washington: Peterson Institute for International Economics.

Polanyi, K. (1944) *The Great Transformation*. London: Gollancz.

Polivka, A. E. and Nardone, T. (1989) 'On the definition of "contingent work"'. *Monthly Labor Review*, December, pp.9–14.

Post-Autistic Economics Network (2000) 'Open Letter From Economics Students to Professors and Others Responsible for the Teaching of This Discipline' www.paecon.net?PAEtexts/a-epetition.htm

Prebish, R. (1949) *El Desarrollo Económico de la América Latina y Algunos de sus Principales Problemas*. Nações Uidas, Cepal http://repositorio.cepal.org/bitstream/handle/11362/40010/prebisch_desarrollo_problemas.pdf?sequence=1

Rama, M. (2003) 'On Globalization and the Labor Market'. *World Bank Research Observer*, Vol. 18, No. 2, pp.159–86.

Rawls, J. (1971) *A Theory of Justice*. Cambridge, MA: Harvard University Press.

Reardon, J. (2006) 'Are Labor Unions Consistent With the Assumptions of Perfect Competition?' *Journal of Economic Issues*, Vol. 40, No. 1, pp.171–81.

Reardon, J. (2009) *The Handbook of Pluralist Economics Education*. London: Routledge.

Reardon, J. (2014) 'Underemployment'. In: Hansen, L. (ed.) *The New Faces of American Poverty: A Reference Guide to the Great Recession*. New York: ABC Clio Books.

Reardon, J. (2017) 'When Will Economics Become Pluralist?' *International Journal of Pluralism and Economics Education*, Vol. 8, No. 1, pp.7–13.

Reed, L., Marsden, J., Rogers, S., Rivera, C. and Ortega, A. (2014) *Resilience: The State of the Microcredit Summit Campaign Report, 2014*. Microcredit Summit Campaign (MCS): Washington. www.microcreditsummit.org/resource/173/resilience-the-state-of-the.html#sthash.H8G9WI7s.dpuf

Reich, R. (2009) *Supercapitalism: the Battle for Democracy in an Age of Big Business*. New York: Icon Books.

Rethinking Economics (2014) www.rethinkeconomics.org/#!our-vision/colf

Reynolds, R. L. (2000) *The Physiocrats: An Outline* http://web1.boisestate.edu/econ/lreynol/web/PDF_HET/Physiocratsoutline.pdf

Ricardo, D. (1817 [2004]) *The Principles of Political Economy and Taxation*. Mineola, NY: Dover Publications.

Rifkin, J. (1995) *The End of Work: The Decline of the Global Labor Force and the Dawn of the Post-Market Era*. New York: Putnam.

Rifkin, J. (2014) *The Zero Marginal Cost Society*. New York: Palgrave Macmillan.

Robinson, J. (1937 [1947]) *Essays in the Theory of Employment*, 2nd edn. Oxford, UK: Basil Blackwell.

Robinson, J. (1954) 'The production function and the theory of capital'. *Review of Economic Studies*, Vol. 21, No. 2, pp.81–106.

Robinson, J. (1980) *What are the Questions And Other Essays?* New York: M.E. Sharpe.

Roberts, G. D. (2003) *Shantaram*, New York: St. Martin's.

Robinson, P. K. (2009) 'Responsible Retailing: The Reality of Fair and Ethical Trade,' *Journal of International Development*. Vol. 21, No. 7, pp.1015–26.

Rockström, J. and Klum, M. (2015) *Big World, Small Planet: Abundance Within Planetary Boundaries*. New Haven, CT: Yale University Press.

Rousseau, J. J. (1755 [1973]) 'Discourse on Inequality'. In: Cole, G. D. H. (ed.) *The Social Contract and Discourses*. London: Everyman.

Ryan-Collins, J. and Greenham, T. (2012) *Where Does Money Come From?* London: New Economics Foundation.

Sahlins, M. D. (1972) *Stone Age Economics*. Chicago: Aldine.

Saunders, A. (1994) Financial Institutions Management: A Modern Perspective. Burr Ridge, IL: Richard D. Irwin.

Schneider, F. and Enste, D. (2000) 'Shadow Economies: Size, Causes and Consequences'. *Journal of Economic Literature*, Vol. 38, March, pp.77–114.

Schneider, F. (2002) *Innovative Policies for the Urban Informal Economy*. UN-Habitat, Nairobi, Kenya: United Nations Human Settlements Programme.

Schumacher, E. F. (1973 [1989]) *Small is Beautiful: Economics as if People Mattered*. New York: Harper Perennial.

Schumpeter, J. (1912 [1934]) *The Theory of Economic Development*. Cambridge, MA: Harvard University Press.

Schumpeter, J. (1918 [1951]) *The Sociology of Imperialism*. New York: Meridian Books.

Schumpeter, J. (1939 [2006]) *Business Cycles: A Theoretical, Historical and Statistical Analysis of the Capitalist Process*. Mansfield Center, CT: Martino.

Schumpeter, J. (1942) *Capitalism, Socialism, Democracy*. London: Routledge.

Schumpeter, J. (1954) *History of Economic Analysis*. New York: Oxford University Press.

Schwab, K. (2015) 'The Fourth Industrial Revolution: What it Means and How to Respond'. *Foreign Affairs*, 12 December 2015. www.foreignaffairs.com/articles/2015-12-12/fourth-industrial-revolution

Scheslinger, A. (1945) *The Age of Jackson*, Boston: Little, Brown and Co.

Sen, A. (1999) *Development as Freedom*. New York: Anchor Books.

Sen, A. (2005b) *The Argumentative Indian—Writings on Indian Culture, History and Identity*. New York: Penguin.

Sen, A. (2009) *The Idea of Justice*. London: Penguin.

Shearman, D. and Smith, J. (2007) *The Climate Change Challenge and the Failure of Democracy*. Westport, CT: Praeger.

Shelley, M. (1818 [1992]) *Frankenstein*, New York: Penguin.

Shlain, L. (1990) *Art and Physics: Parallel Visions in Space, Time, and Light*. New York: Perennial.

Shultz, J. and Draper, M. (2009) *Dignity and Defiance: Stories from Bolivia's Challenge to Globalization*. Berkeley: University of California Press.

Sicsú, J. (2011) 'Lições da Crise de 2008-2009: o que o Brasil Deve Fazer Agora?' Departamento Intersindical de Assessoria Parlamentar. www.diap.org.br/index.php/noticias/artigos/18845-licoes-da-crise-de-2008-2009-o-que-o-brasil-deve-fazer-agora

Sinclair, U. (1906 [1985]) *The Jungle*, New York: Penguin.

Skidelsky, R. (2016) 'The False Promise of Negative Interest Rates'. *The Project Syndicate – The World's Opinion Page*. www.project-syndicate.org/commentary/negative-interest-rates-false-promise-by-robert-skidelsky-2016-05

Smith, A. (1759 [2000]) *The Theory of Moral Sentiments*. New York: Prometheus Books.

Smith, A. (1776 [1976]) *An Inquiry into the Nature and Causes of the Wealth of Nations*. Chicago: University of Chicago Press.

Snyder, G. (1990) *The Practice of the Wild*. Berkeley: Counterpoint.

Soares, S. et al. (2007) *Sergei Soares, Rafael Guerreiro Osório, Fábio Veras Soares, Marcelo Medeiros e Eduardo Zepeda*, Programas de transferência condicionada de renda no Brasil, Chile e México: impactos sobre a desigualdade. Brasília: Ipea, (Texto para Discussão, n. 1.293).

Söderbaum, P. (2008) *Understanding Sustainability Economics: Towards Pluralism in Economics*. London: Earthscan.

Sonenshine, T. (2016) 'U.S. vs the World? Women as Top Political Leaders'. *The Globalist*, 10 February 2016. www.theglobalist.com/women-on-top-of-the-political-world/

Sraffa, P. (1960) *Production of Commodities by Means of Commodities*. Cambridge, UK: Cambridge University Press.

Srnicek, N. (2017) *Platform Capitalism*, London: Polity.

Standage, T. (1998) *The Victorian Internet*, Berkley Books: New York.

Standing, G. (2011) *The Precariat: The New Dangerous Class*. London: Bloomsbury Academic.

Standing, G. (2016) *The Corruption of Capitalism: Why Rentiers Thrive and Work Does Not Pay*. London: Biteback Publishing.

Standing, G. (2017) *Basic Income: And How We Can Make it Happen*. London: Pelican Books

Steinbeck, J. (1939 [1996]) *The Grapes of Wrath*, New York: Penguin.

Stern, N. (2007) *The Economics of Climate Change – The Stern Review*. Cambridge, UK: Cambridge University Press.

Stiglitz, J. (2013) *The Price of Inequality.* London: Penguin.

Stilwell, F. (2012) *Political Economy: The Contest of Economic Ideas.* Oxford, UK: Oxford University Press.

Stockhammer, E. (2008) 'Some Stylized Facts on the Finance-Dominated Accumulation Regime'. *Competition and Change*, Vol. 12, No. 2, pp.189–207.

Stout, L. (2012) *The Shareholder Value Myth.* San Francisco: Berrett-Koehler.

Sukhdev, P. (2013) 'Will 2013 Bring a New, Sustainable World?' *The Guardian.* www.theguardian.com/sustainable-business/2013-new-sustainable-world

Sullivan, S. (2013) 'Banking Nature? The Spectacular Financialisation of Environmental Conservation'. *Antipode*, Vol. 45, No. 1, pp.198–217.

Summers, L. (2015) *Persistent jobless growth: Outlook on the Global Agenda 2015.* World Economic Forum. http://reports.weforum.org/outlook-global-agenda-2015/top-10-trends-of-2015/2-persistent-jobless-growth/

Sundquist, B. (2011) 'The Informal Economy of the Developing World: the Context, the Prognosis, and a Broader Perspective'. December 2008 (last updated 2011). http://home.windstream.net/bsundquist1/ie.html#B

Susskind, D. (2015) 'Robot Doctors and Lawyers? It's a Change We Should Embrace'. *The Guardian*, 2 November 2013. www.theguardian.com/commentisfree/2015/nov/02/robot-doctors-lawyers-professions-embrace-change-machines

Susskind, Richard and Daniel Susskind (2016) The Future of the Professions, Oxford, UK: Oxford University Press.

Taylor, J. B. (1993) *Discretion Versus Policy Rules in Practice*, Carnegie-Rochester Conference Series on Public Policy. 39, pp.195–214.

Thompson, S., Abdallah, S., Marks, N., Simms, A. and Johnson, V. (2007) *The European Happy Planet Index: An Index of Carbon Efficiency and Well-being in the EU.* London: New Economics Foundation.

Thorbecke, W. (2011) 'An Empirical Analysis of East Asian Computer and Electronic Goods Exports'. *Journal of the Asia Pacific Economy*, Vol. 16, No. 4, pp.644–57.

Thorton, T. (2017) *From Economics to Political Economy: The Problems, Promises and Solutions of Pluralist Economics.* London: Routledge.

Tool, M. (2001) *The Discretionary Economy: A Normative Theory of Political Economy.* New Brunswick, NJ: Transaction Publishers.

Toossi, M. (2012) 'Projections of the Labor Force to 2050: a Visual Essay'. *Monthly Review*, pp.4–16.

Triffin, R. (1960) *Gold and the Dollar Crisis.* New Haven, CT: Yale University Press.

Troutman, K. (2013) 'China's Reserve Accumulation: Where Did it Come From, Where Did it Go?' *China Economic Watch*, Peterson Institute for International Economics, www.piie.com/blogs/china/?p=3474

Tudge, C. (2007) *Feeding People is Easy.* Grosseto, Italy: Pari Publishing.

Turgenev, I. (1835 [1990) *Sketches from a Hunter's Album.* London: Penguin.

Tussie, D. and Aggio, C. (n.d.) *Economic and Social Impacts of Trade Liberalization*, United Nations Conference on Trade and Development (UNCTAD) report. www.unctad.info/upload/TAB/docs/TechCooperation/fullreport-version14nov-p106-119.pdf

UN (United Nations) (2000) *World Urbanization Prospects: The 1999 Revision.* New York: United Nations.

UN (2010) *The World's Women 2010: Trends and Statistics.* New York: United Nations Department of Economic and Social Affairs.

UN (2014a) *World Urbanization Prospects: The 2014 Revision*. New York: United Nations. http://esa.un.org/unpd/wup/Publications/Files/WUP2014-Highlights.pdf

UN (2014b) *Localizing the Post-2015 Development Agenda: Dialogues on Implementation*. Report on Stakeholder Dialogue on Implementation. www.uclg.org/sites/default/files/dialogues_on_localizing_the_post-2015_development_agenda.pdf

UN (2015a) 'Sustainable Development Goals'. https://sustainabledevelopment.un.org/?menu=1300

UN (2015b) *The World's Women 2015: Trends and Statistics*. New York: United Nations Department of Economic and Social Affairs, Statistics Division.

UN (2015c) *World Urbanization Prospects: Final Report*. New York: United Nations. http://esa.un.org/unpd/wup/Publications/Files/WUP2014-Report.pdf

UN (2015d) *Fact Sheet: Women, Gender Equality, and Climate Change*. www.un.org/womewatch/feature/climate_change/

UN (2017) 'Facts and Figures: Leadership and Political Participation – Women in Parliaments'. www.unwomen.org/en/what-we-do/leadership-and-political-participation/facts-and-figures

UN Information Service (2013). www.unis.unvienna.org

UNCTAD (United Nations Conference on Trade and Development) (2013) *World Investment Report 2013: Global Value Chains: Investment And Trade For Development*. New Tour Na Geneva: UNCTAD.

UNCTAD (2014) 'Economic Data and Trade Statistics'. May 2014. http://brics.itamaraty.gov.br/about-brics/economic-data

UNDP (United Nations Development Programme) (2001) Towards a New Consensus: Democracy and Human Development in Indonesia. Indonesia Human Development Published with BPS-Statistics Indonesia, Bappenas, http://hdr.undp.org/sites/default/files/indonesia_2001_en.pdfa

UNDP (2013). Human Development Report 2013: *The Rise of the South: Human Progress in a Diverse World*. New York: United Nations Development Programme. http://hdr.undp.org/sites/default/files/reports/14/hdr2013_en_complete.pdf

UNEP (United Nations Environment Programme) (2009) *Global Green New Deal: Update*. Geneva: United Nations Environment Programme.

UNFCCC (United Nations Framework Convention on Climate Change) (2016) *Summary and Recommendations by the Standing Committee on Finance on the 2016 Biennial Assessment and Overview of Climate Finance Flows*. http://unfccc.int/files/cooperation_and_support/financial_mechanism/standing_committee/application/pdf/2016_ba_summary_and_recommendations.pdf

US Census Bureau (various years). www.census.gov

US Energy Information Administration (2016) *International Energy Outlook 2016*. www.eia.gov/forecasts/ieo/

US Department of the Treasury (2017) 'Portfolio Holdings of U.S. and Foreign Securities'. www.treasury.gov/resource-center/data-chart-center/tic/Pages/ticsec2.aspx

Utzig, J. E. (1996) 'Notas sobre o governo do PT em Porto Alegre'. Novos Estudos CEBRAP, 45, pp.209–22.

Vahid, A, Qaddumi, H. M., Dickson, E., Diez, S. M., Danilenko, A. V., Hirji, R. F., Puz, G., Pizarro, C., Jacobsen, M. and Blankespoor, B. (2009) *Water and Climate Change: Understanding the Risks and Making Climate-Smart Investment Decisions*. World Bank. www-ds.worldbank.org/external/default/WDSContentServer/WDSP/IB/2010/02/01/000333038_20100201020244/Rendered/PDF/529110NWP0Box31geowebolargeo1128110.pdf

Van der Berg, H. (2012) *International Economics: A Heterodox Approach*. Armonk, NY: M.E. Sharpe.

Varoufakis, Y. (2012) 'Keynes and Hayek Betrayed: on the Curious Stance of Europe's Keynesian and Libertarian Political Economists in the Context of the Eurozone Crisis'. *International Journal of Pluralism and Economics Education*, Vol. 3, No. 1, pp.71–83.

Varoufakis, Y. (2015) *The Global Minotaur: America, Europe and the Future of the Global Economy*. London: Zed Books.

Vatn, A. (2005) *Institutions and the Environment*. Cheltenham, UK: Edward Elgar.

Veblen, T. (1899 [1991]) *The Theory of the Leisure Class*. New York: Penguin.

Vickery, C. (1977) 'The Time Poor: a New Look at Poverty'. *Journal of Human Resources*, Vol. 12, No. 1, pp.27–48.

Ward, A. (2017) 'Competition for Water Will Make it More Valuable Than Oil, Says Suez Chief'. *Financial Times*, 20 March 2017, p.15.

Waring, M. (1988) *If Women Counted: A New Feminist Economics*. New York: Harper and Row.

WCED (World Commission on Environment and Development) (1987) *Our Common Future*. Oxford, UK: Oxford University Press.

Weber, M. (1930 [1958]) *The Protestant Ethic and the Spirit of Capitalism*. New York: Charles Scribner's Sons.

Weehuizen, R. (2007) 'Interdisciplinarity and Problem-based Learning in Economics Education: The Case of Infonomics'. In: Groenewegen, J. (ed.) *Teaching Pluralism in Economics*. Cheltenham, UK: Edward Elgar, pp.155–88.

Wheat, I. D. (2009) 'Teaching Economics as if Time Mattered'. In: Reardon, J. (ed.) *The Handbook of Pluralist Economics Education*. London: Routledge, pp.69–89.

WHO (World Health Organization) (2013) *Water Quality and Health Strategy 2013–2020*. Geneva: World Health Organization. www.zaragoza.es/contenidos/medioambiente/onu/998-eng.pdf

Wolf, M. (2005) 'Will Globalization Survive?' Third Whitman Lecture. Institute for International Economics, Washington DC, April 5. www.ciaonet.org/attachments/4597/uploads

Wolff, E. N. (2012) *The Asset Price Meltdown and the Wealth of the Middle Class*. New York: New York University Press.

Wong, E. (2013) 'Survey in China Shows a Wide Gap in Income'. *The New York Times*, 19 July 2013. www.nytimes.com/2013/07/20/world/asia/survey-in-china-shows-wide-income-gap.html?_r=0

World Bank (2009) *Global Monitoring Report: The Global Financial Crisis and Its Impact on Developing Countries*. http://siteresources.worldbank.org/INTGLOMONREP2009/Resources/5924349-1239742507025/GMR09_ch01.pdf

World Bank (2012) *Migration and Development Brief 19*. Migration and Remittances Unit, Development Prospects Group.

World Bank (2016a) World Development Indicators. http://data.worldbank.org/indicator/SE.SEC.ENRR/regions? display=default

World Bank (2016b) 'FAQs: Global Poverty Line Update'. www.worldbank.org/en/topic/poverty/brief/global-poverty-line-faq

World Bank (2016c) 'Poverty Overview'. www.worldbank.org/entopic/poverty/overview

World Bank. (2016d) 'High and Dry: Climate Change, Water, and the Economy'. Washington, DC: World Bank.

World Bank (2016e) Development Goals in an Era of Demographic Change: Global Monitoring Report. http://pubdocs.worldbank.org/en/503001444058224597/Global-Monitoring-Report-2015.pdf

World Bank (2017a) 'Doing Business: Starting a Business'. www.doingbusiness.org/data/exploretopics/starting-a-business

World Bank (2017b) *Migration and Remittances. Recent Developments and Outlook. Special Topic: Global Compact on Migration*. http://pubdocs.worldbank.org/en/992371492706371662/MigrationandDevelopmentBrief27.pdf

World Bank (various years) *Commodity Price Data* (aka 'Pink Sheet'). http://data.worldbank.org/data-catalog/commodity-price-data

WTO (World Trade Organization) (2002) *Tourism and Poverty Alleviation*. Geneva: World Trade Organization.

WWAP (World Water Assessment Programme) (2015) *The United Nations World Water Development Report 2015: Water for a Sustainable World*. Paris: United Nations Educational, Scientific and Cultural Organization (UNESCO).

Yang, Y. (2016) 'China's Foreign Exchange Reserves Rise for First Time in Five Months'. *Financial Times*, 7 April 2016.

Yu, F-L. (2009) 'A Human Agency Approach to the Economics of International Trade'. *International Journal of Pluralism and Economics Education*, Vol. 1, No. 1–2, pp.22–36.

Subject Index

Author Index